Dr. Panda has produced a timely tour de force treatment of the most important geopolitical relationship in Asia today. This path-breaking study provides a remarkably comprehensive assessment of China–India relations, analyzing not just bilateral ties, but how the relationship plays out on the subcontinent, in the Asia-Pacific region, within the broader sphere of developing nations and rising powers, as well upon the global stage. I highly commend this up-to-date and thorough volume to anyone seeking to understand the larger twenty-first century seismic forces reshaping the geostrategic landscape of Asia and the world.

Andrew Scobell, *RAND Corporation, USA*

Jagannath Panda has produced an innovative book on India–China relations that goes beyond just bilateral relations to consider sub-regional, regional and cross-continental interactions in groupings ranging from BCIM to IORA to BRICS. The result is a wide-ranging but careful assessment of the increasing complexities and encounters between India and China in a changing international setting. Scholars and students will benefit from this fresh and comprehensive treatment of India–China relations.

Satu Limaye, *East West Center in Washington, USA*

In *India–China Relations* Dr. Jagannath Panda has crafted a comprehensive, thoughtful, and necessary contribution on what has fast become one of the most geopolitically consequential relationships of the twenty-first century. From the origins of the China–India border dispute to contemporary issues like the Dalai Lama succession, China's One Belt One Road Initiative, and disputes over water resources, Dr. Panda shines a bright analytical light on this 'complex web of competition, cooperation, conflict, collaboration, and coexistence'. What's more, his research is supported by a generous helping of detailed maps, graphs and charts that will serve as a reference point for scholars for years to come. For anyone interested in one of the most important, complex, and poorly-understood relationships in the world, *India–China Relations* is a must-read.

Jeff Smith, *Asian Security Programs, American Foreign Policy Council, USA*

In his new book on India–China relations, Jagannath Panda succeeds in bringing new light on a much-debated issue. His goal is ambitious, and rightly so. Combining political, ideological, geopolitical and geo-economic perspectives, and the willingness to reassess international relations theories at the light of what is really happening on the field and in the decision-makers circles, the multilevel approach selected guides the reader step-by-step across the intricate geometries designed by the two great Asian nations. The analysis is well informed, nuanced. A must-read for those concerned by the new Asian dynamics, and by their impact on the rise of multi-polarity in the global world order.

Jean-Luc Racine, *Asia Centre, Paris, France*

India–China Relations

The rise of India and China as two major economic and political actors in both regional and global politics necessitates an analysis of not only their bilateral ties but also the significance of their regional and global pursuits. This book looks at the nuances and politics that the two countries attach to multilateral institutions and examines how they receive, react to and approach each other's presence and upsurge.

The driving theme of this book is to highlight the enduring and emerging complexities in India–China relations, which are multi-layered and polygonal in nature, and both a result and reflection of a multipolar world order. The book argues that coexistence between India and China in this multipolar world order is possible, but that it is limited to a medium-term perspective, given the constraints of identity complexities and global aspirations these two rising powers are pursuing. It goes on to discuss how their search for energy resources, quest to uphold their own identity as developing powers, and engagement in balance-of-power politics to exert authority on each other's presence, are some elements that guide their non-cooperative relationship.

By explaining the foreign policy approaches of Asia's two major powers towards the growing Asian and global multilateralism, and highlighting the policies they carry towards each other, the book is a useful contribution to students and scholars of Asian Politics, Foreign Policy and International Relations.

Jagannath P. Panda is a Research Fellow and Heads the East Asia Centre at the Institute for Defence Studies and Analyses, New Delhi, India.

Routledge Advances in South Asian Studies
Edited by Subrata K. Mitra
South Asia Institute, University of Heidelberg, Germany

South Asia, with its burgeoning, ethnically diverse population, soaring economies and nuclear weapons, is an increasingly important region in the global context. The series, which builds on this complex, dynamic and volatile area, features innovative and original research on the region as a whole or on the countries. Its scope extends to scholarly works drawing on history, politics, development studies, sociology and economics of individual countries from the region as well those that take an interdisciplinary and comparative approach to the area as a whole or to a comparison of two or more countries from this region. In terms of theory and method, rather than basing itself on any one orthodoxy, the series draws broadly on the insights germane to area studies, as well as the tool kit of the social sciences in general, emphasising comparison, the analysis of the structure and processes, and the application of qualitative and quantitative methods. The series welcomes submissions from established authors in the field as well as from young authors who have recently completed their doctoral dissertations.

28 **Globalisation and Governance in India**
New challenges to institutions and society
Harihar Bhattacharyya and Lion König

29 **Indian Muslims and Citizenship**
Spaces for jihad in everyday life
Julten Abdelhalim

30 **China–India Relations in the Contemporary World**
Dynamics of national identity and interest
Yang Lu

31 **Islam, Sufism and Everyday Politics of Belonging in South Asia**
Edited by Deepra Dandekar and Torsten Tschacher

32 **India–China Relations**
Politics of resources, identity and authority in a multipolar world order
Jagannath P. Panda

33 **Indigenous Identity in South Asia**
Making claims in the colonial Chittagong hill tracts
Tamina M. Chowdhury

India–China Relations

Politics of resources, identity and authority in a multipolar world order

Jagannath P. Panda

LONDON AND NEW YORK

First published 2017
by Routledge
2 Park Square, Milton Park, Abingdon, Oxon OX14 4RN

and by Routledge
711 Third Avenue, New York, NY 10017

First issued in paperback 2018

Routledge is an imprint of the Taylor & Francis Group, an informa business

© 2017 Institute for Defence Studies and Analyses (IDSA), New Delhi

The right of Jagannath P. Panda to be identified as author of this work has been asserted by him in accordance with sections 77 and 78 of the Copyright, Designs and Patents Act 1988.

All rights reserved. No part of this book may be reprinted or reproduced or utilised in any form or by any electronic, mechanical, or other means, now known or hereafter invented, including photocopying and recording, or in any information storage or retrieval system, without permission in writing from the publishers.

Trademark notice: Product or corporate names may be trademarks or registered trademarks, and are used only for identification and explanation without intent to infringe.

British Library Cataloguing in Publication Data
A catalogue record for this book is available from the British Library

Library of Congress Cataloging in Publication Data
Names: Panda, Jagannath P.
Title: India-China relations : politics of resources, identity and authority in a multipolar world order / Jagannath P. Panda.
Description: Abingdon, Oxon ; New York, NY : Routledge, 2017. | Series: Routledge advances in South Asian studies ; 32 | Includes bibliographical references and index.
Identifiers: LCCN 2016018280 | ISBN 9781138833593 (hardback) | ISBN 9781315735382 (ebook)
Subjects: LCSH: India–Foreign relations–China. | China–Foreign relations–India. | India–Foreign relations–21st century. | China–Foreign relations–21st century. | International agencies–Asia. | Asian cooperation.
Classification: LCC DS450.C6 P364 2017 | DDC 327.54051–dc23
LC record available at https://lccn.loc.gov/2016018280

ISBN 13: 978-1-138-59301-5 (pbk)
ISBN 13: 978-1-138-83359-3 (hbk)

Typeset in Times New Roman
by Wearset Ltd, Boldon, Tyne and Wear

Dedicated to My Parents

Contents

List of figures	xi
List of maps	xii
List of tables	xiii
Foreword	xiv
Preface and acknowledgements	xvi
List of abbreviations	xix

1 Introduction   1

PART I
The bilateral course   13

2 Between principles and policies   15

3 From *boundary* to *bordering territory*: the enduring
   dispute   34

4 Tibet and post-Dalai Lama contingencies   52

5 The water resource conflict   66

PART II
The sub-regional crescendo   77

6 Beijing's 'one belt, one road' diplomacy and India   79

7 BCIM and sub-regional interaction   98

PART III
Regional contours — 115

8 South Asia, SAARC and sub-regional dynamics — 117

9 The SCO and the competing Central Asian presence — 137

10 China's tryst with IORA: factoring India and the Indian Ocean — 150

11 Between RCEP and TPP: ASEAN+6 and Asia-Pacific intricacies — 164

12 East Asian dynamism: India as a security provider and China — 181

PART IV
Cross-continental contemporaries — 193

13 BRICS and the emerging powers identity — 195

14 BASIC and climate politics — 213

15 Institutionalising the African reach — 224

PART V
The global colloquium — 239

16 The global relationship: from Bretton Woods to alternative institution building — 241

17 Summing up — 256

Index — 263

Figures

1.1	India–China relations: structural convolution	4
2.1	India–China bilateral trade and trade imbalance, 2005–2015	16
7.1	India's trade with China	108
7.2	India's bilateral trade with other BCIM countries	109
7.3	China's bilateral trade with other BCIM countries	109
10.1	Comparison of India, China and US total bilateral trade with IORA, 2011–2015	156
11.1	TPP vs RCEP: economy and trade, 2014	165
11.2	ASEAN total trade with selected trading partners, 1998–2010	169
11.3	Comparative trade contact of China and India with main ASEAN dialogue partners, 2012	169
11.4	India–ASEAN trade, 2002/2003–2012/2013	170
11.5	China, US comparative merchandise trade status with APEC and the world, 2013	174
11.6	Share of Asian and other non-Asian economies in APEC's total GDP (PPP)	175
11.7	China's total merchandise trade with Asian and non-Asian APEC economies, 2013	175
13.1	The rise of the Yuan against US$, 2007–2016	200
13.2	Indian rupee vs US$ (Rs per US$)	203
14.1	Major countries of CO_2 emissions	218
15.1	China–Africa and India–Africa bilateral trade, 2000–2011	226
15.2	Trends of China's trade with BRICS countries, 2000–2012	231
15.3	China's trade figures with IBSA members, 2011	232
16.1	Contribution to WTO budget, 2015	244
16.2	BRICS countries' share in world commercial trade, 2014	245
16.3	BRICS countries' share in world merchandise trade, 2014	245

Maps

3.1	Claims and reclaims in India–China boundary dispute at a glance	36
6.1	India's oil exploration in the South China Sea	88
6.2	CPEC and POK	91
9.1	Chinese design of SCO: Central Asia + South Asia?	142
10.1	China's strategic bases in the Indian Ocean: focus on IORA countries	154
15.1	China, India and Africa: the Indian Ocean connection	228

Tables

2.1	Highest-level political exchange of visits between India and China, 2008–2015	17
2.2	Chronology of India–China dialogue	18
2.3	Chronology of India–China Joint Economic Group (JEG) meetings	20
2.4	India–China comparative profile, 2004–2014	21
2.5	India–China mutual perceptions: (a) Perception of India's democratic elite regarding China; (b) Chinese reflections on India's power of refraction	23
2.6	India–China sister city/province cooperation MoUs/agreements	29
3.1	India–China Joint Working Group meetings	42
3.2	Chronology of India–China Special Representatives meetings	44
3.3	Progress of Working Mechanism for Consultation and Coordination on India–China Border Affairs	46
4.1	Their Holinesses the Dalai Lamas	55
4.2	Sino-Tibetan meetings (since 1978)	57
5.1	India–China experts level mechanism meetings on trans-border rivers	71
5.2	MoUs on water/hydrological data sharing between India and China	71
7.1	BCIM forum so far	100
8.1	SAARC member profile vis-à-vis China	118
8.2	SAARC trade data compared with China	120
10.1	Major chokepoints and key IORA members	152
10.2	China's foreign direct investment to IORA countries	155
12.1	India's naval exercises with ASEAN members	183
13.1	BRICS summits and major issues discussed	196
13.2	China's RMB swap deals	201
14.1	Profile and climate status of BASIC members	215
16.1	India and China in Bretton Woods institutions	241
16.2	Kofi Annan's proposal on UNSC reform and China's reaction	249
16.3	China's perspective on UNSC membership reform	250

Foreword

It gives me great pleasure, and a sense of satisfaction, to contribute the foreword to Dr Jagannath Panda's unique account of India–China relations.

The dynamics of these relations are likely to impact significantly on the evolving world order, given that the two countries account for one-third of the global population, and their economies have been growing in recent decades at a pace faster than that of any other country or region in the world. While China stepped ahead, with its economic reform process accelerating from 1979, both countries are now rising simultaneously, but not at each other's expense.

India and China, as large countries with millennial civilisational inheritance, have a very similar self-image. They have had cultural connectivity between them through itinerant travellers – both monks and businessmen – but their people-to-people contacts have remained modest when seen in the context of their large populations.

They developed, historically, centred unto themselves. When they met, however, on neutral ground, such as in South-East Asia, centred in Sumatra, with the Indonesian Archipelago and the Malay Peninsula at its core, when the Srivijaya Kingdom prospered in the region, there was a Sino-Indic confluence based on culture and commerce. This demonstrates that when India and China came across each other's presence in their contiguities, their interaction was not inimical. Their contemporary relationship has tended to become adversarial because of the unresolved issues between them that touch on their territorial integrity and sovereignty, notwithstanding the secular development of a multi-layered engagement between them.

As a result, both scholarly and popular discourses have tended to use the two binaries of cooperation and conflict to define India–China relations. While these might be treated as the ends of a polarity within which the relationship might slide from one extremity to another, Dr Panda's contribution brings out how, in recent years, their respective national interests have compelled competition, coexistence and convergence on a range of regional and international issues. By focusing exclusively on bilateral relations, existing studies tend to dwell on the contingent and episodic flashpoints, harking back to the 1962 War, missing the longer-term trajectory, which political leaders of the two countries have been quick to grasp.

India–China relations have experienced a consistently upward trajectory since Rajiv Gandhi's visit to China in December 1988 – the first by an Indian Prime Minister in 34 years. The positive narrative has continued, as evident from President Xi Jinping's visit to India in September 2014 and Prime Minister Narendra Modi's visit to China in May 2015. They view their countries as partners in pursuing their ongoing national transformation, see merit in jointly promoting Asia's continued growth and prosperity, and are committed to a global partnership for creating a more equitable international order. While it is debatable whether India and China have actually covered good ground towards 'a new type of relationship between major countries' with each other, there is greater prospect of forward movement in their interactions than at any time since 1962.

The leaderships of both countries are pursuing an economy-centred grand strategy, aware that the real test for it lies at home. They know that it is the domestic success in their development effort that will determine their global standing. With India seeking sustained high growth, following China's example, and China looking to transform its economy and avoid the middle income trap, both countries will gain by preserving strategic peace and forging increased mutual exchanges between them.

Dr Panda brings out how there are growing points of intersection between India and China regionally and globally, besides the United Nations and other multilateral institutions – in the BRICS (Brazil–Russia–India–China–South Africa) Forum, BASIC (Brazil, South Africa, India and China), G-20 (Group of Twenty major economies), EAS (East Asia Summit), NDB (New Development Bank), AIIB (Asian Infrastructure and Investment Bank) and RCEP (Regional Comprehensive Economic Partnership), and potentially in SCO (Shanghai Cooperation Organisation) and APEC (Asia-Pacific Economic Cooperation). Hence, this book looks at India–China ties beyond the bilateral prism, in the context of what the author describes as their 'global polygonal politics'.

For India, arguably, China is its most important external relationship and its biggest foreign and security policy challenge. Their evolving dynamic will shape the future of Asia and the world. I am confident this book will contribute to a greater understanding of the circumstances and processes that embed this vital relationship.

Jayant Prasad
Director General
Institute for Defence Studies and Analyses

Preface and acknowledgements

India–China relations have continually drawn prime interest amongst the strategic community, academia and policymakers. A book aiming to appeal to a variety of communities – be it policymakers or businessmen, academia or journalists – is a meticulous and demanding undertaking. Having emerged predominantly out of discussion, debates and peer-reviewed exercises, this book aims to address the questions that are often raised on India–China relations. Not every argument raised or perspective built into this book is necessarily first-hand. Nevertheless, it lends newness to the prevailing arguments and perspectives and offers new insights and views to ponder. In essence, this book offers a broad picture of India–China relations, covering the current and future outlooks.

Writing a book of this length has been a challenging yet interesting experience. With my interest in India–China strategic affairs primarily in the sphere of multilateralism, this book has emerged as a consequence of sombre academic interest and expertise that I have accumulated over the years in strategic studies and in broader international relations studies. I sincerely thank the Institute for Defence Studies and Analyses (IDSA), New Delhi, for offering itself as a platform to generate this book as part of my research project fellowship. I am thankful to the Director General of IDSA, Shri Jayant Prasad, who has shown keen interest in the book and has been quite forthcoming to share his views on the subject. His encouraging words to examine this relationship from a holistic perspective are a welcome addition to this book. I sincerely thank Dr Arvind Gupta, former Director General (DG) of IDSA, the current Deputy National Security Advisor, for having permitted me to write this book. He encouraged me to explore India–China relations more from the Indian perspective, keeping in mind the policymakers, and write more about emerging intricacies that India–China relations currently invite. I express my gratitude to Brig. (Retd) Rumel Dahiya, the Deputy Director General (DDG) of IDSA, for supporting me throughout the writing of this book and encouraging me to finish the assignment timely. His backing has always fortified me to pursue the manuscript with utmost seriousness. Mr N.S. Sisodia, former DG of IDSA, has equally had a great reassuring influence in pushing me constantly to write a book-length study on India–China relations that would be relevant and referred in the Indian and the global contexts.

This book writing experience has been an enduring one. Some of its chapters have either been presented previously in academic forums or seminars or conferences or have been written after an extensive discussion and debate. Some chapters have been previously published in academic outlets such as *Strategic Analysis, China Report, Asian Perspectives, Georgetown Journal of Asian Affairs, Indian Foreign Affairs Journal, Journal of Contemporary China, Portuguese Journal of International Affairs, China and Eurasia Forum Quarterly* and *Journal of Asian and African Studies*, etc. Copyright permission has either been obtained or due acknowledgement is offered to these original sources of publication.

I owe a multitude of thanks and appreciation to Prof. Subrata Mitra for his guidance and encouragement in writing this book. His productive suggestion to make this book relevant for a wider audience has been the most encouraging aspect. Among the Indian experts who have influenced me are Prof. Alka Acharya, Prof. Srikanth Kondapalli, Prof. Sreemati Chakrabarti and Prof. Manoranjan Mohanty, to all of whom I owe a lot of gratitude. Prof. Acharya, in particular, has always been a guide and encouraged me to write something new and fresh. Her comments and critical inputs were a great contribution to this work. Prof. Kondapalli's constructive suggestions and advice to address this complex subject more from the strategic perspective have been quite beneficial. Prof. Chakrabarti has taken a keen interest in my research and extended timely advice to improve the work in various discussion stages. This work will remain incomplete without recognising Prof. Mohanty's guidance and advice. My long association with him at Delhi University helped me to comprehend India–China relations better, in a more nuanced and objective manner.

This work acknowledges the generous support of the Indian Council of Social Science Research (ICSSR), New Delhi that offered me a field trip study grant to China in December 2014 to January 2015. I sincerely acknowledge the prodigious help and assistance of the universities, institutes and libraries across the world where I have travelled for seminars, conferences and lectures and have interacted with teachers, students, scholars and supporting staff, especially in China, Hong Kong, Taiwan, Singapore, South Korea, Japan, US and various parts of Europe. Several Chinese scholars have also been helpful in generating ideas and helping me to carry out my field trips. Prof. Zhao Gancheng, Dr Liu Zongyi, Prof. Shen Dingli, Prof. Du Youkang, Prof. Chen Dengxiao, Prof. Huang Renwei, Dr Wang Weihua, Prof. Zhang Guihong, Prof. Xia Liping, Prof. Zhang Jiadong, Prof. Song Guoyou, Prof. Wei Zongyou, Prof. Liu Ming, Prof. Ma Jiali, Prof. Sun Shihai, Prof. Hu Shisheng, Dr Li Li, Dr Lan Jianxue, Dr Chen Jianrong, Prof. Zhang Zhejiang, Dr Yang Xiaoping, Dr Wu Zhaoli, Dr Lou Chunhao, Dr Fu Xiaoqiang and Dr Han Hua have particularly been helpful and generous in discussing the topics and offering their comments and views. I thank the Chinese Academy of Social Science (CASS), Beijing, and the Shanghai Institute of International Studies (SIIS) in particular for hosting my stay as a visiting fellow. Among the Taiwanese scholars who also deserve my thanks and appreciation are Prof. Fang-Tien Sze, Prof. Mumin Chen, Prof. Liu Fu-Kuo, Prof. Chih-Yu Shih, Prof. Arthur Ding and Prof. Vincent Cheng.

xviii *Preface and acknowledgements*

I have immensely profited from a few Japanese experts in discussing the matter from regional perspectives. Dr Marie Izuyama of the NIDS in Tokyo, Dr Yasukuni Ishida of JIIA, Prof. Fukunaga Masaki, Dr Rohyei Kasai of Gifu Women's University were forthcoming in offering their perspectives. I am also thankful to Western scholars like Prof. Andrew Scobell, Mr Jeff Smith, Dr Bonnie Glacer, Prof. Suisheng Zhao and Prof. Vincent Wang. I also take this opportunity to offer my special appreciation to Prof. Klaus Lange and Prof. Klara Knapp of the Institute of Transnational Studies (ITS), Germany/Italy for their valuable inputs and comments on the various topics. They have been candid in their academic propositions and have offered me their valuable friendship, which I always cherish. On a personal note, I am thankful to Mr U.S. Bhatia and Mrs Jagjyot Bhatia who have encouraged me to work hard and stay sincere. Their encouragement has always been beneficial.

One person who has been the linchpin behind the editing and completion of this manuscript is Mr Arthur Monteiro. His conscientious and time-bound conclusion of the editing process, especially at a time when he had to go through health treatment, is commendable. I really doubt if I can meet a better copyeditor as professional and committed as him. I offer also a note of appreciation to Mr Vivek Dhankar of the IDSA GIS Lab who prepared the maps of this book. A few interns have also been helpful in providing timely research materials for reading. I mainly acknowledge the assistance of Ms Antara Ghosal, Ms Rinzin Dolkar, Ms Dolma Tsering, Mr Kunga Tsunde, Ms Divya John, Ms Deepika Godara and Mr Shyam Hari in this regard. I must also acknowledge the assistance and help of Mr John Ryan, Qian Zhang and Peter Van Der Hoest for enriching the work.

Last but not least, this work was possible due to the immense patience and encouragement of my family members. I owe my personal gratitude to my mother-in-law for her support and presence during my difficult times. My parents' thrust on my persistence, hard work and competence has always been a huge source of encouragement. Occasionally talking to them during the course of this writing offered me a source of strength and courage. I missed their presence in my workplace during this writing and could not look after their weakening health and wish for more salubrious times to spend more time with them. This book is sincerely dedicated to them. Madhu, my wife, has also been a source of strength, having put up with many inconveniences without a murmur of complaint.

Abbreviations

ADB	Asian Development Bank
ADMM+	ASEAN Defence Minister's Meeting Plus
AIIB	Asian Infrastructure Investment Bank
APEC	Asia-Pacific Economic Cooperation
ARF	ASEAN Regional Forum
ASEAN	Association of Southeast Asian Nations
AU	African Union
BASIC	Brazil–South Africa–India–China
BCIM	Bangladesh–China–India–Myanmar
BCIM-EC	Bangladesh–China–India–Myanmar Economic Corridor
BDCA	Border Defence Cooperation Agreement
BIMST-EC	Bay of Bengal Initiative for Multi-Sectoral Technical and Economic Cooperation
BJP	Bharatiya Janata Party
BRICS	Brazil–Russia–India–China–South Africa
CASS	Chinese Academy of Social Science
CBDR	common but differentiated responsibilities
CBM	confidence-building measure
CDB	China Development Bank
CPEC	China–Pakistan Economic Corridor
EAS	East Asia Summit
EEU	Eurasian Economic Union
EU	European Union
FTA	Free Trade Agreement
G-4	Group of Four
G-20	Group of Twenty
GHG	greenhouse gas
IBSA	India–Brazil–South Africa
IBSAMAR	India–Brazil–South Africa Maritime Exercise
IDSA	Institute for Defence Studies and Analyses
IMF	International Monetary Fund
IONS	Indian Ocean Naval Symposium
IOR	Indian Ocean Rim

IOR-ARC	Indian Ocean Rim Association for Regional Cooperation
IORA	Indian Ocean Rim Association
IPR	intellectual property rights
ISIS	Islamic State of Iraq and Syria
JEG	Joint Economic Group
JWG	Joint Working Group
LAC	Line of Actual Control
MDGs	millennium development goals
MGC	Mekong Ganga Cooperation
MoU	Memorandum of Understanding
MSR	Maritime Silk Road
NDB	New Development Bank
NDRC	National Development and Reform Commission
OBOR	One Belt, One Road
P-5	Permanent Five
PLA	People's Liberation Army
PLAN	People's Liberation Army Navy
POK	Pakistan-Occupied Kashmir
PRC	People's Republic of China
RCEP	Regional Comprehensive Economic Partnership
RIC	Russia–India–China
ROC	Republic of China
SAARC	South Asian Association for Regional Cooperation
SCO	Shanghai Cooperation Organisation
SDR	Special Drawing Rights
S&ED	Strategic and Economic Dialogue
SED	Strategic Economic Dialogue
SREB	Silk Road Economic Belt
SRF	Silk Road Fund
TGIE	Tibetan Government in Exile
TPP	Trans-Pacific Partnership
UNCLOS	Union Nation Convention on the Law of the Sea
UNSC	United Nations Security Council
WTO	World Trade Organization

1 Introduction

What this book is about

India–China relations continue to capture attention in international relations politics. While US–China relations attract discussion, given the political and economic supremacy of the two protagonists, and China–Japan relations are signified by a certain stereotypical power politics of cooperation-conflict that many bilateral relationships in the world represent, India–China relations are distinctive, given the two countries' primacy as 'emerging and enduring powers'. They represent two modes of civilisation, demographically strong societies, and promising economic and geography forte, bringing *cooperation* and *collaboration*, *coexistence* and *convergence*, and *competition* and *conflict* on a single platform, signifying the most complex and dynamic relationship in world politics.

Three mainstream prisms – *realism*, *idealism* and *constructivism* – primarily explain the character of most contemporary bilateral relations. Most scholars and experts have also seen the India–China dynamism through these three prisms. Indian and Chinese scholars and experts have often portrayed this dynamics in the light of their indigenous perspective; non-Indian/non-Chinese scholars have claimed to be more objective. But they ignore that India–China relations are much more complicated than coming under the canvas of the defined theoretical prism of *realism/idealism/constructivism*. This book shuns these mainstream theoretical prisms, and seeks to illuminate the underlying complications characterising this bilateral relationship that go far beyond the *realism/idealism/constructivism* construct through a methodological, orderly and structural analysis.

The *realist* prism of India–China relations explains the power rivalry, antagonism and competition between the two Asian neighbours.[1] It posits that if both countries continue to grow on their current power trajectory, a strong power rivalry between them will be inevitable, given that both stand a sound chance of becoming superpowers in times to come.[2] In contrast, the *liberalist* prism plumps for a cooperative relationship, stable engagement and cooperation. It posits that the strategic rivalry is muted, with a diversity of institutional, bilateral as well as multilateral engagement and economic interdependence[3] in the interest of evolving a 'non-Western' world order that is very much multipolar, thinking alike as Asian powers and as 'emerging powers' (Panda 2013). This discourse of *realism* and *idealism* has further emerged as *neo-realism* and *neo-liberalism*, to depend upon *constructivism* to evaluate and contextualise India–China relations in a more objective and neutral perspective.

Constructivism does offer a nuanced and constructive explanation of India–China ties, following a mid-course, and accepts that cooperation and conflict in these ties are concurrent.[4] But constructivism is often dominated by a liberal mode of thinking, closer to idealism (Bozdaliolu 2007), a result of which has been the coinage of an idea like 'Chindia'.[5] Constructivism overlooks that in a complex relationship such as that between India and China, traditional realities like history, culture and social constructs often play a strong role in state politics along with contemporary realities of present-century world politics. These contemporary realities are mainly national interests: *geographic resources* or *energy resources*, *identity* or image as a nation, or *authority* principle, which is a type of influence that often comes with or without state power. This book essentially seeks to cover these unforeseen and inexplicable characters in India–China relations in an already arrived multipolar world order.

Existing studies mostly focus on the usual bilateral impediments in India–China relations such as their boundary dispute and complexities linked to Tibet and Tibetan affairs, while covering select regional complexities in the neighbourhood region. But the rise of India and China as two major economies and political actors in regional and global politics necessitates scholarly debate and systematic methodological analysis not only regarding their *bilateral* ties; but also the significance of their *sub-regional, regional, cross-continental* and *global* pursuits. The India–China dynamics at the *sub-regional* and *cross-continental* levels is a relatively new area of power dynamics that needs systematic analysis, because they have considerably influenced India–China ties. These polygonal, multifaceted and multilateral parlances call for a strong methodological inquiry.

Defining the concept

The rise of a multilateral mechanism like Brazil–Russia–India–China–South Africa (BRICS), the relative decline of US influence and the 'special' rise of China have connoted a scenario of a multipolar world order. But it needs to be seen whether the current state of India–China relations is a reflection or a result of multipolarity. There is acknowledgement that India–China relations have moved beyond the purview of bilateralism and have become, as Alka Acharya notes, 'one of the most critical relationships not just in Asia but the world' (Acharya 2008: 13). They have become *autonomous* in character, moving beyond their orthodox ambience of bilateral-centrism. Recognising this, the Joint Statement on India–China relations, which was issued on 20 May 2013 on the conclusion of the visit of Premier Li Keqiang, records that:

> There is enough space in the world for the development of India and China.... As the two largest developing countries in the world, the relationship between

India and China transcends bilateral scope and has acquired regional, global and strategic significance.

(MEA 2013)

This endorsement came against the background when the two countries celebrated the 60th anniversary of the Panchsheel discourse in 2014, and commemorated the 10th anniversary of the 'Strategic and Cooperative Partnership for Peace and Prosperity' in 2015. In 2016, when the relationship between the two neighbours has become more 'development' oriented, the question arises: if India–China ties have become autonomous, how do they accommodate each other in this autonomous space of politics? Does the course of Panchsheel of the previous world order have any relevance today? And how well have India–China relations benefited from the decade-old Strategic and Cooperative Partnership, which emphasises peace and prosperity? This book argues that India–China relations are in constant transition, with a new mode of politics and leadership on both sides, where the usual mode of politics is being outdone through new labels of power politics at different stages.

The main premise of this book is about the two emerging contemporary powers and their mutual discourse with and perception of each other. It aims to address a few broad research questions: What is the current nature of India–China relations? What will be their future course? And does the thesis of 'Chindia', which connotes a basis of cooperation and coexistence, have any realistic basis? The 'Chindia' thesis has in a way marginalised India–China relations in a multipolar world order. Without supporting the 'Chindia' discourse, this book aims at the following: (i) inspect the current and future course of India–China relations; (ii) evaluate both countries' geopolitical presence and political nuances in various multilateral mechanisms and institutions; and (iii) examine the strategic fallout in their bilateral, sub-regional, regional, cross-continental and global discourse. Coexistence for the two countries in a multipolar world order is possible, but it will be selective and limited in nature, being further limited to a medium-term perspective, given the constraints of identity complexities of being the two 'prospective world powers': their quest for security and objective of maximising their own national interests stymie any larger prospects of coexistence. Their unremitting search for energy resources, quest to uphold their current identity as developing-world countries but aiming to become world powers, and engaging in a balance-of-power politics to exert authority on each other's presence are some elements that guide their non-cooperative relations.

Figure 1.1 graphically illustrates this India–China convolution. It may not seem most logical, but it helps in presenting and comprehending methodically the India–China intricacy. It also sweeps aside the prejudices adduced by theoretical prisms that idealism, realism or constructivism generally offer. The politics of *resources*, *identity* and *authority* that this book constantly highlights is about the essence, presence and influence of a contemporary state's competing-cooperating reality. These three realities may seem to be distinct and disassociated from each other, but viewed from a rational power political perspective,

4 Introduction

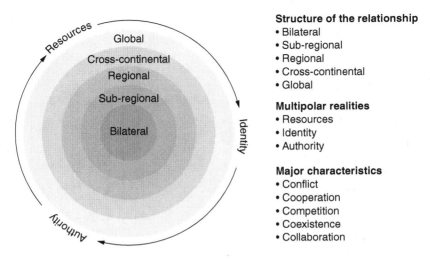

Figure 1.1 India–China relations: structural convolution.

these three are core aspects that contemporary states try to achieve, implement and pursue in order to sustain their global aims and aspirations. The search for energy resources along with constant economic opportunities in different geographic regions of Asia and the world condition their bilateral and multilateral approach towards each other. Identity politics helps them hold on to their status of emerging or developing countries to continue to shape the cross-continental and global politics of their relationship. In between, there is a component of authority politics, involving contention and future outlook, reflected at different stages of their relationship course, and that includes bilateral, sub-regional, regional, cross-continental and global facets. The principle of authority comes with or without power, and is often seen in terms of their influencing capability. These powers or influencing capabilities are linked with both India's and China's political presence and economic stimulus. The politics of authority involves hegemonic state behaviour, dominance character and building influence rather than projecting the pretence of a cooperative endeavour that Panchsheel or the official 'Strategic and Cooperative Partnership for Peace and Prosperity' or the newly 'developmental partnership' promise to produce. The politics of authority in practice represents their economic supremacy, military superiority and rising political presence, which exert influence.

In essence, this book examines three assertions. *First*, opposite to the three prisms – *idealist*, *realist* and *constructivist* – it explores how pragmatism prevails over any pretence of cooperation and conflict at different levels: bilateral, sub-regional, regional, cross-continental and global. As rational and realist actors, the two countries pledge for stronger mutual cooperation but fall short in implementing it in practical circumstances. *Second*, it examines the conventional intellectual discourse that India–China relations are ordained more by competition and conflict than cooperation in their multilateral presence in diverse geographic zones. Cooperation and conflict may be two extremes; but there are new labels and modes of action, which come in the form of competition, coexistence and convergence of mutual interests. *Third*, the book outlines the 'autonomous' or 'explicit' character of India–China relations obtaining today and advancing into the future, arguing that this relationship course has moved beyond its 'orthodox' bilateral character. This autonomous character is linked to their global polygonal politics, third-party outlook and global supply-and-demand politics related to the emerging geopolitics and geo-economics. In sum, this book narrates the current and next course of India–China relations.

Contemporary India–China relations: a reflection or a result of multipolarity?[6]

The conventional argument is that India's and China's rise has been a singular aspect of current world politics and that possibly has driven the core of multipolarism. But have contemporary India–China relations, which have become autonomous or multi-layered, replicated the mode of multipolarism or have they simply been a result of multipolarity? Recent literature suggests that they are both.

William Antholis in *Inside Out, India and China: Local Politics Go Global* (2013) talks about how the two countries have grown and extended their local reach to global outreach and have established their strong footprints in global multilateralism. He provides an excellent account of how local determinants and perspectives in both countries shape the course of their foreign policy actions and global conduct. With a rich and systematic analysis of the two countries' geographic regions, he analyses the diversity of their approaches to business ethics and governance capability that have impacted global politics and economics. He argues that local politics in both India and China are key constituents in their foreign-policymaking. The central government in neither country has absolute control, and the primacy of their domestic boroughs must be understood in the global context. To quote: 'The power outside of their capitals has expanded dramatically in recent decades. Local governments have stepped forward, with global implications' (ibid.: 6).

Carl J. Dahlman in *The World under Pressure: How China and India Are Influencing the Global Economy and Environment* (2012) provides an excellent analysis of how India's and China's rise is influencing the global economic system and geopolitical environment in their favour. Though China's rise and growth has been the flavour of world politics, the picture remains incomplete without assessing India's rise. India harbours the strength and vigour to surpass the US's economic supremacy in the future. In this context, the European Union too would have to reassess its position and standing in the global economic and political setting (ibid.: 227). Besides, the global power dynamics will get complicated further as India and China may collide over water, energy resources, economics and on ideological fronts (ibid.: 2). This book is in agreement with Dahlman's thesis in that it tries to highlight how 'multipolar realities' continue to shape

India–China relations and future world politics. Interestingly, Dahlman contests the premise that India and China together are significant representatives of the 'rise of the rest' (ibid.: 232): together they represent 37 per cent of the world population; the rest of the developing world represents 47 per cent. This could pose the risk of the rest of the developing world getting marginalised in the future (ibid.: 209).

Two other recent publications have highlighted the growing rivalry and competitive aspects of the India–China discourse. Tien-sze Fang, in *Asymmetrical Threat Perceptions in India–China Relations* (2014) locates the two countries' status as 'regional powers' and contextualises their regional rivalry as one aspect of their bilateral relationship (Tien-sze Fang 2014: 126). He deems the 'competitive aspect' of India–China relations to be alive at the regional level and postulates that 'their competition in Asia is not always China-specific or India-specific' (ibid.: 168). He argues that their strategic space is clutched by the extension of each other's influence. In the global context, the India–US alliance, the Russia–India–China (RIC) triangle and the spirit of 'Chindia' are some of the key aspects that are most likely to influence the global discourse of India–China relations (ibid.: 171). These issues, as he argues, are correlated with two special tactics: balancing and bandwagoning, which reduce mutual threat perceptions. To balance each other's opposite needs, interests and considerations of risks, both countries will look to explore opportunities to strengthen their cooperation (ibid.: 197). Tien-sze Fang also examines the so-called asymmetric threat in India–China ties that exists parallel to an 'interactive culture' between the two (ibid.: 8). A range of political and diplomatic interactions exists between the two countries as neighbours, both bilaterally and regionally; but they fall short in checking their growing perceptual gap. Realistically, India's threat perception vis-à-vis China is stronger than vice versa (ibid.: 8).

Jeff Smith in *Cold Peace: China–India Rivalry in the Twenty-First Century* (2014) follows a similar argument to explain the existing complexities and rivalry (a 'civil rivalry') between the two countries. In his view, the mutual antagonistic views and hostile opinions that exist between the two countries are not part of a 'vocal minority' perception (ibid.: 4). The mutual perceptions are somewhat suppressed due to the diplomatic comity. The elements of rivalry in Sino-Indian relations are 'genuine and deep-suited' and are fundamentally central to the bilateral relationship (ibid.: 5). The continuing mutual 'threat perceptions' – which are part of a set of 'fundamental conflict of interests' – are located within the bilateral purview of existing complexities like Territory, Tibet and Tawang. In a wider context, these prevailing conflicts come under a rubric of five Ts: Territory, Tibet, Third Parties, Threat Perceptions and Tawang; and he introduces a sixth T – Turf – in terms of the existing India–China maritime rivalry in the Indian Ocean Region (IOR) (ibid.: 143). At the same time, the India–China rivalry has moved beyond the purview of bilateralism (ibid.: 12), to comprise third-party contexts like the US, Pakistan, the rising complexities in the IOR to East Asia and the rivalry to attain a major share in the global commons. The US factor is currently heavily influencing India–China relations: India's strategic partnership with the US contains a 'most important structural development in Sino-Indian relations' in the current century (ibid.: 115). Since the 1960s, the US has been a factor in India–China relations, which has entrenched the Chinese perception of India as a Western ally.

Dahlman and Antholis have placed in context the fact that countries like India and China, seen previously as developing or transitional countries, have recently been growing faster than developed countries. Accounting for some 40 per cent of the world population, they have increased their combined share of global economic output rapidly in the last three decades. They represented 4 per cent in 1980, but almost 18 per cent by 2010 in terms of purchasing power parity (PPP) (Dahlman 2012: 1). It is widely reckoned that the two countries will together account for almost 50 per cent of world GDP by the year 2050, laying the foundation for them together to heavily influence the world economic geography. This prospect is already causing far-reaching rumblings in the world order, both in regional and global settings and in various global compartments, which are reflected in spheres ranging from finance to trade, intellectual property rights (IPR) to resources competition, governance issues to investments, and security to balance of power (ibid.). The nuances and character of India's and China's rise have not only compelled the major powers to adjust their global bearings but also in their relationship with the two countries (ibid.). In multilateral institutions and vis-à-vis third-party actors, both India and China are strong actors and are intertwined strongly. This explains, partly, why India–China relations are not limited to bilateral complexities but are far wider ranging. The trajectory of their relations will decisively influence the structure and outcome of a multipolar world order.

This multi-layered polygonal system exists at different bilateral, sub-regional, regional, cross-continental and global levels. In these zones, comprising multilateral forums or mechanisms or institutions, India and China are associated directly or indirectly, and either of them holds a predominant position vis-à-vis the other. According to Tien-sze Fang, 'competition for regional leadership remains a significant element in post-Cold War Sino-Indian relations' (Tien-sze Fang 2014: 126). At the same time, cooperation at the sub-regional level is an important aspect of India–China relations now. This has been demonstrated, for example, by India–China interactions in Russia–India–China (RIC), SCO (Shanghai Cooperation Organisation), SAARC (South Asian Association for Regional Cooperation), BCIM (Bangladesh–China–India–Myanmar) and at the Association of South-East Asian Nations (ASEAN) dialogue partners' mechanisms. On the functional side, prospects of cooperation are emerging between the two countries on issues like anti-terrorism, intra-regional trade and economic collaboration. This cooperation cohabits with competition (Tien-sze Fang 2014: 154–68), which Jeff Smith characterises as 'civil rivalry' (Smith 2014: 3).

Multilateral groupings like BRICS, Brazil–South Africa–India–China (BASIC) and the Group of Twenty (G-20), with which India and China are associated, manifest the cross-continental character of multilateralism. Associating with such institutions, India and China attempt 'to protect their own national interests' (Antholis 2013: 179) by interplaying cooperation and competition. The

'Chindia' concept, heralding 'developing country' and 'similar international identities' (Tien-sze Fang 2014: 188), puts the two countries on a single platform to cooperate. On a similar construct, the US factor and trade and global commons compel them to compete and engage in a rational realist world politics (Smith 2014: 115–16). Besides, a seething competition evidenced between the two countries at the cross-continental or global levels, where every country is a priority for them to take on board, propels a case of how power has become diffused in the global structure today (Antholis 2013: 179). Antholis foresees a scenario of a 'G-Zero' world situation having arrived, where he perceives the end of power (ibid.). In this scenario, globalisation has been at the core of the India–China global relationship course. Globalisation has been a 'double-edged sword' that has facilitated both the phenomenon of exchanges and interdependence. Exchanges and multilateral mode of contacts have permitted a greater aura of cooperation, whereas interdependence has propelled tensions and conflicts (Dahlman 2012: 183). India–China interdependence in a globalised world structure has created frictions and tensions in three edifices: economic, environmental and geopolitical or security (ibid.: 185). Therefore, the rise of India and China is not only a vital facet of multipolarism: the future of multipolarity also depends to a great extent on the landscape of this relationship.

Multipolar realities: *resources*, *identity* and *authority*

Tien-sze Fang and Jeff Smith locate their arguments more or less within the premise of bilateral perceptions and misperceptions, whereas Antholis and Dahlman contextualise beyond the orthodox phenomenon that currently exists in India–China relations on a global parameter. We need to stress, however, that the current cooperation and competition between India and China are basically linked to courses of globalisation and competing realities of the current century: these are the *politics of resources, identity and authority*. Issues like boundary, water and Tibet will probably continue to dictate India–China bilateral proceedings. But in this century, India–China complexity will greatly be linked to competing or rational realities of multipolar world politics. Issues like energy, North–South divide and the balance of power will be frontline foci for the two countries. These are the 'competing realities' of a multipolar world order, the 'rational fundamentals' of a multilateral polygonal systemic structure where demographically endowed countries like India and China will cooperate and compete. These elements also propel ethoses like coexistence, competition, collaboration and conflict, prompting a flexible and polygonal character of India–China ties. A methodological analysis of these newly arrived aspects of the India–China course is still missing: the literature that has been reviewed here projects these elements only partially.

Globalisation has increased the demand for energy resources and has intensified the politics over resources. Securing energy resources has become a prime objective of both countries to sustain their economic growth and living standards. Similarly, the mode of multipolarism has intensified the identity politics among the emerging economies. Both India and China seem to be engaged in a similar style of politics here too. The 'developing world' identity is crucial for both countries, as it helps them to pose a strong opposition to the developed world's dominance in the global financial institutions and structures, though as a P-5 (permanent five) country at the United Nations Security Council (UNSC) and as the No. 2 economy in world, China is better placed in the global political and economic structure.

Amidst these paths of resource and identity politics, a politics of authority exists. Authority politics, which pertains to balance-of-power politics, is attached to multilateral bodies or institutions the two countries are associated with. The principle of authority comes with or without power and influence. These powers and influences are primarily economic and political strengths. In Asia or around the region, China carries an enormous influence in bodies like the SCO and ASEAN, whereas India maintains considerable influence in SAARC and the Indian Ocean Rim Association (IORA). These multilateral associations or groupings help them balance each other at the regional level. India's SCO membership largely depended upon China's support; and in turn China's possible entry into SAARC in future will depend on India's manoeuvring. The two countries also need to extend and translate their authority and engage in balance-of-power politics in geopolitical regions that those multilateral bodies particularly represent. A purpose of the need to extend authority as the dominant power from that region is reflected in India's and China's global and regional behaviour. China persists in exerting its authority in the Central and South-East Asian regions as an economic and military/maritime power; and India maintains its authority to an extent in the IOR, which has been a lifeline for global energy resource transport. In this politics, China has an advantage mainly because its economic prominence promotes its interests on many fronts, especially in regard to its energy quest.

Structural edifice

This book is divided into five parts, essentially based on these five aspects, as follows: (i) the bilateral *course*; (ii) the sub-regional *crescendo*; (iii) regional *contours*; (iv) cross-continental *contemporaries*; and (v) the global *colloquium*.

i The bilateral course

Currently prevailing traditional or conformist bilateral subject matters, like the boundary dispute, Tibet and water resource politics are discussed in the first part. These chapters essentially sideline the historical aspect, preferring to examine these matters in the current and future relationship context and how they influence their overall relations. This section has *four* chapters in all.

Chapter 2 deals with India's and China's current bilateral relationship course, their underlying principles and policies towards each other. The other three chapters deal with the boundary dispute, the complexity of Tibet and Tibetans in the context of the post-Dalai Lama phase and the water resource dispute.

10 *Introduction*

Underlying these chapters is the rationale of how *resource* politics is an integral part of India–China bilateral relations. *Chapter 3* signifies how the boundary conflict has become a resource conflict today and how the conflict is not just about land resource, but about the *resources* of the territory which makes it a bordering territorial conflict. *Chapter 4* deals with the complex Tibet issue in today's India–China relations. Given the current and future facet of India–China ties that this book primarily aims to deal with, this chapter narrates the possible post-Dalai Lama scenario and the anticipated intricacies that may arise in India–China ties. It principally notes the identity insecurity that the Tibetans currently live with and how that may complicate India–China relations in the post-Dalai phase. *Chapter 5* deals with another vital resource politics, which is an emergent facet of India–China relations. This chapter pointedly stresses the *authority* character of China in the water conflict with India. It talks about how China as an upper riparian nation carries a posture of a hydro-hegemonic country in water diversion projects in the Yarlung Tsangpo/Brahmaputra River that point to the authoritative politics that exists in India–China relations today.

ii *The sub-regional crescendo*

Associating with multilateral mechanisms, institutions and groupings helps nations to balance each other while aiming to maximise their own foreign policy objectives and interests. India's and China's engagement in multilateral mechanisms, institutions or groupings is conditioned by a variety of third-party factors: the geopolitics of a region, foreign policy dynamism of other countries, and the political and strategic elements of multilateral mechanisms. In this polygonal rendezvous, India and China are not always on an equal footing: their connection and interaction in these multilateral bodies, mechanisms either as members, observers, dialogue partners or co-founders is heavily nuanced. This part has two chapters. *Chapter 6* talks about the Chinese-proposed 'one belt, one road' initiative and its impact on India–China neighbourhood politics. This chapter specifically talks about the corridor and connectivity aspects of China's 'silk road' project in the immediate neighbourhood and how that may affect the future of India–China relations. *Chapter 7* highlights the BCIM and how India–China relations are ordained by the politics of coexistence in the immediate neighbourhood region. This chapter further focuses on how the BCIM Economic Corridor (BCIM–EC) is ensnared in the neighbourhood resource politics.

iii *Regional contours*

At the regional level, the *third* part examines India's and China's accounts in frameworks like SAARC, SCO, IORA and economic frameworks like RCEP, TPP and the EAS, covering key political-security mechanisms such as ASEAN, ARF, ADMM+, etc. Some of these are either orthodox institutions or growing political-economic multiparty models that are linked to an assorted India–China regional political-economic-strategic engagement. *Chapter 8* points to the emerging India–China dynamism in South Asia where Beijing is making a statement to become a member of SAARC and fast emerging as an influential power. Will India concede China's rise in South Asia? *Chapter 9* narrates the emerging India–China dynamism in Central Asia, especially in the context of the SCO. The Ufa SCO summit in 2015 has changed the bilateral contours between India and China in Central Asia. This chapter tests whether cooperative India–China relations will emerge in Central Asia under the premise of SCO and Russia–India–China (RIC) or the relationship will emerge to be more competitive in future. *Chapters 10, 11* and *12* examine the emerging contours between India and China in the Asia-Pacific region to East Asia where the highlight continues to remain on the Indian Ocean and the South China Sea. These three chapters explain how maritime *resource* politics is one prime aspect of India–China regional power politics. They explain how economic and political multilateralism facilitates the two countries' maritime resources and their policy reach in the Indian Ocean Region (IOR) to the South China Sea and to East Asia to Asia-Pacific. The India–China tryst in these regional groupings is shaped by their national interests: power promotion, maximising national interests for resources, identity to uphold predominance as Asian powers, and exerting their influence.

iv Cross-continental contemporaries

The *fourth* part, *Chapters 13, 14* and *15*, debates the cross-continental power politics between India and China. It outlines how in cross-continental groupings like BRICS, BASIC and the African Union (AU), the politics of identity comes into India–China interplay. The two countries employ the label of 'developing world' identity politics to construct the cross-regional and cross-continental politics in their favour. The India–China cooperative drive in these institutions is conditioned by power politics in a rapidly emerging multipolar world order where the two countries share identical concerns vis-à-vis the developed world. This facet prompts India–China relations to move beyond the normal bilateral parameters to cross-continental politics, and touch new geopolitics and subjects of global governance matters like energy, climate change, health, reforming global financial institutions, etc.

v The global colloquium

Discussing the global facets of India–China relations, the *fifth* part emphasises India's and China's international perceptions of each other, how they have factored each other in greater global political and economic multilateral institutions, how they see the evolving politics of multipolarism, and how this is going to shape their relationship discourse at the global level. It deals with their mutual urge to reform the Bretton Woods institutions to establish alternative institutions that have a lasting effect both for world politics and for their bilateral relations. The basic premise of this construct is that India and China are superpowers in the making, and would like to construct and shape a global order in their favour.

Notes

1 The dominant literature that covers India–China realist course comprises Garver 2001; Raja Mohan 2013; and Smith 2014.
2 This perspective and context of India–China relations has been mentioned in Panda 2013.
3 A few readings on these lines are: Tan Chung 2008; Sharma 2009; and Dahlman 2012.
4 A few recent accounts on this aspect of India–China relations include Acharya 2008 and Tien-sze Fang 2014.
5 Jairam Ramesh has popularized the concept of 'Chindia' through his writings. See Ramesh 2005.
6 This section concerning this debate has been published in Panda 2014.

References

Acharya, Alka, 2008. *China and India: Politics of Incremental Engagement*, New Delhi: Har-Anand.
Antholis, William, 2013. *Inside Out, India and China: Local Politics Go Global*, Washington, DC: Brookings Institution Press.
Bozdaliolu, Yucel, 2007. 'Constructivism and identity formation: an interactive approach', *The Journal of Turkish Weekly* (first published by Review of International Law and Politics (RILP), 3(11), pp. 121–44), www.turkishweekly.net/article/310/constructivism-and-identity-formation-an-interactive-approach.html (accessed on 25 November 2014).
Dahlman, Carl J., 2012. *The World under Pressure: How India and China Are Influencing the Global Economy and Environment*, Stanford, CA: Stanford Economics and Finance.
Garver, John W., 2001. *Protracted Contest: Sino-Indian Rivalry in the Twentieth Century*, Seattle: University of Washington Press.
MEA, 2013. 'Joint statement on the State visit of Chinese Premier Li Keqiang to India', Ministry of External Affairs, Government of India, 20 May, www.mea.gov.in/in-focus-article.htm?21723/Joint+Statement+on+the+State+Visit+of+Chinese++Li+Keqiang+to+India (accessed on 2 December 2014).
Panda, Jagannath P., 2013. 'Competing realities in China–India multilateral discourse: Asia's enduring power rivalry', *Journal of Contemporary China*, 22(82): 669–70.
Panda, Jagannath P., 2014. 'Contemporary India–China dynamics: from an orthodox to an autonomous course?', *Strategic Analysis*, 3(4), July, pp. 595–601.
Raja Mohan, C., 2013. *Samudra Manthan: Sino-Indian Rivalry in the Indo-Pacific*, New Delhi: Oxford University Press.
Ramesh, Jairam, 2005. *Making Sense of Chindia: Reflections on China and India*, New Delhi: India Research Press.
Sharma, Shalendra D., 2009. *China and India in the Age of Globalization*, New Delhi: Cambridge University Press.
Smith, Jeff M., 2014. *Cold Peace: China–India Rivalry in the Twenty-First Century*, Lanham, MD: Lexington Books.
Tan Chung, 2008. *Rise of the Asian Giants: Dragon–Elephant Tango* (edited by Patricia Uberoi), Delhi: Anthem Press.
Tien-sze Fang, 2014. *Asymmetrical Threat Perceptions in India–China Relations*, New Delhi: Oxford University Press.

Part I
The bilateral course

2 Between principles and policies

The new official course of India–China ties is termed as 'developmental partnership', which was primarily construed during President Xi Jinping's visit to India in September 2014 (*PIB* 2015). Its essence is to forge a closer economic partnership, enhancing the decade-old Strategic and Cooperative Partnership of Peace and Prosperity. The Joint Statement of the two countries, released on 11 April 2005, outlined the core of the Strategic and Cooperative Partnership as being based on the 'principles of Panchsheel, mutual respect and sensitivity for each other's concerns and aspirations, and equality...' (MEA 2005).[1] This partnership called for 'all-round and comprehensive development' of bilateral ties to be based on 'mutual and equal security, development and prosperity'. The 2005 Joint Statement took note of increased political exchanges, better economic cooperation, stronger connectivity, and strengthening exchanges and interactions in various fields. This expressed vision came within the thrust of the Panchsheel discourse.

Since its formulation officially on 29 April 1954, the Panchsheel doctrine has been a matter of great debate in the international relations discourse. Primarily originated as an 'Agreement on Trade and Intercourse' (MEA 2004a) between the Tibet Region of China and India, it was neither a fully accredited India–China bilateral accord nor was it comprehensive enough to address the India–China–Tibet complexity. The Five Principles of Peaceful Coexistence (Panchsheel) that the agreement envisaged comprised: (i) mutual respect for each other's territorial integrity and sovereignty; (ii) mutual non-aggression; (iii) mutual non-interference; (iv) equality and mutual benefit; and (v) peaceful coexistence. On 28 June 1954, the visiting Premier of China, Zhou Enlai, and the Prime Minister of India, Jawaharlal Nehru, issued a Joint Statement elaborating the course of Panchsheel.

Soon thereafter, the optimism of the Panchsheel vision was put to the test in the context of the Chinese interference in Ladakh in 1954, complication of the Tibetan matter and the rising bilateral differences over the boundary leading to the 1962 war (Madhav 2014). In consequence, Panchsheel has been seen in India's domestic discourse more as a deception principle that is linked with India's territorial loss and national security complexity. For the Chinese, on the other hand, Panchsheel has been a fundamental collection of principles in their

16 *The bilateral course*

outreach policy. Chinese experts have for long envisaged Panchsheel as a useful instrument in their dialogue of a multipolar world order.[2]

Currently, if the two countries' bilateral ties have become more methodical, much of the credit goes to the 2005 agreement. A range of bilateral dialogue mechanisms exists today in India–China relations. Two things that have significantly contributed to enhancing India–China ties are: trade and economic contacts, and political engagement. India–China trade has witnessed a steady rise in the last decade (see Figure 2.1), rising from around US$18 billion in 2004 to $70 billion in 2014 and is set to cross $70 billion by 2016. Political engagement has also been steady (see Table 2.1).

A strategic but not-so-cooperative partnership

A range of dialogue apparatuses – like Financial Dialogue, Defence and Security Dialogues (see Table 2.2) and Strategic Economic Dialogue (SED) – now exists between the two countries. The SED was first mooted in December 2010 when the then Premier Wen Jiabao visited India. Usually held between the planning commissions of the two countries – the Planning Commission of India (now renamed as Niti Aayog) and the National Development and Reform Commission (NDRC) of China – SED is slowly becoming a mechanism of substance.

A number of factors explain the importance of SED interaction. *First*, both countries participate in various regional and global multilateral institutions and frameworks such as RIC, BRICS, BASIC and G-20. This corroborates the spirit of 'strategic and cooperative' aspects that the 2005 Joint Statement speaks about. *Second*, they share a common interest in checking protectionism in the multilateral trading system (MEA 2013). Both also want reform of the Bretton Woods

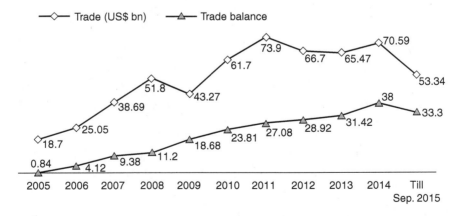

Figure 2.1 India–China bilateral trade and trade imbalance, 2005–2015 (source: data collected from Ministry of Commerce, People's Republic of China (http://english.mofcom.gov.cn), Embassy of India, Beijing (www.indianembassy.org.cn), Ministry of External Affairs, GoI (mea.gov.in) and open sources like *The Hindu*, *Economic Times* and *India Today*).

Between principles and policies 17

Table 2.1 Highest-level political exchange of visits between India and China, 2008–2015

Date of visit	Dignitary visiting	Important joint statements, vision documents or MoUs
13–15 January 2008	Prime Minister Manmohan Singh visited China	A Shared Vision for the 21st Century of the Republic of India and the People's Republic of China
24–25 October 2008	Prime Minister Manmohan Singh visited China	Attended the 7th Asia-Europe Summit Meeting in Beijing
26–31 May 2010	President Pratibha Patil visited China	Important agreements concerning commerce, education and other sectors
15–17 December 2010	Chinese Premier Wen Jiabao visited India	Joint Communiqué of the Republic of India and the People's Republic of China, 16 December 2010
19–21 May 2013	Chinese Premier Li Keqiang visited India	Joint Statement on the State Visit of Chinese Premier Li Keqiang to India, 20 May 2013
22–24 October 2013	Prime Minister Manmohan Singh visited China	Joint Statement – A Vision for Future Development of India–China Strategic and Cooperative Partnership
17–19 September 2014	Chinese President Xi Jinping visited India	Joint Statement between the Republic of India and the People's Republic of China on Building a Closer Developmental Partnership, 19 September 2014
14–16 May 2015	Prime Minister Narendra Modi visited China	Joint Statement between India and China

institutions. *Third*, macroeconomic issues need joint deliberations. The SED creates conditions for them to coordinate in regional and global economic dealings.

The SED is supplemented today by Financial Dialogue and Defence and Security Dialogue mechanisms (Table 2.2) and Strategic Dialogue, Joint Economic Group (JEG) (Table 2.3), etc. These apparatuses comprise stronger global, regional, cross-regional and bilateral contacts in a variety of economic, security and strategic issues. But closer inspection reveals that most of these meetings are yet to offer concrete outcomes in today's practical circumstances in India–China ties.

The SED, for example, requires particular focus on two aspects: cooperation in multilateral economic forums; and collaboration in multilateral political forums. In this context, the principal outlook on forging a common perspective on 'developing country' and 'emerging economies' phenomena needs serious debate. China today is a leading country in many global financial institutions and has also emerged as a big donor in a number of international agencies.

Table 2.2 Chronology of India–China dialogue

Round	Date and venue	Represented by	Major issues discussed
Financial dialogue			
First	7 April 2006, New Delhi	Ashok Jha (Secretary, Department of Economic Affairs, India); Li Yong (Vice Minister of Finance, China)	Macroeconomic situation; promotion of sustainable development strategies for economic growth, etc.
Second	4 December 2007, Beijing	Subba Rao (Finance Secretary, India); Li Yong (Vice Minister of Finance, China)	Macroeconomic situation; fiscal policies that can promote sustainable development
Third	16 January 2009, New Delhi	Ashok Chawla (Secretary, Department of Economic Affairs, India); Liao Xiaojun (Vice Minister of Finance, China)	Global economic conditions; G-20; financial sector reforms in the two countries
Fourth	2 September 2010, Beijing	Ashok Chawla (Finance Secretary, India); Zhu Guangyao (Vice Minister of Finance, China)	Global financial crisis; macroeconomic situation and policy; financial stability and development; G-20; climate change, etc.
Fifth	8 November 2011, New Delhi	R. Gopalan (Secretary, Department of Economic Affairs, India); Wang Baoan (Assistant Minister of Finance, China)	International economic situation; G-20; enhancing bilateral cooperation in global financial institutions
Sixth	26 September 2013, Beijing	Arvind Mayaram, Secretary, Economic Affairs, India); Zhu Guangyao (Vice Minister of Finance, China)	Macroeconomic policies; international economic conditions; IMF quota reforms; BRICS cooperation, etc.

Defence and security dialogue

First	November 2007, Beijing	Bimal Julka, Joint Secretary (G/Air); Ministry of Defence, India; Major Gen. Qian LiHua, Chief of FAO, MND, China	Confidence-building measures (CBMs); peace and stability in the border, etc.
Second	15 December 2008, New Delhi	Vijay Singh, Defence Secretary, India; Lt. Gen. Ma Xiaotian, China	CBMs; peace and stability in the border; bilateral interaction
Third	6 January 2010, Beijing	Pradeep Kumar, Defence Secretary, India; Ma Xiaotian (Dy. Chief of General Staff) and Liang Guanglie, Defence Minister, China	CBMs and joint military exercise
Fourth	9 December 2011, New Delhi	Shashikant Sharma, Defence Secretary, India; Ma Xiaotian, Deputy Chief of General Staff, China	Defence exchanges for 2012; agreed to enhance cooperation and interaction
Fifth	14 January 2013, Beijing	Shashikant Sharma, Defence Secretary, India; Qi Jianguo, Deputy Chief of General Staff, China	Security issues in Asia-Pacific; India-China border
Sixth	24 February 2014, New Delhi	R.K. Mathur, Defence Secretary, India; Lt. Gen. Wang Guanzhong, Deputy Chief of General Staff, China	Military-to-military exchange, security situation in South Asia, Asia-Pacific and the Indian Ocean

Sources: Ministry of External Affairs (MEA), Government of India, *Times of India, The Hindu, Economic Times, China Daily, Global Times, Xinhua, China.org.cn*, Ministry of Commerce, Government of China, etc.

Table 2.3 Chronology of India–China Joint Economic Group (JEG) meetings

Round	Date/venue	Co-chair/representatives
First	18–20 September 1989, New Delhi	Zheng Tuobin, Chinese Minister of Foreign Economic Relations and Trade; V.P. Singh, Indian Minister of Commerce and Industry
Second	6 February 1991, Beijing	Li Lanquing, Chinese Minister of Foreign Economic Relations and Trade; Arun Nehru, Minister of Commerce of India and Ajit Singh, Industry Minister, India
Third	9 December 1991, New Delhi	Li Lanquing, Chinese Minister of Foreign Economic Relations and Trade; Arun Nehru, Minister of Commerce of India and Ajit Singh, Industry Minister, India
Fourth	4 January 1993, Beijing	Li Lanquing, Chinese Minister of Foreign Economic Relations and Trade; Indian Minister and Representatives from Commerce and Industry Ministry, India
Fifth	13 June 1994 New Delhi	Chinese Minister of Foreign Trade and Economic Cooperation; Indian Minister and Representatives from Commerce and Industry Ministry, India
Sixth	19–20 February 2000, Beijing	Shi Guangsheng, Chinese Minister of Foreign Trade and Economic Cooperation; Murasoli Maran, Minister of Commerce and Industry, India
Seventh	16 March 2006, New Delhi	Bo Xilai, Minister of Commerce of PRC; Kamal Nath, Minister of Commerce and Industry, India
Eight	19 January 2010, Beijing	Chen Deming, Chinese Minister of Commerce; Anand Sharma, Indian Minister of Commerce and Industry
Ninth	27 August 2012, New Delhi	Chen Deming, Chinese Minister of Commerce; Anand Sharma, Indian Minister of Commerce and Industry
Tenth	2 September 2014, Beijing	Nirmala Sitharaman, Indian Minister of Commerce; Gao Hucheng, Chinese Minister of Commerce

New Delhi needs to be assured by China that the developing-country formula will continue to be common to both countries in terms of vision and strategy in the foreseeable future. Currently, there is a doubt on this aspect, considering that the Chinese leadership under Xi Jinping is pushing forward the idea of a 'new type of major-power relations', prompting China's status as a power equivalent to the US. This is being promoted concurrently with a strong US–China Strategic and Economic Dialogue (S&ED) (Shambaugh 2013).

Current course of mutual policies

The personality of states matters in international relations. Both India and China are populous and emerging countries and both are Asian powers that shape the dialogue of the Asian Century today. Their foreign policy contours are a reflection of their state personalities: for India, a fragmented 'democratic' character remains the yardstick; and for China, the 'communist and authoritarian' edifice shapes its policy character. In the last decade, the foreign policy of both countries has experienced changes and progress, supplemented by economic ranking improvement (see Table 2.4); their global undertakings have also expanded. India's and China's rise has resulted in 'power shifts and frictions in world governance architecture' (Dahlman 2012: 14). The changing state personality has been augmented with the new leadership personalities too.

Leadership shapes the political course in populous societies. Post-1947, the political trajectory of India and China was driven by strong personalities like Mao Zedong, Zhou Enlai and Jawaharlal Nehru. Panchsheel too was largely a culmination of the strong personality cult of Zhou Enlai and Jawaharlal Nehru (MEA 2004b). This historical trend is also reflected strongly in contemporary India–China ties. Since the enunciation of their Strategic and Cooperative Partnership in 2005, India–China relations have been more or less subjugated to Manmohan Singh and Hu Jintao or Wen Jiabao temperaments. These personalities were contemporaneous leaders. A range of mechanisms and institutional engagements that currently exist in the two countries' bilateral ties were established in the last ten years during the Manmohan Singh–Hu Jintao era. It would appear that given their strong leadership character, the Narendra Modi–Xi Jinping chemistry will likely influence India–China relations in the near future.

India's China dialogue

While the US holds the prime place as the superpower in the Indian strategic outlook, China holds the prime attention in Indian foreign policy and strategic

Table 2.4 India–China comparative profile, 2004–2014

	2004		2014	
	China	India	China	India
GDP per capita, PPP (Current International US$)	4422.65	2576.54	13,216.54	5707.65
GDP (nominal) ranking	6	10	2	9
Bilateral trade (billion US$)	13.6		70.6	
Military expenditure in (constant 2011) million US$	63,503	33,877	190,974	49,999

Sources: World Development Indicators Database, World Bank at http://data.worldbank.org; SIPRI Military Expenditure Database at www.sipri.org/research/armaments/milex/milex_database; and other open sources like *China Daily*, *The Hindu*, etc.

22 *The bilateral course*

deliberation.³ Accounting for this fact are the factors of China's economic pre-eminence, its commanding political image and a strong military presence in the neighbourhood. Perceived as being between the prism of an 'economic opportunity' and security concern, India's China deliberation is divided more between the 'competition-and-cooperation' aspect.

This prism has taken a long time shaping up, beginning with the perception of China as a Panchsheel partner.⁴ The Tibet episode, the 1962 war and the contrasting developmental courses of the two countries over the decades have contributed to changing India's outlook as regards China.⁵ Fundamentally, the current perception of India, which has always been besotted with its Western persuasion of China being a 'mysterious' country (Panda 2015a), is that China is more a powerful neighbour than a reliable partner.

Hitherto, the 'obsessed nationalist' security-centric lookout of its political-strategic community has been the main factor in shaping India's China policy. Unremarkably, most of it is the mental baggage of the trauma of the 1962 India–China war. Compounding the problem to a much greater extent has been China's emergence as a strong military and political power. True, China's military rise does pose some level of security concern for India; yet this aspect is overextended where the objectivity of viewing China in the twenty-first century realm is concerned. Table 2.5 shows how China dominates the Indian strategic prudence more as a concern. Viewing things in a more realistic perspective, however, two concurrent aspects need to shape India's China policy: (i) India's strategic elitist edifice, where China should be seen across multiple prisms in terms of how India–China ties should take shape in the next decade; and (ii) India's changing regional and global foreign policy outlook, in which China is of course important.

Currently, India's China debate is confined to concerns about China's rise as a military and political power, while the process and the trend of China's rise as India's immediate neighbour, as an Asian power and as a global power, have received scant attention, to India's own disadvantage in terms of strategic choices. Currently, like most of the democratic countries, India finds it difficult to form a well-rounded policy on China, hence basing it on the general proposition of 'engage with China, albeit cautiously'. While the business community in India sees China more as an opportunity, the think-tanks and the media visualise that country more as a strategic concern. India currently views China as a powerful neighbour, a vital global economy and an important country in Asian and global politics that India needs to engage with. But amidst this engagement, there is caution that China currently is too strong both politically and militarily vis-à-vis India.

It has been advocated that India must craft a strategic path without entirely rejecting the previously recognised path of non-alignment, which bespeaks 'strategic autonomy' the country has enjoyed over the decades (Khilnani *et al.* 2012). But amidst the numerous challenges and opportunities, the major paradox for Indian foreign policy is how to approach and craft a policy towards the two most important countries of the world, namely, the United States and China. While

Table 2.5 India–China mutual perceptions

(a) Perception of India's democratic elite regarding China

Elites	Predominant view	Assumption
Government	Engage China with caution	China's rise cannot be contained
Media	Alarmist	China is a concern and an obstacle
Think-tanks	China is a security concern	China's approach to India is not so friendly
Business/industrial community	Engage with China	China is an economic opportunity

(b) Chinese reflections on India's power of refraction

Communist construct	Predominant view	Assumption
Media	India is a struggling country	India's democratic path is not on par with China's Communist path
Think-tanks/scholars	India is a pro-USA country	India is not supportive towards China; a key ally of the USA
Business community	India is not business friendly and not an encouraging economy	Indian business approach is not open and friendly towards China
Citizens' perspective	India is land of the Buddha and a culturally rich country	India is a tourist destination
Chinese government	India is a 'potential' country in China's neighbourhood	India is a pro-Western country, not supportive to China's regional and strategic interests

Sources: For Table (a) – modified version of the author's impressions. See Jagannath P. Panda, 2013, 'Competing realities in China–India multilateral discourse: Asia's enduring power rivalry', *Journal of Contemporary China*, 22(2), July, pp. 669–90. For Table (b) – based on the author's impressions gathered in his interactions with Chinese officials, think-tanks/scholars, media personnel, business community and common citizens.

the United States is strategically closer to India at many levels, China remains a partner as well as a security challenge. Implementing a balanced approach towards China could be a desirable policy approach for India. But in practice, the greater quandary in India's broader strategic context is how to deal with China as a 'development partner' at the bilateral level, while coping with China's influence at the regional and global levels. A further challenge is whether to place China as a priority ahead or behind the United States in Indian foreign policy.[6]

The conventional argument notes that India's policy approach towards China should be a 'balance' of competition-and-cooperation (Khilnani *et al.* 2012). It appears, however, that the enterprise of such a balancing policy needs to be more nuanced and subtle.[7] India needs to emerge with a China policy within a

24 *The bilateral course*

'multiple' outlook or prism of competition, cooperation, correlation, coexistence, collaboration and conflict, which would be analogous to China's India policy (Panda 2015b). China on its part views India through multiple prisms, within the evolving progression of a multipolar world order: an Asian partner, a competitor, a developing-world partner as well as a pro-American country that is detrimental to China's security and strategic interests, and more notably, a determined power that poses enormous challenges to China's presence and rise.[8]

Between India and China, correlation has been a relatively new mode engagement. India is connected with China in terms of BRICS grouping and BASIC (Brazil–South Africa–India–China) climate grouping. But India needs to clarify with China as an emerging power on what basis it can establish with it a correlated relationship at the global level when China designs a 'new type of major power relationship' with the US. In terms of coexistence, India must revisit the notion to what extent it values China as a power to coexist with it in Asia and beyond, especially at a time when Prime Minister Modi has spoken about the 'Asian century'. China has usually shown disquiet as regards India's rise in East Asia. India needs to bring clarity in its China outlook in terms of whether China values India's rise in Asia, in East Asia or in Central Asia. India needs also to clarify with China whether their coexistence is possible in the multipolar world politics in the real world, given their diverse understandings.

Collaboration is another domain that needs deliberation in India's China policy. Collaboration is not cooperation: it is more issue specific. India needs to have a discussion on various aspects of collaboration, whether India can actually collaborate with China in third-party sectors or in third-country domains. Afghanistan has been a matter of discussion between the two countries in official parlance. Is there scope for collaboration between them in Afghanistan? Can they also aim to establish collaboration in Africa where both countries' strategic aims are identical, namely, to explore energy and resources? Further, whether both can have collaborative ties on connectivity and corridors proposals? These clarifications need to be entrenched in India's China policy.

Deliberating on these specific aspects, going beyond the competition-and-cooperation dynamic, will help India have a nuanced and comprehensive policy outlook on China. This will also help India anticipate whether a possibility of conflict exists with China. Given China's impressive rise in Asia and beyond, the conflict may not necessarily be military: it is more likely to be subtle, relating to power presence, power influence and resources politics.

China's India dialogue

A consensus is emerging among the experts and academia around the world that Beijing's foreign policy under Xi Jinping is in continuous transition. Core to this transition is China's economic rise and the confidence that it has attained in the recent past. During the world economic slowdown, the Chinese economy was the centre of stability and attraction. Its economic rise has helped China to pursue an 'action'-driven foreign policy, with 'proactive diplomacy' (*zhudongshiwaijiao*) taking over from 'responsive diplomacy' (*fanyingshiwaijiao*) (Zhiqun Zhu 2013: 7; also Zhang Baohui 2010; *Policy Q&A* 2012). Post-18th Communist Party of China (CPC) National Congress replicates a 'new era' in Beijing's foreign policy where new modes of exploration and innovation seem to be the core of its foreign relations practice (see Yang Jiemian 2015). Consequently, there is asynchronous focus on neighbouring as well as remote countries, minor and major powers, developed and developing countries, which was not the case of post-1978 open China (Ruan Zongze 2014; Xu Jian 2014; *The CIIS Blue Book on International Situation and China's Foreign Affairs* 2014).

Unlike most of China's contemporary debate on foreign affairs, the India debate in China remains relatively less known and less perceptible to the outside world. India is debated quite frequently though restrictedly, and unlike in the past, China's India debate is quite serious today. The fundamental notion of this Chinese seriousness is that 'India is rising, and rising steadily'.[9] At the same time, neither does China foresee the supremacy of Indian power as akin to American power; nor as a past power like Japan. If anything, India is seen more as a 'potential power'.[10]

The current Chinese perspective is a culmination of the historical Chinese perspective of India as a neighbour, dating back to the British legacy, where civilisational discourses like Tibet, the Dalai Lama and the McMahon Line were some of the factors. It is basically a culmination of an authoritarian and conservative outlook of a closed society that the Chinese state has pursued over the years as regards its immediate democratic neighbour. Nevertheless, India is being seen afresh as a somewhat 'competitive' and a reasonable power in China's contemporary outlook. Chinese experts foresee India more as a 'pragmatic' rather than an aggressive power and that China must take note of that in its foreign policy. They also hold the view that India's pragmatism has made India–China relations somewhat competitive.[11] Leaders like Xi Jinping and Li Keqiang view India more within the hypothesis of a changing world order. Xi Jinping has written that 'As two important forces in a world that moves towards multipolarity, we need to become global partners having strategic coordination' (Xi Jinping 2014).

Five correlated courses may be observed which more or less form the core of the Chinese state treatise about another country. These are: (i) the Chinese media's perspective; (ii) the intellectual and scholarly perception; (iii) outreach of the economic community and its course; (iv) the citizens' perspective; and (v) the leadership's thinking (Li Xin 2013).[12] The Chinese media reporting on India offers the prime glimpse of China's India debate. It is argued: 'media coverage in China constitutes the gaudy snapshot of the state's outlook on India perception' (ibid.: 14). For the media, India is a matter for close attention. Most of their coverage is based on two versions: one focuses on culture, economics and the social aspects; the other covers India from more of a 'third eye' viewpoint (ibid.). There is occasional direct reporting on the Indian political scene in China. The Chinese media feel more secure in reporting about India's cultural, economic and societal facets, showing India in poor light, struggling as a democracy, vis-à-vis China's success as a communist phenomenon.[13] This works to cast doubt among those Chinese citizens who may seek political change or introduction of more democratic values (ibid.). The 'third eye' perspective is linked with countries or issues that are adverse to China's strategic or foreign policy interests. In this perspective, India is seen to be linked with countries like the US and Japan and in an adversarial position on issues that are linked to China's strategic interests. But as regards emotionally involved issues like Tibet and China's 'most wanted terrorist', the Dalai Lama, the Chinese media are quite vocal against India. The Chinese media outlook on India may be partial, judgemental and restricted; but it surely nurtures and influences the state discourse towards India.

As regards the intellectual and scholarly dialogue, there is a rising flavour to study and research about India, but the India studies curriculum still remains poor. Neither are the existing India study programmes on par with the Japan or Russia or America studies programmes, nor are they strong enough to generate any positive impression about India among the Chinese public or intellectuals. The India study programmes in many universities or think-tanks are typically constructed as part of South Asia study units. Orthodox university departments to study about Indian literature, culture and tradition do exist, but they lack dynamism and policy influence. Only recently, have some mainstream universities and think-tanks started studying India as a separate discipline, but most of these are agenda-centric, being backed either by intelligence units of the government or the Communist Party of China (CPC). Or they are mostly ideological and social science related, and not so much focusing on modern India's contemporary primacies.[14] The usual mindset that India is not affable towards China circumscribes nuanced objectivity.

Modern China is a trading nation, which results in the business and entrepreneurial communities significantly influencing its foreign policy approaches. The Chinese business elite do not usually see India in a positive light. They see the Indian economy as a 'rising' one, but not quite pertinent to China's state or economic interests.[15] There has been some interest among the Chinese business community to reach out to India in recent times, but it remains lukewarm. It sees India more as a nation struggling to take decisions. India's complex bureaucratic and administrative culture in its turn tends to view Chinese business and entrepreneurial outreach with suspicion. This is fostered by the fact that business and economic contacts are part and parcel of China's state political practice.

The Chinese citizens' perspective of India is of a somewhat 'mysterious and complex' country, albeit a graceful land of the Buddha and religion. The attractions of Bollywood cannot compensate for the fact that India is the country where the Dalai Lama resides. The common Chinese citizens generally may see India as deserving respect, but may be apprehensive of their government as regards advocating something that is pro-India or India-friendly. They also lack information to form a correct picture of India.

The current Chinese leadership's account of India is that it is a 'rising' power, and an important power in Asia. India is factored seriously in China's dialogue of building an 'Asian Community' and, notably, India is factored in China's rhetoric of Panchsheel (Liu Zhenmin 2014). The Chinese leaders and officials acutely monitor India's undertaking as a power in the making. Domestic developments, foreign policy courses and India's leadership thinking are taken seriously by the Chinese leaders and their disciples. Think-tank scholars and university teachers also partially help the Chinese leadership to appraise India and its drive.

Li Keqiang's first overseas tour as Premier of China was to India; and that explains India's growing importance in China's foreign policy today. Nevertheless, what remains perplexing in the Chinese political outlook on India is the resistance to an open outlook to see India independently and exclusively beyond the prism of a 'pro-Western country'. Intriguingly, interactions and interviews with Chinese experts suggest that India is watched under China's neighbourhood policy, but more than that, the current leaders see India more as a 'limited Asian partner'. China's connections with India in the BCIM, RCEP negotiation process, and India's joining in the China-led Asian Infrastructure Investment Bank (AIIB) are some indicators that explain that China does see India as an Asian partner, conceivably more as a limited or issue-based partner.[16] The current Chinese leadership has also invited India to join China's proposed 'One Belt, One Road' (OBOR) initiative. It is becoming clear that they foresee India more as a competitive power in Asia, as witnessed in China's approach towards India at the regional level in different segments of Asia, from Central to South-East to South Asia. Between an immediate neighbour to limited Asian partner, China and its leadership see India as a valuable multilateral partner or collaborator. The India–China relationship in BRICS and BASIC evidences this outlook.

The Chinese perspective to locate India as a multilateral collaborator is associated with the fact that India is a developing country, and China's collaboration with India at cross-continental or intercontinental or global levels can be beneficial to China itself (Li Xin 2013). Beijing does comprehend that it is difficult to reform the Bretton Woods institutions single-handed (Glosny 2010).[17] India could be an effective partner in this matter or in establishing alternative institutions in Asia and beyond (ibid.).

In brief, India is debated, watched and prioritised in the Chinese outlook through multiple prisms (Panda 2015a). It is practical for China to do this because of the multipolarity of world politics, and especially, in view of India's emergence as a potential power in world affairs. But the structural edifice of China as a Communist regime restricts its India outlook from being better nuanced.

It has also been rightly argued that even though China wants harmonious relations with India, it would not prevent Beijing from pursuing a 'policy of containment within engagement' (Dutt 2009: 149). Likewise, India may also like to reciprocate to China with harmonious relations but will be 'mindful of its own security needs' with regard to China (ibid.). Their mutual perception is a result of their respective security perception (Li Li 2009: 174).

One does notice, nevertheless, continuity in economic and political engagement.[18] The economic engagement is becoming much more methodological and

28 *The bilateral course*

development-oriented while the political engagement is becoming strong and mature, that prompts to a more 'pragmatic' bilateral relation.[19] The current engagement between the two countries under the leadership of Narendra Modi and Xi Jinping looks promising. Their first meeting at the BRICS summit in Brazil in 2014, Xi's first visit to India as head of state in September 2014, tensions along the border during Xi Jinping's visit, the Chinese invitation to India to attend the Asia-Pacific Economic Cooperation (APEC) preparatory summit meeting in Beijing, and India's decision to join the AIIB are some highlights that indicate concurrent advances in India–China relations.

Under Modi and Xi, notwithstanding persistent tensions along the border, India and China carried forward to sign a few agreements to enhance their bilateral ties. The Joint Statement issued during President Xi's visit to India termed India–China ties as a 'developmental partnership' and the new Joint Statement released during Modi's visit to China endorses that. Studying the varieties of agreements and MoUs that have been signed between the two countries in 2014 and 2015, it is clear that India–China ties perhaps are more of a 'developmental cooperative partnership' or 'development-oriented partnership' today than anytime earlier. Xi Jinping, during his visit to India, contextualised India's and China's situation as 'express trains' for driving regional development. He further endorsed both countries as 'twin anchors' of regional peace (*Xinhuanet* 2014). For China, forging a 'developmental' partnership with other countries has been the crux of its foreign policy in the last decade.[20]

During Xi Jinping's tour of India, the two countries signed a plethora of bilateral agreements/MoUs, to wit, mainly: (i) opening of a new route for Indian pilgrimage for Kailash Mansarovar Yatra to the Tibetan Autonomous Region of China; (ii) action plan of enhancing and reinforcing cooperation in railways; (iii) five-year trade and economic cooperation development plan; (iv) cooperation agreement on customs matters; (v) forging cooperation in the peaceful use of space; and (vi) strengthening cooperation between cultural institutions (MEA 2014b). Each of these deals, or agreements/MoUs points to a new level of progressive understanding between the two countries. Apart from these agreements and MoUs, the two main high points of India–China ties during Xi's visit to India were: (i) agreements on sister-city and sister provincial or state-level ties (see Table 2.6); and (ii) MoUs on establishing industrial parks in Maharashtra and Gujarat with collaboration between Chinese and Indian companies. Mumbai–Shanghai and Ahmedabad–Guangzhou have established 'sister-city' relations; Gujarat and Guangdong have established 'sister-state or province' partnership (MEA 2014b). As per the new MoUs, a 1250 acre Industrial Park near Pune in Maharashtra and an Industrial Park in Gujarat will be set up with the assistance of Chinese enterprises to generate employment in these regions and promote ground-level cooperation between the two business sides (ibid.). There was an interest expressed by both sides to forge a 'broad-based and sustainable economic partnership' (MEA 2014a). To develop a better partnership on economic and commercial matters, it was agreed that the two sides would establish a dialogue mechanism between the Department of Economic Affairs of

Table 2.6 India–China sister city/province cooperation MoUs/agreements

Date/place	Sister city/province (MoUs between)	Representatives
23 October 2013, China	Delhi and Beijing	Dr S. Jaishankar, India's Ambassador to China; Mr Li Shixiang, Vice Mayor, Beijing Municipality
– do –	Bengaluru and Chengdu	Dr S. Jaishankar, India's Ambassador to China; Mr Ge Honglin, Mayor of Chengdu
– do –	Kolkata and Kunming	Dr S. Jaishankar, India's Ambassador to China; Mr Li Wenrong, Mayor of Kunming
17 September 2014, Gujarat	Mumbai and Shanghai	Smt. Snehal Ambekar, Mayor of Mumbai; Mr Tu Guangshao, Executive Vice Mayor, Shanghai
– do –	Ahmedabad and Guangzhou	Dr Guruprasad Mohapatra, Municipal Commissioner, Ahmedabad; Mr Chen Jianhua, Mayor of Guangzhou
– do –	Gujarat and Guangdong	Dr Varesh Sinha, Chief Secretary, Gujarat; Mr Xu Shaohua, Executive Vice Governor of Guangdong
15 May 2015, China	Karnataka and Sichuan Chennai and Chongqing Hyderabad and Qingdao Aurangabad and Dunhuang	During Indian Prime Minister Modi's visit to China

Source: Various Joint Statements signed between China and India. See the website of the Ministry of External Affairs (MEA), Government of India, at http://mea.gov.in.

the Indian Government and the Development Research Centre of the State Council of the PRC. These agreements and MoUs bring the domestic constituents in both countries closer to each other. But practically, trade imbalance, open market collaboration and border trade are some matters that need further deliberation on both sides. Media statistics suggest that even though India–China bilateral trade in 2014 ($70.59 billion) witnessed an increase of $5.02 billion from 2013 (around $65.57 billion), their trade imbalance has been widening (*Economic Times* 2015).

The year 2014 marked the 60th anniversary of the enunciation of Panchsheel between India and China. The year 2015 was designated as 'Visit India Year' and 2016 as 'Visit China Year'. Likewise, the year 2014–2015 marked the 10th anniversary of the India–China Strategic and Cooperative Partnership of Peace and Prosperity. To what extent these symbolic or commemorative occasions strengthen India–China relations are a matter that needs to be observed. If the last decade of India–China relations mostly belonged to Manmohan Singh–Hu Jintao, the next few years will perhaps belong to Modi and Xi.

Notes

1 The Partnership was signed during the state visit of Premier Wen Jiabao to India during 9–12 April 2005.
2 Almost two decades ago, Chinese experts were talking about the usefulness of Panchsheel in an emerging multipolar world. For example, see Qian Jiadong 1996.
3 For a detailed analysis on how China is viewed in Indian foreign policy, see Shourie 2008; Dutt 2009.
4 Prof. Manoranjan Mohanty, former director of the Institute of Chinese Studies (ICS) in New Delhi, still calls India and China Panchsheel partners. See Mohanty 2005.
5 Author's interaction with (Late) Prof. V.P. Dutt.
6 This part is drawn from Panda 2012.
7 Alka Acharya is of the view that the competition-and-cooperation prism is a 'catch-all kind of framework'; that it is 'tactical in nature' and 'does not take us very far or help us in understanding how the relationship has to be actively shaped and guided'. Author's email interview with Alka Acharya, 13 March 2015.
8 Impression gathered from the author's interviews with several Chinese experts on India and South Asia, carried out during his field trip to China under the ICSSR–CASS exchange of scholars from 19 December 2014 to 3 January 2015. The following were interviewed, among others: Prof. Ma Jiali (China Reform Forum), Sun Shihai (Retd. CASS Professor in Beijing), Dr Li Li and Mr Lou Chunhao (CICIR, Beijing), Prof. Shen Dengli (Fudan University, Shanghai), Prof. Du Youkang (Fudan University), Prof. Zhao Gancheng (SIIS, Shanghai), Dr Liu Zongyi (SIIS) and Dr Wang Weihua (SIIS).
9 Impression gathered from the author's interviews with several Chinese experts in mainstream think-tanks like CICIR, CIIS, CASS in Beijing and SASS and SIIS in Shanghai during 18 December 2014 to 4 January 2015.
10 This view is mainly derived from the author's interaction with Dr Liu Zongyi. He is an expert with SIIS, Shanghai.
11 Views of Dr Lou Chunhao of CICIR, Beijing. The author interviewed him on 22 December 2014 in Beijing.
12 This portion is drawn from Li Xin's excellent analysis of China's India outlook. See Li Xin 2013.
13 See the author's compilation on 'Recent important Chinese writings and views on India: a survey of recent media, official and scholarly writings/views' in Panda 2010: 213–16.
14 Impression gathered from the author's interviews during 18 December 2014 to 4 January 2015 with several Chinese experts in mainstream think-tanks like CICIR, CIIS and CASS in Beijing and SASS and SIIS in Shanghai.
15 Prof. Alka Acharya believes that

> China is keen to see India evolving as a major destination for Chinese investment. In the short run the focus would be on addressing the obstacles and to promote smooth flow of trade and commerce. A parallel – and in many ways related – objective would be to ensure that India does not join the US-led efforts to contain China.
> (Author's email interview with Prof. Alka Acharya, 13 March 2015)

16 Impression gathered from the author's interviews during 18 December 2014 to 4 January 2015 with several Chinese experts in mainstream think-tanks like CICIR, CIIS and CASS in Beijing and SASS and SIIS in Shanghai.
17 For an excellent article on this aspect, see Glosny 2010.
18 Alka Acharya is of the view that

> a new momentum and dynamism has been imparted by the new leaderships on both sides wherein the prioritisation of the economic development and

modernisation agenda has also given a more pragmatic turn to the expectations on both sides and has also begun to seep into the general discourse.

(Author's email interview with Prof. Alka Acharya, 13 March 2015)

19 Author's email interview with Prof. Srikanth Kondapalli, 10 September 2015. Prof. Srikanth Kondapalli is currently a professor and chairperson at the Centre for East Asia, School of International Studies (SIS) at the Jawaharlal Nehru University (JNU), New Delhi.
20 There is currently much discussion and debate in China on how to establish worldwide partnership. For instance, see Zhao Minghao 2014.

References

Dahlman, Carl J., 2012. 'Power shifts and rising frictions have implications for the global system and the United States' (Chapter 7), in *The World under Pressure: How China & India Are Influencing the Global Economy & Environment*, Stanford, CA: Stanford University Press, pp. 182–208.

Dutt, V.P., 2009. *India's Foreign Policy Since Independence*, New Delhi: National Book Trust.

Economic Times, 2015. 'India's trade deficit with China rose to $37.8 billion in 2014', *Economic Times*, 13 January, http://economictimes.indiatimes.com/news/economy/indicators/indias-trade-deficit-with-china-rose-to-37-8-billion-in-2014/articleshow/45873415.cms (accessed on 14 January 2015).

Glosny, Michael A., 2010. 'China and the BRICs: a real (but limited) partnership in a unipolar world', *Polity*, pp. 100–29.

Khilnani, Sunil, Kumar, Rajiv, Mehta, Pratap Bhanu, Menon, Prakash, Nilekani, Nandan, Raghvan, Srinath, Saran, Shyam and Varadarajan, Siddharth, 2012. *Nonalignment 2.0: A Foreign and Strategic Policy for India in the Twenty First Century*, New Delhi: Centre for Policy Research, pp. 1–70.

Li Li, 2009. *Security Perception and China–India Relations*, New Delhi: KW Publishers.

Li Xin, 2013. 'India through Chinese eyes', *World Policy Journal*, 30(4), Winter, pp. 13–21, www.worldpolicy.org/journal/winter2013/india-through-chinese-eyes (accessed on 24 February 2015).

Liu Zhenmin, 2014. 'Insisting on win-win cooperation and forging the Asian community of common destiny together', *China International Studies*, A CIIS Journal, March/April, pp. 5–25.

Madhav, Ram, 2014. 'Moving beyond the Panchsheel deception', *Indian Express*, 28 June, http://indianexpress.com/article/opinion/columns/moving-beyond-the-panchsheel-deception/ (accessed on 7 December 2014).

MEA, 2004a. *Panchsheel*, External Publicity Division, Ministry of External Affairs, Government of India, p. 1.

MEA, 2004b. 'Revisiting Panchsheel', Text based on the former President K.R. Narayanan's keynote address at a seminar organized in June 2004 in Beijing to mark the 50th anniversary of Panchsheel, Ministry of External Affairs, Government of India, 20 July 2004, www.mea.gov.in/articles-in-indian-media.htm?dtl/15408/Revitalising+Panchsheel (accessed on 7 September 2014).

MEA, 2005. 'Joint Statement of the Republic of India and the People's Republic of China', Ministry of External Affairs, Government of India, 11 April 2005, www.mea.gov.in/bilateral-documents.htm?dtl/6577/Joint+Statement+of+the+Republic+of+India+and+the+Peoples+Republic+of+China (accessed on 7 December 2014).

MEA, 2013. 'Joint Statement on the State Visit of Chinese Premier Li Keqiang to India, 20 May 2013', Ministry of External Affairs, Government of India, www.mea.gov.in/bilateral-documents.htm?dtl/21723/Joint+Statement+on+the+State+Visit+of+Chinese++Li+Keqiang+to+India (accessed on 11 December 2014).

MEA, 2014a. 'Joint Statement between the Republic of India and the People's Republic of China on building a closer developmental partnership', Ministry of External Affairs, Government of India, 19 September.

MEA, 2014b. 'List of Documents signed during the State Visit of Chinese President Xi Jinping to India', Ministry of External Affairs, Government of India, 18 September, www.mea.gov.in/bilateral-documents.htm?dtl/24012/List+of+Documents+signed+during+the+State+Visit+of+Chinese+President+Xi+Jinping+to+India (accessed on 2 January 2015).

Mohanty, Manoranjan, 2005. 'Panchsheel partner: a new beginning', *Economic and Political Weekly*, 23 April, pp. 1671–75.

Panda, Jagannath P., 2010. *China's Path to Power: Party, Military and the Politics of State Transition*, New Delhi: IDSA and Pentagon Press.

Panda, Jagannath, 2012. *Revisiting India's Policy Priorities: Nonalignment 2.0 and the Asian Matrix*, 10 July, Commentary, Seattle: National Bureau of Asian Research, 10 July, www.nbr.org/downloads/pdfs/Outreach/Panda_Commentary_07102012.pdf (accessed on 27 February 2015).

Panda, Jagannath, 2015a. 'Chinese reflections on India's power of refraction', *The Pioneer*, New Delhi, 21 February, p. 9.

Panda, Jagannath, 2015b. 'India's China policy: go beyond competition-&-cooperation prism', *The Pioneer*, Saturday special, 28 February, p. 9.

PIB, 2015. 'Joint Statement between India and China during Prime Minister's visit to China', Press Information Bureau, Government of India: Prime Minister's Office, 15 May.

Policy Q&A, 2012. 'Continuing a peaceful rise: China's foreign policy after the leadership transition', an interview with Shen Dingli, *Policy Q&A*, National Bureau of Asian Research, 6 September.

Qian Jiadong, 1996. 'Upholding Panchsheel: call of the hour', in Jasjit Singh (ed.), *India–China and Panchsheel*, New Delhi: Sanchar, pp. 35–42.

Ruan Zongze, 2014. 'What kind of neighbourhood will China build?', *China International Studies*, Journal of China Institute of International Studies (CIIS), Beijing, March/April, pp. 26–50.

Shambaugh, David, 2013. 'A big step forward in U.S.–China relations', *China & US Focus*, 19 July, www.chinausfocus.com/foreign-policy/a-big-step-forward-in-u-s-china-relations/ (accessed on 11 December 2014).

Shourie, Arun, 2008. *Self-Deception: India's China Policies: Origins, Premises, Lessons*, Noida: HarperCollins India.

The CIIS Blue Book on International Situation and China's Foreign Affairs, 2014. Preface, 'Characteristics of the international situation and innovations in China's diplomacy in 2013', *The CIIS Blue Book on International Situation and China's Foreign Affairs* (2014), Beijing: China Institute of International Studies, World Affairs Press, pp. 1–7.

Xi Jinping, 2014. 'Towards an Asian century of prosperity', *The Hindu*, 17 September, www.thehindu.com/opinion/op-ed/towards-an-asian-century-of-prosperity/article6416553.ece (accessed on 1 March 2015).

Xinhuanet, 2014. 'China, India should be partners for peace, development: Xi', *Xinhuanet*, 19 September, at http://news.xinhuanet.com/english/china/2014-09/19/c_133653930.htm (accessed on 5 January 2015).

Xu Jian, 2014. 'Rethinking China's period of strategic opportunity', *China International Studies*, Journal of China Institute of International Studies (CIIS), Beijing, March/April, pp. 51–70.

Yang Jiemian, 2015. 'Explorations and innovations of thinking, strategies and practice of China's diplomacy in the new era', *Global Review*, Shanghai Institute for International Studies, Shanghai, pp. 1–16.

Zhang Baohui, 2010. 'Chinese foreign policy in transition: trends and implications, *Journal of Current Chinese Affairs*, 39(2): 39–68.

Zhao Minghao, 2014. 'Developing with global vision', *China Daily*, 26 December, p. 8.

Zhiqun Zhu, 2013. *China's New Diplomacy: Rationale, Strategies and Significance*, Second Edition, England: Ashgate.

3 From *boundary* to *bordering territory*

The enduring dispute

It is a paradox of history that though India and China were the prime architects of the 'Five Principles of Peaceful Coexistence' (discussed in the previous chapter), the novelty of these principles was never executed in the course of their bilateral relationship, particularly in resolving the boundary dispute. Matters bordering on boundary change the complexion of the issue dramatically from its historical perspective, becoming more of a territorial dispute than just a boundary dispute, on account of the *resources* of land territory and the State's military and financial *authority*. Borders also have an important bearing on space and people in a globalised world (Haselsberger 2014; see also Blanchard 2005). This chapter evaluates the current and possible future course of the India–China boundary dispute. It looks at how historical facets have changed with the course of occasion and opportunity. It is divided into three main parts, as follows: (i) the nature of the dispute; (ii) the negotiation process; and (iii) the future of the dispute.

Core vs contiguous: the dispute

Fifty-four years after the India–China war, it is still debated whether it was the technicalities of the boundary that led to the conflict or the matters relating to the bordering regions that are not directly linked to the dispute. The debate points to the fact that the technicalities were as much a factor behind the conflict as the border or bordering regions, with the landscape of the dispute progressively emerging as core vs contiguous. A review of the literature on the subject[1] points to the fact that there are two prevailing aspects to the dispute: (i) differing stance on the length of the border; and (ii) the Line of Actual Control (LAC). This chapter examines how and where the course of these factors has mutated in course of time.

The border: between the claims and reclaims

The Chinese assertion of the India–China border is roughly of 2000 km, which 'has never been formally delineated' (Zhao Shengnan 2015a; see also Zhao Shengnan 2015b). This assertion is based on the deportment that Kashmir being a disputed region, its border must be excluded; and also that of Aksai Chin since

Aksai Chin currently belongs to and is controlled by China.[2] Chinese experts contend that 'China–India boundary has never existed, though each side has made its own territorial claims' (Liu Xuecheng 2011: 153). It is also argued that the border dispute is more a matter of 'zone' than 'line' in the Eastern and Western Sectors (ibid.). This is mainly due to wide desolate tracts in mountainous areas, which were inaccessible in ancient times (ibid.). In the Indian estimation on the other hand, the India–China border is about 4057 km in length, which must include the border of Pakistan-Occupied Kashmir (POK) as well as the Tibet–Sikkim border.

The two countries do not disagree much on the Middle Sector of their border, but have serious differences on the boundary of the Western and Eastern Sectors (see Map 3.1). On the Western Sector, New Delhi accuses China of illegitimately occupying 38,000 sq km of land in the Kashmir region. China also occupies 5180 sq km of land in the Kashmir region which has been ceded to it by Pakistan in 1963. Aksai Chin, which China occupies currently, is part of India's Ladakh region. India has no dispute as far as the Eastern Sector is concerned.

On the other hand, in the Chinese assertion, the Eastern Sector of the border is the most contentious one. In the Chinese contestation, the McMahon Line is illegitimate, which makes the India–China boundary a contested one. On this stance, China claims the Indian state of Arunachal Pradesh (almost 90,000 sq km in area) as its territory. In the Western Sector, the Chinese stance is that Ladakh is a disputed region.

In brief, the Indian stance is that the Western Sector is not really a disputed one but can be considered for negotiation; whereas in the Chinese contestation, both the Western and Eastern Sectors are seriously disputed regions, making the entire existing border an unenforceable entity.

Historically, the India–China boundary discourse is not limited to the two countries' bilateral complexities. It involves 'third party' factors like the British legacy, Tibet, Dalai Lama and the chronological negotiation process of the pre-1950s period, etc.[3] In the Indian contestation, the Western and Eastern Sectors were demarcated and defined in 1842 and 1913–1914 respectively (Tien-sze Fang 2014: 88; also Garver 2001). The western border was demarcated between Tibetan and Kashmir authorities in 1842 and does not need to be re-demarcated; but given the current complexity between the two countries, the matter may be negotiated. The Eastern Sector was demarcated as per the McMahon Line of 1913–1914 of the Simla Conference (Tien-sze Fang 2014: 88).

China in its turn holds that no formal treaty or agreement has taken place between the Indian and Chinese governments historically. China did not send any representative to partake in treaties between India and Tibet; neither did they partake in ratification of the treaties later (ibid.). The McMahon Line is an 'illegal' artefact, an 'imperial conception of British legacy'. The matter of the McMahon Line was never deliberated in the Simla Conference: it was a pact between the British administration and Tibetan representatives, whose original idea was mooted in a secret understanding in Delhi in March 1914 (ibid.). In Chinese contestation, the establishment of Arunachal Pradesh as a state in 1987

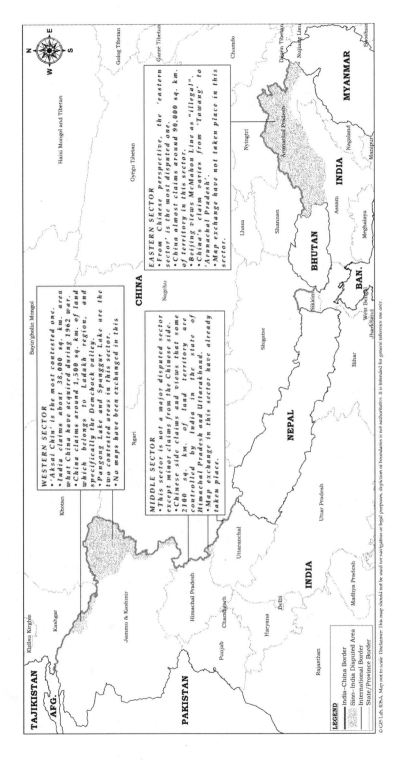

Map 3.1 Claims and reclaims in India–China boundary dispute at a glance.

was a unilateral setup by India,[4] that the so-called Arunachal Pradesh originally comprised three areas of 'China's Tibet' – Monyul, Loyul and Lower Tsayul – which India 'illegally' conquered. These three areas are located between the traditional India–China boundary and China (*Xinhua* 2015).

Interestingly, the Indian understanding before the 1962 war was that there was no border dispute between the two countries. When China released maps that offered a different interpretation to India–China borderlines, Nehru brought up the matter with the Chinese authorities and also expressed his reservations over the Xinjiang–Tibet road. India clarified its position on Tibet in the 1954 Treaty. In the Chinese purview, these Indian reservations were irrelevant since the boundary was never defined, and the boundary was not discussed in the 1954 Treaty.

On 20 October 1962, China launched a two-pronged war against India because of differences on the boundary issue, from both west and east. Six possible major reasons are often cited for the Chinese attack: (i) differences on the McMahon Line; (ii) growing political differences between Mao Zedong and Jawaharlal Nehru; (iii) China's construction of roads in the Aksai Chin area, which were later noticed and patrolled by the Indian military; (iv) Mao's diversionary tactic to take the attention of the Chinese people away from the domestic crisis; (v) China's resentment of India on the refuge given to the Dalai Lama and over the Tibetan issue; and (vi) the global situation, which was not in favour of China (see Panda 2012).

While India lost the war and some territory, for China the war has almost been a non-issue. The Chinese media, which have played a critical role in shaping the public discourse on the issue, have reflected this tendency from the 1960s itself. On 27 October 1962, for example, *Renmin Ribao* published an editorial, which mainly blamed Nehru's 'British legacy' for the war. Nehru was using 'China's Tibet region as an Indian sphere of influence' (*Renmin Ribao* 1962). It further stated: 'Nehru's policy on the Sino-Indian Boundary question and the whole process by which he engineered the Sino-Indian border clashes have shed new light on the expansionist philosophy of the Indian big bourgeoisie and big landlords' (ibid.).

In the post-1962 phase, on 21 November 1963, *Renmin Ribao* in an editorial focused more on starting the negotiation process and finding a 'peaceful' solution to the boundary issue rather than speak about the 1962 war. It noted:

> As far as China is concerned, the door is wide open for reopening Sino-Indian negotiations and for a peaceful settlement of the boundary question. China has patience. If it is not possible to open negotiations this year, we will wait until next year; if it is not possible next year, then the year after next.
>
> (Cited in Chang 1982: 92)

The blame on Nehru and India still continues widely in the Chinese media today, though they have become more open, flexible and articulate in expressing their opinion on conflicting or sensitive issues. A reference can be made to the article 'China won, but never wanted, Sino-Indian war', published in *Global Times* on 28 June 2012. Hong Yuan, its author, who is an expert from the Chinese Academy of Social Science (CASS), mainly traces the event as a political clash of interests and quarrel between Nehru and Mao. In the view of the author, Mao thought that the 'battle with India was also a political combat, and the real target was not Nehru but the US and the Soviets that had been plotting behind the scenes against China' (Hong Yuan 2012). There is certainly great regret among Chinese experts about their government's decision not to gain control over Arunachal Pradesh in the war, that 'it was a costly error on the part of China' to have declared a unilateral cease-fire on 21 November 1962 without really gaining control over Tawang vis-à-vis Arunachal Pradesh.[5]

Line of Actual Control (LAC)

The LAC is possibly the most contested aspect in India–China relations, even more than any specific territorial claims in their boundary dispute (see Panda 2015). Whether the LAC has historically been defined is disputed between the two countries. India holds the view that the LAC is defined, but a disagreement exists over it. For Beijing, clarification of the LAC is important, yet much needs to be discussed before the two sides start negotiating over it;[6] the 'package settlement' is a critical matter, which must help the clarification of the LAC.[7] At the same time, the leaderships and experts in China have not really spoken on how to go about clarifying the LAC, ever since the negotiation process started two decades ago.

Clarification of the LAC is connected with the complex boundary delineation process. Boundary delineation in practice may encompass a three-way process that involves (i) the *clarification* of the boundary, which is the current national boundary of each side, (ii) then agreeing on that to go for an *alignment* of the LAC, and (iii) then implementing the LAC alignment process to resolve the boundary through territorial adjustments or exchanges or through negotiations.

In June 1999, when Jaswant Singh, the then External Affairs Minister of India, visited China, the matter of LAC clarification gathered a new momentum. 'Exchanging maps' was considered as a preliminary step in this regard and in April 2000, during their 12th Joint Working Group (JWG), the two countries agreed to exchange of maps of the Middle Sector of the border. In November 2001, the two sides formally exchanged their respective maps of this sector, which is around 545 km long (Jing-Dong Yuan 2007: 133). India's proposal to implement a timeframe during Jaswant Singh's tour to China in March 2002, for exchanging maps and finally addressing the clarification of the Western and Eastern Sectors, which would be followed in 2002 and 2003 respectively, did not elicit much enthusiasm in the Chinese political circles. The matter stagnates there.

However, in the current Chinese dispensation, the LAC clarification is a matter of 'national security, sovereignty and territorial integrity' as far the PLA is concerned. China's lack of interest in offering a clarification over the LAC is a subject matter that is linked with Beijing's claim over sovereign India's state of Arunachal Pradesh. Beijing has expressed time and again its reservation and unhappiness about the Indian leadership visiting Arunachal Pradesh (see Panda 2008, 2009). Notably, this highlights the fact that China no longer holds sacrosanct the settled principles for boundary demarcation agreed upon in 2005 – that 'in reaching the boundary settlement, the two sides shall safeguard due interests of their settled populations in the border areas'. This provision was renounced as early as 6 June 2007 by the Chinese Foreign Minister Yang Jiechi who stated that 'mere presence' in populated areas would not affect China's claims (Panda 2009; Katoch 2015).

Interestingly, till not long ago, Chinese interest in Arunachal Pradesh – what the Chinese call 'Southern Tibet' – was limited to Tawang, given the spiritual and cultural links between Tibetans and the people of this area. But in recent years the Chinese claim has expanded to encompass the whole state. This expansive interest stems from a number of factors. The Chinese see a lot of scope in Arunachal on the tourism and agricultural fronts. Arunachal is also purportedly endowed with huge mineral deposits and its hydroelectric power potential is immense. At the same time, if seen in the overall context of the boundary settlement, China's official protest on the Indian leadership's visit to Arunachal can be viewed as a bargaining chip within the framework of its 'comprehensive border settlement programme'. Indeed, one can discern a pattern of 'occasional claims at the right time' as part of China's diplomatic practice to deny India any diplomatic gains in the border negotiations.

A mixture of concern and anxiety is also visible among Chinese scholars, party officials and media writers to identify the rationale behind India's strategic decision to revitalise its Northeast region. Two dominant discourses are visible: (i) to understand and evaluate India's strategic or military advancement in the North-East region; and (ii) to gauge India's competitiveness both in protecting Arunachal vis-à-vis the bordering region and in comparison to China's overall progress. For example, referring to India's increasing military presence in the region, China expresses concern that India is trying to make Tezpur an airbase (Qin Mei 2009). The Chinese writings also display concern over India's strategic competitiveness in a range of issues.

This author's interaction with leading Chinese experts from CIIS, CASS, SIIS, SASS, CIIS, CICIR and government officials substantiates that China is in no mood to relax its stance over Arunachal vis-à-vis the boundary issue. There seems to be a consensus of opinion among the Chinese strategic community that 'India is adopting the military means in the north-eastern sector to have a good control over the disputed issue of Arunachal Pradesh.' China has been particularly riled after ADB approved a loan worth US$60 million for infrastructure development in Arunachal Pradesh. On an earlier occasion also, the government had strongly opposed an ADB loan for Arunachal Pradesh, which India resolutely managed to push through with the strong support of the US, Japan and South Korea.

In principle, the public posture in China is to take an official call on Arunachal Pradesh by denouncing the earlier 'agreed official principles' time and again. Interactions with Chinese experts confirm that their understanding is that 'mutually agreed principles' have only a tactical value for them. The Chinese have no hesitation in unilaterally rejecting any principle if it creates barriers to their national interests.

Amidst all this, China constantly refers to Arunachal Pradesh as a 'complex historical chapter' in the China–India border dispute. On the historical account, most Chinese experts refer to the fact that the sixth Dalai Lama hailed from the Monyul area. In the Chinese contention, three parts of this region – Monyul, Loyul and Lower Tsayul – were under the Tibetan administrative and jurisdictional control. For a long time, Beijing has continued its claim to Tawang vis-à-vis Arunachal as a bargaining chip in the overall border negotiation strategy with India. A leading expert in Shanghai, Zhao Gancheng, asserts that 'historically, Tawang belongs to Tibet; and India should realise this fact quickly in order to avoid a situation like 1962'.[8]

Experts cite several assumptions why the 'great political mistake' was made in terms of China winding up the 1962 war without going on to capture the present-day Arunachal Pradesh. Though the Chinese military was short of 'logistical support' in carrying out its momentum in Arunachal, in the Chinese contention, the military decided to retreat because it wanted to uphold the principle of 'peaceful solution' to the boundary issue with India in future. An expert in Shanghai opines that the Chinese political leadership did not set much store over gaining control over Arunachal because it never anticipated that the Tibet crisis would hurt the Chinese as deeply as it does today.[9] A well-known India expert in Beijing holds the view that external factors like the anticipated US support to India and the problematic Sino-Soviet relationship forced the Chinese to retreat.[10]

The negotiation process

The initial years

The political seeds of the boundary negotiation process go back to the late 1970s or early 1980s. Even though formal ambassador-level contact between India and China was resumed in August 1976, it was the visit of India's then Foreign Minister A.B. Vajpayee to China in 1979 that set in motion the political interaction between the two countries. Vajpayee's visit was reciprocated by the Chinese Foreign Minister Huang Hua to India in June 1981. Importantly, the then President Deng Xiaoping proposed a solution to the boundary dispute through a 'package deal' – basically a revival of Zhou Enlai's ideas of the 1960s – during Vajpayee's visit.[11] The 'package deal' offer was more to acknowledge the 'present state of the border' where China made a case that the Eastern Sector of the border must be brought under negotiation. It indicated that 'China would recognise the McMahon Line and accept the Indian claimed Eastern Sector where in return, India must accept to recognise the status quo in the Western Sector' (Tien-sze Fang 2014; see also *archive.org* 1992; Liu Xuecheng 2011).

India was sceptical of the Chinese offer initially (Tien-sze Fang 2014: 92). It was rather more interested in a 'sector to sector' negotiation process. India did not see the need to negotiate on the Eastern Sector as it was never a matter of dispute between the two countries and China did not have a direct claim over any territory in this part of the sector. India was nevertheless open to minor adjustments in the Eastern Sector, but in return insisted that China must make flexible its position on the Western Sector and must return to India the territory it had lost in the war (ibid.; Raghavan 2008).

The formal border talks started in 1981 and eight rounds of these talks were held till 1988. During these talks, there was an acknowledgement by both sides, especially by India, that the existing boundary problem should not be a barrier to the progress of overall bilateral relations (Smith 2014: 30–1; Tien-sze Fang 2014: 92–3). It has been argued, basically by Chinese scholars, that this change in India's stance was brought on by the geopolitical change, which was becoming adverse to India. The Soviet leader of the time, Mikhail Gorbachev, did not seem to offer any support to India in case of another conflict with China (Li Li 2009: 56; Smith 2014: 31). Gorbachev seemed to have made this clear during his visit to India in 1986 (Kalha 2013; Smith 2014: 31). The then Indian Prime Minister Rajiv Gandhi visited China in December 1988 in a 'landmark' visit, which normalised the relationship between the two countries. During this visit, the two countries signed a new border resolution mechanism, of which the highlight was the establishment of the Joint Working Group mechanism. Between 1988/89 and 2002, the JWG met 14 times (see Table 3.1).

The middle years

The JWG had a threefold mandate: (i) offer concrete recommendations for a solution within a stipulated timeframe; (ii) continue maintaining peace and tranquillity till a final resolution was arrived; and (iii) as a joint undertaking, involve military experts, surveyors, communication experts and legal experts from both sides. The ultimate objective was to 'seek a fair, reasonable and mutually acceptable solution'. It was an administrative mechanism between the Foreign Secretary from the Indian side and Deputy Foreign Minister from the Chinese side. In terms of concrete results, however, the JWG, as a complicated 'bureaucratic exercise', was predominantly successful in instituting more confidence-building measures (CBMs) (Smith 2014: 31).

Amidst the JWG meetings between 1988 and 2002, the political exchanges between the two countries improved greatly. They also signed a few CBMs on boundary issues, the two most important of which were: (i) Agreement on the Maintenance of Peace and Tranquillity along the Line of Actual Control in the India–China Border Areas, 7 September 1993; and (ii) Agreement Between the Government of the Republic of India and the Government of the People's Republic of China on Confidence-Building Measures in the Military Field Along

Table 3.1 India–China Joint Working Group meetings

Date	Event	Place	Major development
30 June–4 July 1989	1st meeting	Beijing	The two sides promised to make efforts to maintain peace and tranquillity along the LAC
30–31 August 1990	2nd meeting	New Delhi	Military border personnel would meet from time to time at an appropriate level
12–14 May 1991	3rd meeting	Beijing	The two sides exchanged views on how to maintain peace and tranquillity along the LAC
20–21 February 1992	4th meeting	New Delhi	The two sides agreed that military border personnel would hold regular meetings in the eastern and western sectors in June and October every year. They also agreed to establish telephone links and discussed the issue of prior notification of military exercise.
27–29 October 1992	5th meeting	Beijing	The two sides continued to discuss measures to maintain peace and tranquillity in the regions along the LAC, but no progress was made
24–27 June 1993	6th meeting	New Delhi	The two sides initiated the 1993 CBMs Agreement
6–7 July 1994	7th meeting	Beijing	The two sides agreed in principle to the setting up of more points for meeting between border personnel
18–20 August 1995	8th meeting	New Delhi	The two sides agreed to pull back troops from four forward outposts along the border
16–18 October 1996	9th meeting	Beijing	The two sides agreed to establish two additional meeting sites along the eastern section of the border, and decided to hold a meeting along the middle section
4–5 August 1997	10th meeting	New Delhi	The two sides exchanged the instruments of ratification of the 1996 CBMs Agreement
26–27 April 1999	11th meeting	Beijing	The two sides claimed that there was considerable scope for developing and expanding bilateral relations in economic, commercial and other fields, but no progress was made
28–29 April 2000	12th meeting	New Delhi	The two sides agreed to exchange maps as a further step toward working on the identification of the LAC
31 July–1 August 2001	13th meeting	Beijing	The two sides defined their individual perceptions of the LAC along the middle sector and recorded the differences on the maps
21–22 November 2002	14th meeting	New Delhi	The two sides agreed to exchange the maps in the western sector in January 2003
30 March 2005	15th meeting	Beijing	The two sides reviewed the ongoing process of LAC and CBMs

Source: Tien-Sze Fang, *Asymmetrical Threat Perceptions in India–China Relations*, New Delhi: Oxford University Press, 2014, pp. 94–5. Adopted with the author's consent.

From boundary *to* bordering territory   43

the Line of Actual Control in the India–China Border Areas, 29 November 1996. These two CBMs were not only preliminary comprehensive documents or agreements that talked about the boundary dispute and the problems that exist at the border regions, but also emerged as the two important referring documents for the negotiation process gradually.

The contemporary years

Since 2003, the Special Representatives dialogue mechanism has emerged as the core of the negotiation strategy (see Table 3.2). Through this apparatus the two sides have reached a broad 'consensus' to outline the 'guidelines of settling the boundary dispute'. India's then National Security Advisor (NSA) was recorded as saying that 'on the settlement itself, we are in the second stage of the three stage process of agreeing on principles, a framework and finally a boundary line' (MEA 2013a). The Special Representatives (SRs) talks have gained many highlights over the years: *first*, they are the most important high-level official mechanism that exclusively deals with the boundary negotiation matter; *second*, the decisions made at the SRs talks carry political confidence at the highest leadership levels on both sides; and *third*, the SRs talks are the most representatives dialogue mechanism which are mostly restricted to official dealings and less for public transparency (the outcomes of the SRs talks have never been made public). As a supporting mechanism, the Working Mechanism for Consultation and Coordination on India–China Border Affairs (WMCC) was established during the 15th round of SRs talks in January 2012. A positive aspect of the WMCC is that it is a special mechanism to address and manage the tensions and matters that arise in the border regions.

The 2005 Protocol between India and China on the Modalities for the Implementation of Confidence-Building Measures in the Military Field along the Line of Actual Control on the India–China Border Areas is in many ways a reiteration of the 1993 and 1996 CBMs agreements. This protocol recognises the need to actualise the process of 'early clarification and confirmation of the alignment' of the LAC (MEA 2005). Article II (a) prohibits 'holding large scale military exercises involving more than one division (approximately 15,000 troops) in close proximity' to the LAC. Article V (a) mentions various border meetings each year at Spanggur Gap in the Western Sector, Nathula in the Sikkim Sector and Bomla in the Eastern Sector; Article V (b) talks about expanding 'the mechanism of border meeting points', which include Kibithu-Damai in the Eastern Sector and Lipulekh Pass/Qiangla in the Middle Sector. Some of these stated objectives are, however, inappropriate today, the situation in the border areas having become more complicated than in 2005.

The Agreement dated 11 April 2005 between the two countries, titled *The Political Parameters and Guiding Principles for the Settlement of the India–China Boundary Questions*, also still stands for many as a reference document in the boundary negotiation strategy. Its highlights are in Articles V, VI, VII, VIII, IX and X (MEA 2005). These articles not only talk about finding a settlement to

Table 3.2 Chronology of India–China Special Representatives meetings

Date	Event	Place	Major developments
23–24 October 2003	1st meeting	New Delhi	The two sides formulated guiding principles
12–13 January 2004	2nd meeting	Beijing	The two sides formulated guiding principles
26–27 July 2004	3rd meeting	New Delhi	The two sides reviewed the guiding principles
18–19 November 2004	4th meeting	Beijing	The two sides exchanged views on the principles that could form the framework of a possible boundary agreement
9–12 April 2005	5th meeting	New Delhi	The two sides worked out the finalised documents on guiding principles
26–28 September 2005	6th meeting	Beijing	The two sides worked out an agreed framework for a boundary settlement on the basis of the 'Agreement on Political Parameters and Guiding Principles for the Settlement of India–China Boundary Question'
11–13 March 2006	7th meeting	New Delhi and Kumarakom	The two sides devised an agreed upon framework for the basic framework for settlement
25–27 June 2006	8th meeting	Xi'an and Beijing	The two sides continued their discussions on an agreed framework for a boundary settlement
16–18 January 2007	9th meeting	New Delhi	The two sides continued their discussions on an agreed framework for a boundary settlement
20–22 April 2007	10th meeting	New Delhi and Connor	The two sides continued their discussions on a framework for a boundary settlement
24–26 September 2007	11th meeting	Beijing	The two sides exchanged views on the boundary issues
19 September 2008	12th meeting	Beijing	The two sides exchanged views on a framework to solve the boundary issue
7–8 August 2009	13th meeting	New Delhi	The two sides exchanged views on the boundary issue
29–30 November 2010	14th meeting	Beijing	Both sides agreed to seek a 'fair deal' as they made 'steady progress' on a framework to solve the dispute
16–17 January 2012	15th meeting	New Delhi	The two countries signed an 'Agreement on the Establishment of a Working Mechanism for Consultation and Coordination on India–China Border Affairs'
28–29 June 2013	16th meeting	Beijing	The two sides exchanged views on improving bilateral ties
11 February 2014	17th meeting	New Delhi	Both sides expressed satisfaction that 2014 would be marked as the Year of Friendly Exchanges; framework for a resolution of the Boundary Question, the early implementation of the Border Defence Cooperation Agreement; discussed on cooperation in the East Asia Summit process as well as developments in West Asia and Afghanistan
22–24 March 2015	18th meeting	New Delhi	Both sides reaffirmed to properly manage and control conflicts and join efforts to maintain the peace and tranquillity in the boundary area before the boundary issue is finally settled

Source: same as Table 3.1, pp. 111–12. Adopted with the author's consent. More information has been added and updated further by the author of this book.

the boundary question, but about addressing issues in the border areas. The current situation on the ground, however, does not jell with these expressed sentiments, with hegemonic political statements sporadically emerging from China.

The matter of border incursions has been primarily addressed by 'border management' talks under the institutional base of the WMCC. Mostly seen as standard official practice, the seventh round of WMCC met on 27 August 2014, to address a fresh set of reported border incursions and perceptual differences relating to patrolling along the LAC. It may be noted that border incursions have been taking place even after the Agreement on Border Defence Cooperation Talks (BDCA) was signed on 23 October 2013 after the Depsang valley incident (see Table 3.3 for the progress of WMCC).

The framework of the BDCA is based on three perspectives: the basic course of Strategic and Cooperative Partnership for Peace and Prosperity between the two sides must serve the fundamental interests of the common people; not to use military capability against each other; and not to use force against each other to gain unilateral superiority. The BDCA also stresses the aspect of 'principles of mutual and equal security' (MEA 2013b). The fundamental explanation for border incursions is that these take place 'due to the difference of perception about boundary'.[12] No matter what is the political hue of the Indian government, the general line of approach that has so far been followed is that there is an absence of a mutually agreed LAC, still the border so far has been peaceful, but from time to time, on account of differences in the perception regarding the LAC, incursions have happened.

The future[13]

'Package settlement' through 'sectoral' approach

The boundary negotiation process rests on a 'package settlement' through a 'sectoral' approach. Recent bilateral agreements and MoUs emphasise these principles. The 1993 and 1996 CBMs have been the main reference texts of the boundary negotiation process, while the 2005 Protocol, Agreement and Joint Statement along with the 2012 and 2013 Agreements and Joint Statements have primarily worked as safeguards of the negotiation process. The 2005 Agreement states that both India and China must 'make meaningful and mutually acceptable adjustments to their respective positions on the boundary question' to arrive at a 'package settlement' to the dispute, and to reach a final settlement, 'all sectors of the India–China boundary' must be taken into account or bounded for negotiation (MEA 2005, Article III). The 'package settlement' aspect is vital to China's border assertion; the Indian viewpoint is linked to the 'sectoral' approach. The Chinese option is intended to have a portion at least in the Eastern Sector without compromising on the Aksai Chin area that India lost to China in 1962; the Indian approach is based on the principle that it must compel China to return Aksai Chin without India having to compromise on Arunachal Pradesh.

Table 3.3 Progress of Working Mechanism for Consultation and Coordination on India–China Border Affairs

Meeting	Date	Venue	Main representatives	Major issues discussed
8th Round	16–17 October 2014	New Delhi	Pradeep Kumar Rawat (India) and Ouyang Yujing (China)	• Regular interaction between the Army Headquarters and Field Commands of the two sides • Additional border personnel meeting points; and more telecommunication linkages between forward posts of the two sides at mutually agreed locations
7th Round	27 August 2014	Beijing	Pradeep Kumar Rawat (India) and Ouyang Yujing (China)	• Operationalising BDCA
6th Round	28–30 April 2014	Beijing	Gautam Bambawale (India) and Ouyang Yujing (China)	• Implementation of BDCA • Additional CBMs • To find an alternative route for Kailash-Mansarovar Yatra
5th Round	10 February 2014	New Delhi	– do –	• Developments in the border areas in the Western sector • Implementation of BDCA • Additional CBMs
4th Round	29–30 September 2013	Beijing	– do –	• Review of developments on border, mainly in the Western sector • Measures to maintain stability on the border
3rd Round	23–24 July 2013	New Delhi	– do –	• Developments in the border areas • Additional CBMs • Improvement of the functioning of the Working Mechanism
2nd Round	29–30 November 2012	New Delhi	Gautam Bambawale (India) and Wang Xiaodu (China)	• Developments in border areas • Establishment of additional measures for maintaining peace and tranquillity • Liberalisation of border trade across Nathu La • Additional routes for Kailash Mansarovar Yatra
1st Round	5–6 March 2012	Beijing	Gautam Bambawale (India) and Deng Zhonghua (China)	• Working Mechanism Rules and Mode of Functioning • Emergency consultation over telephone and video conferencing • Additional items for border trade • Possibility for exploration of possible alternative route for Kailash Mansarovar Yatra

Source: various open sources like Ministry of Foreign Affairs of the People's Republic of China, Ministry of External Affairs of the Government of India, *China Daily*, *Xinhua*, *Times of India*, *The Hindu*, etc.

From boundary *to* bordering territory   47

Beijing has repeatedly used 'package settlement' as a yardstick in its negotiation strategy since the 1960s, without really offering any concrete ideas or proposals for a settlement. Neither have the Chinese exchanged maps to inform where they stand on this matter; nor have they agreed to a proposition of status quo. The Indian approach in the negotiation process has also been somewhat obtuse. Though India has expressed support for the Chinese maxim about an 'early solution', it has remained too dependent on the institutional mechanisms on this matter.

From a realist prism, after 18 rounds of talks at the SRs level, the two countries have not agreed upon the LAC and are yet to exchange maps that will clarify their respective perceptions and stances on the matter. The two sides have exchanged maps with regard to the Middle Sector only, more than a decade ago. In fact, constant tensions in both the Western and Eastern Sectors have even raised serious doubts over the validity of the previously signed MoUs and agreements of 1993, 1996, 2005 and, more predominantly, the BDCA of 2013.

Swap deal or maintaining status quo?

Is it feasible for the two countries to resolve the boundary dispute without actually attempting to define the LAC? The Chinese, given their assertion on 'Southern Tibet', would like to have a portion of Arunachal, which is an integral part of India, constituting part of its sovereign architecture as a state. New Delhi would also like China to return Aksai Chin in the Western Sector. The recent Chinese incursions and the PLA's recent activity in the Western Sector indicate that Beijing may like to have territory in the Ladakh region too, or at least bring the matter to the negotiating table to have a better deal or say. Neither 'nationalist China' nor 'nationalist India' can ideally afford to do that. In China's case, given the PLA's dominant role in national security affairs – mainly matters concerning sovereignty and territory – these cannot be compromised. As Chinese experts explain, contemporary China may seem flexible and open as far as diplomatic and foreign policy matters are concerned, but it can hardly make any compromise on matters relating to national security, territory or sovereignty.[14] Besides, the intricacy of civil–military relations in China today is such that the country can hardly go for an exchange or swap deal, where the PLA will have a major say on most of these matters as compared to the Communist Party of China (CPC). There have been several occasions in the last decade that suggest that differences of opinion exist between the PLA and the party, making them function differently at times, but without really prompting a conflict. The course of civil–military relations in China suggests that the party does concede that the PLA must have a greater role and opinion on matters relating to national security, while ensuring at the same time that it remains under the full control of the CPC. More notably, the PLA does enjoy a relative autonomy in China under the 1997 National Defence Law (NDL). Given the Chinese military temperament towards India, not many within the PLA would be persuaded to give up their claim on what they call 'Southern Tibet'. Therefore, the PLA will have a say over the India–China boundary resolution, and it is expected that it would hardly make any big concession for or support territorial exchange through a swap deal that will satisfy India.

Further, nationalism has overtaken any perception of pragmatic thinking in China today. The CPC will find it challenging to propose any territorial exchange, as nationalism has become its strategy for survival. Also, what would actually prevent China from going for any sort of territorial exchange or swap is Tibet and the Dalai Lama. The Chinese government is highly sensitive to the India–China boundary dispute due to its historical links with Tibet. The Chinese government and the CPC have always projected negatively to the Chinese public the Dalai Lama and the Tibetan Government in Exile (TGIE) and have blamed them for complicating the India–China boundary dispute further. It consequently seems far-fetched to expect that China would propose or agree to a territorial exchange when it is preparing to consolidate its outlook and position on Tibet, once the Dalai Lama dies.

For New Delhi, the challenge is to overcome the visible inconsistency reflected in its approach in addressing the boundary dispute: whether it wants an early political solution to the dispute or would it like to wait and negotiate till it reaches any acceptable technical solution, where territorial exchange could be an option. Even though India is mainly concerned about the PLA's repeated border incursions, it has kept the issue separate from its normal engagement discourse with China. No political party in India would like to propose a territorial exchange with China without risking its own electoral prospects, as the memories of the 1962 war will take a long time to fade, and China itself remains an adversarial neighbour for India. Nationalism is at the forefront in both countries.[15]

Meanwhile, negotiation on the boundary dispute itself seems to have taken a backseat amidst the *border issues*. Border trade, growing water dispute between the two sides, Silk Road Economic Belt (SREB), border tourism, the Kailash Mansarovar Yatra, the BCIM (Bangladesh–China–India–Myanmar) economic corridor, etc., explain the reality that the border issues today are rapidly changing. Matters like India's concern over China's water diversion project in Yarlung Tsangpo/Brahmaputra and the China–Pakistan Economic Corridor of the SREB, further spoil the bonhomie at the border. Some of these issues indicate that resolving the boundary dispute through either territorial exchange by a swap deal or political settlement may become a daunting task in the future. The boundary dispute involves history, the India–Tibet–China political context and, more importantly, the contemporary positioning of both sides along the border.

There is subtle acceptance, given the two countries' military and economic strength, among the strategic communities of both countries that perhaps maintaining status quo would be the most plausible option. Even in China, there is tacit acknowledgement among the strategic experts that it would be practical for Beijing not to aspire for any territory from India. Many of them are of the view that China's claim on Arunachal Pradesh today may remain a reverie only. Not many in India's strategic community foresee China returning Aksai Chin to

India. The future of the India–China boundary dispute, therefore, may continue to remain with the current reality of the bordering areas and upholding the status quo.

Notes

1 For instance, Rama Rao 1984; Maxwell 2006; Raja Mohan 2007; Chaudhuri 2009; Soni and Marwah 2011.
2 Chinese expert Hu Shisheng made this assertion in clarifying this Chinese stance. See Krishnan 2010; see also Smith 2014: 22–3.
3 A review of the literature on the boundary dispute points to that. For instance, see Garver 2001; Li Li 2009; Maxwell 2011; Liu Xuecheng 2011; Tien-sze Fang 2014.
4 Many Chinese official views in this regard are available in public nowadays, for example, the view of Vice Foreign Minister Liu Zhenmin; see *Xinhua* 2015; see also *China Daily* (Asia) 2015.
5 This is based on the author's numerous interviews and interactions with Chinese experts in premier think-tanks. See Panda 2009.
6 Impression based on the author's numerous interviews and interactions with Chinese experts in premier think-tanks like CICIR, CIIS, SIIS, SASS, CASS, Fudan University, etc. The author is particularly thankful to the following for their insights on the subject: Prof. Zhao Gancheng, Dr Liu Zong yi, Prof. Zhang Jiadong, Dr Li Li, Dr Lan Jianxue, Dr Lou Chunhao, Prof. Ma Jiali, Prof. Sun Suhai, Dr Yang Xiaoping and Dr Mao Yue.
7 Impression based on the author's numerous interviews and interactions with many Chinese experts in premier think-tanks like CICIR, CIIS, SIIS, SASS, CASS, etc.
8 Interview with Prof. Zhao Gancheng, a leading expert on South Asian affairs.
9 Based on the interviews, interactions and discussion with the scholar. Name withheld on request.
10 A leading scholar from CICIR holds this opinion. Name withheld on request.
11 See, for example, Garver 2001: 79–109; Raghavan 2008; Tien-sze Fang 2014.
12 This is a remark made by India's Home Minister Rajnath Singh on the reported attempt at border incursion on 13 July 2014. See *Economic Times* 2014.
13 This part of the chapter has been published as a commentary in Panda 2015.
14 Author's interviews with experts from CICIR and CIIS at Beijing, 23–24 December 2014.
15 Chinese experts acknowledge that nationalism overshadows the boundary negotiation process. Prof. Sun Sihai, an expert on South Asia at CASS, Beijing, confirms in an email interview that 'Given the high nationalist sentiments in both countries, officials, scholars and journalists should take a responsible attitude to tell the truth to their people about the origin of the problem and the conflict in 1962.' Author's email interview with Prof. Sun Shihai, 15 December 2014.

References

archive.org, 1992. 'Promote the friendship between China and India and increase South-South cooperation: October 22', Full text, *Selected Works of Deng Xiaoping: Vol. 3*, https://archive.org/stream/SelectedWorksOfDengXiaopingVol. 3/Deng03_djvu.txt (accessed on 16 May 2015).

Blanchard, Jean-Marc F., 2005. 'Linking border disputes and war: an institutional–statist theory', *Geopolitics*, 10: 688–711.

Chang, Luke T., 1982. *China's Boundary Treaties and Frontier Disputes*, London: Oceana.

Chaudhuri, Rudra, 2009. 'Why culture matters: revisiting the Sino-Indian border war of 1962', *The Journal of Strategic Studies*, 32(6), December, pp. 841–69.
China Daily (Asia), 2015. 'China protests Indian PM's visit to disputed border region', *China Daily* (Asia), 21 February, www.chinadailyasia.com/nation/2015-02/21/content_15230079.html (accessed on 30 June 2015).
Economic Times, 2014. 'Incursions along China border due to perception difference about boundary: Rajnath Singh', *Economic Times*, 17 July, http://articles.economictimes.indiatimes.com/2014-07-17/news/51656862_1_chumar-chinese-troops-pla (accessed on 4 September 2014).
Garver, John W., 2001. *Protracted Contest: Sino-Indian Rivalry in the Twentieth Century*, Seattle: University of Washington Press.
Haselsberger, Beatrix, 2014. 'Decoding borders. Appreciating border impacts on space and people', *Planning Theory & Practice*, 15(4): 505–26.
Hong Yuan, 2012. 'China won, but never wanted, Sino-Indian war', *Global Times*, 28 June, www.globaltimes.cn/content/717710.shtml (accessed on 4 September 2014).
Jing-Dong Yuan, 2007. 'The dragon and the elephant: Chinese–Indian relations in the 21st century', *The Washington Quarterly*, 30(3), Summer, pp. 131–44.
Kalha, R.S., 2013. 'The Chinese message and what should the reply be?', *IDSA Comment*, 21 May, www.idsa.in/idsacomments/TheChineseMessageIndiareply_rskalha_210513 (accessed on 16 May 2015).
Katoch, Prakash, 2015. 'Arunachal Pradesh – China's fallacious claims', *Indian Defence Review*, 23 February, www.indiandefencereview.com/news/arunachal-pradesh-chinas-fallacious-claims/ (accessed on 30 May 2015).
Krishnan, Ananth, 2010. 'Officials dismiss China's Kashmir border claims', *The Hindu*, 20 December, www.thehindu.com/news/national/officials-dismiss-chinas-kashmir-border-claims/article963655.ece (accessed on 29 May 2015).
Li Li, 2009. *Security Perception and China–India Relations*, New Delhi: KW Publishers.
Liu Xuecheng, 2011. 'Look beyond the Sino-Indian border dispute', *China Report*, 47(2): 147–58.
Maxwell, Neville, 2006. 'Settlements and disputes: China's approach to territorial issues', *Economic and Political Weekly*, 41(36), 9–15 September, pp. 3873–81.
Maxwell, Neville, 2011. 'Why the Sino-Indian border dispute is still unresolved after 50 years: a recapitulation', *China Report*, 47(2): 71–82.
MEA, 2005. *Bilateral Documents*, 'Agreement between the Government of the Republic of India and the Government of the People's Republic of China on the Political Parameters and Guiding Principles for the Settlement of the India–China Boundary Questions, April 11, 2005', www.mea.gov.in/bilateral-documents.htm?dtl/6534/Agreement+between+the+Government+of+the+Republic+of+India+and+the+Government+of+the+Peoples+Republic+of+China+on+the+Political+Parameters+and+Guiding+Princip les+for+the+Settlement+of+the+IndiaChina+Boundary+Question (accessed on 19 May 2015).
MEA, 2013a. 'Speech by NSA on "Developments in India–China Relations"', Ministry of External Affairs, 9 January, www.mea.gov.in/Speeches-Statements.htm?dtl/17101/Speech+by+NSA+on+Developments+in+IndiaChina+Relations (accessed on 19 May 2015).
MEA, 2013b. 'Agreement between the Government of the Republic of India and the Government of the People's Republic of China on border defence cooperation', Ministry of External Affairs, Government of India, 23 October, www.mea.gov.in/bilateral-documents.htm?dtl/22366/Agreement+between+the+Government+of+the+Republic+

of+India+and+the+Government+of+the+Peoples+Republic+of+China+on+Border+Defence+Cooperation (accessed on 29 August 2014).
Panda, Jagannath P., 2008. 'China's designs on Arunachal Pradesh', *IDSA Strategic Comment*, 12 March, www.idsa.in/idsastrategiccomments/ChinasDesignsonArunachalPradesh_JPPanda_120308.html (accessed on 31 May 2015).
Panda, Jagannath P., 2009. 'China's eagle eye on Arunachal', *IDSA Strategic Comment*, 10 July, www.idsa.in/strategiccomments/ChinaseagleeyeonArunachal_JPanda_100709 (accessed on 31 May 2015).
Panda, Jagannath P., 2012. 'The 1962 War: will China speak about it?', *IDSA Strategic Comment*, 16 October, www.idsa.in/~idsa/idsacomments/The1962WarWillChinaspeakaboutit_jppanda_161012.html (accessed on 30 June 2015).
Panda, Jagannath P., 2015. 'Future of India–China boundary: leadership holds the key?', *Strategic Analysis*, 39(3): 287–92.
Qin Mei, 2009. 'Indian Air Force deploys Sukhoi-30 fighters in NE region', *Xinhua* (CRI English), 15 June, http://english.cri.cn/6966/2009/06/15/2001s493501.htm (accessed on 31 May 2015).
Raghavan, Srinath, 2008. 'The boundary dispute with China', *Seminar*, no. 548, www.india-seminar.com/2008/584/584_srinath_raghavan.htm (accessed on 16 May 2015).
Raja Mohan, C., 2007. 'Soft borders and cooperative frontiers: India's changing territorial diplomacy towards Pakistan and China', *Strategic Analysis*, 31(1), January–February, pp. 1–23.
Rama Rao, T.S., 1984. 'India's international disputes', *Archiv des Völkerrechts*, 22(1), *Indien Und Das Völkerrecht/India and International Law*, pp. 22–44.
Renmin Ribao, 1962. 'More on Nehru's philosophy in the light of the Sino-Indian boundary question', *Renmin Ribao*, Editorial Department, 27 October.
Smith, Jeff M., 2014. *Cold Peace: China–India Rivalry in the Twenty-First Century*, Lanham, MD: Lexington Press.
Soni, Sharad K. and Reena Marwah, 2011. 'Tibet as a factor impacting China studies in India', *Asian Ethnicity*, 12(3), October, pp. 285–99.
Tien-sze Fang, 2014. 'Chapter 3: The Sino-Indian border problem', in *Asymmetrical Threat Perceptions in India–China Relations*, New Delhi: Oxford University Press.
Xinhua, 2015. 'China "unhappy" on Modi's visit to disputed territory', *Xinhua*, 21 February, www.chinadaily.com.cn/china/2015-02/21/content_19630982.htm# (accessed on 30 June 2015).
Zhao Shengnan, 2015a. 'Fresh talks begin on border issue', *China Daily*, 24 March, www.chinadaily.com.cn/china/2015-03/24/content_19889843.htm (accessed on 29 May 2015).
Zhao Shengnan, 2015b. 'Modi seeks further ties with Beijing', *China Daily*, 25 March, www.chinadaily.com.cn/china/2015-03/25/content_19901769.htm (accessed on 29 May 2015).

4 Tibet and post-Dalai Lama contingencies

Literature on the dynamics of Tibet and the Tibetan community is prolific. It has appeared regularly in tandem with the course and verve of the Tibetan cause, and more consistently in keeping with Tibet's political legacy and complexity as a region in Asia's history, especially in the India–China historical as well as contemporary context. Most of it has looked at the historical and modern course of Tibet and Tibetan people and has tried to link it to and rationalise it within the continuing realities.[1] But most of this literature has ignored Tibet's geographic context and the Tibetans' relationship with India and China in the context of identity, ethnicity and state discourse. As the crux of this book is to evaluate the *next* trajectory of India–China relations, this chapter looks at the emerging complexity between the two countries where both the region of Tibet and Tibetans are an integral part. Tibet as a contemporary subject in India–China bilateral discourse has come of age.

A 'perpetual' and 'perceptual' dispute

What brings Tibet to the core of India–China disputes is the identity insecurity of Tibetans, mutual misperceptions of the two countries regarding Tibet and Tibetan affairs, and the course of the succession of the Dalai Lama.[2]

Historically, Tibet emerged as a matter of political contention between China and Great Britain in the early twentieth century. India became a factor in the matter in later years especially in the context of the Lhasa Convention on Tibet, signed between Tibet and Great Britain in 1904, with the focus on facilitating greater trade in the Yadong, Gyantse and Gartok areas. This treaty also recognised the Sikkim–Tibet border, which virtually offered an image that Tibet was a sovereign country. The Chinese have severely opposed the sovereign character accorded to Tibet in the Lhasa Convention (*china.org.cn* 2008; see also *au.china-embassy.org* 2008). The Simla Convention of 1914 to settle the boundaries between (the British) India and Tibet and between China and Tibet, settling the inner and outer Tibet, further complicated matters.[3] China expressed its reservation on accepting the settlement line of inner and outer Tibet; that neither outer Tibet should be given autonomy nor there should be inner Tibet (*china.org.cn* 2015). The McMahon Line, which was an outcome of the Simla Convention, was therefore never recognised by the Chinese government, which became the most contested aspect of the India–China boundary dispute in later years.

Post-1949, with the establishment of the People's Republic of China (PRC), the signing of the 17-point agreement with Tibet on 23 May 1951 to some extent implied China's sovereignty over Tibet. The PLA's eventual capturing of Tibet in the 1950s tensed Sino-Tibetan relations. The Dalai Lama's deteriorating relationship with the Chinese leadership, the Tibetan protests and the rising revolt, and the Dalai Lama's escape to India in 1959 further complicated the India–Tibet–China tripartite relations.

India's Tibet policy and China

Post-independence India's approach towards Tibet is based on the premise that Tibet must enjoy autonomy, 'as an autonomous buffer between India and China, while recognising China's suzerainty not sovereignty' (Tien-sze Fang 2014: 53; see also Norbu 1997). Nevertheless, India was not in favour of allowing the Tibet matter to affect India's relations with China (ibid.). Notably, India officially acknowledged in the 1954 Agreement that 'Tibet region is a part of China' (*commonlii.org* 1954) but refused to renew it when the time came up for its renewal in later years. The Dalai Lama's asylum in India in 1959 changed the complexion of the matter and became one of the prime reasons behind the India–China war (Deepak 2011: 302). However, with normalisation in relations starting in 1988, India recognised 'Tibet as an autonomous part of China', even signing an agreement to that effect during the then Prime Minister A.B. Vajpayee's visit to China in 2003 (*fmprc.gov.cn* 2003). India's fundamental approach towards the Tibet issue has been one of 'non-interference'. If anything, as a neighbour, India has limited itself to advocating 'greater autonomy' for the Tibetans all these years.

To what extent is the Tibet issue alive as an irritant in India–China relations? And more importantly, will India continue its 'non-interference' and 'non-political' approach towards Tibet? From India's political standpoint, Tibet as a territorial matter is settled, that Tibet is an 'autonomous part of China'. From China's viewpoint, however, the matter of Tibet is not yet over with India. In other words, Tibet continues to exist as a 'perpetual' dispute between India and China, and also as a 'perceptual' dispute. Given these differences, will India revisit its standpoint on Tibet?

On the territorial aspect, India may find such a revisit difficult. China is an immediate neighbour and, given that India is currently engaged with that country on a range of bilateral, regional as well as global multilateral mechanisms, India may not wish to allow the Tibet matter to remain an irritant in future Sino-Indian relations. Nonetheless, a more nuanced change remains a possibility. The Tibet issue has not been mentioned in the India–China bilateral official proceedings for some time. Does this imply a silent policy change on the part of India regarding the Tibet issue? Not really. India is not worried on the territorial aspect of the Tibet issue. But the issue remains a card in India's hands to build pressure

54 *The bilateral course*

on China, given that the Tibet matter is linked to the India–China boundary dispute and the post-14th Dalai Lama period may bring complications in India's relationship with China.

As regards the boundary dispute, China's claim on India's Arunachal Pradesh is based on the sixth Dalai Lama's connection with the region. As regards the post-Dalai Lama contingencies, the current Dalai Lama turned 80 years old in 2015.[4] Given his age, finding his successor has occupied the prime cosmos in India and China, including the Tibetans.[5] The succession process has not taken place since 1933 and the China–India region has witnessed many turbulent decades in the interim. Three important issues that dominate the post-Dalai Lama scenario are: (i) the succession issue and its legitimacy; (ii) the unity and identity of the Tibetans and their future; and (iii) the fallout of these developments on India–China bilateral relations.

In the Tibetan assertion, the institution of the Dalai Lama (known as *Gaden Phodrang Labrang* in the Tibetan language) was established in the fifteenth century.[6] Both the Gedun Gyatso and the reincarnated Gedun Drub, the two first Lamas, established the institution of the Dalai Lama and made the practice of reincarnation customary (*dalailama.com* 2011; see Table 4.1 for the chronology of the successive Dalai Lamas). Consent from the Mongol rulers to this institution was important at that time. Sonam Gyatso, the third in the line, was offered the title of Dalai Lama by the Mongol Khans due to his wisdom and spirituality. The Gaden Phodrang government was established in 1642 by the fifth Dalai Lama, Ngawang Lobsang Gyatso. He was given the political authority and he continued to enjoy the confidence of the Mongol rulers. Consequently, in the Tibetan assertion, the institution of the Dalai Lama goes back to the fifteenth century (*dalailama.com* 2011; see also Wolff 2010: 45–56; Frossard 2013).

China on its part asserts that the institution of the Dalai Lama was granted by the central government of the Chinese dynasties; that the institution has a multi-ethnic language connotation attached to it (Liu Wei 2009); that until the Mongol invasion of Tibet in the 1240s AD, Tibet was an organic 'administrative unit' of the Chinese empire and China's sovereignty over Tibet is a story of more than 700 years. In other words, the independence of Tibet has no historical basis (Yan Liang 2008; *xinhuanet.com* 2008; see also *china.org.cn* 1992). This Chinese assertion is, however, dubious both in the Tibetan view and the wider academic world.[7]

The reincarnation matter became a story in the spotlight after the current Dalai Lama's decision to surrender his political authority in March 2011 and bestow it on the office of the Prime Minister of the TGIE (Tibetan Government in Exile), which has existed in India since 1960. Many view this as a prelude to the erosion of the institution of the Dalai Lama; others view it as a right decision to bestow executive authority to the TGIE to decide the political future of Tibet and Tibetans. The Dalai Lama still remains the final authority in matters concerning the spiritual world of Tibet and retains the authority to appoint special envoys and participate in TGIE meetings. Currently, Lobsang Sangay, the Harvard-educated Prime Minister of the TGIE, exercises the political authority.

Table 4.1 Their Holinesses the Dalai Lamas

S. No.	Name	Period	Birthplace	Status of China
1	Gendun Drupa	1391–1474	Shabtod (U-tsang)	Ming dynasty
2	Gedun Gyatso	1475–1542	Tanag Segme (U-tsang)	Ming dynasty
3	Sonam Gyatso	1543–1588	Tolung (U-tsang)	Ming dynasty
4	Yonten Gyatso	1589–1617	Mongolia	Ming dynasty
5	Ngawang Lobsang Gyatso	1617–1682	Chingwar Taktse (U-tsang)	Ming and Qing dynasties
6	Tsangyang Gyatso	1682–1706	Mon Tawang, India	Qing dynasty
7	Kelsang Gyatso	1708–1757	Lithang (Kham)	Qing dynasty
8	Jamphel Gyatso	1758–1804	Thobgyal (U-tsang)	Qing dynasty
9	Lungtok Gyatso	1805–1815	Dan Chokor (Kham)	Qing dynasty
10	Tsultrim Gyatso	1816–1837	Lithang (Kham)	Qing dynasty
11	Khedrup Gyatso	1838–1856	Gathar (Kham)	Qing dynasty
12	Trinley Gyatso	1856–1875	Lhoka (U-tsang)	Qing dynasty
13	Thupten Gyatso	1876–1933	Dagpo Langdun (U-tsang)	Qing dynasty and Republic period
14	Tenzin Gyatso	1935–onwards	Taktser, Kumbum (Amdo)	Republic period

Source: compiled from open sources.

Will the Panchen Lama take the lead?

The Panchen Lama is the second-highest Lama in the Tibetan tradition after the Dalai Lama. In the past, he served to guide in the selection of the Dalai Lama incarnation. Historically, power rivalry between the Dalai Lama and Panchen Lama has not been uncommon. China has from time to time exploited this rivalry to promote the school of Panchen Lama at the cost of the institution of Dalai Lama. The 10th Panchen Lama opted to stay in China in 1959; he was found dead in 1989 (Kristof 1989). After a search for several years, the current Dalai Lama recognised a seven-year old Gendun Choekyi Nyima from Lhari, Nagchu in Tibet and declared him as the 11th Panchen Lama on 14 May 1995. Within a few days, he was abducted by the Chinese government and was censured from the position of Panchen Lama; it is not known whether he is still alive. When Gendun Choekyi Nyima went missing, Beijing declared Gyaltsen Norbu as the new Panchen Lama (*savetibet.org* 2015).

The Chinese government has offered Gyaltsen Norbu political privileges. For instance, in March 2013, he became a member of the Standing Committee of the Chinese People's Political Consultative Committee (CPPCC) (*tibetanreview.net* 2015). On 4 March 2015, he delivered a speech at the CPPCC meeting, profoundly appreciating the development work in Tibet carried out by the Chinese government and declaring that the Tibetans were enjoying full religious freedom (ibid.). In practice, there are two Panchen Lamas now: the missing one and Gyaltsen Norbu.

China today keeps the option open of declaring its own Panchen Lama as the successor to the current Dalai Lama if he declares that the Panchen Lama may take over from him. But the Panchen Lama succeeding the Dalai Lama may not be acceptable to the majority of the Tibetan people. This will be the first time in Tibetan history where a successor to the Dalai Lama will be found or decided outside Tibet.

In the meanwhile, China has tried to stack the cards in its own favour. For instance, Regulations on Religious Affairs (RRA), promulgated by the State Council of the People's Republic of China, states that

> the succession of living Buddhas in Tibetan Buddhism shall be conducted under the guidance of Buddhism bodies and in accordance with the religious rites and rituals and historical conventions, and be reported for approval to the religious affairs department of the people's government at...
>
> (*Chinese Journal of International Law* 2006)

In September 2007, China's State Administration for Religious Affairs declared: 'All the reincarnations of living Buddhas of Tibetan Buddhism must get government approval, otherwise they will be declared illegal and invalid' (*chinadaily. com.cn* 2008). The Chinese government asserts that 'The authority of the central government has always been important in the reincarnation process. Historical precedents have clearly shown the central government's vital role in the process' (*xinhuanet.com* 2015a, 2015b).

The Tibetan–Chinese dialogue

Two mainstream debates dominate the entire spectrum of Tibet, the Dalai Lama and the succession issue (Tsering 2014; see also Frossard 2013; Chonzom 2015). The first debate is whether there is scope for resolution of the Tibet issue through dialogue and negotiation with the Chinese government during the current Dalai Lama's tenure. The second debate is about the future of Tibet and Tibetans once he passes away.

Given Beijing's authoritarian approach to the Tibet issue, not much prospect is visible as regards its resolution through dialogue. The dialogue process between the Chinese government and the Dalai Lama's special envoys has been stalled since 2010 (Table 4.2). As regards the future of Tibet in the post-Dalai Lama future, the entire Tibetan community has been united because of the charismatic role and leadership of the current Dalai Lama. One is not sure whether this unity will hold after his demise.[8] That may seal the future of Tibet permanently in favour of China (Gautam et al. 2012).

Beijing's White Paper, titled *Tibet's Path of Development Is Driven by an Irresistible Historical Tide*, released in April 2015, eloquently explains the Chinese outlook on Tibet under its new leadership (*xinhuanet.com* 2015c). Denouncing the 'middle path' advocated by the Dalai Lama, it remarks that this is a tactic insinuated by him to gain independence, to create a 'state within a state' (ibid.). Three approaches that are central in China's approach towards Tibet in the post-Dalai Lama future are: (i) constantly pursue an 'economic oriented' Tibet policy where economic developments will gradually consolidate its political reach and control over Tibet; (ii) denounce the 'middle path' tactic, and

Table 4.2 Sino-Tibetan meetings (since 1978)

S.N.	Date	Place
1	February 1979	Beijing
2	August 1979	Tibet and Beijing
3	May 1980	Tibet and Beijing
4	June 1980	Tibet and Beijing
5	April 1982	Beijing
6	October 1984	Beijing
7	June 1985	Beijing
8	July 1993	Beijing
9	September 2002	Beijing and Tibet
10	May 2003	Beijing and Tibet
11	September 2004	Beijing and Tibet
12	June 2005	Berne, Switzerland
13	February 2006	Guilin, China
14	June 2007	Shanghai and Nanjing, China
15	June/July 2008	Beijing
16	October/November 2008	Beijing
17	January 2010	Beijing

Source: compiled from open news sources.

open only partially a conditions-based talk with the Dalai Lama's representatives; and (iii) promote Tibet internationally as a 'developmental region' of China and connect infrastructural modes with India and Nepal.

Economic-oriented Tibet policy. China's 'economic oriented' policy towards Tibet came into the limelight through the 'Western Development' Scheme.[9] This is a classic policy of the Chinese government, which is aimed at achieving concurrent goals of bringing fast-track development and controlling the Tibetan region through economic means (Cooke 2003). One of its integral parts is to promote investment, expand market and allow the Chinese Han population to migrate to Tibet to settle down and promote China's state enterprises and agendas (Hillman 2008). Even though these aims were not achieved initially, Tibet is slowly becoming a 'marketable' province of China where the Han people see a future for personal prosperity. Recent Chinese reports suggest that the Tibetan plateau maintains a high growth rate comparable to other provinces of China due to the high-scale investment by the Chinese government (*chinadaily.com.cn* 2015). But the actual reason why Tibet's economy is booming at a time when other provincial economies are struggling is an intense and constant focus on 'commercialising' Tibet through robust economic investment and stiff policy measures which will allow the Chinese government to exercise a better control over the region. There is heavy Chinese government investment particularly in traditional industries like metals and mining and exploring hydro and solar power resources (Heinrich 2015). Tourism and high-scale infrastructural development have brought huge progress to Tibet's economy (ibid.).

Conditions-based talks. As regards dialogue with the Dalai Lama's representatives, there is no scope for compromise in the post-14th Dalai Lama phase.[10] Most officials, experts and scholars in China are of the view that Beijing will choose a separate spiritual leader as the next Dalai Lama for 'China's Tibet': this will be carried out under the new laws and regulations that have been passed in 2007. An expert from the Chinese Academy of Social Science (CASS) argues that under the current Dalai Lama, any kind of compromise between the central government of China and the TGIE – which China characterises as an 'illegitimate government' – is impossible.[11] Conversely, some argue that the central government in China may be open to dialogue and compromise and may conditionally reconsider the 'middle path' if the Dalai Lama publicly apologises for his past actions and recognises Chinese sovereignty on Tibet; and may even consider greater autonomy for Tibet under the Chinese government.[12] Elaborating, an official in Beijing said: (i) the Dalai Lama must publicly apologise to the Chinese government; (ii) he must publicly give up the demand for independence of Tibet, which is hidden in the 'middle path' approach or his 'greater autonomy' dialogue; and (iii) he must acknowledge publicly that 'Tawang' or 'Arunachal Pradesh' belongs to China traditionally.[13] Beijing further cautions that even if hypothetically it agrees to carry forward a dialogue process with the TGIE to handle the post-Dalai Lama contingencies, no third party will be allowed to influence this dialogue process.

Promoting Tibet internationally as a 'developmental region' of China and integrating it with the neighbouring region. The new leadership under Xi Jinping aims to integrate Tibet as a region with the rest of China and also promote it as a greater connectivity zone for the greater neighbouring region, including the India–Nepal border. Tibet is an important region for China's 'One Belt, One Road' initiative, to be strategically linked with India and Nepal. The ambitious Sichuan–Tibet railway link is one aspect that explains this undertaking. This enterprise will directly link Lhasa with Chengdu, the capital of Sichuan province. It will branch out from the Lhasa–Shigatse rail line, which ends at the Nepal border. The Chinese government has been pondering this railway link for years (Dai Xu and Huang Zhiling 2009). Reports suggest that the Sichuan–Tibet railway and its Lhasa–Chengdu connection 'would integrate Tibet with China's corridor to Europe' (Aneja 2015). For India, this remains a concern, since infrastructural upgradation in the Tibetan Autonomous Region (TAR) will offer a strategic advantage to the PLA.

Three factors in particular explain the Chinese government's seriousness about the Tibet issue, namely, the question of 'national prestige', Tibet's strategic location and Tibet's resource endowment.

National prestige. In the Chinese perspective, the Dalai Lama and the Tibetans who have fled out of Tibet and China, have brought national shame to mainland China. Tibet has remained the most problematic aspect of China's domestic problem.

Tibet's strategic location. The 965,000 square mile area of the Tibetan plateau, which is spread across the Himalayas and is located at the centre of Asia, acts as a buffer for China with regard to the immediate neighbouring countries like India, Nepal and Bangladesh. Uncontested domination of Tibet will also enable China to think about a future where it could employ hawk-eye vigilance over the neighbouring countries.

Tibet's resource endowment. The largest reserve of uranium in the world, Tibet is not only home to Asia's largest rivers but also acts as a water-supplying region.

China's approach to Tibet and Tibetans has become severe since the outbreak of the protest march in March 2008 just before the Beijing Olympics. There has been a massive Chinese military presence in the TAR since then to closely monitor Tibetan activities.[14] Beijing's concern about the aspects of Tibetan religious celebrations in and outside Tibet is clearly evidenced in its official deliberations. For example, the July 2011 White Paper, *Sixty Years since Peaceful Liberation of Tibet*, carries a special section about religious freedom in Tibet, noting that religious freedom is 'respected and protected in Tibet' (*xinhuanet. com* 2011). Article 36 of the Chinese constitution states that

> No one may make use of religion to engage in activities that disrupt public order, impair the health of citizens or interfere with the educational system of the state. Religious bodies and religious affairs are not subject to any foreign domination.
>
> (*hkhrm.org.hk* n.d.)

There is not only a check on religious freedom but securitisation and militarisation of Tibet has also taken place. Yet the fragility of China as regards Tibet is still vividly reflected in its concern about how to absolutely control Tibet as a region in times to come (see Arpi 2014).

India's next course and India–China relations

The primary challenge for India is how to manage the Tibet issue without giving an impression that it is interfering in the succession matter of the Dalai Lama. For India, this is a bilateral matter between the Tibetan communities and the Chinese government. Nevertheless, India's future standpoint and outlook both towards Tibet and Tibetans will invariably depend upon who becomes the next Dalai Lama. India will be in a quandary whom to recognise as the Dalai Lama if, as seems likely, two concurrent Dalai Lamas emerge, one declared by the Chinese government and one by the Tibetan community. The Indian government, at least the top leadership, has maintained a distance from the Dalai Lama. This public posture may continue with the new Dalai Lama too. That will also allow India to flag its Tibet card.

In extreme circumstances, given China's persistent claim over Arunachal Pradesh or Tawang, India may like to revisit its stance on Tibet. This may not be a judicious approach, but the dynamism of the India–China boundary dispute is such that Tibet will continue as an issue between the two countries. Receiving the Tibetans in 1959 demonstrated the forte of Indian democracy. Tibetan communities living in India not only signify India's soft-power image but also the courage and strength of India's democracy. These strengths will be tested again amidst the post-Dalai Lama complexities.

Three specific challenges may emerge for India in the post-14th Dalai Lama period. The *first* challenge will be how to manage the roughly 100,000 Tibetans in India. The current Dalai Lama possesses a charismatic leadership quality to hold the Tibetan communities in India and elsewhere united. That may not be the case with the new Dalai Lama. The Tibetan communities in India and away have become somewhat pragmatic. They do not see any more the spiritual way of living life as a singular mode. They see the arrival of globalisation as an opportunity for them. India will also be in a dilemma whether to allow the Tibetans to live in India permanently or induce them to return to their homeland. If they decide to stay on, a further challenge for India would be whether to allow them to live under both the TGIE and Indian government.

The *second* challenge for India is the potential security concern. The radical elements in the Tibetan exile community in India have in the past sporadically engaged in intense protest activities against the Chinese Embassy in New Delhi but are currently silent (Gautam *et al.* 2012: 'Chapter 8: Tibetan refugees and India's security', pp. 159–61). Yet, their activities will be a factor that India must learn to deal with.

Third, India faces an ethical dilemma whether it can have a view on the succession issue of the Dalai Lama. India initially did not wish to welcome

Karmapa. The time has come for India to have a talk with the TGIE Prime Minister over the succession issue. India must make a strong case that the TGIE must take India into confidence before the next Dalai Lama is found or chosen. The challenge for New Delhi is how to promote a trust-building network with the TGIE Prime Minister and the Panchen Lama. Besides, India needs to decide whether it wants to give its future Tibet policy a 'strategic direction' or not. This Tibet policy can have two dimensions: one with regard to the territorial matter of Tibet and the other on how to manage the challenges that will emerge from the Tibetan episode.

Implications for Sino-Indian relations

In the post-14th Dalai Lama scenario, three issues will remain the main aspects of India–Tibet–China tripartite dynamics, posing considerable challenges to India. These are: (i) the insecurity of the identity dilemma of Tibetans around the world, including in Tibet and in India, over the future of Tibet; (ii) China's authoritative approach towards Tibet and Tibetans; and (iii) India's own indecisiveness towards the matter of Tibet, Tibetans and the course of Tibetan affairs, principally towards the TGIE. Behind these issues, there are greater governance issues that will affect this tripartite dynamics.

The future course of the Tibetans' protest movement is one important factor in this context. The Tibetan protest movements so far have been both peaceful and violent. After the demise of the Dalai Lama, one is not sure how the Tibetan protest movements will unfold. There are enough signals that in the absence of a strong leadership like the current Dalai Lama, the Tibetan movements may not remain united and wither away. It is also possible that the protest movement may continue and take a violent course, in which case, India will come under stress to manage the activities of the Tibetans. But more than a violent course, what the Chinese government will actually worry about is the non-violent means of protest, including self-immolation. Even though the Dalai Lama has publicly criticised the self-immolation phenomenon, the Chinese government has blamed him and his followers for it (An Lu 2015). This is one aspect of the Tibetan protests that the Chinese government will always find difficulty in dealing with.

The greater challenge for India–China relations is, however, the unity of Tibetans after the current Dalai Lama and their future course of action. The Tibetans in India, living mainly as exiles or refugees, are still hopeful of going back to Tibet. Neither is there any formal administrative mechanism between India and China, which can specifically discuss the Tibet issue or the Tibetans' return to Tibet. Nor will China allow India to talk about such a sensitive matter that has brought it years of humiliation and has propelled a war with India.[15] Hence, the post-14th Dalai Lama phase will emerge as one of the most important aspects of India–China relations.

Notes

1 A review essay on the subject has been published by the author in *Asian Ethnicity* (Routledge). See Panda 2013.
2 The title Dalai Lama translates in the Tibetan language as 'Ocean of Compassion'. The word Dalai derives from the Mongolian 'Gyatso'; 'Lama' means 'high priest'. The Dalai Lama is found, not chosen. After a Dalai Lama dies, the Panchen Lama, a council of senior lamas, or a specially appointed person, search for his reincarnation as a young boy. When he is identified, he is groomed to become the Dalai Lama. This is so far as the Tibetan tradition goes. China on the other hand holds the view that this search must be carried out through the 'golden urn' process where several potential boys' names, written on paper, are placed in a special golden urn where the lamas appointed for the process pick up one name and send it for the approval of the Chinese central administration after the approval and consent of the Tibetan National Assembly.
3 Illustrative of the literature on the subject is Deepak 2011.
4 He was born on 6 July 1935 to a family of horse traders and farmers in Taktser of the Tibetan hamlet and was named as Lhamo Thondup. He was taken to Lhasa at the age of four and was conferred the spiritual leadership where his name was changed to Ngawang Lobsang Yeshe Tenzin Gyatso. The Tibetan Government bestowed temporal political power and authority on him in November 1950 in the wake of Tibet's invasion by China's PLA. The Dalai Lama fled to India in 1959.
5 For illustrative literature on the subject, see Arpi 2013; Lhamo 2013; Virk 2013; Topgyal 2013; Tsering 2014.
6 The office of the Dalai Lama claims,

> Since the omniscient Gedun Gyatso was recognised and confirmed as the reincarnation of Gedun Drub in the fifteenth century and the Gaden Phodrang Labrang (the Dalai Lama's institution) was established, successive reincarnations have been recognised. The third in the line, Sonam Gyatso, was given the title of the Dalai Lama. The Fifth Dalai Lama, Ngawang Lobsang Gyatso, established the Gaden Phodrang Government in 1642, becoming the spiritual and political head of Tibet. For more than 600 years since Gedun Drub, a series of unmistaken reincarnations has been recognised in the lineage of the Dalai Lama.
> (See *dalailama.com* 2011)

7 For instance, Diane Wolff argues:

> Because Tibet accepted Chinggis Khan's rule, it was never garrisoned nor was it subject to rule by a Mongol military governor. Chinggis Khan designated the Sakya branch of the Tibetan Buddhist faith to rule as his surrogates. Tibet was not assigned a Mongol *darugachi*. It fell under the authority of the regional khan who made his military camp in southwest China adjacent to Tibet (in Ogodei's time, this was Godan), but a member of the Sakya sect ruled it internally. As has been noted, Chinggis Khan revered Speakers to Heaven and recognised Tibetan Buddhist clerics as holy men. Only in cases where taxes were not remitted did Mongol troops enter Tibet.
> (Wolff 2010: 53)

Therefore, Tibet was not in Chinese historical dynastic territorial control.
8 A field trip was made to Dharmasala in India in the second week of April 2009. The author interviewed and interacted with several TGIE and Central Tibetan Administration (CTA) officials. Names withheld on request. Some of these interviews and impressions gathered from the interaction have been published in Gautam *et al.* 2012.
9 This 'Great Western Development' (*Xibu da kaifa*) strategy was introduced in March 1999 and launched in January 2000. One of its main objectives is to address the

regional economic disparities by robust investment and bringing new scales of infrastructural development, to bridge the disparity gaps that exist between different provinces and the centre. The strategy covers six provinces, five autonomous regions (Tibet among them) and one municipality. In view of its problematic domestic standing, special importance has been given to Tibet. See Ogutcu and Taube 2002; Cooke 2003; Huang *et al.* 2010).
10 The author carried out a series of interviews and interactions on the post-Dalai Lama scenario in Beijing, Shanghai, Sichuan and Guangzhou during July–September 2009. These interviews have been partially published in Gautam *et al.* 2012.
11 Interview conducted on 24 December 2014. Name withheld on request.
12 Based on interviews with experts from CIIS, CASS, CIIR, SIIS and SASS in China, during a field trip conducted from 16 December 2014 to 4 January 2015. The field trip was sponsored by ICSSR, New Delhi.
13 Interview with a Chinese official in Beijing on 24 December 2014; name withheld on request.
14 See, for example, Xing'an *et al.* 2011.
15 Impression gathered from interviews and interactions with the CASS (Beijing) and SASS (Shanghai) scholars. The author has interacted with Chinese experts like Xiong Aizong, Wu Zhaoli, Wang Xiaoping, Zhao Gancheng, Yang Danzhi, Liu Zongyi and Wang Dehua a number of times.

References

An Lu, 2015. 'Dalai Lama incites lamas and followers to engage in self-immolation: white paper', *Xinhua*, 15 April, http://news.xinhuanet.com/english/2015-04/15/c_134152496.htm (accessed on 21 July 2015).
Aneja, Atul, 2015. 'Integrating Tibet with the world', *The Hindu*, 13 July, p. 11.
Arpi, Claude, 2013. 'China's leadership change and its Tibet policy', *Strategic Analysis*, 37(5): 539–57.
Arpi, Claude, 2014. 'China's Tibet policy under a new leadership', *Pentagon's South Asia Defense and Strategic Year Book*, New Delhi: Pentagon Press, pp. 26–33.
au.china-embassy.org, 2008. '"Lhasa Convention" not proof of sovereign Tibet', Embassy of The People's Republic of China in Australia, 29 May, http://au.china-embassy.org/eng/zt/zgxz/t459635.htm (accessed on 9 July 2015).
china.org.cn, 1992. *Tibet – its ownership and human rights situation*, Information Office of the State Council of The People's Republic of China, September, Beijing, www.china.org.cn/e-white/tibet/ (accessed on 13 July 2015).
china.org.cn, 2008. '"Lhasa Convention" proves nothing', 3 June, www.china.org.cn/china/tibet_democratic_reform/content_17363552.htm (accessed on 9 July 2015).
china.org.cn, 2015. 'Tibet's path of development is driven by an irresistible historical tide', *White Paper*, State Council Information Office: People's Republic of China, 15 April, Beijing, www.china.org.cn/china/2015-04/15/content_35325433.htm (accessed on 13 July 2015).
chinadaily.com.cn, 2008. 'Reincarnation of living Buddha needs govt's approval', *Xinhua*, 4 August, www.chinadaily.com.cn/china/2007-08/04/content_5448242.htm (accessed on 15 July 2015).
chinadaily.com.cn, 2015. 'Tibet maintains ambitious growth target with strong investment', *China Daily*, 18 January, www.chinadaily.com.cn/china/2015-01/18/content_19343334.htm (accessed on 21 July 2015).

Chinese Journal of International Law, 2006. 'Regulations on Religious Affairs (promulgated by the State Council of the People's Republic of China: effective as of March 1, 2005)', *Chinese Journal of International Law*, 5(2): 475–85.

Chonzom, Tsering, 2015. 'Will he or won't he? recent Sino-Tibetan exchanges over the Dalai Lama's reincarnation', *ICS Analysis*, no. 27, February, pp. 1–8.

commonlii.org, 1954. *Agreement Between the Republic of India and the People's Republic of China on Trade and Intercourse Between Tibet Region of China and India*, Ministry of External Affairs, New Delhi, 29 April, www.commonlii.org/in/other/treaties/INTSer/1954/5.html (accessed on 13 July 2015).

Cooke, Susette, 2003. 'Merging Tibetan culture into the Chinese economic fast lane', *China Perspectives*, November–December, pp. 1–17.

Dai Xu and Huang Zhiling, 2009. 'Sichuan-Tibet railway project delayed', *China Daily*, 3 September, www.chinadaily.com.cn/business/2009-09/03/content_8649487.htm (accessed on 13 July 2015).

dalailama.com, 2011. 'Reincarnation' (Translated from the original Tibetan), The Dalai Lama: His Holiness the 14th Dalai Lama of Tibet, Dharmasala, 24 September, www.dalailama.com/biography/reincarnation (accessed on 13 July 2015).

Deepak, B.R., 2011. 'India, China and Tibet: fundamental perceptions from Dharamsala, Beijing and New Delhi', *Asian Ethnicity*, 12(3), October, pp. 301–21.

fmprc.gov.cn, 2003. *Declaration on principles for relations and comprehensive cooperation between the People's Republic of China and the Republic of India*, Ministry of Foreign Affairs of the People's Republic of China, 25 June, www.fmprc.gov.cn/mfa_eng/wjdt_665385/2649_665393/t22852.shtml (accessed on 13 July 2015).

Frossard, Adrien, 2013. 'Reincarnation under stress: the Dalai Lama's succession and India–China Relations', *Strategic Analysis*, 37(4): 463–73.

Gautam, P.K., Jagannath P. Panda and Zakir Hussain (eds), 2012. *Tibet and India's Security: Himalayan region, refugees and Sino-Indian relations*, IDSA Task Force Report, May.

Heinrich, Eric, 2015. 'Tibet's economy booms as rest of China slows', *Global Finance*, 6 April, https://www.gfmag.com/magazine/april-2015/tibets-economy-booms-rest-china-slows-milestones (accessed on 21 July 2015).

Hillman, Ben, 2008. 'Money can't buy Tibetans love', *Far Eastern Economic Review*, April, pp. 8–12.

hkhrm.org.hk, n.d. 'Chapter Two – The fundamental rights and duties of citizens', *International Human Rights Treaties & Documents Database*, hkhrm.org.hk, www.hkhrm.org.hk/english/law/const03.html (accessed on 21 July 2015).

Huang, Nancy, Joie Ma and Kyle Sullivan, 2010. 'Economic development policies for central and western China', *China Business Review*, 1 November, www.chinabusinessreview.com/economic-development-policies-for-central-and-western-china/ (accessed on 16 July 2015).

Kristof, Nicholas D., 1989. 'The Panchen Lama is dead at 50: key figure in China's Tibet policy', *New York Times*, 30 January, www.nytimes.com/1989/01/30/obituaries/the-panchen-lama-is-dead-at-50-key-figure-in-china-s-tibet-policy.html (accessed on 13 July 2015).

Lhamo, Tseyang, 2013. 'The Tibet issue under China's new leadership: changes and continuity', *Defence and Diplomacy*, 3(1), October–December, pp. 59–70.

Liu Wei, 2009. 'Origin of the title of "Dalai Lama" and its related backgrounder', *xinhuanet*, 1 March, http://news.xinhuanet.com/english/2009-03/01/content_10921943.htm (accessed on 13 July 2015).

Norbu, Dawa, 1997. 'Tibet in Sino-Indian relations: the centrality of marginality', *Asian Survey*, 37(11): 1078–95.

Ogutcu, Mehmet and Markus Taube, 2002. 'Getting China's regions moving', *Observer*, no. 231/232, May, pp. 13–15.

Panda, Jagannath P., 2013. Book Review of Dianne Wolff edited *Tibet Unconquered: An Epic Struggle for Freedom* (New York, Palgrave Macmillan 2010); and John B. Roberts II and Elizabeth A. Roberts (eds), *Freeing Tibet: 50 Years of Struggle, Resilience, and Hope* (New Delhi: Pentagon Press, 2009), published in *Asian Ethnicity*, 14(3): 383–7.

savetibet.org, 2015. 'China attempts to legitimize its Panchen Lama through a major speech as the real Panchen Lama's birthday approaches', *International Campaign for Tibet*, 21 April, www.savetibet.org/china-attempts-to-legitimize-its-panchen-lama-through-a-major-speech-as-the-real-panchen-lamas-birthday-approaches/ (accessed on 13 July 2015).

tibetanreview.net, 2015. 'China's Panchen calls for socialist-society Tibetan Buddhists', *Tibetan Review*, 9 March, www.tibetanreview.net/chinas-panchen-calls-for-socialist-society-tibetan-buddhists/ (accessed on 13 July 2015).

Tien-sze Fang 2014. 'The Tibet issue in Sino-Tibetan relations', in *Asymmetrical Threat Perceptions in India–China Relations*, New Delhi: Oxford University Press.

Topgyal, Tsering, 2013. 'Identity insecurity and the Tibetan resistance against China', *Pacific Affairs*, 86(3), September.

Tsering, Dolma, 2014. 'Dalai Lama central to resolution of the Tibet issue', *Strategic Analysis*, 38(1): 19–24.

Virk, Simrat Kaur, 2013. 'Institution of the Dalai Lama and the Sino-Tibetan conflict', *Defence and Diplomacy*, 2(3), April–June, pp. 77–85.

Wolff, Diane, 2010. *Tibet Unconquered: An Epic Struggle for Freedom*, New York: Palgrave Macmillan.

Xing'an, Liu, GuoFengkuan and Liu Yinghua, 2011. 'PLA holds first air and ground forces joint drill on plateau', *The China Times*, 26 October, http://thechinatimes.com/online/2011/10/1738.html (accessed on 22 July 2015).

xinhuanet.com, 2008. 'Tell you a true Tibet – origins of so-called "Tibetan Independence"', 16 April, http://news.xinhuanet.com/english/2008-04/16/content_7987719.htm (accessed on 13 July 2015).

xinhuanet.com, 2011. 'Sixty years since peaceful liberation of Tibet', *White Paper*, Information Office of the State Council, China, 11 July, at http://news.xinhuanet.com/english2010/china/2011-07/11/c_13978644.htm (accessed on 21 July 2015).

Xinhuanet.com, 2015a. 'China voice: For reincarnation, it takes more than just the words of Dalai Lama', *Xinhuanet*, 19 July, at http://news.xinhuanet.com/english/2015-07/19/c_134426032.htm (accessed on 19 August 2015).

Xinhuanet.com, 2015b. *Tibet's Path of Development Is Driven by an Irresistible Historical Tide*, The State Council Information Office of the People's Republic of China, Beijing, April, http://news.xinhuanet.com/english/china/2015-04/15/c_134152612_2.htm (accessed on 15 July 2015).

Xinhuanet.com, 2015c. 'Xinhua insight: China issues white paper on Tibet, denouncing Dalai Lama's "middle way"', *Xinhuanet*, 15 April, http://news.xinhuanet.com/english/2015-04/15/c_134154123.htm (accessed on 15 July 2015).

Yan Liang, 2008. 'China publishes historical records that show Tibet an inalienable part of country', *Chinaview.com*, 8 April, http://news.xinhuanet.com/english/2008-04/08/content_7935999.htm (accessed on 13 July 2015).

5 The water resource conflict

As emerging economies, both India and China have entered a phase of 'perennial water scarcity' where industrial outfits, irrigation pattern, agricultural sector and people's livelihood demand more water resources.[1] Exploitation of transboundary water resources, however, can cause serious conflict when an upper riparian country overlooks the needs and concerns of trans-national economies. The growing discord between India and China on the trans-boundary water resources is both a bilateral and trans-national problem. China has the edge in water politics, being an upper riparian state. Although India is both an upper and lower riparian country in regard to various rivers, most of the extended rivers flowing from the Himalayan region and Tibetan glacier make it largely a lower riparian state.

The Ganga–Brahmaputra–Meghna/Barak (GBM) basin involves India, Tibetan Autonomous Region (TAR) of China, Bangladesh, Nepal and Bhutan and extends up to 1.7 million km roughly (*fao.org* 2011; see also *india-wris.nrsc.gov.in* n.d.; Rasul 2015). Importantly, the Ganges and Brahmaputra headwaters originate from the Tibetan plateau, which is a Greater Himalayan mountain range. The Ganges headwaters flow south-west, and after entering India turn south-east to join major tributaries. After entering Bangladesh, they join the Brahmaputra and the Meghna to flow inside the Bay of Bengal. The Brahmaputra originates near Kailash Mansarovar in Tibet, flows east from the headwaters, and moves through the southern areas of TAR. It then enters eastern India, turns south-west and enters Bangladesh before merging with the Ganges. The Greater GBM basin amalgamates and compounds many socio-economic facets and environmental problems and concerns. The populace of the region is multi-religious, multi-ethnic and mostly poor. Frequent floods, poor drainage and lack of water management system characterise the ecology of this water basin (*fao.org* 2011; Rasul 2015). For India, though the river waters originating from the Tibetan plateau are a great resource for its agricultural economy and renewable water supplies, they also pose a serious problem in managing the flow of the waters.

The Brahmaputra/Yarlung Tsangpo, whose water is a matter of discord between India and China, originates from the Tibetan glacier, enters into Arunachal Pradesh and Assam in India and flows to Bangladesh. It takes a bend on the India–China border, known as the Great Bend, and rushes between the Namcha Barwa and Gyala Pelri mountains (IDSA Task Force Report 2010: 45).

China has an ambitious water diversion project in the Tibetan plateau, from south-western China to the dry lands of northern China, popularly known as the Grand Western Water Diversion Plan. This plan facilitates the South–North Water Diversion Project (SNWDP) (*CCTV English* 2011; *chinadaily.com.cn* 2015). SNWDP is one of Beijing's largest infrastructure projects since the Three Gorges Dam. Mao Zedong conceived this project in 1952. It was formally approved in December 2002 after intense debate (Deng Shasha 2012). Guo Kai, a famous water expert, proposed this 'Grand Western Water Diversion Plan'. The SNWDP became operational in 2014.

The project consists of three routes – eastern, middle and western. India has a problem with the western route, which is connected through the Brahmaputra. If China decides to divert water from the Brahmaputra, the water flow is likely to be affected substantially, making most of north-eastern India drought prone. Currently, India has a data sharing MoU with China. The Chinese have been adamant about not entering into a dialogue with India on this issue (He Shan 2012). A range of Chinese media and government reports have indicated that China is serious about pushing the hydropower projects in the Brahmaputra's Great Bend. The State Council of China in 2006 indicated planning of Yarlung Tsangpo water diversion projects after the near completion of the Three Gorges Dam (*gov.cn* 2006).

Non-Chinese experts foresaw a nuclear detonation being linked to this programme (Christopher 2013: 15). Even though China ratified the Comprehensive Test Ban Treaty (CTBT) in the 1990s, the interest in a nuclear detonation in water diversion was still kept alive, and Beijing persistently argued for a Peaceful Nuclear Explosion (PNE), where the clandestine aim was to use nuclear detonations for such a challenging water diversion programme (ibid.).

Beijing's five-year energy plan, released in January 2013, mentioned three dam-building projects in the Yarlung Tsangpo basin. When India expressed its concern about the possible adverse fallout on India of these plans, China assured India that these projects did not have a direct concern for India since the initial dam construction in Zangmu in Tibet was a run-of-the-river project (Parsai 2013). To India's concern, however, hydrologists in China, for example Wang Guangqian, have been reported expressing the view that 'even though we thought that the western route construction may not be possible for 50 years, it is necessary now' (Xuyang Jingjing 2011). According to Chinese reports, SNWDP is expected to divert an estimated 44.8 billion cubic metres of water every year to almost ten provinces and cities (Yang Yi 2014a). According to these reports, 'the western route of the SNWDP will flow from three tributaries of Yangtze River near the Bayankala Mountain' (Yang Yi 2014b).

The prime Indian concern about this matter has been that North-East India, which is heavily dependent on the Brahmaputra water for agricultural needs, may have substantial water shortage if China continues to divert water in the western bend of Yarlung Tsangpo/Brahmaputra; and if the water overflows, that may cause floods. The initial Indian concern arose in 2000 when India's northeast was flooded due to a dam burst in Tibet. Indian officials and experts presumed a Chinese hand behind this calamity and urged the Chinese government to compensate for it (*BBC World* 2000; Gogoi 2000). It turned out later that the flood occurred due to a natural dam burst. Nevertheless, India's concern over China's water diversion plan was validated when China in its *National Defence White Paper*, released in 2006, mentioned about the possibility and potentiality of the SNWDP (*fas.org* 2006).

Indian concern and Chinese explanation

Since 2006, the Chinese government has denied that the water conservation expert Guo Kai's idea will not be implemented or accepted completely. Guo Kai's idea behind the Great Western Route Water Diversion Project is to divert 200 billion cubic metres of water annually from the Yarlung Tsangpo (Zangbo), Mekong (Nujiang) and Salween (Lancang) to the Yellow River and finally to northern China (*China Daily* 2006). Criticising this project proposal as 'dramatic', the then Water Resources Minister Wang Shucheng stated that it was 'unnecessary, unfeasible and unscientific'. Liu Jianchao, the then Chinese Foreign Ministry spokesman, denied publicly that China had any plan of building a dam on Yarlung Tsangpo and diverting water to the Yellow River (ibid.). It was further stated that this kind of project would require 'international cooperation'.

In the Chinese assertion, the SNWDP is the world's largest water diversion project (Yang Yi 2014a). Its main intent is to divert water from south to north China. The main aim is to divert and supply water from the Yangtze to northern China, including the capital city Beijing. This is planned in three routes: eastern, middle and western. Reports indicate that even though the eastern and middle routes have been in operation, the western route is still in its 'pre-construction stage' (ibid.). The western line is not linked with the Grand Western Diversion Plan (Zhang Hongzhou 2015). It is also practically impossible to build or construct alone, as it requires regional coordination or consent. Also, it is not environmentally friendly and it may affect China's neighbouring provinces (ibid.).

The Indian perception of the SNWDP is a progressing one. In the initial years, the strategic community in India saw its implementation in alarming terms and linked it with China's approach to troubling India's North-East and an attempt to reshape the boundary dispute in its favour (Mukherjee 2014). The fear was that if China decided to divert the water in the Yarlung Tsangpo/Brahmaputra, then north-eastern India, especially Assam, would face severe drought. However, slowly, there has been a serious and nuanced debate in India about the SNWDP. Even though the alarmist viewpoint still dominates, India currently appears to be more sensible in expressing its opinion on the water row.

What becomes problematic in India's perception is a lack of clarity and transparency on China's part to address India's concern (Wall 2013). Lower riparian countries including India primarily perceive China as an 'uncooperative water hegemon' (Zhang Hongzhou 2015). Beijing's passive role in global water governance and its non-cooperative outlook explain this perception to some extent. China has, for example, voted against the 1997 UN Convention on Non-Navigational Uses of International Watercourses (ibid.). Strategic experts contend that there are reasons why China has taken this stand, including the mention of mandatory involvement of 'third party' in dispute settlement, responsibility of upper riparian states and the involvement of national security issues (ibid.).

Search for a 'watershed' agreement?

Three rivers – Brahmaputra, Indus and Sutlej – originate from China and enter India. Discussions over these rivers have often been from the ecological perspective and have been limited to scholarly and academic persuasions. However, only Yarlung Tsangpo/Brahmaputra has occupied political continuum in India–China bilateral bearings. The first MoU on hydrological data sharing between the two countries was crafted in 2002; it was relevant till the year 2007. By this MoU, China agreed to share with India hydrological information on Yarlung Tsangpo/Brahmaputra water level in the flood season from 1 June to 15 October every year (*wrmin.nic.in* 2014). These data were mainly concerning the water level discharges and rainwater volume in three stations – Nugesha, Yangcun and Nuxia (ibid.). A fresh MoU was signed for five years in 2008. During Premier Li Keqiang's visit to India in May 2013, this MoU was renewed for a further five years. In October 2013, during the Indian Prime Minister's visit to China, a separate MoU on 'Strengthening Cooperation on Trans-Border Rivers' was signed. By this MoU, it was agreed that China would provide hydrological information data from 15 May to 15 October every year (ibid.; see also GoI 2013). Similarly, MoUs between the two countries exist on Sutlej/Langquin Zangbu on hydrological data sharing. These MoUs were crafted in 2005, 2010 and 2011 (*wrmin.nic.in* 2014). Besides, there is an Experts Level Mechanism (ELM) that mainly addresses matters concerning flood season hydrological data, emergency management and trans-border rivers.

Notably, there has been a political recognition of the ELM and MoUs at the bilateral level. For instance, the Joint Statement released during Prime Minister Narendra Modi's visit to China notes, 'The Indian side expressed appreciation to China for providing flood-season hydrological data and the assistance in emergency management' (*pib.nic.in* 2015). Similarly, the Joint Statement signed on 23 October 2013 noted about the trans-border river management and data sharing (*mea.gov.in* 2013). But these expressed statements are mostly rhetoric. Neither are any enforcement mechanisms in place nor is there any express avowal to address India's concerns.

It needs to be asked here: why is there no bilateral agreement between China and India on the water issue? Apparently, not only is water a trans-border matter that is indirectly linked to India–China bordering affairs but it is also based on India–China dynamisms in the neighbourhood. Water as a bordering affairs matter may continue to prevail in India–China boundary undertaking in future. India insists on a bilateral agreement on the issue of trans-border waters, but China refuses, because it will have a legal enforcement mechanism.

A possible extreme scenario – which Chinese scholars and experts discount in the author's interactions with them – presents itself in the context of the sensitivity of Tibet in India–China ties and China's mounting claim over Arunachal. In this scenario, one may gradually witness China becoming more authoritarian and non-cooperative as an upper riparian country. This, however, may force India's hand to revisit its stand on Tibet as well as reword its one-China policy stance. Obduracy in this matter could also go against China's achieving its 'One Belt, One Road' and BCIM economic corridor ambitions.

That prompts one to ask: will China eventually enter an agreement on water sharing with India on Yarlung Tsangpo/Brahmaputra? The answer is, quite unlikely. For China, national security issues like Tibet are non-negotiable whether at the bilateral or regional level. Controlling the water resources in Tibet allows China to become resource-independent as far as water is concerned. It may be noted in this context that neither has China actively supported the Mekong River Commission nor has it shown any inclination for an agreement with India on the water issue. Most importantly, data and information concerning water are seen as state secrets in China (Zhang Hongzhou 2015). Above all this, what remains challenging is the contention of Chinese scholars and experts that India is exaggerating the matter for propaganda mileage[2] and that the Indian media distort this issue to give it a political connotation, which becomes problematical.[3]

Possible emerging scenarios

Four scenarios are conceivable as regards the future of the water conflict surrounding Yarlung Tsangpo/Brahmaputra, as follows.

One. Contrary to many forecasts of a 'water war' (Chellaney 2013a; Mukherjee 2014; Ramachandran 2015), one may actually see India and China forging a *cooperative* bilateral understanding on the issue. Given that the two countries have a 'developmental partnership' currently, the idea of establishing a cooperative relationship on a governance issue like water does not seem far-fetched. The Indian government has stated expressly that India has no objection to a run-of-the-river project since it will not affect inflows into India (Parsai 2013). It has also been stated that India must carefully study the water flowing from China to the Brahmaputra before raising the matter officially with China (Krishnan 2014). At the moment, there are only ELMs for dialogue and MoUs on river waters or hydrological matters. One may see the two countries signing more MoUs with regard to the water flow in Yarlung Tsangpo/Brahmaputra or hydrological matters. Issues like generating hydropower jointly, joint action plan to face and mitigate floods and use water jointly for trans-national energy resources may eventually be discussed between the two countries. It is also possible that they may enhance some understanding on sharing flood management system, planning to have an early warning system and developing joint data sharing mechanisms to address concerns on flood and drought. The water issue has not been a major issue in the India–China dialogue yet: it has only been limited to discussion at ELMs and a few MoUs (see Tables 5.1 and 5.2). Neither are there any concrete diplomatic forums or discussions between the two

Table 5.1 India–China experts level mechanism meetings on trans-border rivers

Name of agreement/MoU	Date of signing	Place
1st Expert Level Mechanism	19–21 September 2007	Beijing
2nd Expert Level Mechanism	10–12 April 2008	New Delhi
3rd Expert Level Mechanism	21–25 April 2009	Beijing
4th Expert Level Mechanism	26–29 April 2010	New Delhi
5th Expert Level Mechanism	19–22 April 2011	Beijing
6th Expert Level Mechanism	17–20 July 2012	New Delhi
7th Expert Level Mechanism	14–18 May 2013	Beijing
8th Expert Level Mechanism	24–27 June 2014	New Delhi
9th Expert Level Mechanism	May 2015	Beijing

Source: Ministry of Water Resources, Government of India; South Asia Network on Dams, Rivers and People (SANDRP), etc.

Table 5.2 MoUs on water/hydrological data sharing between India and China

Name of agreement/MoU	Date of signing	Key issues
MoU on Brahmaputra/Yaluzangbu River	2002	To share hydrological information for flood forecast on Nugesha, Yangcun and Nuxia stations located on Yaluzangbu and Brahmaputra rivers
MoU on Sutluj/Langquin Zangbo River	April 2005	For supply of hydrological information in respect of Sutlej and Langquin Zangbo rivers
MoU on Brahmaputra/Yaluzangbu river	5 June 2008	To share hydrological information for flood forecast on Yaluzangbu and Brahmaputra rivers
MoU on Sutluj/Langquin Zangbo River	16 December 2010	For provision of hydrological information of Sutluj and Langqen Zangbo rivers in flood season by China to India with a validity of five years
MoU on Sutluj/Langquin Zangbo River	5th ELM meeting on April 2011	Technical details of provision of hydrological information, data transmission method and cost settlement
Implementation Plan of MoU on Brahmaputra/Yaluzangbu River	30 May 2013	To extend the data provision period of the Yaluzangbu and Brahmaputra rivers

Source: Ministry of External Affairs and Ministry of Water Resources, River Development and Ganga Rejuvenation, Government of India, http://wrmin.nic.in/forms/list.aspx?lid=349#.

countries; nor are there any serious political undertakings that will prevent the water issue becoming a matter of serious conflict. For India, the challenge will be how to push China towards a dialogue forum, at least at the bilateral level.

Two. A *confrontational* scenario may equally emerge, if the Chinese government continues to push ahead on the water diversion project. Xi Jinping's 'Chinese dream' seeks to offer 'equal opportunities' to all citizens of China and address the regional disparities. Water is one source through which the political leadership is trying to bridge the existing gap in prosperity between southern and northern China. Water is seen as a renewable energy source and the promotion of ecological entities is one of China's current priorities (Qu Xing 2013). General Zhao Nanqi has stated: 'Even if we do not begin this water diversion project, the next generation will. Sooner or later it will be done' (*china.org.cn* 2006). Currently, the debate in China concerns fears that any construction on Yarlung Tsangpo/Brahmaputra will affect the ecological balance in the Tibetan plateau (Xuyang Jingjing 2011). Given the challenge that China faces technically and from environmental risks, there is difference of opinion whether China must continue the western route of the SNWDP project (ibid.). In terms of its regional perspective, China has a more cooperative drive towards the Mekong River Basin than towards Yarlung Tsangpo/Brahmaputra (Ho 2014). South-East Asia has been a priority region in China's foreign policy perspective and that compels Beijing to approach the Mekong River Basin under a more cooperative form than the Brahmaputra/Yarlung Tsangpo water basin. Neither has South Asia been a priority region in Chinese foreign policy all these years nor does India's 'power parity' with China encourage Beijing to pursue a cooperative drive (ibid.).

Three. A *consultative* scenario could also emerge. Even though the India–China water conflict is a transnational issue, there is no regional or international framework or mechanism or charter currently that can effectively address the conflict. The most appropriate international framework on watercourse management is the UN Convention of 1977 (*legal.un.org* 1997). Article 24 of the convention talks about the 'management' of watercourses among states. It states: 'Watercourse States shall, at the request of any of them, enter into consultations concerning the management of an international watercourse, which may include the establishment of a joint management mechanism' (ibid.). This UN convention takes note of the management of watercourses only. South Asian countries like India, Bangladesh, Nepal and Bhutan are not signatories to it (Bisht 2009). In the absence of a credible regional or international watercourses agreement that can address the possible tensions or conflicts arising over water sharing, one may eventually see Yarlung Tsangpo/Brahmaputra basin countries proposing a watercourse mechanism to address the issue. But one needs to watch whether this mechanism will evolve more as a consultative mechanism or enforcement mechanism. Above all, it also needs to be seen whether China will agree for regional watercourses mechanisms or agreement concerning Yarlung Tsangpo/Brahmaputra (Svensson 2012; Chellaney 2013b). So far, Beijing has not shown any interest for water-sharing or joint mechanism, or to a rule-based mechanism for water sharing. It has rejected the 1997 UN Convention and has asserted that as an upper riparian state it holds absolute rights and territorial sovereignty to manage or divert water in Yarlung Tsangpo/Brahmaputra (Chellaney 2013b). China has bilateral water treaties with several neighbours, but not with India. Neither has it been open to a regional approach to water sharing mechanisms.

Four. A scenario of *containment* or *conflict*-prone situation may emerge between India and China. Hitherto, the water row between the two countries has not been linked with the boundary problem, even though the Yarlung Tsangpo/Brahmaputra involves Tibet and India's North-East where Arunachal Pradesh is an issue. But given the nature of the India–China boundary dispute, which has extended from being purely a boundary dispute to a bordering dispute, there is enough indication that the water row will continue to be linked with the boundary dispute in coming times. China's rise as a power and its rising maritime posture in the neighbourhood are also factors in this regard. Other lower riparian states also hold this suspicion and lack trust in China (Gautam 2008: 973). The role and approach of Bangladesh will be crucial in this regard. Though Bangladesh will be severely affected if China decides to divert the water through the western line of SNWDP, not many in India are sure if Bangladesh will be supportive of India's stance on the issue. If China decides not to go ahead with the diversion, it will abate most of the suspicion in its neighbourhood. It will also encourage India to share the Himalayan rivers' water data with its lower riparian neighbours like Nepal, Pakistan and Bangladesh. This will greatly prompt a regional water sharing structure or mechanism (ibid.).

Among the four plausible scenarios, a cooperative or a consultative scenario may well materialise. Nonetheless, mutual suspicion will prevail and restrict any realistic cooperative relationship between India and China.

Notes

1 See, for instance, Gautam 2008; Chellaney 2009: 38–9; Christopher 2013; Sanwal 2015.
2 Reported views of Wang Dehua. He is a senior South Asia specialist based in Shanghai and is associated with many Chinese think-tanks and forums. See Wall 2013.
3 Author's interactions with Wang Dehua, Liu Zongyi, Li Li, Yang Xiaoping and Lan Jianxue in Beijing and Shanghai between 19 December 2014 and 4 January 2015. Most of the Chinese experts blame the Indian media for sensationalising the matter.

References

BBC World, 2000. 'Flood disaster in India', *BBC World*, 4 August, http://news.bbc.co.uk/2/hi/south_asia/865884.stm (accessed on 3 August 2015).
Bisht, Medha, 2009. 'Diversion of Yarlung Tsangpo: a probability analysis', *IDSA Comment*, 11 November, www.idsa.in/idsacomments/DiversionofYarlungTsangpo_MBisht_111109.html (accessed on 5 August 2015).
CCTV English, 2011. 'China water diversion project accelerates', *CCTV English*, 4 October, http://english.cntv.cn/program/newshour/20111006/103541.shtml (accessed on 3 August 2015).

Chellaney, Brahma, 2009. 'Beware the future: coming water wars', *The International Economy*, Fall, pp. 38–9.
Chellaney, Brahma, 2013a. 'The coming water wars', *Washington Times*, 8 October, www.washingtontimes.com/news/2013/oct/8/the-coming-water-wars/?page=all (accessed on 5 August 2015).
Chellaney, Brahma, 2013b. 'China's hydro-hegemony', *New York Times*, 7 February, www.nytimes.com/2013/02/08/opinion/global/chinas-hydro-hegemony.html (accessed on 5 August 2015).
China Daily, 2006. 'Dam proposal rubbished by critics', *China Daily*, 22 November, www.chinadaily.com.cn/china/2006-11/22/content_739379.htm (accessed on 4 August 2015).
China.org.cn, 2006. 'Controversial plan to tap Tibetan waters', *China.org.cn*, (Translated from *Southern Weekend* by Shao Da), 8 August, www.china.org.cn/english/MATERIAL/177295.htm (accessed on 5 August 2015).
chinadaily.com.cn, 2015. 'Report on the Implementation of the 2014 Plan for National Economic and Social Development and on the 2015 Draft Plan for National Economic and Social Development', Third Session of the Twelfth National People's Congress, 5 March 2015, National Development and Reform Commission, 17 March, www.chinadaily.com.cn/china/2015twosession/2015-03/17/content_19835944.htm (accessed on 3 August 2015).
Christopher, Mark, 2013. 'CIWAG case study on irregular warfare and armed groups: water wars: the Brahmaputra River and Sino-Indian relations', Centre on Irregular Warfare & Armed Groups (CIWAG), Newport, Rhode Island: US Naval War College, pp. 2–38.
Deng Shasha, 2012. 'China's water diversion project to be operational next year', *Xinhua*, 4 February, http://news.xinhuanet.com/english/china/2012-02/04/c_131391611.htm (accessed on 15 March 2012).
fao.org, 2011. 'Ganges–Brahmaputra–Meghna river basin', *Irrigation in Southern and Eastern Asia in figures – AQUASTAT Survey – 2011*, pp. 1–17, www.fao.org/nr/water/aquastat/basins/gbm/gbm-CP_eng.pdf (accessed on 3 August 2015).
fas.org, 2006. 'V. People's Armed Police Force', *China's National Defence in 2006*, Information Office of the State Council of the People's Republic of China, 29 December, http://fas.org/nuke/guide/china/doctrine/wp2006.html (accessed on 4 August 2015).
Gautam, P.K., 2008. 'Sino-Indian Water Issues', *Strategic Analysis*, 32(6), November, pp. 969–74.
Gogoi, Nitin, 2000. 'Army suspects Chinese hand behind flash floods in N-E', The *Rediff Special*, www.rediff.com/news/2000/aug/22assam.htm (accessed on 3 August 2015).
GoI, 2013. 'Memorandum of Understanding between the Ministry of Water Resources, the Republic of India and the Ministry of Water Resources, the People's Republic of China on Strengthening Cooperation on Trans-border Rivers, 2013', Government of India, New Delhi, 23 October.
Gov.cn, 2006. 'Three Gorges Dam nears completion', *Gov.cn*, 16 May, www.gov.cn/english/2006-05/16/content_281417.htm (accessed on 15 August 2015).
He Shan, 2012. 'Western route of water transfer project very much possible', *China.org.cn*, 13 March, www.china.org.cn/china/NPC_CPPCC_2012/2012-03/13/content_24883931.htm (accessed on 12 March 2012).
Ho, Selina, 2014. 'River politics: China's policies in the Mekong and the Brahmaputra in comparative perspective', *Journal of Contemporary China*, 23(85): 1–20.

IDSA Task Force Report, 2010. 'Chapter 3: Water issues in India–China relations', *Water Security for India: The External Dynamics*, IDSA Task Force Report, Institute for Defence Studies and Analyses, New Delhi, September.

india-wris.nrsc.gov.in, n.d. 'Brahmaputra', Water Resources Information System of India: India-WRIS Wiki, www.india-wris.nrsc.gov.in/wrpinfo/index.php?title=Brahmaputra (accessed on 3 August 2015).

Krishnan, Ananth, 2014. 'China puts first Brahmaputra dam into operation', *India Today*, 23 November, http://indiatoday.intoday.in/story/brahmaputra-dam-india-vs-china-zangmu-yarlung-tsangpo-zangbo-hydropower-project/1/403379.html (accessed on 5 August 2015).

legal.un.org, 1997. Convention on the Law of the Non-navigational Uses of International Watercourses, 1997, Adopted by General Assembly, 21 May 1997, http://legal.un.org/ilc/texts/instruments/english/conventions/8_3_1997.pdf (accessed on 5 August 2015).

mea.gov.in, 2013. 'Joint Statement – A vision for future development of India–China strategic and cooperative partnership', Ministry of External Affairs, Government of India, 23 October, http://mea.gov.in/bilateral-documents.htm?dtl/22379/Joint+Stateme nt+A+vision+for+future+development+of+IndiaChina+strategic+and+cooperative+par tnership (accessed on 9 August 2015).

Mukherjee, Amitav, 2014. 'Water wars: the next clash between India and China', *Oil Price. com*, 20 April, http://oilprice.com/Energy/Energy-General/Water-Wars-The-Next-Clash-between-India-and-China.html (accessed on 4 August 2015).

Parsai, Gargi, 2013. 'Run-of-the-river dams won't affect inflows into India', *The Hindu*, 31 January, www.thehindu.com/news/national/runoftheriver-dams-wont-affect-inflows-into-india/article4362027.ece?ref=relatedNews (accessed on 7 August 2015).

pib.nic.in, 2015. 'Joint Statement between India and China during Prime Minister's visit to China', Press Information Bureau, Government of India, Prime Minister's Office, 15 May, http://pib.nic.in/newsite/PrintRelease.aspx?relid=121755 (accessed on 9 August 2015).

Qu Xing, 2013. 'An emerging China in pursuit of peace and prosperity', *China Institute of International Studies*, 2 May, www.ciis.org.cn/english/2013-05/02/content_5919530. htm (accessed on 5 August 2015).

Ramachandran, Sudha, 2015. 'Water wars: China, India and the Great Dam push', *The Diplomat*, 3 April, http://thediplomat.com/2015/04/water-wars-china-india-and-the-great-dam-rush/ (accessed on 5 August 2015).

Rasul, Golam, 2015. 'Water for growth and development in the Ganges, Brahmaputra, and Meghna basins: an economic perspective', *International Journal of River Basin Management*, 13(3), September, pp. 387–400.

Sanwal, Mukul, 2015. 'Why water politics matter', in Uttam Kumar Sinha (ed.), *Emerging Strategic Trends in Asia*, New Delhi: Pentagon Press and IDSA, pp. 176–89.

Svensson, Jesper, 2012. 'Managing the rise of a hydro-hegemon in Asia: China's strategic interests in the Yarlung Tsangpo River', *IDSA Occasional Paper No. 23*, New Delhi: Institute for Defence Studies and Analyses, April.

Wall, Kim, 2013. 'Chinese dam concerns raise fears of future water conflict', *South China Morning Post*, 5 September, www.scmp.com/news/china/article/1303506/chinese-dam-concerns-raise-fears-future-water-conflict (accessed on 5 August 2015).

wrmin.nic.in, 2014. 'India–China cooperation: Memorandum of Understanding on hydrological data sharing on River Brahmaputra/Yaluzangbu', Ministry of Water Resources, River Development & Ganga Rejuvenation, Government of India, 19 September, http://wrmin.nic.in/forms/list.aspx?lid=349 (accessed on 7 August 2015).

Xuyang Jingjing, 2011. 'Making rivers run north', *Global Times*, 28 June, www.globaltimes.cn/content/663664.shtml (accessed on 9 August 2015).

Yang Yi, 2014a. 'Backgrounder: the South-to-North water diversion project's middle route', *Xinhuanet*, 12 December, http://news.xinhuanet.com/english/china/2014-12/12/c_133851139.htm (accessed on 8 August 2015).

Yang Yi, 2014b. 'China's water transfer project begins', *English.news.cn*, 12 December, http://news.xinhuanet.com/english/video/2014-12/12/c_133851268.htm (accessed on 9 August 2015).

Zhang Hongzhou, 2015. 'China–India water disputes: two major misperceptions revisited', *RSIS Commentary*, no. 015, 19 January.

Part II
The sub-regional crescendo

6 Beijing's 'one belt, one road' diplomacy and India

No proposition in Chinese foreign policy explains better the outward transformation that is taking place in it today than President Xi Jinping's 'One Belt, One Road' (popularly also known as 'belt and road') initiative. After assuming power in 2013, Xi Jinping spoke about the 'Silk Road Economic Belt' (SREB) and the '21st Century Maritime Silk Road' (MSR) in September and October 2013 (*caixin* 2014).[1] This is considered one of the most ambitious strategies by the President of China along with his 'Chinese Dream' (*zongquo meng*) proposition which is basically aimed at consolidating China's domestic conditions and global positioning (*CRIENGLISH.com* 2014). Many have seen a resilient and resolute China behind the 'belt and road' initiative. Seen sceptically as China's 'Marshall Plan' in many quarters initially,[2] the geopolitical implications of this initiative have been massive, including in India. This chapter assesses the Indian outlook towards 'One Belt, One Road' (OBOR) and its impact on India–China ties.

OBOR: more than a 'Marshall Plan'?

Essentially, OBOR is still an abstract concept, without any clearly articulated geographical lines or routes. It is more of a roadmap currently which aims to integrate China with the regional and global economies through greater connectivity, trade and economic contacts. This 'visionary conception' of Xi Jinping is primarily aimed at reviving China's historical contacts and revitalising sociocultural as well as economic contacts through the ancient Silk Road maps (*CRIENGLISH.com* 2014). In the Chinese formulation, OBOR is based on 'win-win' prospects by offering a chance of 'peaceful coexistence and mutual development' for China and the world (ibid.). Concretely, the key components of this initiative appear to be: economic corridor, transportation connectivity, infrastructure development, establishing better trade and economic contacts, exploring energy and natural resources, and generating financial security (ibid.). Three types of objective targets are meant to be achieved by the Chinese leadership through this grand strategy: demographic target, geographic target and resource objective targets.

In terms of *demographic* objectives, the OBOR initiative targets to establish direct contacts with 4.4 billion people – which is almost 63 per cent of the world population – through connectivity and economic corridor linking (ibid.). For *geographical* objectives, this strategy is not limited to China's immediate neighbourhood or Asian continent. It also factors in Africa, Europe and Latin America. With regard to *resource* objectives, it aims to take along a total GDP of US$2.1 trillion that accounts for 20 per cent of world capital and wealth (ibid.). The OBOR is supposed to guide China's national investment strategy too (Kennedy and Parker 2015). Most of its salient features are still being worked out, but the initiative has been officially approved and will be implemented in China's 13th Five Year plan (2016–2020).

The OBOR is not a replication of the Marshall Plan (Liu Ying 2015; see also Dingding Chen 2014; *Diplomat* 2015). The purpose and idea behind the latter was to augment the strategic influence of the United States in Europe in the post-World War II phase to limit and confront the Soviet influence (Liu Ying 2015) and to engender goodwill for the US, which would facilitate its strategic interests. The OBOR is much more multifaceted, being linked with Beijing's national interests, foreign policy objectives and global ambition that it has unveiled from time to time. It is unlike the Marshall Plan for the additional reason that though China continues to remain an economic attraction for many countries around the world, mistrust endures about China as a power in the neighbourhood and remote regions. Some of the causes of this mistrust are disputes in the South China Sea, China's problematic relations with Japan on the Senkaku/Diaoyu island dispute, boundary disputes with India, and attitude among the Central Asian countries about China as a 'suspect power'. Nonetheless, the prime aim of the OBOR initiative is to position China as the epicentre of regional as well as global economics and geopolitics. 'One Belt' implies land corridor connectivity from China to Central Asia and Western Asia, going all the way to Europe; whereas 'One Road' implies maritime connectivity through the Strait of Malacca to India, the Middle East and East Africa.

India and SREB

India factors prominently in China's exposition of the SREB. Gao Zhenting, Councillor of the Department of International Economic Affairs, has stated, for example:

> From the historical point of view India is the converging point of MSR and the ancient Silk Road on land. For more than 2,000 years, India had very good exchanges with China through the passage of the South Silk Road.
> (*Beijing Bulletin* 2014; see also *The Hindu* 2014)

Dai Bingguo elucidated in July 2014 in Guiyang how South Asia and India are an integral part of SREB (Dai Bingguo 2014).

By inviting Prime Minister Narendra Modi to Xi'an, Shaanxi province, during his recent China trip in May 2015, which broke the protocol of receiving a state guest in Beijing, the Chinese President sought to cajole India to rethink its silence on China's invitation to India to join its Silk Road project. Shaanxi province traditionally has been the epicentre of China's Silk Road diplomacy, at a time when Xi'an was known as Chang'an. Shaanxi is also politically significant because political leaders from that province have played a conspicuous role in China's policymaking. To receive the Indian Prime Minister in Xi'an and offer him a grand reception was an occasion for China to explain to him the merits of the SREB project and how and where the two countries can cooperate in the endeavour. Shaanxi plays a significant role in pushing forward the SREB project (Lu Hongyan et al. 2014) just like China's coastal provinces – Shandong, Jiangsu, Zhejiang, Fujian and Guangdong – play an important role in China's MSR project. These provinces have acted on behalf of the central government to host events, public relations exercises and academic forums, meeting business contacts overseas and campaigning with international bodies in the recent past for China's SREB enterprise. There is no reason, in the view of the Chinese strategic community, why India should not offer support to the SREB, given that China in principle has welcomed India's application for full membership in the Shanghai Cooperation Organisation (SCO).

The Chinese planning with regard to Xi'an is huge. The city aims to become the stationing point for almost 40 consulates in the next five years (Zhang Yi 2014). Xi'an not only wants to push ahead the SREB but also aims to act as a bridge between China and Central Asia. Shaanxi may not be important for India as far as security matters are concerned, but provinces individually do play a strong role in China's foreign policy planning and diplomacy. Especially in the current context, President Xi Jinping aims to empower most of China's provinces through his vision of a 'Chinese dream'.

SREB challenges and opportunities for India

In terms of opportunities for India, the SREB offers greater infrastructural linkages in the regional and neighbourhood contexts. The key components of SREB will involve an extended network of road and rail connection routes between Xi'an and Central Asia, eventually reaching Moscow, Rotterdam and Venice (*xinhuanet.com* 2015). These networks will also encompass greater oil and gas connections, new avenues for pipeline projects, and infrastructural projects for a greater connection between China and Central Asia, West Asia and Europe. The SREB is linked to China's 'Eurasian Pivot' strategy, where the objective is to establish linkages with 40 countries in Central Asia and South Asia, Middle East and in Eastern and Western Europe. India could benefit from these linkages.

In terms of challenges for India from the SREB, the biggest challenge comes from the China–Pakistan Economic Corridor (CPEC), which is an integral part of SREB. The challenge is fourfold.

First, the investment involved. The CPEC project is estimated to involve an initial grant of $46 billion to establish linkages between China and Pakistan. China had announced earlier that a corpus of $40 billion Silk Road Fund (SRF) would be generated initially to support the SREB projects. Reports indicate that

China has now announced that it will run a Karot hydropower project for the next 30 years, which is roughly estimated to cost $1.65 billion, before handing it over to Pakistan (*CHINAREALTIME* 2015). The Karot project is supposed to be in operation by 2020.

Second, the CPEC project is meant to connect Kashgar in China's Xinjiang province with the strategic port of Gwadar in Pakistan. India has always been concerned about the China–Pakistan understanding over the Gwadar port. India may have the Chahbahar port with Iran; yet the volume of financial backing that Gwadar port receives from China is far superior to what India can match.

Third, the outlay of the CPEC project that intends to run through the Pakistan Occupied Kashmir (POK) region of India is a challenge for India. It even portends that China may emerge as a silent 'third party' in the Kashmir dispute in future. Even though China has maintained a somewhat 'neutral' position on the Kashmir dispute in recent years after the Kargil conflict between India and Pakistan, terming it mostly as a 'bilateral historical dispute', the Chinese pursuit of the CPEC project may impel China to revisit its position on Kashmir on a future date. The CPEC will run through the strategic Gilgit-Baltistan, which is a region adjacent to India.

Fourth, the Chinese endeavour is to encourage India to get involved in the neighbourhood region without being generous on conflicting issues. This is a classical Chinese strategy of connecting with countries that are detrimental to China's strategic interests.

The Indian response

India waited a decade before expressing strongly its reservation on the embryonic understanding that was taking shape between China and Pakistan on infrastructural construction activities in POK, which was crafted in 2006 when the then Chinese President Hu Jintao visited Pakistan. However, recently, New Delhi has officially taken note of the CPEC. Sushma Swaraj, India's External Affairs Minister, stated in the Indian Parliament in December 2014:

> Government has seen reports with regard to China and Pakistan being involved in infrastructure building activities in POK, including construction of China–Pakistan Economic Corridor. Government has conveyed its concerns to China about their activities in Pakistan Occupied Kashmir, and asked them to cease such activities.
>
> (*MEA* 2014a)

On the other hand, the Indian High Commissioner to Pakistan was recently quoted stating that 'India has no worry over the construction of Pakistan–China Economic Corridor as an economically strong Pakistan would bring stability in the region' (*Economic Times* 2015a).

Three aspects mainly explain India's reservations on the SREB as well. *First*, both the SREB and CPEC put the Kashmir problem on a new platform. *Second*,

India is uneasy that a new strategic calculus may emerge between China, Pakistan and Russia at a time when the SCO is on the verge of expansion. Moreover, the US 'pivot' to Asia policy has compelled the Chinese and Russians to look for new regional allies where Pakistan may fit into this possible triangular relationship and that may impact India. *Third*, given India's strategic interest in the neighbourhood, particularly in the immediate maritime regions, supporting China's SREB would be a tactical imperfection. The challenge will further compound after India's possible induction in the SCO as a member where New Delhi may have to eventually join and back some of the infrastructural and energy-related projects in the Central Asian region.

India and MSR

In October 2013, while addressing the Indonesian Parliament, President Xi Jinping proposed the formation of a new MSR in the South-East Asian region (Wu Jiao and Zhang Yunbi 2013). Xi's thrust was on building a stronger China–ASEAN community, based on strong political foundation and economic cooperation between the two sides. In making this proposal, Xi Jinping highlighted two aspects: *first*, the geographic proximity between China and ASEAN members and how cooperation and development should bring them closer; and *second*, the economic potential of China and ASEAN as emerging markets in Asia, which are important not only for Sino-ASEAN bilateral relations but also for regional economic growth and integration (ibid.). Going by this spirit, the introduction of MSR was limited to the ASEAN region initially but has now become 'pan-global' in character.

The 'silk road' concept has a hoary ancestry in Chinese foreign policy planning. Beijing has used the idea of the 'silk road' concept traditionally to expand its overseas business and commercial deals and linkages. But Beijing's orderly employment of this notion in the maritime sector reflects fresh thinking in China's foreign policy in terms of overseas commercial as well as maritime interests. The MSR scheme is attached to China's ever-growing security awareness in the surrounding region and validates the Chinese dialogue of 'harmonious world' or 'harmonious ocean' thinking (*Xinhuanet* 2015a). In recent years, the developments, disputes and growing tensions both in the South China Sea and in the East China Sea region have prompted Beijing to constantly search for new methods of policy planning in the maritime sector. The core behind implementing the 'silk road' ideas into the maritime sector expounds a serious interest in Chinese strategic thinking to emerge as an important maritime power, particularly in the South China Sea, East China Sea and Indian Ocean region (IOR).

Beijing had invited India to join and support the MSR in 2014 during the Special Representatives (SRs) level dialogue. India has asked China for more details about the MSR, especially about the broader 'belt and road' initiative. The *Vision and Action on Jointly Building Belt and Road*, released in March 2015, unveils some details about Beijing's grand initiative, but these details are still hazy. Most of the regional or neighbouring countries around India have extended their support for MSR while New Delhi has maintained a strategic silence so far. Beijing has gone beyond the South Asian region, and has pursued the matter of MSR also with Gulf Cooperation Council (GCC) and African countries.

Implications for India

MSR poses two broad challenges to India. *First*, to India's presence and authority as a maritime power in the context of the South China Sea and Indian Ocean respectively; and *second*, to the maritime understanding that has been unfolding in IOR among India, the US, Australia, Japan and South-East Asian countries. ASEAN has seen India in a higher order than earlier in the recent past. The Americans have in their turn urged India to pursue an active policy in the ASEAN region. The MSR will certainly test this aspect of India's presence.

Historically, China has preferred to promote the spirit of economic multilateralism with the ASEAN region. Xi Jinping, while promoting the Silk Road concept, delved upon the fifteenth-century bonding between China and ASEAN, when the famous Chinese navigator Zheng He made seven expeditions to the Western Seas. Beijing's current approach to ASEAN is to establish its economic and political posture in the region, and consolidate its positioning and claim over the South China Sea. Despite tensions between China and ASEAN over the South China Sea dispute, ASEAN–China trade is flourishing and has exceeded $400 billion (*Xinhua* 2015). In October 2013, Beijing floated the idea of a number of maritime cooperation projects with ASEAN and allocated three billion Yuan ($484 million) to the China–ASEAN Maritime Cooperation Fund, whose primary objective is to promote marine research, rescue, navigation safety, etc. (Wang Qian and Li Xiaokun 2013). Neither has India such a forceful approach towards ASEAN nor is India's 'Act East' policy inclusive enough to determinedly match the Chinese strength in the region.

Underlying China's MSR strategy is an orderly diplomatic, economic and maritime quest for power. A core aim behind this strategy is to re-brand China as an economic, political and maritime power in IOR as well as in the neighbouring region. The bigger challenge and implication for India is on how to restrict the implementation of MSR in the IOR. There are many powers that are stationed in the Indian Ocean, including the US and Australia. India holds the authority in IOR as a 'local power'. That is now being severely challenged when Beijing is constantly pushing its presence by signing new contracts, agreements and understanding with the IOR countries. Sri Lanka, Maldives and Djibouti have shown massive interest in China's MSR, with China being on the verge of setting up a naval base in Djibouti in the Horn of Africa (Parashar 2015). India is in a dilemma whether to forge a strategic understanding with countries like the US, Australia and Japan to counter China's MSR in the IOR or to pursue its own plan of practising an independent maritime presence in the region. India's response to MSR challenge, albeit indirect, is in terms of 'Project Mausam', 'Cotton Route' and 'Spice Route'.

Project Mausam

Some in the strategic community in India see Project Mausam as a sound initiative to oppose China's MSR and limit Beijing's maritime activities in the IOR. Others have seen it as a converging point of cooperation in the IOR with China's MSR. In India's official perspective, Project Mausam is a cultural project and not a strategic initiative. A Ministry of Culture project, it is aimed at revitalising India's cultural heritage across IOR (*ignca.nic.in* 2014–2019; see also *pib.nic.in* 2014). 'Mausam' refers to 'weather'. Given the difficult weather conditions in the Indian Ocean, the idea behind Project Mausam is to follow a regular wind pattern where the ships can sail safely, and return when the wind condition change or reverse. The idea is to use natural wind, mainly monsoon wind, to maritime or sailing purpose for maritime trade cooperation. The nodal agency of Project Mausam is the Archaeological Society of India (ASI) and its core research body is the Indira Gandhi National Centre for Arts (IGNCA) (*ignca.nic. in* 2014–2019; see also *pib.nic.in* 2014). The theme of Project Mausam is not only to revitalise connections and communications between India and Indian Ocean countries but to enhance and promote national sentiments and understanding with the regional maritime corridors. The whole idea is to revive ancient maritime routes for cultural and trade practices (ibid.). There have been some sporadic talks between the Ministry of Culture and the Ministry of External Affairs of the Government of India to work concurrently and offer a strategic context to this project.

But Project Mausam is hardly a counter to China's MSR in the Indian Ocean, given its limited mandate. Four practical distinctions can be made between Project Mausam and MSR. *First*, Project Mausam is a maritime cultural scheme to revitalise India's cultural heritage across the IOR, whereas the MSR is an integral part of Beijing's SREB or the broader OBOR initiative that is integrated to China's 'silk road' diplomacy and is essential to China's foreign policy practice. The MSR is an initiative under the State Council of Chinese government, which makes it opaque (Chang Ching 2015). *Second*, the volume of Project Mausam is much more limited than the MSR. Further, it is maritime bound, whereas MSR supplements the land corridor of the SREB (ibid.). *Third*, the financial backing to MSR is massive from the Chinese government, whereas Project Mausam is just a culture-oriented project that enjoys lesser financial backing. None the less, is there scope for cooperation between China's MSR or the silk road projects and India's Project Mausam and 'Spice Route'? The Chinese Ambassador to India, Le Yucheng, was quoted saying that 'China is willing to strengthen communication and coordination with India, to link the "Belt and Road" initiatives with India's "Spice Route" and Mausam projects' (*The Hindu* 2015).

Beijing's MSR initiative has induced India to start thinking about how to renew its Indian Ocean strategy. Just like Project Mausam, India is currently pondering how to revive its ancient 'Spice Route' that is meant to revive the old trading route across the countries of Asia and Europe, placing the state of Kerala as the epicentre of this trading route. The 'Spice Route' is supposed to complement Project Mausam. It is expected to revitalise India's trading routes with almost 31 countries in Asia, Africa, Europe and South-East Asia. There are also reports about India mooting the revival of the ancient 'Cotton Route', which will revitalise Indian presence in the IOR and possibly create some strategic challenge to MSR diplomacy (*Economic Times* 2015a).

Implications for neighbourhood dynamics[3]

China's unilateral decision to engage with Pakistan to invest in POK under the CPEC is a matter that affects India's sovereignty over POK, and brings into question India's historical claim on POK. Sovereignty and history have universal context in international politics, but in Beijing's strategic foreign policy setting, the logic of sovereignty and history are employed or applied selectively. This is clear in the context of its reservation on India's oil exploration in the South China Sea vis-à-vis its unilateral engagement with Pakistan to implement the CPEC project in POK, which India opposes. Both oil exploration in the South China Sea and infrastructure construction in the POK may be two different substances involving different regions; but the Chinese and Indian approaches, reactions and their pursuit of 'national interests' in these matters compel one to draw a parallel. An appraisal of these two conflicts indicates an irreconcilable Chinese approach to which India must respond cogently. All the more so, when China has released its document *Vision and Actions on Jointly Building Silk Road Economic Belt and 21st Century Maritime Silk Road* in March this year (*xinhuanet.com* 2015) and Beijing desires India to join and support its SREB initiative.

China opposes India's oil exploration in the South China Sea at Vietnam's request, calling it a 'disputed' area and asserts 'Chinese sovereignty' over the South China Sea in the 'historical' context, whereas Beijing casually shrugs off the issue of addressing India's sovereignty over POK in the historical context, where it is currently engaged with Pakistan on a variety of investment and infrastructural building activities in the Gilgit–Baltistan region under CPEC. This matter was raised by this author as a query to the Chinese government. The query was: 'To what extent is Chinese investment in POK – which India calls a disputed region – under CPEC legitimate, whereas China objects to India's oil exploration in the South China Sea calling it a "disputed" area?' In response to the query, Huang Xilian, Deputy Director General of Asian Affairs of the Foreign Ministry of the PRC, replied:

> China will oppose India's drive for oil exploration in the South China Sea as the South China Sea is a disputed area. But China's standpoint with regard to its investment in POK is in valid agreement with Pakistan which is a 'livelihood project' in the POK region.[4]

China further explains that the Sino-Pak understanding to implement CPEC through POK is based on a range of bilateral agreements and understanding, including the 1963 Agreement.[5]

Meanwhile, China has been continually expressing its reservations on India's oil exploration in the South China Sea in the last few years, and sometimes quite belligerently. India has taken note of the Chinese reservation and has carefully gone ahead in signing a few agreements with Vietnam in the South China Sea. Regarding China's construction activities in POK, India has raised the matter at the highest political level, between Prime Minister Narendra Modi and President Xi Jinping. Before Prime Minister Modi's visit to China, India officially expressed reservation over CPEC with the Chinese Ambassador in New Delhi.

Indian concern over the Sino-Pakistan understanding in its neighbourhood is a longstanding matter. There are often debates in India, which have been mostly episodic and lacking vigour, about Sino-Pak relations. India must have a nuanced deliberation on the matter, as the scope and direction of the CPEC projects are quite futuristic and may have strategic implications for India. To China, India's occasional protest and expressions of concern have little relevance. CPEC is for China an important strategic initiative. It is key to China's Silk Road diplomacy, which nevertheless has massive strategic bearings on India. China's response to India's reservation on the CPEC has been a cautious one and measured. Importantly, the South China Sea is a matter of 'core' national interest for China; whereas CPEC is critical to China's Silk Road diplomacy under President Xi Jinping.

The propriety of 'sovereignty' and 'history' in the South China Sea

The South China Sea (SCS) is a multiparty maritime conflict involving bigger and smaller powers like China, Vietnam, Philippines, Malaysia, Brunei and Taiwan in South-East Asia. Of the 3.5 million sq km area of the SCS, almost 70 per cent is disputed. Essentially, at the core of these disputes are five sets of islands covering atolls, cays, shoals, reefs and sandbars. These five sets of islands are known as Spratlys, Paracels, Scarborough Shoal, Pratas and Maccelsfield Bank. There are many aspects to Chinese and South-East Asian claims to these islands (see Map 6.1 for reference to the claims). It is still being debated among the Chinese strategic community whether China must exert its claim over the entire South China Sea or only on its main islands.[6] There are also conflicting reports that suggest that China claims 80 per cent of the entire South China Sea.[7] But in principle, China claims the whole of the South China Sea, based on the 'nine-dash line', which is in turn based on historical claims that the Republic of China (ROC) and subsequently the PRC demarcated. The Chinese claims on some of the islands in South China Sea are also based on ancient historical times (*Xinhuanet* 2014a, 2014b).

Based on the nine-dash line, the Chinese have taken many military, administrative and jurisdictional initiatives recently to maximise their control over these islands. The main target is to have better control over Paracels (*Xisha*), Spratlys (*Nansha*) and Macclesfield Bank (*Zhongsha*). These Chinese claims and recent initiatives are contested by other South-East Asian nations who are parties to the dispute. Outside powers like the US have also taken an interest, have opposed

88 The sub-regional crescendo

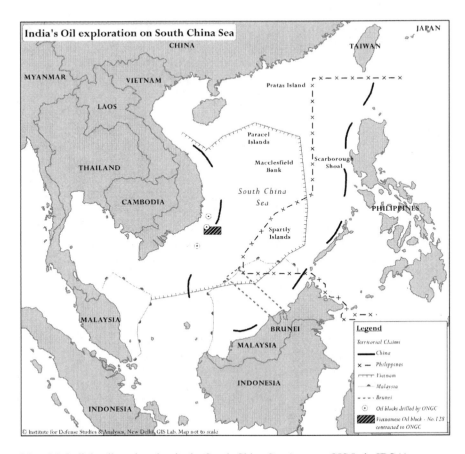

Map 6.1 India's oil exploration in the South China Sea (source: GIS Lab, IDSA).

the Chinese claims and have proposed freedom of navigation. The Chinese have reacted aggressively to this American intervention. India is neither a 'claimant' nor a party in the maritime dispute. Still, the Chinese reservation over India's ambition for oil exploration in the South China Sea has intensified gradually. Two pointed questions need to be asked here: Why did China object to India's oil exploration in the South China Sea? Is China's objection about India's activities in the region consistent and rational? An appraisal of the Chinese reaction points to an unjustifiable Chinese standpoint, which is neither logical nor consistent.

The Chinese reservation has been more regional than bilateral. Unlike its provocative and direct reactions towards Vietnam which is a party to the conflict, and towards the United States, an influential outside power in the South China Sea region, the Chinese reactions on Indian oil companies' activities in the South China Sea have been less antagonistic and are mostly linked with Vietnamese claims. For instance, reacting to a question on how India and Vietnam's joint oil and gas exploration in the South China Sea infringed on China's sovereignty and territorial integrity, the Chinese Foreign Ministry spokesperson Hong Lei stated on 22 September 2011 that China has 'indisputable sovereignty over the Nansha Islands and their adjacent waters' (*china-embassy.org* 2011). Stating Beijing's claim over this area on 'historical' and 'jurisdictional' context, he stated: 'Any foreign company's oil and gas exploration activity in the waters under China's jurisdiction without China's permission is illegal and invalid' (ibid.). The Chinese authorities have stated that the 'relevant foreign company' must stay away from oil and gas exploration in the South China Sea. None the less, there are statements made by the Chinese authorities that are a little more nuanced than those made earlier. For example, commenting on a question about the Vietnamese Prime Minister's invitation to India to jointly explore oilfields in the South China Sea, Hong Lei's recent reply was somewhat candid. Asserting China's 'indisputable sovereignty over the Nansha Islands and the adjacent waters', he said that 'China doesn't have any problem with oilfield exploration by relevant countries in uncontested waters if such cooperation is legitimate and lawful' (*fmprc.gov.cn* 2014); but 'if such cooperation undermines China's sovereignty and interests, we are firmly opposed to that' (ibid.).

Overall, the Chinese objection to India's presence in the South China Sea has been gradual and intense. And since 2011, it has been categorical. On 22 July 2011, INS *Airavat* was contacted by a Chinese naval unit around 45 nautical miles from the Vietnamese coast in the South China Sea to express reservation that it was a disputed area. Similarly, in September 2011, China reacted to the three-year agreement between ONGC Videsh Limited (OVL) and Petro Vietnam on oil exploration in certain South China Sea areas. Stating that 'China enjoys indisputable sovereignty' over the South China Sea and the island, Beijing added that its stand was based on the 'historical facts' and 'international law' and that 'we hope that the relevant countries refrain from taking unilateral action to complicate and expand the issue' (*ke.chineseembassy.org* 2011). Dismissing the relevance of the UN Convention on the Law of the Sea (UNCLOS), the statement noted that UNCLOS 'does not entitle any country to extend its exclusive economic zone or continental shelf to the territory of another country, and it does not restrain or deny a country's right which is formed in history and abidingly upheld' (ibid.).

At first glance, Beijing's reaction to India's oil exploration in the South China Sea is not direct. It is connected with a number of regional factors. *First*, among all the six claimants in the South China Sea dispute, China has direct hostility with Vietnam. *Second*, the US factor. Chinese experts and strategic groups have continually felt that the US is engaged in destabilising the South China Sea dispute by offering support to Vietnam and other South-East Asian countries and encouraging other outside powers to pursue the matter of freedom of navigation in the South China Sea. *Third*, Beijing has openly stated that the South China Sea is a matter of China's 'core' interest along with the East China Sea and is linked to China's 'sovereignty' (*Xinhuanet* 2013, 2015b). In other words, China aims emphatically to 'enhance enforcement to match its national strength' (Wang Qian and Zhang Yunbi 2013).

The official Indian position with regard to oil exploration in the South China Sea has been quite consistent and moderate. For instance, on the OVL-Petro Vietnam joint oil exploration deal, New Delhi has stated: 'The Chinese had concerns, but we are going by what the Vietnamese authorities have told us and have conveyed this to the Chinese' (Airy and Jacob 2011), that the Indian interest in the South China Sea is 'purely commercial' and as per freedom of navigation and maritime international law, and that it is not a party to the South China Sea dispute. The then External Affairs Minister of India, Salman Khurshid, on 20 December 2012 said that 'there are fundamental issues there which do not require India's intervention' (MEA 2012) and that India's reach to the South China Sea was purely 'commercial' in nature and primarily aimed at exploring for oil and energy resources in the region (MEA 2014b). More recently, the Minister of State of External Affairs, Dr V.K. Singh, stated: 'India supports freedom of navigation in international waters while maintaining that sovereignty issues must be resolved peacefully by the countries which are parties to the dispute in accordance with accepted principles of international law', including UNCLOS 1982 (ibid.).

Denouncing 'sovereignty' and 'history' in CPEC

Sovereignty and history become secondary, somewhat extraneous, to China's jurisprudence in the context of CPEC projects in POK. The primary Chinese standpoint in this regard is based on the same 'commercial' reason that India puts forward in the context of the South China Sea. Chinese officials call their investment and activities in POK as 'livelihood project'; not being 'political', but just 'commercial' in nature. Hitherto, to what extent Beijing appreciates the Indian concern over the disputed POK that are linked to history and sovereignty, is a matter of contest. CPEC, a part of China's SREB, runs through a territory that is historically a disputed region between India and Pakistan (see Map 6.2). Notably, India asserts that Gilgit-Baltistan is part of the historical princely state of Jammu and Kashmir, which acceded to India.

Beijing does acknowledge the historical nature of the POK dispute and that it is a dispute essentially between India and Pakistan. Hua Chunying, the spokesperson of the Chinese Foreign Ministry, has clarified that the CPEC is an important corridor for 'common development' between China and Pakistan, which will boost regional connectivity (*fmprc.gov.cn* 2015a). He stated that 'Kashmir issue is primarily an issue left over by history between India and Pakistan' and that the cooperation between China and Pakistan in the relevant region is for the 'sole purpose of boosting local economic and social development' (ibid.). In April 2015, on the sidelines of Xi Jinping's visit to Pakistan, the spokesperson of the Chinese Foreign Ministry, Hong Lei, stated that CPEC will be connected with Gwadar port in four key areas, namely, port, energy, infrastructure and industrial cooperation, aiming to boost development of the

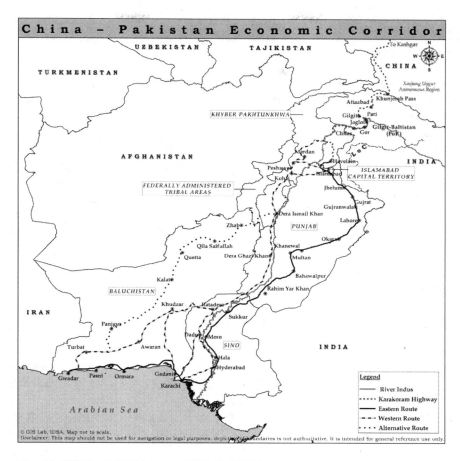

Map 6.2 CPEC and POK (source: GIS Lab, IDSA).

Pakistani people (*fmprc.gov.cn* 2015b). Answering a pointed question 'whether the CPEC deal covers relevant projects in the Kashmir region over which India and Pakistan have disputes', he said that 'friendly cooperation between China and Pakistan will have no India–Pakistan disputes involved' (ibid.).

Three narratives can be extracted from this Chinese standpoint. *First*, even though Beijing acknowledges that Kashmir is a 'historical' dispute between India and Pakistan, there is little reverence to India's historical claim to POK. *Second*, China defends CPEC, calling it a 'commercial' or 'livelihood' project. How is India's 'commercial' ambition for oil and energy exploration in the South China Sea different from that of Beijing's 'commercial' projects with Pakistan in the disputed POK region? *Third*, China's explanation of the CPEC project puts the vital matter of sovereignty into doubt, as far as India is concerned. This obscures the India–China–Pakistan geopolitical calculus on Kashmir too.

92 *The sub-regional crescendo*

The Chinese justification with regard to the CPEC harbingers the prospect that China may in future emerge as a silent 'third factor' in the Kashmir dispute. From the Indian viewpoint, claiming stake on territory or having a legal jurisdiction over land through financial investments, construction and economic dealings do exist in Chinese foreign relations strategy. This is especially noticed in China's recent attempt at land reclamation in the South China Sea to reinforce its claim of sovereignty (Dolven *et al.* 2015). Reports suggest that China will soon complete the land reclamation process in some islands and reefs in Nansha Island. Beijing defends this construction activity by stating that they 'fall within the scope of China's sovereignty, which are lawful, reasonable and justified' (*Xinhuanet* 2015c).

Charting a course of action

Undeniably, these matters explicate an emerging complex chapter in India–China relations. This is critical at a time when China is still at a primary stage of implementing its SREB and MSR. Without India's support, the SREB implementation could become bumpy. Can India capitalise on this fact? Three options present themselves.

First, the legality of these matters must be stressed and India must compel China to have an open and publicly clarified position, mainly on Kashmir and urge China intently to reconsider the execution of CPEC-related projects. The entire Chinese rationale for carrying out the construction activities in the POK is based on the Boundary Agreement between China and Pakistan (2 March 1963) and other bilateral dealings between the two countries. India has never acknowledged the legitimacy of the 1963 agreement. Besides, articles One, Two and Six of the agreement are completely irreconcilable and illegal. Article Six states that 'after the settlement of the Kashmir dispute between Pakistan and India, the sovereign authority concerned will reopen negotiations with the Government of the People's Republic of China on the boundary'. Per this chapter, no matter what happens to the Kashmir issue, either Pakistan or India will have to deal with China at a later date, that China is a silent 'third party' in the Kashmir dispute.

Second, POK is in illegal occupation of Pakistan, a matter that is linked to India's sovereignty. The matter of the Kashmir dispute is with the UN, and India has never been hesitant to raise the matter at the UN. Does China appreciate this fact as a Permanent Member of the UN Security Council? China must be responsible as a permanent member of the UNSC and distance itself from involvement in the dispute.

Article One of the 1963 Agreement states,

> In view of the fact that the boundary between China's Sinkiang and the Contiguous areas, the defence of which is under the actual control of Pakistan, has never been formally delimited, the two Parties agree to delimit it on the basis of the traditional customary boundary.
>
> (*Pakistan Horizon* 1963)

Per this chapter, China concedes that the India–Pakistan boundary in this area is not 'delimited' or 'defined'. By this, China concedes that the area is not entirely under the sovereign control of Pakistan. India must underline to China that having 'actual control' and 'sovereign' control are two distinct matters. This has relevance also with regard to India's oil exploration in the South China Sea. Viewed from a relative prism, the reason of 'actual control' in the context of India's oil exploration with Vietnam must compel Beijing to reconsider its own approach to these two issues. India's oil exploration drive in the South China Sea area is under Vietnam's control currently. Besides, it is beyond the 'nine-dash line' which is supposed to be the benchmark of the Chinese claim in the South China Sea. Moreover, the claims in the South China Sea overlap, and India could actually enter into similar agreements within the areas which are under the 'actual control' of Vietnam or Philippines or other nations in South-East Asia, going beyond the Chinese-claimed 'nine-dash line'. The strategic implication of this matter for China will be huge, since the South China Sea is a regional dispute. Besides, the accent on freedom of navigation needs a little more pondering from China. China's interest in the Indian Ocean is based on freedom of navigation; it cannot employ the dialogue of freedom of navigation selectively.

Third, India must have a deliberate discussion with China on both the SREB. Beijing's reconsideration of the Indian interest on both these conflicting issues may create a win-win situation for India–China engagement at the regional level, where India may offer support to China for the SREB. After all, India was one of the first countries to support the Chinese-led AIIB. Beijing must comprehend that its irrational approach towards India on both the South China Sea and CPEC may affect and limit the scope of regional cooperation. From a bilateral perspective, this is in juxtaposition to the spirit of the new official pronunciation of an 'Asian century' with the lead of India and China. The Joint Statement of 15 May 2015 between the two countries, released during Prime Minister Modi's visit to China, does recognise the emergence of India and China as 'two major powers' in regional as well as world politics, which indicates that their cooperative relations will be a key to an 'Asian century'.

Notes

1. MSR stands for Maritime Silk Road projects of China. The Chinese government have used both the word 'road' and 'route' interchangeably. These words have also been used by the author interchangeably throughout the book.
2. Some called it China's 'Marshall Plan'. However, now it seems, the Chinese initiative of 'one belt, one road' is much more than just a 'Marshall Plan'. See Dingding Chen 2014; Shannon Tiezzi 2014; *Diplomat* 2015.
3. This part of this chapter has been published as an *IDSA Policy Brief*, jointly with Brig. Rumel Dahiya. See Dahiya and Panda 2015.
4. The author met Huang Xilian in Beijing on 3 June 2015 during the Think-Tanks Forum meeting organised by the Public Diplomacy Division of the Ministry of Foreign Affairs of the Chinese Government. A number of Indian journalists were present. Details of this interaction have been reported in mainstream Indian media. See *Indian Express* 2015; Varma 2015.

5 Author's interaction with Huang Xilian in Beijing. Even though a direct public statement is missing currently on the part of the Chinese officials that China's current activities and investment in POK under the CPEC are based on the 1963 Agreement, the Chinese officials and scholars often refer to this agreement as a benchmark of Chinese involvement and construction in POK. Besides, Pakistan always refers openly to the 1963 Agreement as the basis of China's involvement in POK.
6 For instance, see Li Mingjian 2012.
7 Chinese reports indicate that the 'nine-dash line' covers almost 80 per cent of the South China Sea on Chinese maps. In the Chinese estimation, the entire South China Sea zone is a total of 3.5 million sq km. China states that this 'nine-dash line' boundary was first published on an official map in 1948. Since then, China has officially based its claim on this map, and all the official maps released subsequently by the Chinese government carry this 'nine-dash line'. See *Xinhua* 2012.

References

Airy, Anupama and Jayanth Jacob, 2011. 'China objects to oil hunt, India says back off', *Hindustan Times*, 15 September, www.hindustantimes.com/newdelhi/china-objects-to-oil-hunt-india-says-back-off/article1-745854.aspx (accessed on 20 June 2015).

Beijing Bulletin, 2014. 'China invites India to join its ambitious Silk Road projects', *Beijing Bulletin*, 11 August, www.beijingbulletin.com/index.php/sid/224611565 (accessed on 10 May 2015).

caixin, 2014. 'One Belt, One Road', *caixin*, 12 October, http://english.caixin.com/2014-12-10/100761304.html (accessed on 29 April 2015).

Chang Ching, 2015. 'India's Project Mausam not intended to counter China', *Want China Times*, 18 March, www.wantchinatimes.com/news-subclass-cnt.aspx?id=20150318000002&cid=1703 (accessed on 29 June 2015).

china-embassy.org, 2011. 'Foreign Ministry spokesperson Hong Lei's regular Press Conference on September 22, 2011', Embassy of the People's Republic of China in the United States of America, 23 September, www.china-embassy.org/eng/fyrth/t861644.htm (accessed on 17 June 2015).

CHINAREALTIME, 2015. 'China makes multibillion-dollar down-payment on Silk Road Plans', *CHINAREALTIME*, 21 April, http://blogs.wsj.com/chinarealtime/2015/04/21/china-makes-multibillion-dollar-down-payment-on-silk-road-plans/ (accessed on 19 June 2015).

CRIENGLISH.com, 2014. 'Xi's strategic conception of "One Belt and One Road" has great significance', *CRIENGLISH.com*, 11 October, http://english.cri.cn/12394/10/11/53s47421.html (accessed on 2 April 2015).

Dahiya, Rumel and Jagannath Panda, 2015. 'A tale of two disputes: China's irrationality and India's stakes', *IDSA Policy Brief*, 29 June, pp. 1–14.

Dai Bingguo, 2014. 'Jointly build the Silk Roads for the 21st century with openness and inclusiveness' (Speech by H.E. Dai Bingguo, 11 July 2014), Ministry of Foreign Affairs of the People's Republic of China, Guiyang, 12 July, www.fmprc.gov.cn/mfa_eng/zxxx_662805/t1173754.shtml (accessed on 12 May 2015).

Dingding Chen, 2014. 'China's "Marshall Plan" is much more', *The Diplomat*, 10 November, http://thediplomat.com/2014/11/chinas-marshall-plan-is-much-more/ (accessed on 2 April 2015).

Diplomat, 2015. 'One belt, one road', *The Diplomat*, 20 January, http://country.eiu.com/article.aspx?articleid=1252682109&Country=China&topic=Economy (accessed on 29 April 2015).

Dolven, Ben, Jennifer K. Elsea, Susan V. Lawrence, Ronald O'Rourke and Ian E. Rinehart, 2015. 'How China's "land reclamation" helps Beijing to exert more purposely its claim over South China Sea', in *Chinese Land Reclamation in the South China Sea: Implications and Policy Options*, Congressional Research Service, 16 June.

Economic Times, 2015a. 'To counter China's Silk Road, India is working on Cotton Route', *Economic Times*, 23 March, http://articles.economictimes.indiatimes.com/2015-03-23/news/60404017_1_indian-ocean-rim-maritime-trade-silk-road-economic-belt (accessed on 30 June 2015).

Economic Times, 2015b. 'India not worried over Pakistan–China economic corridor: High Commissioner TCA Raghavan', *Economic Times*, 22 April, http://articles.economictimes.indiatimes.com/2015-04-22/news/61417320_1_indian-high-commissioner-bilateral-trade-enhanced-trade (accessed on September 3, 2015).

fmprc.gov.cn, 2014. 'Foreign Ministry Spokesperson Hong Lei's regular Press Conference on October 28, 2014', Permanent Mission of the People's Republic of China to the UN, 28 October, www.fmprc.gov.cn/mfa_eng/xwfw_665399/s2510_665401/t1204813.shtml (accessed on 17 June 2015).

fmprc.gov.cn, 2015a. 'Foreign Ministry Spokesperson Hua Chunying's regular Press Conference on June 1, 2015', Ministry of Foreign Affairs of the People's Republic of China, 1 June, www.fmprc.gov.cn/mfa_eng/xwfw_665399/s2510_665401/2535_665405/t1269123.shtml (accessed on 19 June 2015).

fmprc.gov.cn, 2015b. 'Foreign Ministry Spokesperson Hong Lei's regular Press Conference on April 20, 2015', Ministry of Foreign Affairs of the People's Republic of China, 20 April, www.fmprc.gov.cn/mfa_eng/xwfw_665399/s2510_665401/t1256093.shtml (accessed on 19 June 2015).

The Hindu, 2014. 'China wants India to play key role in "Silk Road" plan', *The Hindu*, 10 August, www.thehindu.com/news/international/world/china-wants-india-to-play-key-role-in-silk-road-plan/article6301227.ece (accessed on 10 May 2015).

The Hindu, 2015. '"Building ties for the 21st century", Srinivasan Ramani's interview with the Chinese Ambassador to India, Le Yucheng', *The Hindu*, 1 April, www.thehindu.com/opinion/op-ed/building-ties-for-the-21st-century/article7054501.ece (accessed on 30 June 2015).

ignca.nic.in, 2014–2019. 'Project "Mausam"– Mausam/Mawsim: Maritime routes and cultural landscapes', Indira Gandhi National Centre for Arts (IGNCA), New Delhi, http://ignca.nic.in/mausam.htm (accessed on 29 June 2015).

Indian Express, 2015. 'China defends projects in POK, opposes India's oil exploration in South China Sea', *Indian Express* (PTI), 4 June, http://indianexpress.com/article/world/asia/china-justifies-projects-in-pok-objects-to-indias-oil-exploration-in-south-china-sea/99/ (accessed on 18 June 2015).

ke.chineseembassy.org, 2011. 'Foreign Ministry Spokesperson Jiang Yu's regular Press Conference on September 15, 2011', Embassy of the People's Republic of China in The Republic of Kenya, 16 September, http://ke.chineseembassy.org/eng/fyrth/t860126.htm (accessed on 20 June 2015).

Kennedy, Scott and David A. Parker, 2015. 'Building China's "One Belt, One Road"', *Critical Questions*, Centre for Strategic and International Studies (CSIS), 3 April, http://csis.org/print/5496 (accessed on 29 April 2015).

Li Mingjian, 2012. 'Chinese debates of South China Sea policy: implications for future developments', *RSIS Working Paper*, No. 239, 17 May.

Liu Ying, 2015. '"Marshall Plan" copycat allegations misleading', *Beijing Review*, No. 6, 5 February, www.bjreview.com.cn/special/2015-02/02/content_667594.htm (accessed on 29 April 2015).

Lu Hongyan, Ma Lie and Zhong Nan, 2014. 'Shaanxi in good position to anchor Silk Road', *China Daily*, 22 May, www.chinadaily.com.cn/china/2014-05/22/content_17546545.htm# (accessed on 27 June 2015).

MEA, 2012. 'Transcript of media interaction of External Affairs Minister following the conclusion of the plenary session of the ASEAN–India Commemorative Summit 2012', Media Centre, Ministry of External Affairs, Government of India, 20 December, www.mea.gov.in/Speeches-Statements.htm?dtl/20984/Transcript+of+media+Interaction+of+External+Affairs+Minister+following+the+conclusion+of+the+plenary+session+of+the+ASEANIndia+Commemorative+Summit+2012 (accessed on 17 June 2015).

MEA, 2014a. 'Q. NO. 260: Projects of China and Pakistan in neighboring countries', Lok Sabha, Starred Question No. 260 To Be Answered On December 10, 2014, Ministry of External Affairs: Government of India, www.mea.gov.in/lok-sabha.htm?dtl/24458/QNO260PROJECTS+OF+CHINA+AND+PAKISTAN+IN+NEIGHBOURING+COUNTRIES (accessed on 20 June 2015).

MEA, 2014b. 'Dispute over islands in South China Sea', Lok Sabha Unstarred Question No. 563, To Be Answered on November 26, 2014, Parliament Q & A, Ministry of External Affairs, Government of India, www.mea.gov.in/lok-sabha.htm?dtl/24339/Q+NO+563+DISPUTE+OVER+ISLANDS+IN+SOUTH+CHINA+SEA (accessed on 17 June 2015).

Pakistan Horizon, 1963. 'Boundary Agreement between China and Pakistan, 2 March, 1963', *Pakistan Horizon*, Pakistan Institute of International Affairs, 16(2), second quarter, pp. 177–82.

Parashar, Sachin, 2015. 'China in South China Sea and Indian Ocean: a quest for pre-eminence in Asia', *Times of India*, 24 May, http://timesofindia.indiatimes.com/world/china/China-in-South-China-Sea-and-Indian-Ocean-A-quest-for-pre-eminence-in-Asia/articleshow/47406036.cms (accessed on 27 June 2015).

pib.nic.in, 2014. 'Project "Mausam" launched by Secretary, Ministry of Culture', Press Information Bureau, Government of India, Ministry of Culture, 21 June, http://pib.nic.in/newsite/PrintRelease.aspx?relid=105777 (accessed on 29 June 2015).

Shannon Tiezzi, 2014. 'The New Silk Road: China's Marshall Plan?', *The Diplomat*, 6 November, http://thediplomat.com/2014/11/the-new-silk-road-chinas-marshall-plan/ (accessed on 29 April 2015).

Varma, K.J.M., 2015. 'China defends projects in Gilgit-Baltistan region, justifies its objections in SCS', *Live Mint*, 4 June, www.livemint.com/Politics/pXSgtK0xZOMaWiCfeSIUlN/China-defends-projects-in-GilgitBaltistan-region-justifies.html (accessed on 18 June 2015).

Wang Qian and Li Xiaokun, 2013. 'Premier vows to lift maritime cooperation', *China Daily*, 12 October, www.chinadaily.com.cn/china/2013livisiteastasia/2013-10/12/content_17025992.htm (accessed on 27 June 2015).

Wang Qian and Zhang Yunbi, 2013. 'Xi vows to protect maritime interests', *China Daily*, 1 August, http://usa.chinadaily.com.cn/china/2013-08/01/content_16859216.htm (accessed on 18 June 2015).

Wu Jiao and Zhang Yunbi, 2013. 'Xi in call for building of new "maritime silk road"', *China Daily*, 4 October, http://usa.chinadaily.com.cn/china/2013-10/04/content_17008940.htm (accessed on 25 June 2015).

Xinhua, 2012. 'China dismisses Vietnam's sovereignty claim for South China Sea islands', *Xinhua*, 12 December, http://news.xinhuanet.com/english/china/2014-12/12/c_133848818.htm (accessed on 20 June 2015).

Xinhua, 2015. 'China focus: change and hope, five years after China–ASEAN Free Trade Area established', *Xinhua*, 9 January 9, http://news.xinhuanet.com/english/2015-01/09/c_133908521.htm (accessed on 27 June 2015).

Xinhuanet, 2013. 'Core interests at heart of new US ties', *Xinhuanet*, 20 May, http://news.xinhuanet.com/english/china/2013-03/20/c_132247867.htm (accessed on 20 June 2015).

Xinhuanet, 2014a. 'Chinese envoy rebuts Vietnamese, Philippines accusations over South China Sea', *Xinhuanet*, 14 June, http://news.xinhuanet.com/english/china/2014-06/14/c_133407129.htm (accessed on 21 June 2015).

Xinhuanet, 2014b. 'Commentary gives China's reasons for refusing arbitration on South China Sea issue', *Xinhuanet*, 1 April, http://news.xinhuanet.com/english/china/2014-04/01/c_133228152.htm (accessed on 21 June 2015).

Xinhuanet, 2015a. 'Full Text: Vision and actions on jointly building Belt and Road', *Xinhuanet*, 28 March, http://news.xinhuanet.com/english/china/2015-03/28/c_134105858_2.htm (accessed on 26 June 2015).

Xinhuanet, 2015b. 'China dismisses recent tension in South China Sea as "old tricks"', *Xinhuanet*, 26 May, http://news.xinhuanet.com/english/2015-05/26/c_134271366.htm (accessed on 20 June 2015).

Xinhuanet, 2015c. 'China to complete land reclamation of construction on some Nansha Islands soon', *Xinhuanet*, 16 June, http://news.xinhuanet.com/english/2015-06/16/c_134330406.htm (accessed on 19 June 2015).

xinhuanet.com, 2015. Issued by the National Development and Reform Commission, Ministry of Foreign Affairs, and Ministry of Commerce of the People's Republic of China, with State Council authorization, March, Beijing, http://news.xinhuanet.com/english/china/2015-03/28/c_134105858.htm (accessed on 16 June 2015).

Zhang Yi, 2014. 'Xi'an planning to attract more Silk Road diplomats', *China Daily*, 20 August, http://usa.chinadaily.com.cn/china/2014-08/20/content_18452066.htm (accessed on 27 June 2015).

7 BCIM and sub-regional interaction

The BCIM (Bangladesh–China–India–Myanmar) construct is based on the core concept of sub-regional cooperation among the four immediate neighbours for enhancing trade and investment contacts, and convergence of their interests. Started primarily as a Track-II process under the Kunming Initiative, momentum is developing currently to enhance BCIM into a higher-order mechanism, especially to upgrade it from Track-I to a level of ministerial mechanism. Underlying India's and China's policy approaches to BCIM are three vital strategic priorities, namely, infrastructural connectivity, security concerns and neighbourhood politics. Both countries' approaches towards BCIM have an underlying soft-power economic bearing, which is the key to their regional as well as sub-regional power politics. This chapter aims to evaluate the progress and influence of the BCIM mechanism on India–China sub-regional interaction.

The idea and construct of BCIM: a 'growth zone' concept?

Growth zone is a relatively new concept in the parlance of development economics. Its core idea is to involve three or more neighbouring countries for common economic and socio-political progress and development (Rahman *et al.* 2007: 2; see also Bin Alam 2012). Taking advantage of the resources of adjacent regions, a growth zone aims to foster economic development between partaking countries (ibid.; see also Bhattacharya and Akbar 2012: 4). There are a number of growth zone initiatives in the region such as the South China Growth Triangle, Greater Mekong Sub-region Growth Triangle, South Asian Growth Quadrangle, etc. (Rahman *et al.* 2007; see also Landingin and Wadley 2005; Bin Alam 2012). Started as the 'Kunming initiative'[1] in the 1990s, BCIM has evolved from an informal scholarly forum to Track-II mechanism and has been upgraded to Track-I level gradually. Table 7.1 shows the progress of BCIM over the years. Recent BCIM meetings on establishing an economic corridor suggest that BCIM is slowly emerging as an intergovernmental dialogue mechanism, mainly on trade, economics, tourism and infrastructural bonding.

While the spirit of BCIM is closely linked with the growth zone concept, its nuances, politics and backdrop suggest that its scope goes beyond the standard realm of growth zone concept. This is for two strategic reasons: *first*, BCIM involves two largest economies of the world today, namely China and India, and it functions within their balance-of-power dynamics and neighbourhood politics; and *second*, it involves two adjacent strategic regions, namely South Asia and South-East Asia, which involves land and Maritime Silk Road politics. More importantly, it involves power promotion and economic diplomacy, which combines a soft-power approach.

BCIM is one of those sub-regional groupings that empower the local or provincial administration to play a strong role. The role of Yunnan is an example. Its economic and geostrategic primacy in the South Asian–South-East Asian zone propels it to undertake a leading role in BCIM. Likewise, there is a huge scope for India's north-eastern states to take a leading approach and stimulate sub-regional economic integration (Uberoi 2008: 310). The distinction that BCIM holds in regional politics is that it is a forum of transnational cooperation that tries to address regional development through a cooperative agenda rather than conformist or orthodox multilateral assignation through a defined, narrow or concrete geopolitical outlook (ibid.: 307). As a whole, BCIM combines together 9 per cent of the total geography of the world and brings together around 40 per cent of the world population (*Daily Star* 2013). BCIM's additional attraction is its 7.3 per cent GDP of the global GDP (ibid.).

Though BCIM currently accounts for only 2 per cent of global trade, given economic interdependence and the scope of greater connectivity, it is poised for exponential growth (Lal 2013). It is expected to get combined with the India–ASEAN Free Trade Area (FTA), China–ASEAN FTA and ASEAN FTA in coming times, prompting robust trade interactions at the regional level and moving gradually to become one of the biggest FTAs in the world (ibid.).

Trade and investment cooperation, energy cooperation, enhancing tourism potential and upgrading infrastructural facility in terms of better connectivity – road, rail and communications – are the overriding themes of the BCIM spirit. To these aspirations, three main strategic elements are attached: instituting better political relations; establishing closer geographical proximity through connectivity; and addressing economic complementarities in neighbourhood regions. Crucial behind these strategic elements is the BCIM Economic Corridor (BCIM-EC), which has been under discussion for some time now. The first Joint Study Group (JSG) meeting to establish BCIM-EC was held on 18–19 December 2013 in Kunming (*indianembassy.org.cn* 2013).[2]

The economic corridor will be beneficial for a few correlated reasons. *First*, it would create economic opportunities in the four countries through greater business transactions (Bi Shihong 2013). *Second*, it will be a capital point for most Asian markets for greater regional dealings and economic collaboration. *Third*, it will also enhance the BIMSTEC and MGC (Mekong Ganga Cooperation) initiatives and further the cooperation among the adjacent countries at the sub-regional level. *Fourth*, it will enhance ASEAN's cooperation with China, India and Bangladesh (ibid.). *Fifth*, enhanced foreign trade dealings may eventually lead to (sub-)regional economic integration.

Table 7.1 BCIM forum so far

	Date	Venue	Key issues
1st Round (Kunming Initiative)	15–17 August 1999	Kunming	Trade, economic, infrastructure, communication, technology, tourism, agriculture, and industrial cooperation
2nd Round	4–7 December 2000	New Delhi	Trade, economic and infrastructural cooperation, how to push forward sub-regional cooperation, etc.
3rd Round	6–7 February 2002	Dhaka	Trade, economic, infrastructure, communication, tourism cooperation, etc.
4th Round	19–21 March 2003	Yangon	Sub-regional cooperation, trade and economic contacts, technological and infrastructural cooperation, etc.
5th Round	21–22 December 2004	Kunming	Improving commercial and trade links with focus on rich natural resources of the member countries; enhancing cultural exchange; enhancing transport by opening direct flight routes, infrastructure, tourism; boost cooperation in all fields including agriculture, technology, communication, information, environment protection, human resource development
6th Round	30–31 March 2006	New Delhi	Prepare a plan for developing multi-modal transport links from Kunming to Kolkata via Myanmar and Bangladesh; improve connectivity between major cities of the four countries, including Guwahati, Kolkata, Kunming, Dhaka, Mandalay; cooperation in the field of health and medical care; governments to work towards facilitating the visa process; each country to appoint a specific liaison officer and name a liaison institution for better coordination; each member country will head a specific subject for two years

7th Round	31 March – 1 April 2007	Dhaka	Develop ties by positioning officials of member countries in partner countries; identify entrepots to facilitate trade; conduct a study to promote smooth transportation among countries based on ADB initiative for Regional Transport Study for BIMSTEC; support from UN World Tourism Organisation (UNWTO) and Tourism Unit of UN-ESCAP to promote tourism; improve Trans-Asian Railway (TAR) route
8th Round	23–24 July 2009	Nay Pyi Taw (Myanmar)	Improve trade cooperation, tourism, transport connectivity, set up Business Council and progress in car rally initiative
9th Round	18 January 2011	Kunming	MoUs for establishing BCIM Business Council and route survey of BCIM car rally were signed; agreement on renaming the 'Forum on regional economic cooperation among BCIM' as 'Forum on BCIM Cooperation'
10th Round	18–19 February 2012	Kolkata	BCIM Business Council meetings to promote dialogue; economic cooperation and exchange of information; ensure optimum utilisation of water resources, academic exchanges between institutions
11th Round	23–24 February 2013	Dhaka	Flagged off a car rally from Kolkata to Kunming

Sources: The Forum on Regional Cooperation among Bangladesh, China, India, Myanmar, www.bcim-forum.com/en/index.aspx. BCIM (Kunming Initiative), Regional Dynamics, Online Burma/Myanmar Library, updated on 25 February 2008, www.burmalibrary.org/show.php?cat=2144 (accessed on 31 May 2014).

The idea of establishing BCIM-EC was mooted during Chinese Premier Li Keqiang's visit to India in May 2013. The joint statement on the visit also recognised the progress of the BCIM Regional Forum (*mea.gov.in* 2013). It pointed out two aspects: strengthening connectivity and developing BCIM-EC. Reports suggest that BCIM-EC aims to include Yunnan province in China, Bangladesh, Myanmar, and the Indian states of West Bengal, Bihar and the North-East (Bi Shihong 2013). It will cover almost 1.65 million sq km and will benefit almost 440 million people at the sub-regional level (ibid.; see also Lal 2013).

BCIM between Chinese and Indian perspectives

Location, geographical proximity and relations among member states mostly decide the course of a multiparty forum. Bangladesh and Myanmar, with their strategic and geographic location, facilitate the spirit of BCIM hugely. Compared to Myanmar, Bangladesh seems to be taking more interest in BCIM. Prime Minister Sheikh Hasina, for example, recently lauded China's 'proactive role' in promoting BCIM-EC. BCIM has also often been discussed by China and Bangladesh in their bilateral dialogue (*Financial Express* 2014; see also *chinadaily.com.cn* 2013). From Bangladesh's perspective, the BCIM north–south transport corridor will help enhance its trade and economic contacts with India and China (Rahman 2014). Bangladesh is a connecting bridge among India, China and Myanmar. Myanmar, with rich natural resources, in its turn, also shares borders with India (1463 km), China (2185 km), Bangladesh (193 km) and other South-East Asian countries like Laos and Thailand (Bhattacharya and Akbar 2012: 3). Given its regional strategic location, Myanmar is actively involved with ASEAN, BIMSTEC, MGC and BCIM.

China and BCIM

BCIM is vital to China as it facilitates China's southern provincial connections to other neighbouring countries. Beijing's approach to BCIM is closely linked with its strategy of 'peripheral diplomacy' (Fu Mengzi 2013: 43), which has always been central in Chinese foreign policy and has been a crucial factor in Beijing's rise on the global horizon.[3] In a new exposition of this philosophy, President Xi Jinping has proposed a 'three-dimensional, multi-element perspective' to establish contacts and relations with neighbouring countries.[4] The BCIM construct is not only seen as an 'international gateway to South Asia' (Lal 2013) but also as an important sub-regional grouping that enhances China's strategic movement at the regional level. Beijing sees BCIM as a mechanism that facilitates its maritime strategy in the Greater Mekong Sub-Region (GMS) (Lee 2013), comprising, besides Myanmar, Vietnam, Laos, Cambodia and Thailand (ibid.). Chinese officials are vigorously promoting the idea of BCIM-EC as a priority, and aiming to promote it along the Maritime Silk Road proposal (Li Jun 2014).

BCIM offers a number of strategic advantages to China. *First* is to develop a 'win–win' strategy for Yunnan along with neighbouring regions, which will be key factors for the Chinese economy. The basic aim is to enhance China's southern provincial or geographical contacts, mainly of Yunnan, with adjacent regional economies like India, Bangladesh, Myanmar and Vietnam. The idea is to promote the Kunming model for regional economic contacts and regional reach, which would be beneficial to China's southern regions. The Yunnan model is a replication of China's Yunnan Gateway project that was launched in December 2009, aiming to push Yunnan as a key province for China's inter-regional cooperation with South Asian and South-East Asian neighbouring countries (Li Yingqing *et al.* 2011). Its goal is not limited to South Asia and South-East Asia: the Chinese media report that its scope covers more than 50 countries, more than 2.8 billion people and extends to West Asia and East Africa.[5] By backing BCIM and other sub-regional leads, China has regularly stressed the potential of Yunnan's economic growth model. The key thrust behind this has been Yunnan's ever-expanding trade and economic contacts. Yunnan's annual trade contacts with Bangladesh, India and Myanmar were worth around US$2.8 billion in 2012 compared to $416 million in 2000 (Hu Yongji 2014). Chinese trade with Bangladesh, India and Myanmar had also reached $82 billion by 2012, which is 18 times that in 2000 (ibid.).

Second, BCIM is testimony to China's contemporary diplomatic drive to revive its historical trade and economic contacts with the greater South Asian and South-East Asian region. Yunnan facilitated these trade and economic contacts. Since the Tang Dynasty (AD 618–907), China's greater tea and salt trade was conducted from Yunnan, which historically ran through the Tibetan Autonomous Region and then towards neighbouring regions of India, Myanmar and Bangladesh. These ancient trade contacts are sought to be revived through BCIM-EC projects like the Southern Silk Road initiatives. Kunming currently has air linkages with Kolkata in India, Yangon and Mandalay in Myanmar and Dhaka in Bangladesh.

The *third* reason behind China's strategy vis-à-vis BCIM is to steadily improve its influence in the South Asian region. Recently, Beijing has started the China–South Asia Expo in Yunnan as part of its diplomatic initiative to impress South Asian traders and promote China's linkages with the region. Both India and Bangladesh are factors in China's 'Southern Silk Road' and 'Going Out Strategy'.[6]

There are *three* main constructs on which Beijing capitalises on its South-East and South Asian contacts under BCIM: (i) Southern Silk Route, which links the Kunming–Myanmar Road, China–India Road and Guangtong–Dali railway that links Kunming with Myanmar, India and Bangladesh; (ii) the Lancang–Mekong River where three highways link Kunming with the port of Mohan, and Xishuangbanna airport which helps establish contacts with Laos, Myanmar, Thailand, Malaysia and Singapore; and (iii) Kunming–Vietnam railway, Kunming–Hekou highway and the Honghe River which runs to Hanoi, Haiphong and to other parts of Vietnam (Li Yingqing *et al.* 2011). Through this connectivity, Beijing follows a 'going outside' strategy, in which Yunnan plays a strong role.

104 *The sub-regional crescendo*

Fourth, China's BCIM conception is a soft-power phenomenon where economic diplomacy predominates over political proceedings. Trade, education, cultural and services cooperation have been the foremost highlights of Yunnan's regional engagement and that is noticed in China's annual plan for Yunnan (Hu and Li 2014). Speaking at the Yunnan People's Congress Annual Conference, Li Jiheng stated that Yunnan would invest almost 300 million Yuan ($49 million) to boost the cross-border economic cooperation zone between Hekou and Lao Cai (ibid.).

The importance of Yunnan along with Sichuan and Guizhou is increasing in China's overall Centre-State dynamics, with these provinces being promoted as strategic regions in China's overall 'peripheral diplomacy', at a time when China's peripheral diplomacy has evolved from 'reactive to proactive' (Shen Dingli 2013). The notion and spirit of BCIM is prompted in China within a broader concept of Asia-hood to propel the Chinese leadership in the region (*bdnews24.com* 2014).[7]

India and BCIM

The spirit and notions of BCIM come more in the context of India's Look East policy or the current 'Act East' policy and have been linked to India's north-eastern region. Advocates of BCIM in India argue that India will be geographically more open and closer to the South-East Asian region by a successful achievement of this project, that the Yunnan model is a grand strategy in itself, and will be beneficial for India's north-eastern states and intra-regional developmental initiatives (Aiyar 2006). North-East India totals around 1.65 million sq km, with nearly 440 million people (Lal 2013). It is also projected that these states will boost investments and propel economic prowess, which may eventually challenge the Chinese supremacy. BCIM will also enhance New Delhi's bearing in Bangladesh and Myanmar. In relative terms, however, India's approach to BCIM has been cooler and slower than to BIMSTEC. Possibly, this is because China is not a member of BIMSTEC. BIMSTEC permits India to gather some tactical advantage to maximise its own posture at the sub-regional level in South-East Asia and enhance its Act East policy. Through BIMSTEC, India maximises its political as well as commercial contacts in the Bay of Bengal region, where Myanmar is very important (ibid.).

Given that BCIM is essentially a Chinese proposition, the strategic community in India has been divided over what it offers to India in realistic terms. Orthodox thinkers see the proposition sceptically; liberals and economic communities support the idea. The view has also been expressed that apart from providing the north-east Indian states massive economic advantages, BCIM provides scope for a huge market at the sub-regional level, which is currently stalled due to high tariff/non-tariff barriers (Masood 2013). In promoting the case for BCIM, the main ideas in India have been the following. *First*, the geographical advantage. India's national interests will be enhanced, in terms of both physical and non-physical connectivity, by attaching north-east India with

Yunnan mainly, and neighbouring countries like Bangladesh and Myanmar. Most of the current and proposed road or physical connectivity linkages across the BCIM countries pass through north-east India. *Second*, BCIM is expected to enhance trade, economic and energy contacts between India's north-east and the neighbouring region. So far, the trade barrier has been one of the biggest challenges for sub-regional cooperation in the region. *Third*, the BCIM members are important to India's regional political as well as non-political strategic dealings. Bangladesh and Myanmar are important countries for India (ibid.), offering India a strategic balance to implement a delicate policy between South Asia and South-East Asia.

At the same time, the BIMSTEC is vital to India's strategic interests and remains at the crossroads between SAARC and ASEAN. As a Bay of Bengal mechanism it offers India a range of strategic benefits in the South-East Asian region. Bangladesh and Myanmar are part of this grouping,[8] which keeps India's interests floating. Compared to BCIM, New Delhi's approach to BIMSTEC has been rather progressive. The then Prime Minister Manmohan Singh visited Thailand to attend the first BIMSTEC summit in 2004. India promotes BIMSTEC in two important areas, namely connectivity and sub-regional cooperation. India needs to consider FTA negotiations among BIMSTEC countries seriously, but the difficulty, as argued by the then Foreign Secretary Sujata Singh, is that some of the BIMSTEC countries are already clubbed under SAFTA (South Asian Free Trade Area), for which the negotiation process will be complex and time-consuming (*Economic Times* 2014).

China's interests and objectives in BIMSTEC, either as a possible observer member or as a future partner, are also progressively becoming a subject matter of discussion. With the support of the Centre for Policy Dialogue (CPD), Dhaka, the policy option of involving China in BIMSTEC has grown in the last few years. Reports suggest that the CPD, which is Bangladesh's focal institute for BCIM, submitted a concept note in 2013, which urged inclusion of China in BIMSTEC.

India's stance on BCIM is surrounded more by the China factor. Recent trade statistics suggest that China has emerged as a leading economic partner of Myanmar and has become the principal investor in that country. Beijing is effectively executing a number of infrastructure, hydropower and pipeline projects in Myanmar. Port building, pipeline projects and exploiting energy resources has been China's principal objective in Myanmar (Panda 2010). Many Indian companies find difficulty in matching the Chinese companies' lucrative projects there. The Chinese reach towards Myanmar is to influence the Bay of Bengal region and get access to the Indian Ocean Region (IOR) (Gupta 2013; see also Panda 2010). In terms of its security constraints, the instant policy challenge for India is: should it focus more on BCIM promotion or should it capitalise on securitising its border regions in its north-eastern states? This is in view of the fact that China poses a stronger challenge to it not only in South-East Asia but also in adjacent maritime regions.

Between connectivity and conflict

Reviving the Ancient Silk Route. A principal element of the BCIM agenda is to revive the ancient Silk Route connectivity between India and China. The ancient course of this Silk Route originates from Chengdu in the Sichuan province of China, passes through Myanmar and enters finally Bangladesh and India. This route is also extended to West Asia. Chinese strategists and lobby groups see this route as a 'channel access' to India and South Asia (Ren Jia 2013: 1) and as a revival of the bonding point between the two regions. It allows China to have greater physical and political access or connectivity not only to North-East India but permits a better presence in the neighbourhood politics. Further, it permits the Chinese strategists to launch multimodal access and connectivity, politically and physically, with Bangladesh, India and Myanmar, with the accompanying investment advantages.

India's stance on the proposal, on the other hand, is caught between a forward-looking and security-caution approach. One major concern for New Delhi is that perhaps the Chinese economic supremacy will dominate the BCIM chronicle and Yunnan will emerge as the epicentre of BCIM proceedings. Revival of the Southern Silk Route could also expose India's border regions with China, providing China direct access to states like Arunachal Pradesh. Given this strategic concern, Chinese experts and the strategic community have proposed a route that is longer than the ancient Southern Silk Route, connecting Kunming in Yunnan to Imphal in Manipur in India through Ruili in Yunnan and Mandalay in Myanmar, but Indian strategic thinkers do not see this option as entirely safe: it not only exposes India's north-east directly but also allows China to influence rebel or insurgent groups in the region that comprises 440 million ethnically different people in a 1.65 million sq km area.

Stillwell Road and *Car Rally.* Within BCIM, there has been an attempt to revitalise physical connectivity, especially through the road linking India and China through Bangladesh and Myanmar. During the 11th BCIM forum meeting, held in Dhaka during 23–24 February 2013, a car rally was initiated from Kolkata and Kunming, similar to the India–ASEAN car rally in 2013 (*bcimcarrally.com* 2013). Meanwhile, a doubt arose about Stillwell Road, that it was incapable of managing 20–25 per cent of the India–China bilateral trade (Ahmed 2013). There is keen interest in China and Bangladesh in reviving Stillwell Road, also known as Ledo Road, constructed during World War II, which directly connects India and China. But India is not keen on it; negotiations on the matter have been stalled.

India has major reservations on this matter, concerning two points: China's repeated assertion of its claimed suzerainty on India's state of Arunachal Pradesh and the internal insurgency in India's north-east region. The Chinese claim over Arunachal Pradesh has made India cautious over the BCIM connectivity projects in the region. The Myanmar side of Stillwell Road is being upgraded, but India has reservations on it. The security syndrome may continue to prevail over India's connectivity approach with BCIM. In January 2008, India announced launching a two-lane mega Trans-Arunachal Highway project, signalling to negate the Chinese claim over Arunachal but also to upgrade connectivity in its north-east region. Ledo Road, with its Tirap-Changlang corridor, has much potential for commercial activities along the bordering regions, but rebel activities and insurgency in this region affect the progress of this corridor. India also remains worried about possible Chinese involvement in supporting insurgent groups in this area. India is also concerned about the adverse effect of opening this geographically difficult region, particularly over the flood of Chinese goods to North-East India. Most rivers in this region originate from the Chinese side and flow to the Indian Ocean through India and Bangladesh. Given the ever-growing India–China differences on the Brahmaputra River, it is difficult to estimate in the near future whether the BCIM projects in these regions will actualise.

Economic interdependence vs security syndrome

Economic interdependence is a predominant factor in sub-regional cooperation. Cross-border trade, resource potential of neighbouring regions and extent of FTAs are focal elements behind this interdependence. The BCIM mechanism prompts some of these aspirations, but most of them have been restricted to discussion and debate. The Chinese media state that the border trade in the Renqinggang market in the Tibet Autonomous Region grew by 54 times over the figure in 2006 after Nathu La was opened (Kong and Liang 2013); Renqinggang market witnessed a 23.3 per cent rise in business in 2013, and the total trade figure reached 86.6 million yuan (about $14.3 million) (ibid.). Neutral statistics are not available, however (*in.china-embassy.org* n.d.).

Nathu La is a major trading pass for India–China border trade contacts.[9] About 90 per cent of India–China trade takes place through the sea route; 80 per cent of the land trade is carried out at Nathu La (*Hindu Business Line* 2012). The reopening of Nathu La has raised the spirit of reviving the Silk Route concept between India and China. Given the feasibility and scope of Nathu La border trade, the road connection between India and China through Sikkim-to-Tibet, touching Lhasa, is supposed to benefit not only India–China local people but also the neighbouring region's people from Bangladesh, Bhutan and Nepal (Srinivasan 2006). The Nathu La pass aims to boost linkages, both economic and infrastructure, between India's north-east region and western China (ibid.). From the Chinese perspective, Nathu La facilitates its 'periphery policy' (*zhoubianzhengce*). India's concern is that the absence of quantitative safeguards may allow local businessmen to import cheaper Chinese goods and dump them in the Indian market. The Development Institute of the Ministry of Macro, Small & Medium Enterprises of the Government of India clarifies that:

> IEC [Import Export Code] is not required for the border trade because persons importing from or exporting to TAR China are authorised to trade in Indian currency value of Rs.25,000 per trader (2006–2007) only. The

term border trade is to be construed as trade is open for the people of the border area only for items produced in the local area of limited value. Government of India increased the Indian currency value limit from Rs.25,000 to Rs.100,000 per day per trader (2007–2008).

(*sikkim.nic.in* n.d.)

The dilemma behind these quantitative measures is that while they restrict illegal imports, they also remain a stumbling block against the free flow of border trade sentiments. It is also argued that the present list of items that can be traded does not have much commercial value. Besides, the road infrastructure in this sector is sub-standard. Meanwhile, trade imbalance between India and China has been rising constantly in the last few years (see Figure 7.1).

BCIM between political cooperation and contradictions

Even after its existence for more than a decade, BCIM as a credible sub-regional grouping is struggling to generate sufficient trust, political will and interest among its member countries, mainly between India and China. Also, the geographical standing of Bangladesh and Myanmar generates an ambience of competition between India and China for various reasons: resource politics to regional influence, trade and economic contacts to maritime politics. Fundamental to these influences and competition are India's and China's different

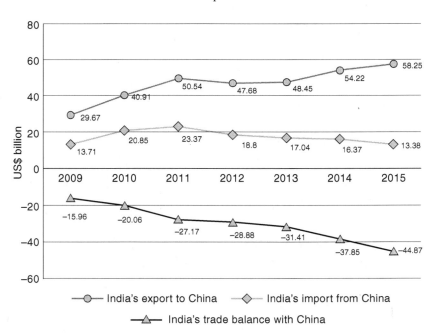

Figure 7.1 India's trade with China (in US$ billion) (source: United Nations Commodity Trade Statistics Database, *comtrade.un.org*, and various open sources).

outlooks and strategies towards the sub-regions of South-East and South Asia. In terms of comparative trade contacts that China and India have with Bangladesh and Myanmar (Figures 7.2 and 7.3), Beijing has the upper hand. The current Chinese drive is to push forward these trade and economic contacts and pursue a better posture for strategic advantages. India is one factor in this context where China uses an 'engage but deny' strategy through BCIM.

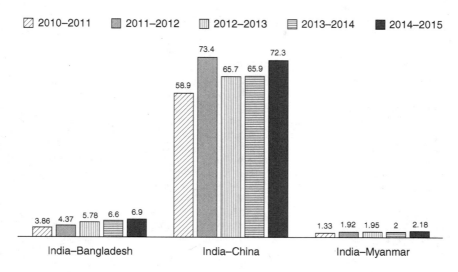

Figure 7.2 India's bilateral trade with other BCIM countries (in US$ billion) (source: data compiled from various open sources such as Ministry of External Affairs, Government of India; Embassy of People's Republic of China in the People's Republic of Bangladesh; *The Economic Times, World News Network, China Daily, China Daily Asia*, etc.).

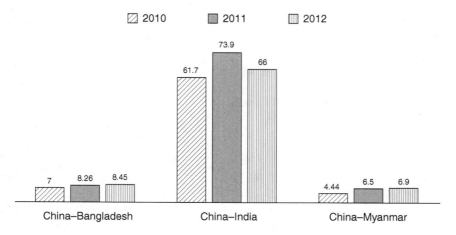

Figure 7.3 China's bilateral trade with other BCIM countries (in US$ billion) (source: same as Figure 7.2).

110 *The sub-regional crescendo*

Both India and China are connected with Myanmar and Bangladesh in the Asian Land Transport Infrastructure Development (ALTID) project, which comprises vital connectivity schemes like the Asian Highway Network (AHN), Trans-Asian Railway (TAR) and a few land, rail and road transport connectivity proposals. Implementing these infrastructural projects will continue to remain a challenge for these BCIM countries, especially given their political contradictions and complexities of relationship. Hitherto, differences in outlook and security syndrome have overridden sub-regional economic integration.

Notes

1 The BCIM forum was formally instituted in a meeting held in 1999 in Kunming, Yunnan province of China. Earlier, there used to be informal discussions among subject experts and scholars of the four countries. Originally, the idea was mooted among Indian and Chinese institutes and developed as a collaborative research network among experts from the Institute of Chinese Studies (ICS), New Delhi, and the Indira Gandhi National Centre for the Arts, New Delhi along with institutes from Yunnan and Sichuan provinces of China in 1998. There was a view that Chinese scholars wanted to generate this kind of forum and lobbied hard for it. Many Indian strategists viewed the Kunming Initiative sceptically. Today also it is primarily seen as a Chinese concept where security issues remain the prime obstacle for its progress and implementation. See Uberoi 2008.
2 Besides, the 11th BCIM Business Forum meeting, which was organised in Dhaka under the auspices of the Centre for Policy Dialogue (CPD), emphasised establishing a 'multimodal transport network', easing out visa norms and attracting 'intra-regional' trade cooperation. Supporting this idea, the Indian business community has agreed with the importance of launching a multimodal transport system with Myanmar. Chittagong and Mongla port of Bangladesh will be two key points in this context. See *Daily Star* 2013.
3 There are a series of articles from Chinese think-tank scholars about this. These include Fu Mengzi 2013; Liu Zhenmin 2013; Wang Taiping 2013. See also Zhang Ming 2013.
4 'Three-dimensional perspective' is a diplomatic network that has been proposed to facilitate China's strategic connections with neighbouring countries. It implies 'strengthen[ing] top-level design, strategic planning and promot[ing] deeper official and non-official exchanges and understandings between China and neighbouring countries'. The notion of 'multi-element perspective' implies initiatives and measures that would be conducive to local and regional conditions and facilitate China's interests. BCIM along with 'Silk Road Economic Belt' and the 'Maritime Silk Road' initiative are parts of this 'three-dimensional, multi-element perspective' strategy. For details, see Zhao Kejin 2013; see also Shen Dingli 2013.
5 Chinese media reports suggest that the 'Yunnan Gateway' project consists of five ideas: *channel, window, platform, base* and *barrier*. *Channel* implies an international thoroughfare linking Yunnan to South-East and South Asia; *window* implies cultural contacts; *platform* is to enhance trade and economic contacts; *base* implies Yunnan as a manufacturing and processing base; and *barrier* implies Yunnan's role as an 'ecological barrier'. See Li Yingqing *et al.* 2011.
6 'Going out strategy' has been a key strategy of China for the last two decades. The current leadership in China continues with it. For example, see Zhong Shan 2013.
7 For a perspective on what Chinese experts are saying about building an Asian Community, see Liu Zhenmin 2013.
8 The BIST-EC (Bangladesh, India, Sri Lanka and Thailand Economic Cooperation) grouping was established in June 1967. Myanmar joined in 1997, upon which the group

was renamed BIMSTEC (Bay of Bengal Initiative for Multi-Sectoral Technical and Economic Cooperation). Nay Pyi Taw, the capital of Myanmar, hosted the third summit of BIMSTEC on 4 March 2014. Earlier, senior officials of BIMSTEC held the 16th round of their meeting and agreed to establish a permanent secretariat in Dhaka. The establishment of regional centres, involving three in India, is in progress. Collectively, BIMSTEC represents 20 per cent of the world population and $2.5 trillion worth of GDP.

9 The Nathu La border trade pass was opened officially on 6 July 2006. The other two border trading passes are Lipulekh pass/Gunji in Uttarakhand and Namgiya Shipki La in Himachal Pradesh, which cover both 'overland trade' and 'exchange of commodities by the residents' along the border between Sikkim and TAR. As per the Nathu La border trade agreement, people from Sikkim can export some 29 items to China while 15 items can be imported from China. For more details, see *pib.nic.in* 2006. Reports in 2012 suggested that the Directorate-General of Foreign Trade (DGFT) has increased the number of items that can be imported from China to 20. See *Hindu Business Line* 2012.

References

Ahmed, Syed Miraz, 2013. 'Open Stillwell Road, push NE-Kunming trade corridor: Pradyut', *Assam Times*, 13 November, www.assamtimes.org/node/9020 (accessed on 8 May 2014).

Aiyar, Pallavi, 2006. 'Yunnan model', *Frontline*, 23(21), 21 October–3 November, www.frontline.in/static/html/fl2321/stories/20061103000306300.htm (accessed on 8 May 2014).

bcimcarrally.com, 2013. 'Welcome to BCIM Car Rally 2013', BCIM Car Rally 2013: Kolkata to Kunming: Building Bonds, Fostering Friendship, 22 February–5 March 2013, www.bcimcarrally.com (accessed on 5 September 2013).

bdnews24.com, 2014. 'China for peaceful, prosperous and open Asia: Li Jun', 23 April, http://bdnews24.com/economy/2014/04/23/china-for-peaceful-prosperous-and-open-asia-li-jun (accessed on 30 April 2014).

Bhattacharya, Debapriya and Mashfique Ibne Akbar, 2012. *Recent Developments in Myanmar and New Opportunities for Sub-Regional Cooperation: A Bangladesh Perspective*, Dhaka: CPD, September.

Bi Shihong, 2013. 'Trade corridor helps rejuvenate Asia', *Global Times*, 3 June, www.globaltimes.cn/content/786402.shtml (accessed on 8 June 2014).

Bin Alam, Jahangir, 2012. 'BCIM: more of economic cooperation and less of political gimmicks', *Financial Express*, 20(348), 20 March, www.thefinancialexpress-bd.com/old/more.php?news_id=124001&date=2012-03-20 (accessed on 30 May 2014).

chinadaily.com.cn, 2013. 'China, Bangladesh to progress BCIM Economic Corridor', *China Daily*, 20 October, www.chinadaily.com.cn/china/2013-10/20/content_17046669.htm (accessed on 27 May 2014).

Daily Star, 2013. 'Multimodal transport is a must for BCIM to boost trade', *Daily Star*, 24 February, http://archive.thedailystar.net/newDesign/news-details.php?nid=270216 (accessed on 2 September 2013).

Economic Times, 2014. 'PM leaves for Myanmar on Monday to attend BIMSTEC Summit', *Economic Times*, 26 February, http://articles.economictimes.indiatimes.com/2014-02-26/news/47705622_1_bimstec-summit-myanmar-foreign-secretary-sujatha-singh (accessed on 8 June 2014).

Financial Express, 2014. 'Hasina greets Chinese PM, lauds BCIM push', *Financial Express*, 1 February, www.thefinancialexpress-bd.com/2014/02/01/16600/print (accessed on 27 May 2014).

112 The sub-regional crescendo

Fu Mengzi, 2013. 'Reflections on China's peripheral strategy', *Contemporary International Relations*, 23(6), November–December, pp. 42–5.

Gupta, Ranjit, 2013. 'China and its periphery: Beijing's Myanmar strategy', *Issue Brief*, Institute of Peace and Conflict Studies, No. 215, May, pp. 1–8.

Hindu Business Line, 2012. 'Duty-free import of Chinese garments, shoes via 3 more border points', *The Hindu Business Line*, 20 July, www.thehindubusinessline.com/industry-and-economy/dutyfree-import-of-chinese-garments-shoes-via-3-more-border-points/article3662315.ece (accessed on 8 June 2014).

Hu Yongji, 2014. 'Yunnan border trade to get boost from new links', *China Daily*, 7 January, http://yunnan.chinadaily.com.cn/cultureindustry/2014-01/07/content_17225833.htm (accessed on 4 May 2014).

Hu Yongqi and Li Yingqing, 2014. 'Yunnan puts economic zone atop priority list', *China Daily*, 24 January 2014, www.chinadaily.com.cn/business/2014-01/21/content_17247639.htm (accessed 4 May 2014).

in.china-embassy.org, n.d. 'China–India bilateral relationship', Embassy of the People's Republic of China in India, http://in.china-embassy.org/eng/ssygd/errorpath/t247108.htm (accessed 29 May 2014).

indianembassy.org.cn, 2013. 'Minutes of the First Meeting of the Joint Study Group of Bangladesh–China–India–Myanmar Economic Corridor (BCIM EC)', 20 December, Embassy of India, Beijing, www.indianembassy.org.cn/newsDetails.aspx?NewsId=455 (accessed on 29 April 2014).

Kong Defang and Liang Jun, 2013. 'China–India border trade booms', *English.people.cn*, 12 December, http://english.people.com.cn/business/8482387.html (accessed on 29 May 2014).

Lal, Neeta, 2013. 'India and China seek economic integration via Burma, Bangladesh', *The Irrawaddy* (Asia Sentinel), 6 November, www.irrawaddy.org/china/India–China-seek-economic-integration-via-burma-bangladesh.html (accessed on 8 June 2014).

Landingin, Nathaniel and David Wadley, 2005. 'Export processing zones and growth triangle development: the case of the BIMP-EAGA, Southeast Asia', *Journal of International Development*, 17(1), January, pp. 67–96.

Lee, John, 2013. 'Ambitious China goes land roving', *Business Spectator*, Hudson Institute, 30 October, www.businessspectator.com.au/article/2013/10/30/economy/ambitio US-China-goes-land-roving (accessed on 8 June 2014).

Li Jun, 2014. '"Belt" and "Road" initiatives BCIM-EC should be on top of agenda', *Daily Star*, 20 March, www.thedailystar.net/op-ed/bcim-ec-should-be-on-top-of-agenda-16338 (accessed on 27 May 2014).

Li Yingqing, Guo Anfei and Liu Yujiao, 2011. 'Yunnan opens all its borders', *China Daily*, 1 June, www.chinadaily.com.cn/regional/2011-06/01/content_12637045.htm (accessed on 4 May 2014).

Liu Zhenmin, 2013. 'Build an Asian Community of shared destiny', *Foreign Affairs Journal*, Winter, pp. 17–29.

Masood, Asma, 2013. 'India and the BCIM: Should the "I" stand up?', 6 June, www.foreignpolicyjournal.com/2013/06/06/india-and-the-bcim-should-the-i-stand-up/ (accessed on 29 April 2014).

mea.gov.in, 2013. 'Joint Statement on the State Visit of Chinese Premier Li Keqiang to India', 20 May, www.mea.gov.in/bilateral-documents.htm?dtl/21723/Joint+Statement+on+the+State+Visit+of+Chinese++Li+Keqiang+to+India (accessed on 2 August 2013).

Panda, Jagannath, 2010. 'The pipeline dynamics in the Sino-Myanmar honeymoon: regional contention and strategic fallout', *Policy Brief*, Institute for Development & Security Policy, Sweden, No. 35, 13 September, pp. 1–3.

pib.nic.in, 2006. 'Trade between India and China through Nathu La Pass', Press Information Bureau, Ministry of Commerce and Industry, Government of India, 23 August, http://pib.nic.in/newsite/PrintRelease.aspx (accessed on 29 May 2014).

Rahman, Mustafizur, 2014. 'BCIM-economic corridor: an emerging opportunity', *Daily Star*, 15 March, www.thedailystar.net/23rd-anniversary-2014-economy-investment-and-business/bcim-economic-corridor-an-emerging-opportunity-15533 (accessed on 27 May 2014).

Rahman, Mustafizur, Habibur Rahman and Wasel Bin Shadat, 2007. *BCIM Economic Cooperation: Prospects and Challenges*, Occasional Paper 64, Dhaka: Centre for Policy Dialogue (CPD), September.

Ren Jia, 2013. 'Some thoughts on strengthening transport connectivity and communication in BCIM region', *Recent Developments in BCIM Countries: New Opportunities and New Challenges for BCIM Cooperation*, 11th BCIM Forum, Session II: Strengthening Multimodal Connectivity, Centre for Policy Dialogue: Bangladesh, BRAC Centre Inn, Dhaka, 23–24 February.

Shen Dingli, 2013. 'China's upgraded peripheral diplomacy' (translated by Li Huiru), *China.org.cn*, 26 November, www.china.org.cn/opinion/2013-11/26/content_30709098.htm (accessed on 29 April 2014).

sikkim.nic.in, n.d. '8. Trade Fair', MSME-Development Institute, Ministry of Macro, Small & Medium Enterprises, Government of India, http://sikkim.nic.in/msme-di/html/trade.html (accessed 30 May 2014).

Srinivasan, G., 2006. 'Nathula Pass: a springboard for India–China trade ties', *The Hindu Business Line*, 5 July, www.thehindubusinessline.in/bline/2006/07/06/stories/2006070602020700.htm (accessed on 29 May 2014).

Uberoi, Patricia, 2008. 'India–China initiatives in multilateral fora: two case studies', *China Report*, Sage, 44(3): 307–18.

Wang Taiping, 2013. 'China's peripheral situation and countermeasures', *Foreign Affairs Journal*, Spring, pp. 15–28.

Zhang Ming, 2013. 'The current status and prospects of China's relations with developing countries', *Foreign Affairs Journal*, Winter, pp. 30–40.

Zhao Kejin, 2013. 'Common destiny needs stability', *China Daily*, 31 December, http://usa.chinadaily.com.cn/epaper/2013-12/31/content_17207489.htm (accessed on 29 April 2014).

Zhong Shan, 2013. 'Advancing mutually beneficial economic cooperation to promote prosperity and development', Speech at the Luncheon of the Second World Peace Forum: 28 June, *Foreign Affairs Journal*, Autumn, pp. 24–30.

Part III
Regional contours

8 South Asia, SAARC and sub-regional dynamics

This chapter examines India–China power politics in South Asia in a context where India's 'localism' or influence in the region is tested by China's 'proximity localism' or 'neighbourhood localism'. The premise is that China is rapidly emerging as a power in the South Asian context, seeking closer involvement in the region.[1] The chapter examines the evolving India–China power politics in South Asia against three broad aspects, namely, (i) by examining the usual and contemporary policy approach of India and China towards South Asia; (ii) to what extent the modes of refining relationship through 'bilateralism' and 'multilateralism' contribute to the overall India–China balance of power politics; and (iii) whether resource politics will remain a constant factor in their broader power dynamics.

Modi, Xi and their contemporary South Asia policy

As a 'local power', India's strategic interests in the region are closely linked with the political, economic and security dynamics of South Asia, though India has recently moved beyond its sub-regional tag and has been projecting itself as an Asian power. On the other hand, China has over the decades shaped its course in Asia as a 'greater regional power', where it placed South Asia below Central Asia and East or South-East Asia. Chinese experts acknowledge that 'South Asia has long been a weak link in China's peripheral diplomacy' (Zhao Minghao 2014). But the geographical unit and economic profile of South Asia or the South Asian Association for Regional Cooperation (SAARC) members (see Table 8.1) is a factor that is difficult for India and China to overlook.

Under the Modi government at the centre, India's South Asia policy seems to be receiving a renewed life through a strong diplomatic engagement. Narendra Modi's decision to invite all the SAARC members to attend his oath-taking ceremony as the new Prime Minister is an indication of this, which the Chinese media saw as a part of India's 'stronger regional diplomacy' (Wu Qiang 2014) and as 'an extraordinary step'. Three factors probably explain this new policy boldness. *First*, the economic potential of the South Asian market in terms of enabling India to brighten up its economy. Even though India is a local power and the biggest economy in South Asia, its exports to the SAARC countries

Table 8.1 SAARC member profile vis-à-vis China

	Population (2013)	Surface area (sq. km)	GDP (current US$), billion 2013	GDP growth (annual %) 2013	HDI ranking	Youth literacy 2005–2012	Unemployment (% of labour force)* 2012
Afghanistan	30.55 million	652,860	20.72	4.2	169	–	8.6
Bangladesh	156.6 million	148,460	129.9	6	142	78.7	4.5
Bhutan	753,900	38,394	1.884	5	136	74.4	2.1
India	1.252 billion	3,287,260	1.877 trillion	5	135	81.1	3.4
Maldives	345,000	300	2.3	3.7	103	99.3	11.3
Nepal	27.80 million	147,180	19.29	3.8	145	82.4	2.7
Pakistan	182.1 million	796,100	236.6	6.1	146	70.7	5.1
Sri Lanka	20.48 million	65,610	67.18	7.3	73	98.2	4.8
Total SAARC	1.67 billion	5,136,164	2.355 trillion				
China	1.357 billion	9,562,911	9.240 trillion	7.7	91	99.6	4.5

Source: World Development Indicators, The World Bank database at http://data.worldbank.org (accessed on 3 October 2014).

Note
* Modelled ILO estimate.

account for a meagre 4.9 per cent of its global exports (*EXIMIUS: Export Advantage* 2013: 1). In 2012–2013, India's exports to the other South Asian countries were around US$17.3 billion, compared to its global exports, which totalled around $312 billion (see Table 8.2) (*BBC News India* 2014). India seems to be pursuing a strategy where economic diplomacy will simultaneously move with strategic reach.

Second, the strategic significance of South Asia is realised well enough in Indian diplomacy. Prime Minister Modi travelled to Bhutan in his first overseas trip after taking over as the Indian government's leader, and thereafter made an official visit to Nepal in August 2014.

Third, the new Indian government's South Asia policy factors in China. A clear reflection of this was Modi inviting the Prime Minister of the Tibetan Government in Exile (TGIE), Lobsang Sangay, to attend his swearing-in ceremony, clearly intended to pass on a strategic signal to China that India values the cause of Tibet and the Tibetan community. The Chinese government sent a demarche to India protesting this move. Also, though India does not have any diplomatic ties with Taiwan, the new government invited Taiwan's Economic and Cultural Council (TECC) representative in New Delhi, seating him with other ambassadors.

Looking from the Chinese perspectives, in recent times, South Asia has acquired a new 'strategic focus' in the Chinese power building exercise (Li Zhang 2009). Most of the South Asian states share land borders with China, totalling about 4000 km, in Chinese assessment (Du Youkang 2002: 126). In the recent Chinese foreign policy understanding, the strategic milieu of South Asia as a region and the standing of the countries in this region have also increased in regional politics (Lan Jianxue 2014). SAARC member countries like India, Pakistan, Bangladesh and Afghanistan are catalogued as important in China's transnational projects under a 'neighbourhood strategy' (Yang Jiechi 2014; also see Ruan Zongze 2014). A number of other factors that have shaped China's South Asia outlook in the process are: the strategic and economic standing of South Asia in today's context; connections between China's two arduous regions – Xinjiang and Tibet – with the South Asian region; tactical dynamism of Pakistan and India in its strategic interests; and the vitality of infrastructural linkages along with economic tie-ups with the South Asian countries (Panda 2010: 305).

It would appear that under the leadership of Xi Jinping neither has China an entirely new South Asia policy nor is China's strategic thrust on India in its South Asia policy anything new. The newness seems to be only in the strategic focus, the mode of contacts and the channels of understanding. Essentially, China has always pursued its South Asia policy under two broad terminologies: through a dialogue of 'good neighbour diplomacy' (*mulinwaijiao*) and through a dialogue of 'peripheral or regional diplomacy' (*zhoubianwaijiao*). Both essentially imply a similar approach: take your neighbours seriously. In both these constructs, India has been a major factor in China's overall South Asia outlook. Policymakers in Beijing have mostly seen India as a regional power in the South Asian context (Ho 2014: 1). Currently, Beijing accommodates India under its

Table 8.2 SAARC trade data compared with China

	Export (US$), 2013 est.	Import (US$) 2013 est.	Major export partners	Major import partners
Afghanistan	376 million*	6.39 billion*	Pakistan 32.2%, India 27%, Tajikistan 8.5%, US 6.2% (2012)	Pakistan 24.3%, US 18%, Russia 8.7%, India 5.8%, China 5.6%, Germany 4.4% (2012)
Bangladesh	26.91 billion	32.94 billion	US 18.7%, Germany 15.8%, UK 10.2%, France 6.2%, Spain 4.6%, Canada 4.3%, Italy 4% (2013 est.)	China 21.7%, India 16.3%, Malaysia 5.2%, Republic of Korea 4.5%, Japan 4.1% (2013 est.)
Bhutan	721.8 million*	1.28 billion*	India 83.8%, Hong Kong 10.8% (2013 est.)	India 72.3%, South Korea 6% (2013 est.)
India	313.2 billion	467.5 billion	UAE 12.3%, US 12.2%, China 5%, Singapore 4.9%, Hong Kong 4.1% (2012)	China 10.7%, UAE 7.8%, Saudi Arabia 6.8%, Switzerland 6.2%, US 5.1% (2012)
Maldives	283 million*	1.406 billion*	France 18.9%, Thailand 15.8%, UK 11.4%, US 9.4%, Sri Lanka 8.6%, Italy 8.1%, Germany 6.4% (2012)	Singapore 21.7%, UAE 20.9%, India 9.6%, Malaysia 7.6%, China 6%, Thailand 5.6%, Sri Lanka 4% (2012)
Nepal	1.06 billion	6.329 billion	India 93.9%, Bangladesh 4%, Italy 0.4% (2013 est.)	India 79.4%, South Korea 3.1%, China 2.5% (2013 est.)
Pakistan	25.05 billion	39.27 billion	US 13.6%, China 11.1%, UAE 8.5%, Afghanistan 7.8% (2012)	China 19.7%, Saudi Arabia 12.3%, UAE 12.1%, Kuwait 6.3% (2012)
Sri Lanka	10.39 billion	18 billion	US 20.4%, UK 9.9%, India 5.8%, Italy 4.7%, Belgium 4.3%, Germany 4.3% (2012)	India 22.7%, Singapore 8.8%, UAE 7.7%, China 7%, Iran 6.1%, Malaysia 4.5% (2012)
Total SAARC	378 billion	573 billion		
World	18.71 trillion	18.59 trillion		
China	2.21 trillion	1.95 trillion	Hong Kong 17.4%, US 16.7%, Japan 6.8%, South Korea 4.1% (2013 est.)	South Korea 9.4%, Japan 8.3%, Taiwan 8%, United States 7.8%, Australia 5%, Germany 4.8% (2013 est.)

Source: The World Fact book, CIA at www.cia.gov/library/publications/the-world-factbook/ (accessed on 5 October 2014).

Note
* 2012 est.

great-power diplomacy (*daguowaijiao*) (Chen and Guan 2014), partly because India has emerged as a power both at the regional and the global levels.

President Xi Jinping has invested strong focus on 'neighbourhood' or 'peripheral' diplomacy (see Liu Zhenmin 2014; Ruan Zongze 2014; Wang Yi 2014) in his endeavour to establish a 'prosperous, strong, democratic and culturally advanced, harmonious and modern socialist country by 2049', as set out by the 18th CPC National Congress in November 2012 (Wang and Zhang 2013). Xi has attempted to employ a multipronged strategy to establish stronger bilateral as well as multilateral relationships with the neighbouring regions across Asia and its sub-regions. He emphasises that recently there have been many changes in China's relations with its neighbours, which must induce China to revitalise its neighbourhood policy through win-win diplomacy, capitalising on economic bonding with the neighbouring region through interconnectivity and Silk Road Economic Belt (SREB) and Maritime Silk Road (MSR) projects (ibid.). More importantly, as part of China's focus on institutionalising its regional and neighbourhood diplomacy in the context of South Asia, SAARC has become an anchor in China's engagement with South Asia.

Factoring SAARC: prospective China membership; guarded India?[2]

New Delhi institutionalises its South Asia policy through SAARC, which in its perception facilitates and addresses the broader governance issues in South Asia. SAARC has also helped India carry forward its identity of being a South Asian power. For China, SAARC may currently be less significant in its foreign policy perspective than the Shanghai Cooperation Organisation (SCO) and ASEAN; but its regular engagement with SAARC as an observer since November 2005 has augmented China's interest in this South Asian body.[3] More than anything else, India's growing influence within SAARC has induced Beijing to aim for better involvement with this South Asian body, in a power balancing game.

Beijing has steadily gained clout within SAARC as an observer member and also with its member countries individually. Imaginatively, it floated two constructive dialogues within SAARC: (i) the dialogue of developing countries and (ii) the dialogue of 'common interests'. At the 14th SAARC summit, the year after China was admitted as an observer member, the Chinese Foreign Minister Li Zhaoxing said: 'We all belong to the developing world, are experiencing fast growth and facing geographical location and popular support will greatly boost China–SAARC cooperation, which serves our common interests and peace, stability and development of the region' (*in.chineseembassy.org* 2007). This articulation allows China to pursue a twofold strategy of establishing bilateral or multilateral/institutional contacts with South Asia through SAARC. This is a classic foreign policy strategy that China has articulated in the post-Deng Xiaoping era. The contemporary Chinese foreign policy course suggests that Beijing is open to the idea of multilateral practices and membership in institutional institutions and regional bodies (Wu and Lansdowne 2008). China's presence and experience in regional bodies is primarily a post-Cold War phenomenon, coinciding with its larger interests in Asia (Dittmer 2008). To deal with the post-Soviet world situation, China embarked on a 'policy of good neighbourliness' (*mulinzhengce*) (ibid.: 27), in which the diplomatic primacy was to establish institutional linkages with different parts of Asia.[4]

The Chinese effort to tie up with South Asia institutionally through SAARC incorporates two objectives: *first*, to remain an active player in the neighbourhood politics; and *second*, to maximise its strategic interests by integrating into the region. Qi Huaigao rightly notes that 'Southeast Asia and South Asia involve important economic interests of China, so China can play a guiding role by participating in the existing ASEAN and SAARC institutions.' In effect, institutionalising its regional engagements remains a priority in China's contemporary thinking (Qi Huaigao 2009: 130).

In the last few years, China has steadily increased its economic connections with SAARC. In December 2006, the China–South Asia Commercial Affairs Council was founded in Kunming for promoting this economic collaboration. China's trade contacts with the South Asian countries have also seen a constant rise. The principal Chinese effort vis-à-vis SAARC is to capitalise on and make the most of its bilateral links with select SAARC members (Saez and Chang 2010). China sees some of these developing states either as political heavyweights or main sources of raw materials. This is one of the reasons why China has entered into 'strategic partnerships' (*zhanluehuobanguanxi*).

What paves the road for China to acquire a larger influence in SAARC is India's dithering over this body vis-à-vis South Asia (Raja Mohan 2010). India has overlooked its outreach potential in South Asia as well as in SAARC in contrast to the way it has accosted the South-East Asian neighbours under its two-decade-old Look East policy or new 'Act East' policy. Under Modi, India has now recognised that it must realise the usefulness of its neighbours and upgrade its South Asia reach.

In India's perception, inviting China to be a SAARC member would change the dynamics of SAARC since China is not a South Asian country. To perhaps impede China's entry into SAARC, India has raised the issue of 'institutional reform within SAARC' (MEA 2014a; see also Ramachandran 2014). India's then Minister for External Affairs, Salman Khurshid, stated in February 2014:

> SAARC needs to clarify its thinking on the nature and direction of its relationships with partner States who have observer status. Some of the Observer States have done commendable work with our Association, but it is important that we define a clear set of policies and objectives for these relationships and their future direction, before we move further.
>
> (MEA 2014b)

Bhutan, which does not have diplomatic relations with China, may accept this stance of India, but other SAARC members may not, perhaps seeing China as an equipoise to India's influence within SAARC (Ramachandran 2014).

Most of SAARC's institutional mechanisms operate and function consensually, where members have veto. Article X, General Provisions of the SAARC Charter, lays down that decisions within SAARC at all levels will be taken on the basis of 'unanimity' and 'bilateral and contentious issues shall be excluded from the deliberations' (*saarc-sec.org* 1985). If China becomes a full-fledged SAARC member, its veto could become inconvenient to India's interests, barricading many of India's regional planning and infrastructural activities in South Asia. Therefore, India may be open to the idea of granting a more institutionalised dialogue mechanism facility to China rather than SAARC membership.

Rationale, resources and relationships

India's keenness to uphold its status as a dominant South Asian power and China's ambition to emerge as a Greater South Asian power is the main factor in the current India–China bilateral dynamism. Important factors that shape this balancing propensity are: resource politics, bilateral connectivity or regional infrastructural projects and conflicting issues. For China, this dynamism along with the significance of each of the South Asian countries is central to its regional standing. It has been argued that China's relations with the South Asian countries are much weaker than its relations with other Asian nations (Mu Chunshan 2014).

Pakistan: Beijing's all-weather partner and New Delhi's arch rival

Pakistan was the third country to recognise the People's Republic of China in the early 1960s. For China, ties with Pakistan, customarily described as all-weather friendship, remain a stable proxy factor in its India policy, making this relationship a 'special one' (Garver 2001a; see also Smith 2014). The principal Chinese outlook on Pakistan is that it is a struggling state and needs China's assistance to overcome its difficulty.[5] Three elements that merit appraisal in the India–China–Pakistan tripartite dynamics are: (i) China's standpoint on Kashmir and recent approach on Pakistan-Occupied Kashmir (POK); (ii) infrastructural and economic engagements between China and Pakistan and their implications for India; and (iii) the strategic and political dynamics among the three neighbours.

Beijing's position on the Kashmir issue has been far from consistent and has evolved over the years, occasionally being pro-Pakistan or pro-Kashmiris, and sometimes a somewhat neutral one. China's stance towards Kashmir has been based on its shared strategic interests with Pakistan, its shared interests in the region of POK and its overall strategic interests in Asia. China's traditional stance on Kashmir is connected with a range of issues such as the Kashmir dispute itself, the issue of terrorism and China's 'special' relationship with Pakistan on a range of security issues. The current and future China's stance on Kashmir is linked with Beijing's regional economic planning as well as infrastructural connectivity with the region.

John Garver points out that even during the heydays of the India–China ties, when the sentiment of Panchsheel was at its peak, Beijing decided not to endorse

India's position on Kashmir, probably anticipating a conflict with India over Tibet and the boundary issue. During the Tibetan crisis, China chose not to openly state its position on Kashmir. Between 1964 and 1979, until Atal Bihari Vajpayee's visit to China as India's Minister for External Affairs, Beijing consistently talked about the 'Kashmiri people's right to self-determination'. Later on, the Chinese leadership started linking the Kashmir issue with the India–Pakistan Simla agreement and maintained that the Kashmir dispute should be resolved as per the relevant UN resolutions. Garver argues that by mentioning the Simla agreement and UN resolutions, China fundamentally 'straddled the Pakistani and Indian positions' on Kashmir. In the 1990s, China seemed to be frequently changing its position on Kashmir from a 'neutral' to a pro-Pakistani one (Garver 2001b). During the Kargil war between India and Pakistan, China maintained 'perceived neutrality' and urged the two countries to resolve the Kashmir issue peacefully. In 2009, the Chinese foreign ministry spokesperson Ma Zhaoxu stated that the Kashmir issue is 'left over from history' and 'as a neighbouring country and friend of both India and Pakistan, China always maintains that the issue should be properly settled through dialogue and consultation by the two countries' (*china-un.org* 2009).

Even though China acknowledges that the Kashmir dispute is essentially a bilateral dispute between India and Pakistan, the geographical merits of the region are linked to China's strategic interests and it considers Pakistan as the legitimate owner of this region. It may be recalled that in the China–Pakistan 'border agreement' that was signed on 2 March 1963, Pakistan ceded to China approximately 5180 sq km of the area under its occupation (*pib.nic.in* 2014).

On the security front, China anticipates terrorism-related problems from the Pakistan–Afghanistan region. The Sino-Pakistani ties have solidified against the background of China's fear of *terrorism, extremism and separatism* (*san gushili*) in Xinjiang, which is adjacent to the Kashmir and Central Asian region. China aims to keep Pakistan briefed about any anticipated threat from the Uyghurs in Xinjiang, who may have linkages with the extremist Islamic forces in the region. The magnitude of Xinjiang is vital to China's security and strategic interests (Panda 2010). China wants to have greater control over this region through infrastructural linkages so that its security interests can be better protected.

The economic nuances of China's construction activities in POK are even greater than the security mandate. China brings a stimulating viewpoint with regard to Kashmir as well as in its relationship discourse towards Pakistan through regional economic dealings. Gone is that period when China used to look at the South Asian region simply as a 'periphery'. South Asia is now seen as a significant strategic location in the Chinese foreign policy. The immediate construct that Beijing employs with regard to South Asia is to include the region under its pan-regional outlook. Xi Jinping's advocacy of 'One Belt, One Road' implies that South Asia is an important construct in China's greater regional planning, which includes Central Asia, South-East Asia and the Indian Ocean as well (Zhao Minghao 2014).

Three implications may be noted here. *First*, though China officially maintains that the Kashmir dispute is a bilateral matter between India and Pakistan, it has de facto approved Pakistan's annexation of a part of Kashmir. *Second*, China's stance over Kashmir is no more India–Pakistan centric, rather it is 'regional' centric and is linked with China's broader foreign policy design. *Third*, in any future episode in the Kashmir dispute, Beijing will play the role of a silent 'third party'.

The stapled visa issue further exposes the so-called neutrality that China claims to maintain vis-à-vis the Kashmir issue. In the recent past, the Chinese authorities began issuing stapled visas to Indians hailing from the state of Jammu and Kashmir. This policy approach indicates two things. *First*, China wants to make the conflict of Kashmir a 'tripartite' one. *Second*, China wants to aggravate the conflict by questioning India's sovereignty over the region (*Hindustan Times* 2010). Also, Beijing seems to be resorting to a tit-for-tat approach with India, as New Delhi earlier refused to allow the Chinese diplomats to visit North-East India.

The 2005 Treaty for Friendship and Cooperation and Good Neighbourly Relations between China and Pakistan continues to be the central base of their current bilateral ties. The core of this treaty is mutual recognition of each other's strategic concerns. Pakistan acknowledged one-China policy by taking note of China's 'great cause of national reunification'. The Chinese side in its turn acknowledged Pakistan's 'independence, sovereignty and territorial integrity' (see, for details, *People's Daily* 2006). Today the Sino-Pakistani ties have become multi-dimensional. Hu Jintao, the then Chinese President, outlined the core fundamentals of this 'multi-dimensional' relationship as follows: (i) deepening strategic ties and consolidating customary friendship; (ii) improving trade and business ties which will create 'win-win' conditions for both countries; (iii) improving socio-cultural understanding; (iv) maximising understanding on regional and global strategic affairs; and (v) promotion of ideas for world harmony (*China Daily* 2006). China's arms supplies to Pakistan, military-to-military collaboration, growing trade and economic asymmetry and the Chinese strategic investment in the adjacent India–China–Pakistan region are important factors that currently shape the India–China dynamism in South Asia.

The Afghanistan fulcrum

Factoring Afghanistan, which strategically and regionally connects with India and China in SAARC and the SCO, in the India–China dynamics connotes a mixed cooperative endeavour. Afghanistan was not an important aspect in the India–China ties till recently. However, recent developments in that country have offered a cooperative option for India and China rather than a competing one. The post-2014 US troops withdrawal from Afghanistan, the strategic significance of this country for India's and China's security concerns mainly emanating from terrorist forces in the region, and the geographical location of Afghanistan as a bridge between South Asia and Central Asia have developed a new dynamism between India and China, most of which is cooperative and seems to be complying with each other's strategic interests. The two countries started an official dialogue in April 2013 on Afghanistan. The India–China 2014 Joint Statement also takes note of bilateral consultations on Afghanistan (MEA 2014b). Three strategic nuances explain this cooperative drive.

First, countering terrorism is a common interest for India and China (Pantucci 2014; see also Schwarck 2014). The rise of ISIS (Islamic State of Iraq and Syria) further mandates such cooperation. India's prime concern comes from the Taliban's Islamic Emirate or the extremist forces that are closely associated with ISIS and al-Qaeda outfits. China may not face the same security threat or concern from these forces, but Beijing does feel concerned over the constant instability in Afghanistan. The extremist forces in the region may have strong linkages with poorly governed spaces in Central Asia or in Pakistan, and that will eventually influence the Uyghurs in Xinjiang. But the prospect for cooperation in this regard is limited, given the India–Pakistan dynamics on the issue of terrorism.

Second, Afghanistan facilitates India's and China's connectivity to reach further. For India, Afghanistan is the key to its Central Asia reach. India's main target is not only to reach Central Asia for further energy exploration but also to bring Afghanistan on board for its gas pipelines. For China, Afghanistan is a key to its energy supplies and economic opportunities. Of particular importance for Beijing is to actualise its newly launched SREB. Even though SREB does not pass through Afghanistan, it is an inter-regional connectivity proposal that pushes forward China's cross-border logistic infrastructure linkages between its western region to Central Asia, via POK, and finally touching the markets in Europe.

Third, Afghanistan's strategic location and its presence in SAARC and SCO make it important for India and China. Multilateral organisations often prompt dialogue of cooperation and win-win conditions. India needs Afghanistan in its fold to keep its influence intact both within SAARC and in South Asian as well as Central Asian affairs. China facilitated Afghanistan's induction into the SCO to keep track of the evolving security situation in South Asia as well as in Central Asia.

Despite their common interests, genuine cooperation between India and China with regard to Afghanistan is limited. Strategic communities contend that there is scope for India–China cooperation in Afghanistan, where Beijing could take advantage of India's cultural fluencies in Afghanistan for Afghanistan's reconstruction activities; that both can further cooperate in training the Afghan National Army (ANA) and push further Afghanistan's defence competencies (Stobdan 2013). The topic of forming a cooperative 'strategic partnership' with regard to Afghanistan has been propelled in the India–China official bilateral parlance for some time now, but has remained only at the level of talk. Both countries have shown a commitment for the reconstruction of Afghanistan and have supported an 'Afghan-led, Afghan-owned' reconciliation process (MEA 2013). India and China may cooperate in a few issue-based affairs in

Afghanistan, but a stable cooperative drive does not appear on the horizon at the moment. Afghanistan may on the other hand become a country where both India and China will exert themselves to make their own space and presence as regional powers.

Bhutan: boundary, resources and politics[6]

Though it is one of the smallest countries on the world map, Bhutan has always been an influential political figure in South Asian politics, especially between India and China. Customarily seen as a nation closer to India's historical, strategic and political trajectory, Bhutan today faces an unenviable dilemma to choose between India and China, and more notably, how to maintain a fine balance in their rivalry. Bhutan's course in the India–China imbroglio is usually linked with the state of Sikkim, the Tibetan complexity and the India–China boundary dispute. Two correlated pointers explain the growing India–China antagonism with regard to Bhutan: (i) political partnership and potential relationship competition surrounding Bhutan; and (ii) competition for resources. However, at the core of India–China dynamics are the ongoing boundary negotiations between China and Bhutan. The recent political engagement between the two countries indicates a growing political bonhomie, which could eventually result in the establishment of formal diplomatic ties, which might worry India.

Bhutan and China have 470 km of unresolved border. China's attempt is to negotiate and demarcate a border with Bhutan's north-western areas in exchange of some specific central areas. Bhutan's north-western region is close to the Chumbi Valley and India's state of Sikkim. Chumbi Valley, located in the Yadong county of Tibet Autonomous Region, is close to the Siliguri corridor of India's north-east. China will have an edge over India if its border negotiations with Bhutan succeed. China and Bhutan have had more than 22 rounds of boundary talks.

Bhutan remains central to India's broader Himalayan sub-regional politics. The India–Bhutan relationship is based on the 1949 Treaty of Friendship, updated in February 2007, when King Jigme Khesar Namgyel Wangchuk visited India. The 2007 treaty is fundamentally different from its predecessor treaty, and puts Bhutan internationally on a different track. In 1949, the government agreed 'to be guided by the advice of the Government of India in regard to its external relations'. The revised version states that both countries need to 'cooperate closely with each other on issues relating to their national interests' (*mea.gov.in* 2007).

Many Chinese have shown an interest in touring and investing in Bhutan. Bhutan has pursued a one-China policy, and has started seeing China as an economic opportunity. Bhutan's holding bilateral border talks with China is linked to India's national interests in the Eastern Himalayan region. Therefore, it is expected that Bhutan would consult India on the matter.

Strategic Nepal

As a landlocked nation, Nepal's political trajectory has heavily been associated with the India–China bilateral dynamism, particularly in the context of Tibet. Seen as 'strategically vulnerable' to both Indian and Chinese tactical influence, Nepal has maintained a measured policy of 'equi-cordial' ties with the two countries, while steadily increasing its strategic standing in the two countries' foreign policy parameters. Geographically, it has always been a buffer between India and China along with Tibet.

The contemporary political outreach of India and China towards Nepal appears to be robust. The relatively new leaderships in India and China have exhibited a strong interest in reaching out to Nepal. Prime Minister Narendra Modi's visit to Nepal soon after taking office reflects the seriousness that the new Indian government holds as regards Nepal. Modi was the second leader to address the Nepalese Constituent Assembly during his trip to Nepal in the first week of August 2014; the then German Chancellor Helmut Kohl was the first to address it in 1990. China's new leadership under Xi Jinping also prioritises its outreach to Nepal.

Nepal's hydropower potential makes it strategically important for both India and China. After Prime Minister Modi's visit to Nepal in August 2014, a new deal between the Investment Board of Nepal and GMR has been signed, under which the Nepal government has cleared GMR's plan for the $1.4 billion hydroelectric plant project on the Upper Karnali River belt. This is a 900 MW dam-and-tunnel system and is the first of four projects. There is, however, a glitch in the understanding between Nepal and India for increasing trade of hydropower. The Nepalese want a power trade agreement (PTA), because without it, investors may shy from collaborating with India (Celestine 2014).

Since 2012, China has intensified its commercial and business-related links in hydrological search in Nepal. Nepal has approved a project worth $1.8 billion in the Three Gorges Corp. in the West Seti River hydropower project. It was reported in 2012 that more than $400 billion worth of investment was offered to Nepal by the Chinese government to carry out future endeavours. Reports suggest that Indian companies have lost to Chinese companies in Nepal's hydrological sector. Most of the Chinese enterprises are state-owned and are backed by their government; whereas the competing Indian companies have to plough their lonely furrow without any clear governmental support.

Security concerns vis-à-vis the Tibetan community in Nepal are a prime factor in China's bilateral interaction with Nepal. Connecting with Tibet through better road and railway connections has been a prime focus in the Chinese policy in recent times. The Nepalese have noticed China's huge capability in building infrastructure in Tibet and realise that China can help Nepal improve its infrastructure as well. For India, this becomes a headache. The recent Chinese proposal to establish a new engineering marvel connecting Lhasa with Tibet's second city Shigatse is a case in point. This railway line will extend towards Arunachal Pradesh, near the Indian boundary (Moore 2014). In response to this

Chinese initiative, India has announced recently that it would establish 54 border posts in Arunachal Pradesh in addition to the existing 30 posts in this region.

The Tibetan community in Nepal has maintained a strong linkage with the Dalai Lama and the Tibetan Government in Exile (TGIE) in India's Dharmasala. Since the end of monarchical rule in Nepal in 2008, China has taken a serious interest in checking the Tibetan community's activities in Nepal through a set of political, economic and social contacts. The post-Dalai Lama phase is also a prime concern in the Chinese security outlook (Patel 2013).

The India–China power dynamism in Nepal involves four layers of politics, as follows. *First*, India and China are emerging as strong contenders for Nepal's hydrological resources. *Second*, Nepal will remain on the radar in the Indian and Chinese foreign policy stratagems. Nepal may well exploit this advantage, which will impact hugely on South Asian politics. *Third*, the Tibet factor will continue to dominate the India–China dynamics with regard to Nepal. *Finally*, Nepal's role in the India–China South Asia power politics will grow. The Nepalese community may actively see China as a brighter option as an economic power, which may not go well with India.

Bangladesh bonding

For both India and China, Bangladesh is vital in being a Bay of Bengal country. Bangladesh perceives China as a more stable power at the regional level than India. China in its turn, by offering a stable connection to Dhaka, is taking benefit of Bangladesh's land corridors for resource exploration and maritime inroads into the Bay of Bengal and the Indian Ocean. The evolving China–Bangladesh ties are further strengthened by the trust deficit that exists between India and Bangladesh, involving the Farakka Barrage and Teesta River, boundary dispute, maritime border, territorial waters, refugee matters and drug trafficking in the border areas. In contrast with the low trade and economic contacts between India and Bangladesh, China–Bangladesh trade and economic ties have grown rapidly. China has also emerged as a prominent investor in Bangladesh.

China's defence ties with Dhaka and exports of military equipment to Bangladesh are causing concern for the Indian government. In India's perception, through this kind of defence cooperation China is strategically making forays into the Indian Ocean waters. A recent $203 million defence deal between the two countries for China to sell two Ming-class submarines is a pointer to this concern (Miller 2014). This development comes at a time when New Delhi is aiming for a greater Bay of Bengal presence. China is also attempting to develop Chittagong port as an operational port just like Gwadar port in Pakistan, which Beijing can utilise for its naval vessels in the Bay of Bengal region and in its forays into the Indian Ocean.

In the recent past, Bangladesh opinion-makers have argued strongly for a greater Chinese role in South Asia. They have not opposed, for example, the Chinese announcement of hydropower dam construction in Dagu, Jiacha and Jiexy along the middle reach of the Brahmaputra, which India has strongly opposed. The recent meeting between President Xi Jinping and Prime Minister Sheikh Hasina Wajed also suggested a new level of trust and confidence evolving between the two countries both on bilateral and regional issues. Bangladesh seems to be a key country for China's SREB and MSR. Beijing's grand design is to gain the confidence of Bangladesh and take it into its fold to realise these projects. The year 2015 marks the 40th anniversary of the establishment of China–Bangladesh diplomatic ties, and there are indications that both will further deepen their bilateral and regional understanding (Shen Jie 2014).

Three types of undertakings may be seen with regard to India–China politics around Bangladesh. *First*, they recognise Bangladesh's standing in South Asia and seek to intensify their connections with that country. In this endeavour, China has an advantage. *Second*, even though Bangladesh is connected with India and China in BCIM, China will like to arrive at a unilateral understanding with Bangladesh on infrastructural development issues and themes that are principal to China's national interests. Bangladesh will agree; and this may affect India–Bangladesh relations. *Third*, India–China dynamism in connection with Bangladesh will grow particularly regarding issues of maritime security and defence. The Chinese exertion to take advantage of Bangladesh to reach the Bay of Bengal region and eventually the IOR will intensify.

Sri Lanka's prevalence

Sri Lanka is an important littoral state for India's Indian Ocean maritime politics; and for China, it is an important partnering country not only for South Asian affairs but also for its Indian Ocean drive. Three nuances are attached to the India–China dynamics with regard to Sri Lanka: partnership politics, maritime politics concerning the Indian Ocean, and MSR.

China's MSR and its security and defence partnership with Sri Lanka that is taking shape complicate India–China bearings in and around Sri Lanka. Xi Jinping visited Sri Lanka in September 2014, in the first trip to that country by a Chinese President in 28 years. The maritime understanding that was brokered between the two countries during his visit carries obvious implications for India and many other countries like the US and Japan. The MSR is meant to negate the American, Indian and Japanese influence in the Indian Ocean (Jayasekera 2014). After Xi's visit, Sri Lanka has openly supported MSR, whereas India has maintained silence over it, considering it as a strategic initiative by China to carve out a better space for itself in the Indian Ocean (Goodman 2014).

The Strategic Cooperative Partnership between China and Sri Lanka has amplified the defence understanding between the two countries, and China has gained enormous confidence in Sri Lanka's foreign as well as strategic context. The new Plan of Action between the two countries endorses investments and cooperative courses in Hambantota port. The two sides have also agreed to establish a joint committee on coastal and marine cooperation, under which the two sides aim to explore cooperation in areas like ocean observation, marine and coastal zone management, ecosystem conservation, search and rescue operations, maritime security, navigation security, anti-piracy, etc. Chinese naval activities have also increased in the Sri Lankan territorial waters. For instance, recently the Chinese Navy type-039 (Song class) and PLA Navy type-093 nuclear submarine visited the Indian Ocean along the Sri Lankan coast (*China Military Online* 2014). Even though it is acceptable that the PLA Navy visits the Indian Ocean and touches the Sri Lankan coast, it is difficult to comprehend why a nuclear submarine undertook this trip. Media reports also suggest that almost 230 Chinese warships have travelled to Colombo port in the recent past for refuelling and crew refreshment (Rupasinghe 2014). Chinese naval presence in Sri Lanka, including in Trincomalee, is detrimental to India's strategic interests and violates the 1987 Peace Accord between the two countries, which lays down that they will refrain from allowing their territory to be used against each other's unity, integrity and security (*peacemaker.un.org* 1987). Recent reports also suggest that China Merchants and China Harbor Engineering has entered into an agreement with the Sri Lankan Port Authority to construct a container terminal at Hambantota port (Yung 2014). Sri Lanka also has expressed an interest in joining the SCO as an observer. In return, China seems to expect Sri Lanka's support for China's SAARC membership.

The Maldives concurrence

The Maldives, as a small archipelagic nation in the middle of the IOR, is strategically important for India's and China's maritime drives, supplies, ferry or shipping transportation and maritime politics.

Commencing November 2014, India and Maldives celebrated the 50th year of their diplomatic ties. Given the geographic and ethnic proximity with the island nation, India has traditionally taken an interest in Maldives politics and has maintained strong cultural, economic and security links with that country. The current Maldives government under President Abdulla Yameen Abdul Gayoom, however, seems to be more China-friendly. Maldives acknowledges that its ties with China today are 'very close', but its ties with India are 'far more precious' (*Daily News Analysis* 2014).

In September 2014, Xi Jinping visited the Maldives, the first Chinese President to visit that country in 42 years (*fmprc.gov.cn* 2014). Maldives is an important country in China's MSR proposal. The importance that the Maldives attaches to China can be surmised from the fact that President Gayoom along with his wife received Xi Jinping at the Male international airport.

Xi Jinping's recent trip to Sri Lanka and Maldives before travelling to India signifies that China intends to convey the message that these smaller countries are as strategically important for China as India as a neighbour. During Xi Jinping's tour, the Maldives and China signed several agreements. On its part, the Maldives has declared its intention to join the MSR. Like the other smaller South Asian powers, the Maldives stands to gain a lot of importance from the India–China dynamism, especially in terms of making its demands on the India–China maritime rivalry.

The emerging course

Why does China merit a better space in SAARC today? The reasons are twofold. The *first* is shared understanding and goodwill that Beijing has garnered among SAARC members. In this Beijing has outsmarted other SAARC observer members, benefiting considerably from its geographic proximity to South Asia. Given Beijing's strong political system and economic track record, most SAARC members would unequivocally advocate a bolstered Chinese presence in South Asia, including as a full-fledged SAARC member.

The Chinese profile in South Asia bears comparison with three other powerful SAARC observer members, namely, the US, Japan and the EU. The US's primary interest in South Asia has been security-centric, being either busy in an India–Pakistan balancing game or scrutinising the maritime developments in the Indian Ocean vis-à-vis its juxtaposition to South Asia. Throughout Asia, the sole American preoccupation has been to obstruct Chinese progress. For perspective, it may be noted that in 2000 President Bill Clinton merely saw South Asia as 'the most dangerous place in the world today' (*BBC News* 2000). Japan has reached out to South Asia as an economic power, investing in India and in some other SAARC members, but Japan's domestic political uncertainty, coupled with Prime Minister Shinzo Abe's recent advocacy of a stridently nationalist policy, has not generally induced SAARC countries to view Tokyo as a burly anchor in Asia.

The *second* reason why South Asia attaches great value to its relationship with China is the importance that South Asia has always had in the Chinese foreign policy construct. A decade ago, neither was South Asia attractive as a region to draw the Chinese priority attention nor was the Chinese economy strong enough to offer investments, but that did not discourage Beijing from emphasising its South Asian outreach. China could not also afford to relax its thrust on South Asia, principally because its biggest enemy, the Dalai Lama, was housed in India. Matters like the Tibetan refugees, India–China boundary and energy resources in South Asia did not allow China to look away from this region. The Western Development Strategy also helped Beijing keep a vigilant eye on Tibet and the adjacent regions of Pakistan and India. India missed the vision to position South Asia on the same pedestal as China did, even though it always had an opportunity to lead the South Asian politics as a regional power. India focused mainly on South-East Asia in the last decade, enunciating a modest Look East policy.

Should India prepare to accept China as a permanent SAARC member in times to come? China leads the Asian power politics, no matter how much the US 'pivot' Asia policy tries to limit its outreach. Ironically, Beijing is balancing the American reach in Asia, leading regional politics with a number of arrangements like the Asian Infrastructure Investment Bank (AIIB), SREB and MSR. In its conflict with Japan on the East China Sea, China holds the strategic edge through joint maritime exercises with Russia to counter any possible joint eventuality from Japan and the US. Further playing to China's advantage is the current recession in Japan, with the Japanese business and industrial lobbies advocating closer engagement with the Chinese economy. Similarly, in the South China Sea dispute, no matter how much Vietnam and other South-East Asian powers grumble, China's economic supremacy outmanoeuvres them, particularly when China and ASEAN members along with dialogue partners are engaged in RCEP (Regional Comprehensive Economic Partnership) negotiations.

After the Kathmandu summit, China is likely to emerge as 'lead dialogue partner' with SAARC. In the circumstances, India needs to follow, at least in the short term, a prudent middle path for a more constructive engagement between China and SAARC. Can something be retrieved from this situation? To welcome China as a SAARC member, India could play for its own stakes: (i) a more structured engagement in Central Asia through the SCO; (ii) asking Beijing to publicly declare its position on the India–China boundary dispute, mainly in terms of officially retracting its claim on Tawang or Arunachal Pradesh. Also, India must wait and observe how the India–China boundary negotiations progress in the Modi–Xi regimes, which holds the key to most of the two countries' bilateral and regional problems. In the alternative, India can block China's formal entry into SAARC.

Notes

1 Chinese analysts argue that South Asia should be a key region for China's energy needs and strategic interests. See, for example, Zhao Minghao 2014.
2 This section draws heavily on Panda 2010.
3 China was accorded observer status along with Japan in SAARC at the 13th Dhaka SAARC summit in 2005. At this summit, Afghanistan was welcomed as a full-fledged new member.
4 For a detailed analysis of China–SAARC relations, see Panda 2010.
5 Author's discussions with several Chinese experts at CICIR and CIIS in Beijing, and SIIS in Shanghai on various occasions.
6 This section draws mainly on Panda 2012.

References

BBC News, 2000. 'Analysis: Clinton's disappointments in South Asia', *BBC News*, 26 March, http://news.bbc.co.uk/2/hi/south_asia/691339.stm (accessed on 24 November 2014).
BBC News India, 2014. 'Can India's Modi integrate South Asia?', *BBC News India*, 29 May, www.bbc.com/news/world-asia-india-27572992 (accessed on 2 October 2014).
Celestine, Avinash, 2014. 'Will a PTA really give the boost needed for India–Nepal hydropower trade?', *Economic Times*, 10 August, http://articles.economictimes.indiatimes.com/2014-08-10/news/52648198_1_pta-hydropower-power-exchange (accessed on 28 October 2014).
Chen Qi and Guan Chuanjing, 2014. 'New vitality in peripheral diplomacy', *China Daily* (Asia Weekly), 26 September–2 October.
China Daily, 2006. 'China, Pakistan to enhance strategic partnership', *China Daily*, 24 November, www.chinadaily.com.cn/china/2006-11/24/content_742389.htm (accessed on 24 October 2014).

China Military Online, 2014. 'PLA Navy submarine visits Sri Lanka', *China Military Online*, 24 September, http://eng.chinamil.com.cn/news-channels/china-military-news/2014-09/24/content_6152669.htm (accessed on 20 November 2014).

china-un.org, 2009. 'Foreign Ministry Spokesperson Ma Zhaoxu's regular Press Conference, November 3, 2009', Permanent Mission of the People's Republic of China to the UN, 4 November, www.china-un.org/eng/fyrth/t624696.htm (accessed on 10 October 2014).

Daily News Analysis, 2014. 'Ties with China "very close", "far more precious" with India: Maldives President', *Daily News Analysis*, 5 January, www.dnaindia.com/world/report-ties-with-china-very-close-far-more-precious-with-india-maldives-president-1945682 (accessed on 13 November 2014).

Dittmer, Lowell, 2008. 'China's new internationalism', in Guoguang Wu and Helen Lansdowne (eds), *China Turns to Multilateralism: Foreign Policy and Regional Security*, London: Routledge, pp. 21–34.

Du Youkang, 2002. 'South Asian security situation and its impacts on China', *Contemporary World Configuration*, Shanghai: SIIS.

EXIMIUS: Export Advantage, 2013. 'India's engagement in SAARC', *EXIMIUS: Export Advantage*, Exim Bank, XXVII(II), June.

fmprc.gov.cn, 2014. 'Xi Jinping arrives in Male, starting his state visit to Maldives', Ministry of Foreign Affairs of the People's Republic of China, 15 September, www.fmprc.gov.cn/mfa_eng/zxxx_662805/t1191505.shtml (accessed on 13 November 2014).

Garver, John W., 2001a. 'The Sino Pakistan entente cordiale', in *Protracted Contest: Sino Indian Rivalry in the Twentieth Century*, Seattle: University of Washington Press, pp. 187–215.

Garver, John W., 2001b. 'Managing the contradiction between maintaining the Sino-Pakistani entente and furthering Sino-Indian rapprochement', in *Protracted Contest: Sino Indian Rivalry in the Twentieth Century*, Seattle: University of Washington Press, pp. 216–42.

Goodman, Jack, 2014. 'Sri Lanka's growing links with China', *The Diplomat*, 6 March, http://thediplomat.com/2014/03/sri-lankas-growing-links-with-china/ (accessed on 19 November 2014).

Hindustan Times, 2010. 'India watches shift in China's Kashmir policy with concern', *Hindustan Times*, 13 October, www.hindustantimes.com/StoryPage/Print/61252.aspx?s=p (accessed on 13 October 2014).

Ho, Selina, 2014. 'China's shifting perceptions of India: the context of Xi Jinping's visit to India', *Asia Pacific Bulletin*, East West Centre, No. 279, 2 October, pp. 1–2.

in.chineseembassy.org, 2007. 'Remarks by Foreign Minister Li Zhaoxing at the Opening Ceremony of the Fourteenth SAARC Summit, April 3, 2007', Embassy of the People's Republic of China in India, http://in.chineseembassy.org/eng/ssygd/zygx/zysj/t308596.htm (accessed on 3 October 2014).

Jayasekera, Deepal, 2014. 'Chinese President visits Sri Lanka to strengthen strategic ties', *World Socialist Web Site*, 20 September, www.wsws.org/en/articles/2014/09/20/jings20.html (accessed on 19 November 2014).

Lan Jianxue, 2014. 'Developments in South Asia in 2013: accelerated transformation and overlaying risks' (Chapter 9), *The CIIS Blue Book on International Situation and China's Foreign Affairs*, CIIS, World Affairs Press.

Li Zhang, 2009. 'To manage conflict in South Asia: China's stakes, perceptions and inputs', *Asia Paper*, Institute for Security and Development Policy, October, pp. 6–15.

Liu Zhenmin, 2014. 'Insisting on win win cooperation and forging the Asian community of common destiny together', *China International Studies*, vol. 45, March/April, pp. 5–25.

MEA, 2013. 'Joint Statement on the State Visit of Chinese Premier Li Keqiang to India', Ministry of External Affairs, Government of India, 20 May, http://mea.gov.in/bilateral-documents.htm?dtl/21723/Joint+Statement+on+the+State+Visit+of+Chinese++Li+Ke qiang+to+India (accessed on 27 October 2014).

MEA, 2014a. 'Statement by External Affairs Minister at SAARC Foreign Ministers' Meeting held in Maldives', Ministry of External Affairs, Government of India, Male, 20 February, www.mea.gov.in/bilateral-documents.htm?dtl/22962/Statement+by+Exte rnal+Affairs+Minister+at+SAARC+Foreign+Ministers+Meeting+held+in+Maldives (accessed on 5 October 2014).

MEA, 2014b. 'Joint Statement between the Republic of India and the People's Republic of China on building a closer developmental partnership', 19 September, Ministry of External Affairs, Government of India.

mea.gov.in, 2007. 'India–Bhutan Friendship Treaty, February 2007, Thimphu, March 2, 2007', http://mea.gov.in/Images/pdf/india-bhutan-treaty-07.pdf (accessed on 6 October 2014).

Miller, J. Berkshire, 2014. 'China making a play at Bangladesh?', *Forbes*, 3 January, www.forbes.com/sites/jonathanmiller/2014/01/03/china-making-a-play-at-bangladesh/ (accessed on 1 November 2014).

Moore, Malcolm, 2014. 'China to extend railways to borders with India and Nepal', *Telegraph*, 24 July, www.telegraph.co.uk/news/worldnews/asia/tibet/10988714/China-to-extend-railways-to-borders-with-India-and-Nepal.html (accessed on 13 November 2014).

Mu Chunshan, 2014. 'China's choice: India or Pakistan?', *The Diplomat*, 27 September, http://thediplomat.com/2014/09/chinas-choice-india-or-pakistan/ (accessed on 6 October 2014).

Panda, Jagannath P., 2010. 'The Urumqi crisis: effect of China's ethno-national politics', *Strategic Analysis*, 34(1), January, pp. 9–13.

Panda, Jagannath P., 2012. 'Bhutan eyes China, but bond with India remains stronger', *Global Times*, 17 September, www.globaltimes.cn/content/733673.shtml (accessed on 6 October 2014).

Pantucci, Raffaello, 2014. 'Afghanistan a building block for China–India ties', *Reuters*, 30 July, http://blogs.reuters.com/archive/tag/afghanistan/ (accessed on 27 October 2014).

Patel, Dharmesh, 2013. 'The entangled triangle of Nepal, India and China', *Culture Mandala: Bulletin of the Centre for East-West Cultural and Economic Studies*, vol. 10, October–December, pp. 41–4.

peacemaker.un.org, 1987. 'India–Lanka Accord, July 29, 1987, Colombo', http://peacemaker.un.org/sites/peacemaker.un.org/files/IN%20LK_870729_Indo-Lanka%20 Accord.pdf (accessed on 20 November 2014).

People's Daily, 2006. 'China, Pakistan sign treaty of friendship, cooperation and good-neighbourly relations', *People's Daily*, 6 April, http://english.peopledaily.com.cn/200504/06/eng20050406_179629.html (accessed on 24 October 2014).

pib.nic.in, 2014. 'Bilateral issues with China', Press Information Bureau, Government of India, 16 July, http://pib.nic.in/newsite/PrintRelease.aspx?=106775 (accessed on 24 October 2014).

Qi Huaigao, 2009. 'Multilateral cooperation and bilateral alliance', *Contemporary International Relations*, 19(3), May–June, pp. 114–32.

Raja Mohan, C., 2010. 'Welcoming China into SAARC', *Khaleej Times*, 19 April, www. khaleejtimes.com/DisplayArticle09.asp?xfile=data/opinion/2010/April/opinion_April 169.xml&section=opinion (accessed on 4 October 2014).

Ramachandran, Shastri, 2014. 'China in SAARC: time to weigh the pros and cons', *DNA India*, 24 February, www.dnaindia.com/analysis/column-china-in-saarc-time-to-weigh-the-pros-and-cons-1964516 (accessed on 5 October 2014).

Ruan Zongze, 2014. 'What kind of neighbourhood will China build?', *China International Studies*, vol. 45, March/April, pp. 26–50.

Rupasinghe, Wasantha, 2014. 'India criticises Chinese submarine visits to Colombo', *World Socialist Web Site*, 10 November, www.wsws.org/en/articles/2014/11/10/slch-n10.html (accessed on 20 November 2014).

saarc-sec.org, 1985. 'SAARC Charter', 8 December, http://saarc-sec.org/saarc-charter/5/ (accessed on 6 October 2014).

Saez, Lawrence and Crystal Chang, 2010. 'China and South Asia: strategic implications and economic imperatives', in Lowell Dittmer and George T. Yu (eds), *China, the Developing World, and the New Global Dynamics*, Boulder, CO: Lynne Rienner.

Schwarck, Edward, 2014. 'Can China and India cooperate in Afghanistan?', *The Diplomat*, 1 October, http://thediplomat.com/2014/10/can-china-and-india-cooperate-in-afghanistan/ (accessed on 27 October 2014).

Shen Jie, 2014. 'China, Bangladesh pledge joint efforts to build economic corridor', *CCTV.com English*, 10 June, http://english.cntv.cn/2014/06/11/ARTI1402442898062762.shtml (accessed on 1 November 2014).

Smith, Jeff M., 2014. 'Sweeter than honey: Pakistan in Sino-Indian relations', *Cold Peace: China India Rivalry in the Twenty First Century*, Boulder, CO: Lexington Books, pp. 129–42.

Stobdan, P., 2013. 'India and China: exploring partnership in Afghanistan', *IDSA Policy Brief*, 3 December, pp. 1–4.

Wang Xin and Zhang Qian, 2013. 'Xi Jinping: China to further friendly relations with neighbouring countries', *People's Daily*, 23 October, http://english.peopledaily.com.cn/90883/8437410.html (accessed on 2 October 2014).

Wang Yi, 2014. 'Peaceful development and the Chinese dream of national rejuvenation', *China International Studies*, vol. 44, January/February, pp. 1–44.

Wu Guoguang and Helen Lansdowne, 2008. 'International multilateralism with Chinese characteristics: attitude changes, policy imperatives, and regional impacts', in Guoguang Wu and Helen Lansdowne (eds), *China Turns to Multilateralism: Foreign Policy and Regional Security*, London: Routledge, pp. 3–18.

Wu Qiang, 2014. 'India showcases stronger regional diplomacy at Modi swearing in ceremony', *Sina English*, 26 May, http://english.sina.com/world/2014/0526/703764.html (accessed on 2 October 2014).

Yang Jiechi, 2014. 'China's new foreign relations for a complex world', *China International Studies*, vol. 44, January/February, pp. 5–17.

Yung, Chester, 2014. 'Chinese firms to invest in $601 million Sri Lanka port project', *Wall Street Journal*, 17 September, http://blogs.wsj.com/frontiers/2014/09/17/chinese-firms-to-invest-in-601-million-sri-lanka-port-project/ (accessed on 20 November 2014).

Zhao Minghao, 2014. 'China understands South Asia's needs better', *Global Times*, 16 September, www.globaltimes.cn/content/881774.shtml (accessed on 22 October 2014).

9 The SCO and the competing Central Asian presence

Regional politics and regional order find themselves in a paradoxical juxtaposition today, against the political announcement of expansion of the Shanghai Cooperation Organisation (SCO) membership, which took place at the 15th SCO leadership summit in Ufa, Russia, in July 2015. This summit was a landmark event for a number of regional and global advances. It took place in Ufa at a time when Russia's relations with the West are still on a difficult track, the Chinese have launched their ambitious Silk Road Economic Belt (SREB) under the OBOR, and the formal launch of BRICS's New Development Bank (NDB) and the Chinese-led Asian Infrastructure Investment Bank (AIIB) which have been introduced. The SCO summit in the Ufa was concurrently hosted with the BRICS summit and simultaneously, the announcement was made of SCO membership expansion. India partook in the Ufa summit as a BRICS member and prospective member of the SCO. India's Prime Minister Narendra Modi, while partaking in the BRICS and SCO summits, also met the leaders of the Central Asian Republics (CARs).

The question arises in this context: Will its inclusion in SCO as a full member allow India to emerge as a greater power in the Central Asian region and change the balance of power there? To what extent will China, as the predominant power in the SCO, accommodate India's presence? This chapter argues that post-Ufa, a 'soft balancing' is taking place between India and China, where Russia as well as the region of Central Asia are significant factors in their relationship discourse.[1]

Ufa summit: spurring the SCO ahead

Crafting a ten-year long strategy for 2015–2025, the Ufa summit ratified a comprehensive programme for the progress of SCO (*Asia Times* 2015; Chen Yue 2015). As part of the programme, an official accession procedure was commenced for India and Pakistan to become full-fledged SCO members in the next two or three years. Also, the status of Belarus was upgraded from a dialogue partner to an observer, and Azerbaijan, Armenia, Cambodia and Nepal were included as new dialogue partners (ibid.). The membership expansion extends the SCO's horizon from Central Asia to South Asia; and with India's inclusion, the SCO is no longer Sino-Russian centric.[2] India's potential membership was being backed by Russia for several years, and Pakistan's by China.

Unlike in the South-East Asian and South Asian regions, India–China dynamism in Central Asia has not amounted to direct power contestation. China is a 'local immediate' and predominant power in the region; India is an outsider reaching out to the region through an 'extended neighbourhood' policy. China has basked for 15 years in the achievement of having promoted the SCO. But can the SCO become a better foreign-policy instrument for China, even including India, its strategic competitor, as a member? To Beijing, expanding the SCO beyond Central Asia amounts to cobbling together a constituency for its own influence and to restrict the reach of the United States.[3]

India's 'connect Central Asia' outlook post-Ufa

Morgenthau and Thompson maintain that

> the aspirations for power of individual nations can come into conflict with each other – and some, if not most of them, do at any particular moment in history – in two different ways ... the *pattern of direct opposition* and the *pattern of competition*.
>
> (Morgenthau and Thompson 1985: 192, emphasis added)

To make the best of this competition-conflict portent, a State has to rely on its own diplomacy and power factors, the relative competence of which must be its invariable concern.

Central Asia, a treasure trove of oil and energy resources, has for long been the prime focus of 'great game' politics. Local powers like Russia and China are concerned primarily with resisting the global supremacy of the US and its regional presence. The US's 'pivot' Asia policy has made the two countries rethink their strategy that will be conducive to both. India, under its new government led by Prime Minister Narendra Modi, is in the process of redrafting its strategic interests in the region. New Delhi's newfound orientation towards the region is summed up in the slogan 'Connect Central Asia' (*mea.gov.in* 2012). The purpose is to expand a comprehensive linkage combining political, economic, security and cultural connections with the region (ibid.).

New Delhi's policy approach towards this region is a Central Asia plus South Asia construct. It consequently outlines a 'cooperative approach' where Afghanistan is contemplated as a trade and energy centre and acting as a connecting point between Central Asia and South Asia (ibid.). The Turkmenistan–Afghanistan–Pakistan–India (TAPI) pipeline that India promotes is a reference of that. India's approach of reactivating the International North–South Transport Corridor (INSTC) is another illustration of how India wants to connect with the region physically (ibid.). Connectivity, energy exploration, sharing security concerns on terrorism and establishing political presence are some of the factors that shape India's Central Asia policy.

Post-Ufa summit, the SCO bids fair to emerge as one of the most significant bodies in the Eurasian region. Following the *Joint Statement* between Xi Jinping and Vladimir Putin in May 2015, there also seems to be better convergence between China's SREB and Russia's Eurasia Economic Union (Tian Shaohui 2015). This convergence is noticeable in areas like local-currency settlement in bilateral trade, financial cooperation through the Silk Road Fund (SRF) and AIIB (ibid.). The greater Sino-Russian purpose here is to establish an economic understanding that will be equivalent to the Asia-Pacific economic and security undertaking, which has been the key of the US's 'pivot' Asia strategy (Stobdan 2015a).

For India, the greater challenge is how to participate intently in a Sino-Russian regional design while advancing its own strategic interest without abandoning its partnership with the US and without necessarily pursuing a 'China containment' strategy in Eurasia. The bigger test for India is how to integrate and accept the SCO's future undertaking where 'connectivity' is one of the most important aspects. India has maintained 'strategic silence' over the SREB and has opposed the China–Pakistan Economic Corridor (CPEC) that is planned through Pakistan-Occupied Kashmir (POK). Can India realistically oppose the SCO undertakings involving these connectivity issues where Pakistan is also joining the SCO as a member? Terrorism also may well emerge as a matter where India may have difficulty in generating a consensus within SCO. Given the stronger China–Pakistan understanding on security affairs, India will face an uphill task in discussing terrorism, ISIS and Afghanistan within SCO. China's blocking of India's attempt to seek action against Pakistan on the release of LeT (Lashkar-e-Toiyaba) commander Zaki-ur-Rehman Lakhvi for his role in the Mumbai terrorist attack in 2008 is a case in point. The Sino-Russian chemistry and Sino-Pakistani bonhomie is certainly a matter that India will have to reckon with both within and outside the SCO.

Intriguingly, among the important group of actors in the Central Asian region – Russia, the US, China, Iran and the European Union (EU) – India's commonality is with China (see Bhadrakumar 2009). The Chinese design in Central Asia to explore energy resources has encouraged India to initiate a similar strategy (Bhadrakumar 2009). As the local immediate power in the region, China has managed to outmanoeuvre India on many energy-related deals. India's core aim in this region has been how to push TAPI and Iran–Pakistan–India (IPI) pipelines. China has lately shown an interest in IPI, whereas despite India's push, TAPI remains somnolent. Consensus over the routes, price of the gas and securitising the pipelines remain stumbling blocks to progress in the matter. The 20th steering committee meeting of TAPI failed to select a consortium leader in February 2015, which implies that India is finding it difficult to implement this project (Tanchum 2015).

Given India's geographical distance from Central Asia, connectivity is an issue between India and the region. Land route connectivity through China, reviving the traditional Ladakh–Xinjiang route is an option (Stobdan 2015b), but may not be feasible given India's reservation about China's SREB. India did share traditionally a greater bonding with Eurasia through the Silk and Spice trade routes. The time seems to have arrived to consider enlivening these traditional modes of connectivity and try to identify if India can have a greater understanding with China with regard to Central Asia and SCO.

The source of the pre-eminence of geopolitics in Central Asia is primarily twofold: the continuous arrival of outside powers to the region; and the existence of balance of power there, especially among its constituent countries (Vlad *et al.* 2010: 116; see also Panda 2011: 111). Taking note of these phenomena, India for its part is in the process of not only redrafting its newfound influence to spread and defend its strategic interests in Central Asia but to advocate a broader regional institutional order. China would certainly appreciate the Indian perspective of a SCO-led order; yet to what extent Beijing will welcome India's greater role in Central Asia needs to be seen.

Beijing's pragmatism, SCO and India

The SCO is a shining example of China's identification with multilateralism and its brilliant ascent in this sphere. Established in 2001, the SCO became the first regional multilateral organisation of the current century, and also the first multilateral security organisation (Yu Jianhua 2003). China's pre-eminence in SCO is indicated by the fact that the organisation is named after the Chinese city of Shanghai, that the first SCO Secretary-General was Chinese, and that the SCO secretariat is located in Beijing. In the course of one and a half decades since its inception, China has pushed the SCO as one of the most vital organisations and tried to instil 'Asian-ness' into this body (Panda 2012a).

At the same time, there is an alternative view regarding the SCO. Often seen as an anti-Western and anti-NATO alliance, SCO's constant growth is seen by many as being conducive to China's rise and partaking in a new world order, whereas others believe that the SCO must expand to emerge as a strong Eurasian body to stabilise the greater international balance of power (Kumar 2011). It is further argued that the SCO has emerged definitely as a 'delicate equilibrium through a cooperative framework among the participants in the post-bipolar structure' (Stobdan 2009: 219). It is also disparagingly argued that there is a lack of trust among SCO members and it

> is also an old-style organisation, an attempt at a bloc or a counter-bloc, to help protect the encroachment of other blocs (or states) on geopolitical and domestic interests of the members, as well as a forum for regulating shared security concerns.
>
> (Olcott 2008: 249)

The fact nevertheless remains that the SCO has remained one of those regional organisations where the United States and its allies have hardly any influence (Kumar 2011). The SCO has probably arrived as an alternative multilateral architecture to address most of the security problems in the greater Eurasia region (Stobdan 2009: 219).

Beijing's perspective on SCO expansion may be explained in terms of realism and idealism in the international relations theory. In the realist discourse, survival is the main goal of a nation-state in an anarchic and perilous world (Dittmer 2008). Security has so far been the main ingredient of China's interest in the SCO, and economic security (*jingjianquan*) is going to guide its policy towards it in the future. On the other hand, the liberalist discourse, more often considered as 'neo-liberal institutionalism', talks about trade, investment and social and cultural engagements to identify mutual motives and divert any possible conflict (ibid.). Beijing seems to follow this course in its link with Central Asia. The SREB is an illustration of this.

Over the years, China's multilateral approach to the SCO has facilitated it to construct various cultural, economic, political and security ties with the Central Asian countries (Pan Guang 2007: 45). To prevent the emergence of an anti-China alliance in the region, Beijing originally wanted a well-knit organisation that would emphasise economic cooperation. China supported Mongolia's membership as an observer in 2004, and was open to the inclusion of Iran, Pakistan and India, all of which joined later.[4] Afterward, the PRC's clout within the organisation increased when the SCO adopted RATS (Regional Anti-Terrorist Structure) and formed a Business Council and Inter-bank SCO Council. Beijing has supported the inclusion of SCO members, mainly Russia, in the World Trade Organisation (WTO). It has also sought to establish free trade agreements (FTAs) among SCO members and regional transportation networks (Paramonov 2010). However, in the current Chinese perspective, Beijing visualises that SCO expansion will actually be beneficial to it and help construct a greater 'Eurasian' policy, which combines Central Asia with South Asia (see Map 9.1).

From the outset, China was not entirely adverse to the idea of expanding SCO. Though hesitantly, China did see merit in expanding the SCO to South Asia. But Beijing was worried over two aspects where India's membership in the SCO was concerned: (i) how India's inclusion would change the balance-of-power politics in SCO, where a stronger India–Russia rapport might subdue China's influence; and (ii) India's inclusion in SCO might eventually augment New Delhi's regional standing and India might ultimately emerge as a stronger power in Central Asia (Panda 2012a: 508). Chinese experts' writings have always suggested that China sought to persuade more powers from greater Asian regions to be with it in checking the US influence in Asian strategic affairs (Yan Wei 2008; Ma Zhengang 2010).

The everlasting well-known complexities in India–China relations may offer an impression that Beijing was quite conservative in its approach to supporting India's candidature because of their rivalry. But the recent maturity in the India–China discourse has indicated strongly that China would take a pragmatic call on India's inclusion in SCO as a full member. This Chinese standpoint needs to be further located within its dialogue on globalisation (*quanqiuhua*) and multi-polarisation (*duojihua*), where the central concerns are power relations and the global structure that features 'one superpower and several great powers' (*yichao duoqiang*) (Xu Xin 2009). Despite seeing India as a pro-US country in the region

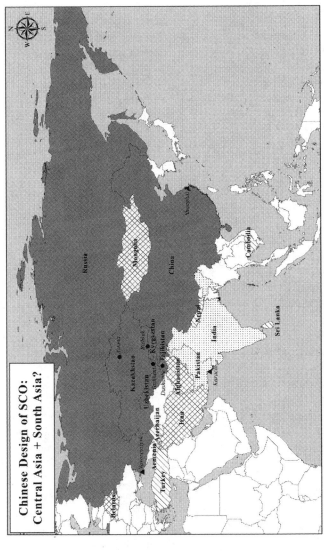

Map 9.1 Chinese design of SCO: Central Asia + South Asia? (source: GIS Lab, IDSA).

in strategic matters, the Chinese have been open in associating with India in multilateral mechanisms at regional and global spheres. Regional multilateral ties give China a political opportunity to work with India to counter the US unilateralism. The RIC (Russia–India–China) forum, for instance, is said to be the result of the post-Cold War international system under which the United States is the sole superpower and holds absolute superiority in the global power structure (Zhao Gancheng 2009: 128). Consequently, strategic compulsions dictate the need for multilateral cooperation among the RIC countries, according to Chinese sources. Their conviction is that the United States still wants to 'prevent the rise of other large developing countries ... what it opposes is that the emerging countries represented by China, Russia and India may conceivably challenge its hegemony' (ibid.). Thus, the consensus among Chinese scholars appears to be that the scope for RIC institutional engagement at a broader level has widened (ibid.; Rong Ying 2009), and it must be further enhanced. China's aim to have cooperation in some areas is not genuinely to offer India greater space in Central Asia, but rather to contain India's presence through multilateral contacts and cooperative participation.

An emerging course between cooperation and containment?

India's inclusion in the post-Ufa SCO prompts a new wave of opportunities for India and China at the regional level of Central Asia. The scope of these opportunities is limited, being placed between cooperative measures and containment strategies. A case-by-case analysis of opportunities that the SCO and Central Asia offer for India and China indicates that. Four different issues invite deliberation between the two countries in the post-Ufa Central Asia, namely, security, Afghanistan, connectivity and regional order.

Security

The Shanghai Five, from which the SCO has evolved, was initially planned as a bilateral mechanism between China and Russia, with the three Central Asian countries on the sidelines. The Shanghai grouping was basically intended to promote security confidence building, whereas its offspring, the SCO, has increasingly moved into the economic domain. In the Chinese perception, the SCO has made progress in three areas: establishing laws and regulations in the security field; institutionalising cooperative mechanisms; and steering joint military exercises (Liu Wanyun 2011). The principal thinking in the Chinese military, however, is not to develop the SCO as a counter to NATO (Guo and Lv 2010), but to use it as a platform for security and military purposes. The joint military exercises that China has been conducting with Russia under the 'Peace Mission' exercises all these years, and other law enforcement exercises complement China's long-time effort to counter the security risks it faces from the Uyghurs in Xinjiang and stabilise matters within and around the Xinjiang Uyghur Autonomous Region (XUAR).

Significantly, the Chinese have carried out joint military exercises in the last few years, though on different scales, with both Pakistan and India. India needs to study this aspect carefully and see whether a realistic scenario of cooperation exists for it with China on the issue of terrorism and carry this exercise under the SCO. Given the security risk China faces in the Xinjiang–Central Asian region, the Chinese would ideally like to expand the ambit of these exercises; to what extent India can cooperate in them needs to be seen. To begin with, India may find it difficult to involve itself in any SCO exercises on counterterrorism, given the differences that exist between India and Pakistan.

The withdrawal of Western troops from Afghanistan in 2014 has also raised Chinese anxieties with regard to peace and stability in the greater Central Asian region. The 12th SCO Prime Ministers meeting, held during 28–29 November 2013 in Tashkent, Uzbekistan, discussed this concern. The Chinese participants stressed the importance of countering terrorism through SCO mechanisms and robust bilateral measures in the region, and expressed specific concern regarding the 'East Turkistan Islamic Movement' (ETIM) and Xinjiang Uyghurs (Mo and Zhao 2013). China will undoubtedly try to make sure that the SCO addresses its security concerns. But can a broader understanding evolve on terrorism, particularly among India, China and Pakistan? Given the differing perspectives they have on the issue of terrorism, it is most unlikely that these three countries will develop a common understanding on terrorism.

Afghanistan

In Afghanistan, most powers' strategic interests converge, whether of China, the United States or India. It is to create and maintain stability so that Afghanistan's metal and mineral reserves can be extracted. The SCO and China have shown great interest in Afghanistan recently in this matter. As stated in the Ufa SCO summit, the SCO is looking for greater engagement in Afghanistan (*Sputnik* 2015). Can India and China cooperate under the premise of SCO on Afghanistan? Chinese experts have long contended that to attain shared interests, the regional players must have a shared security vision to deal with the changing geopolitical situation in Central Asia and South Asia (Rong Ying 2009). India is a factor in this 'shared security vision'. India and China have bilaterally discussed issues – but only at the talking-shop level – regarding Afghanistan such as terrorism, national construction in that country, shared connectivity with Afghanistan, etc.

But what is the Chinese rationale for possible cooperation with India in the ambit of South Asia? Primarily, Beijing does not see South Asia and Afghanistan in isolation from the SCO perspective. In fact, an immediate factor that has urged the Chinese to expand both the mandate and membership of the SCO is the current status and future of Afghanistan in the regional context (Ma Zhengang 2010). Chinese experts have tried to establish strategic linkages between Afghanistan, RIC and SCO. Advocating three Cs (*consensus* on policy dialogue, *coordination* in Eurasia and *connectivity* among regional states), Chinese strategists have argued that the RIC's interactions and involvement in Afghanistan make political and pragmatic sense if it closely coordinates with and is incorporated into the SCO framework (Rong Ying 2009).

What makes Afghanistan regionally important for China is that Afghanistan is a member of SAARC and shares stable relations with India. Afghanistan–India relations have strengthened in the recent past. Beijing does see India as a partner, but not a collaborator. This partnership is limited to security concerns over terrorism. China believes that tying up with India as regards Afghanistan helps it not only to reach the country regionally but also bind it in various modes for China's own benefit. In the post-US troops withdrawal phase, China has emerged as a key player in Afghanistan with greater economic and energy interests, without ignoring the security concerns. Therefore, it is anticipated that India and China may have a shared understanding on Afghanistan within SCO; but this understanding will mainly be China-driven and will not be feasible for India for practical cooperation.

Connecting Central Asia

After Prime Minister Modi's visit to Central Asia in July 2015, India has placed connectivity as a top priority of its Central Asia policy outlook. There is no doubt that India will face a test from China's greater Eurasian reach where the bordering South Asian countries are taken seriously along with Central Asia and Russia. Given India's reluctance to support China's SREB, there will be new dynamics emerging between the two countries in the region.

For several years now, China has prioritised Central Asia and Russia in its foreign policy agenda. Russia was the first country Xi Jinping visited after taking over as President in March 2013. In September 2013, he travelled to Turkmenistan, Kazakhstan, Uzbekistan and Kyrgyzstan when he attended the G-20 summit at St Petersburg in Russia and the SCO summit at Bishkek in Kyrgyzstan. This tour by the Chinese President witnessed multi-layered engagements at various political, diplomatic and economic levels, as well as security and military-to-military understanding. Beijing pushed several mega trades as well as economic proposals in the region, with thrust on enhancing energy cooperation. The current and future aspects of the China–Central Asian engagement were outlined in Xi Jinping's speech on 'China's Central Asia Strategy' at the Nazarbayev University in Astana, Kazakhstan. Xi proposed the establishment of an 'economic belt along the Silk Road' between China and the Central Asian region as a joint construction initiative, a 'trans-Eurasian project spanning from the Pacific Ocean to the Baltic Sea' that would benefit about three billion people in the region (Wu and Zhang 2013). The success of this proposal would depend upon the extent to which both sides enhanced cooperation in areas of connectivity, communication, trade in local currencies and greater monetary cooperation (ibid.). Therefore, the challenge for India would be how to maximise its strategic interests, given China's supreme reach towards Central Asia.

A post-Ufa triangular order in the making?

New Delhi's inclusion in the SCO is supposed to coagulate India's relations with China and Russia. A triangular mechanism already exists among the three immediate neighbours in the form of the RIC. RIC meets often to discuss common issues of concern. However, RIC is basically a soft network that lacks the strength to forge any concrete understanding among the partners on key global issues (Panda 2015). Both the Ufa SCO and the BRICS summits offered an occasion for these three countries to rethink about the scope of the RIC mechanism in terms of strengthening the triangularity. The emphasis of this triangularity must not only be on how to increase the space and influence of the three neighbouring countries, but on how to reduce the dominance of the Western powers in global financial decision-making.

The RIC is not security or military-centric. It is 'power' centric, combining posture and political perspective at a time when there is a need for South–South formulation to excel in global politics and to unite for reforming the global institutions (Panda 2012b). The vitality of RIC as a possible scope for a triangular order is understood against three constructive realities: (i) the rise of BRICS; (ii) expansion of SCO membership; and (iii) the American 'pivot' to Asia. Neither the rise of BRICS nor the possible expansion of SCO membership has really reduced the influence and vitality of RIC. Rather, there are fresh contours that need to be understood within the current context of Asian power politics, which further enhances the importance of the RIC. The rise of BRICS has adequately indicated that the three mainstream powers of the RIC are the centre of the South–South politics and North–South divide. RIC members are the leading figures not only for cross-continental developing countries but also for the construction of the unity of the social underpinnings of developing societies, for whom unity among themselves is an essential requisite.

Individually, all the three RIC countries have problematic financial concerns with the Western world. Russia is currently searching for suitable mediums and trying to overcome the financial burden that has arisen out of the Western pressure from the Ukraine crisis. India along with China is trying hard to increase its voting rights in global financial institutions. India may have a greater parallel understanding with the US on global security and strategic matters, but finds it difficult to raise its presence and influence at the IMF, the World Bank and Asian Development Bank (ADB). This may propel a new triangular order among the RIC countries. But it is also hard to have this triangular order, given the three countries' differing foreign policy perspectives and objectives. Russia and China have improved their mutual understanding in the recent past. Even though mistrust still exists between the two, a new chemistry of power sharing seems to be evolving between them on weakening the American 'pivot' to Asia.

Meanwhile, India–China relations are marked by a range of conflict, cooperation and competition elements. A greater India–China understanding for a regional order is a common forte that must bring these two countries together. Likewise, India–Russia ties must be upgraded from their usual standing of being pleasant to each other. Given the traditional bonding and depth of India and the Soviet World, relations with Russia must merit the first choice for India. Russia on its part need to accept India on a pragmatic note that, even though India has a strategic understanding with the US, it is purely based on India's national interest, and not intended against Russia. More than these labels of relationships, the most important determinants are the Indian and Chinese mutual perceptions of each other in the compass of Russia. China still believes that the current India–Russia relations are not favourable to itself. It should be expected that a common and equal sharing platform under the SCO between these three countries in coming times will become an exciting aspect of regional politics.

Notes

1 Some portions of this chapter have appeared earlier, as arguments or write-ups. See for example, Panda 2009, 2010, 2012a, 2011.
2 Quoted media views of Alexander Lukin, an expert from Russia. See Strokan and Mikheev 2015.
3 This part of the chapter has been published as Panda 2012a.
4 The request of Belarus for observer membership in the SCO was declined in 2006 on the ground that it was a non-Asian country. However, in June 2009, Belarus was granted dialogue partner status. See Paramonov 2010: 74–5.

References

Asia Times, 2015. 'SCO adopts 10-year plan, admits India, Pakistan', *Asia Times*, 10 July, http://atimes.com/2015/07/sco-adopts-10-year-plan-admits-india-pakistan/ (accessed on 16 August 2015).

Bhadrakumar, M.K., 2009. 'India plays catch-up in the great game', *Asia Times*, 18 July, www.atimes.com/atimes/South_Asia/KG18Df04.html (accessed on 20 August 2015).

Chen Yue, 2015. 'SCO begins expansion with ratification of 10-year development strategy', *CCTV English*, 11 July, http://english.cntv.cn/2015/07/11/ARTI1436580705823658.shtml (accessed on 16 August 2015).

Dittmer, Lowell, 2008. 'China's new internationalism', in Guoguang Wu and Helen Lansdowne (eds), *China Turns to Multilateralism: Foreign Policy and Regional Security*, London: Routledge, pp. 21–34.

Guo Jianyue and Lv Desheng, 2010. 'SCO enjoys bright prospect in defence security cooperation', *PLA Daily*, 25 September, *eng.chinamil.com.cn*.

Kumar, Sanjay, 2011. 'Why the SCO matters', *The Diplomat*, 29 June, http://the-diplomat.com/indian-decade/2011/06/29/why-the-sco-matters/ (accessed on 17 August 2015).

Liu Wanyun, 2011. 'SCO defence security cooperation enters into new stage', 26 April, *eng.mod.gov.cn*.

Ma Zhengang, 2010. 'Shanghai Cooperation Organisation: in good shape and with better prospect', in *The CIIS Blue Book on International Situation and China's Foreign Affairs: 2009–2010*, China Institute of International Studies, World Affairs University, January.

mea.gov.in, 2012. 'India's "Connect Central Asia Policy"', Keynote address by MOS Shri E. Ahamed at First India-Central Asia Dialogue, Ministry of External Affairs,

Government of India, 12 June, www.mea.gov.in/Speeches-Statements.htm?dtl/19791/Keynote+address+by+MOS+Shri+E+Ahamed+at+First+IndiaCentral+Asia+Dialogue (accessed on 18 August 2015).

Mo Jingxi and Zhao Yinan, 2013. 'SCO meeting to focus on battling terrorism', *China Daily* (Asia), 21 November, www.chinadailyasia.com/news/2013-11/21/content_15100374.html (accessed on 12 January 2014).

Morgenthau, Hans J. and Kenneth W. Thompson, 1985. *Politics among Nations: The Struggle for Power and Peace*, New Delhi: Kalyani.

Olcott, Martha Brill, 2008. 'Central Asia: carving an independent identity among peripheral powers', in David Shambaugh and Michael Yahuda (eds), *International Relations of Asia*, Lanham, MD: Rowman & Littlefield, pp. 234–57.

Pan Guang, 2007. 'A Chinese perspective on the Shanghai Cooperation Organization', in Alyson J.K. Bailes, Pal Dunay, Pan Guang and Mikhail Troitskiy, *Shanghai Cooperation Organization*, SIPRI Policy Paper, No. 17, May, pp. 45–58.

Panda, Jagannath P., 2009. 'India's approach to Central Asia: strategic intents and geopolitical calculus', *China and Eurasia Forum Quarterly*, 7(3): 103–13.

Panda, Jagannath P., 2010. 'The Urumqi crisis: effect of China's ethno-national politics', *Strategic Analysis*, 34(1): 9–13.

Panda, Jagannath P., 2011. 'India's new look at Central Asia policy: a strategic review', in Marlene Laruelle and Sebastien Peyrouse (eds), *Mapping Central Asia: Indian Perceptions and Strategies*, London: Ashgate, pp. 109–22.

Panda, Jagannath P., 2012a. 'Beijing's perspective on expansion of the Shanghai Cooperation Organization: India, South Asia, and the spectrum of opportunities in China's open approach', *Asian Perspective*, 36: 493–530.

Panda, Jagannath P., 2012b. 'The import of Russia–India–China: still a valid entity?', *Russia & India Report*, 16 April, http://in.rbth.com/articles/2012/04/16/the_import_of_russia-India–China_still_a_valid_entity_15484.html (accessed on 18 August 2015).

Panda, Jagannath P., 2015. 'Will a triangular Russia–India–China order emerge at Ufa?', *Russia & India Report*, 8 July, http://in.rbth.com/opinion/2015/07/08/will_a_triangular_russiaIndia–China_order_emerge_at_ufa_44107.html (accessed on 18 August 2015).

Paramonov, Vladimir, 2010. 'China in Central Asia', *Central Asia and the Caucasus*, 11(4): 66–79.

Rong Ying, 2009. 'Stabilising Afghanistan: the role of China–India–Russia (RIC) trilateral cooperation', *China Report*, 45(2): 145–51.

Sputnik, 2015. 'SCO discusses Afghan security as tension in Middle East grows', *Sputnik*, 11 July, http://sputniknews.com/politics/20150711/1024483679.html (accessed on 21 August 2015).

Stobdan, P., 2015a. 'Talking heads: Modi in Ufa', *IDSA Comment*, 7 July, www.idsa.in/idsacomments/TalkingHeadsModiinUfa_pstobdan_070715.html (accessed on 18 August 2015).

Stobdan, P., 2015b. 'Modi's visit to Central Asia', *IDSA Comment*, 6 July, www.idsa.in/idsacomments/ModisVisittoCentralAsia_pstobdan_060715.html (accessed on 21 August 2015).

Stobdan, Phunchok, 2009. 'Shanghai Cooperation Organisation and Asian multilateralism in the twenty-first century', in N.S. Sisodia and V. Krishnappa (eds), *Global Power Shifts and Strategic Transition in Asia*, New Delhi: Academic Foundation, pp. 219–45.

Strokan, Sergey and Vladimir Mikheev, 2015. 'Inclusion of India and Pakistan set to be a game-changer for SCO', *Russia & India Business Report, The Economic Times*, 12 August, p. 19.

Tanchum, Micha'el, 2015. 'TAPI and India's future in Eurasia', *The Diplomat*, 27 February, http://thediplomat.com/2015/02/tapi-and-indias-future-in-eurasia/ (accessed on 22 August 2015).

Tian Shaohui, 2015. 'China, Russia agree to integrate Belt initiative with EAEU construction', *Xinhuanet*, 9 May, http://news.xinhuanet.com/english/2015-05/09/c_134222936.htm (accessed on 18 August 2015).

Vlad, L. Bogdan, A. Josan and G. Vlasceanu, 2010. 'Active geo-strategic players, geopolitical pivots and the changing balance of power in Eurasia,' *Revista Romana de Geografie Politica*, XII(1), May, pp. 116–25.

Wu Jiao and Zhang Yunbi, 2013. 'Xi proposes a "new Silk Road" with Central Asia', *China Daily*, 8 September, http://usa.chinadaily.com.cn/china/2013-09/08/content_16952304.htm (accessed on 23 December 2013).

Xu Xin, 2009. 'The Chinese concept of "twenty years' strategic opportunities" and its implications for Asian security order', in N.S. Sisodia and V. Krishnappa (eds), *Global Power Shifts and Strategic Transition in Asia*, New Delhi: Academic Foundation, pp. 59–92.

Yan Wei, 2008. 'Establishing regional rapport', *Beijing Review*, September, pp. 11–17.

Yu Jianhua, 2003. 'The development of SCO and the exploration of new interstate relations', *Chinese Diplomacy*, No. 7: 127–33.

Zhao Gancheng, 2009. 'China–Russia–India trilateral relations: realities and prospects', *China Report*, 45(2): 127–33.

10 China's tryst with IORA

Factoring India and the Indian Ocean[1]

The 13th meeting of the Council of Ministers of the Indian Ocean Rim Association for Regional Cooperation (IOR-ARC), held on 1 November 2013 at Perth, resulted in the IOR-ARC being renamed as the Indian Ocean Rim Association (IORA). The Perth communiqué outlined how IORA member countries must reaffirm their trust and commitment to build 'stability, security and prosperity' in the IOR region and boost prospects of regional economic growth and collaboration (*mea.gov.in* 2013). Notably, as the only comprehensive multilateral body in the Indian Ocean, IORA binds together 20 countries, six dialogue partners, and two observers, namely, the Indian Ocean Research Group (IORG) and the Indian Ocean Tourism Organisation (IOTO). As a dialogue partner, China has been participating in IORA deliberations ever since it was inducted in 2000.

Engaging with a multilateral body requires constructive foreign policy forethought, especially for a country that is not its full-fledged member. China's overtures to IORA exemplify this approach. With 20 member states, extra-territorial major powers as important dialogue partners, and the increasing importance of energy politics in the region, IORA becomes a significant multilateral body today in China's calculus. For India, China's power construct in this matter poses three challenges: Beijing as a maritime power, Beijing as a marine economy and Beijing as a polygonal power.

China's tryst with IORA: the course so far

China is the second-largest economy after the US, among the current dialogue partners of IORA (China, Egypt, Japan, US, United Kingdom and France).[2] China has participated regularly in the IORA meetings and has pursued a constructive agenda of promoting its political, economic and diplomatic clout among IORA member countries. Recently, China is even reported to have expressed its interest in becoming a full member of IORA (Dikshit 2012).

Dialogue based on *economic globalisation* and *regional economic integration* has been at the core of China's global activism, especially in its approach to multilateral bodies. The speeches and interventions by the Chinese representatives at the IOR-ARC Council of Ministers Meetings in 2004, 2007, 2009 and 2010 suggest that as regards IORA too, China follows the same dialogue of economic globalisation and regional economic integration in policy thrust (see *iora.net* 2004, 2007, 2010; Zweig 2010).[3] The Chinese representative's address at the Perth meeting was more nuanced. Terming China as a 'sincere partner' of IORA, Ambassador Lu Shaye announced that China was contributing US$100,000 to IORA for project implementation of the Regional Division on Desalination Technologies (*focac.org* 2013). All this indicates China's intensified attention to IORA in terms of its 'going global' strategy, with the IOR countries providing a key input. Most of China's strategic motives and policy interests vis-à-vis IORA are not restricted to IORA simply but are more realistically related to China's wider geopolitical interests concerning the Indian Ocean.[4]

Beijing as a maritime power, marine economy and polygonal power

The Indian Ocean (*yinduyangqu*) along with the Taiwan Strait, the South China Sea, the Strait of Malacca and the Arabian Sea is seen as being the 'maritime lifeline' of China in terms of its importance to China's national economy and national defence (Wang Xianglin 2010: 97). The demand for energy to sustain China's robust economy, combined with the emerging military presence and geopolitics in IOR has forced Beijing to accord utmost priority to this region. Chinese vigilance and activism is noticeable in the public articulation of Chinese scholars, that the Indian Ocean is not India's Ocean. China has also published its first ever bluebook, in 2013, on developments around the Indian Ocean. This publication talks exclusively about: (i) the political, economic and security situation in IOR; (ii) China's Indian Ocean strategy; (iii) India's Look East policy (now Act East) in the context of major powers like China and the US; and (iv) Sino-Myanmar relations in the context of the Indian Ocean (*wantchinatimes.com* 2013a). Surprisingly, it claims that China does not have an Indian Ocean strategy (Krishnan 2013). To China's attention what matters are the strategic chokepoints in the Indian Ocean. The Strait of Hormuz, Bab el-Mandeb and the Strait of Malacca connect the IOR with the Persian Gulf, the Red Sea and the South China Sea respectively. They have seven adjacent IORA member countries, namely, Oman, UAE, Iran (Strait of Hormuz), Yemen (Bab el-Mandeb) and Indonesia, Malaysia and Singapore (Strait of Malacca) (Table 10.1). Almost 85 per cent of China's oil and gas supplies and most of its maritime cargo, trade and transport pass through these chokepoints.

Strait of Hormuz. Almost a fifth of the world's oil supply passes through this strait. Data for 2012 suggest that 17 million barrels of crude pass through it every day (Zhou Yan 2012). China imports almost 40 per cent of its crude requirements from Iran, Saudi Arabia and Oman. The importance of this strait for China is also linked with the Abu Dhabi Crude Oil Pipeline, of which the China National Petroleum Corporation (CNPC) is a main contractor. When Iran threatened to close the Strait of Hormuz supply routes, following its nuclear tensions with the West, Chinese Premier Wen Jiabao asked Iran not to take any 'extreme action' (Wang and Hu 2012).

152 *Regional contours*

Table 10.1 Major chokepoints and key IORA members

Major chokepoints	Significance in China's energy transport	IORA countries
Strait of Hormuz	Almost 40 per cent of China's total crude oil transport from three IORA countries passes through it	Iran, UAE, Oman
Bab al-Mandeb	China is dependent on oil transport from South of Sudan on the Red Sea	Yemen
Strait of Malacca	Almost 37 per cent of China's LNG imports, 46 per cent of gas imports and 59 per cent of oil imports pass through IOR and enter this strait	Indonesia, Malaysia, Singapore

Bab el-Mandeb. Most of the trade between the European Union and China, India, Japan and to the rest of Asia passes through this narrow passage that connects the Red Sea with the Indian Ocean (Mountain 2011). Beijing is heavily dependent upon the oil transported from the south of Sudan on the Red Sea. In addition, Yemen, which has some of the world's largest untapped oil reserves, attracts China as a future energy hub. Djibouti, located on the west coast of the Gulf of Aden and facing Bab el-Mandeb, is also strategically important for China.[5] China proposes to have a military base in Djibouti, a proposal that the latter is reported to have welcomed (Anquan and Zhang 2013).

Strait of Malacca. While the Strait of Hormuz and Bab el-Mandeb are the key to China's maritime transport through the IOR, the Strait of Malacca, which is one of the shortest shipping channels between the Indian Ocean and the Pacific Ocean, serves as a transit point to the South China Sea. Beijing's economic and geopolitical security is closely attached to this strait.[6] Almost 10 per cent of the oil carried by foreign-owned tankers passes through the IOR region, enters the Strait of Malacca and the South China Sea and is finally transported to China (Lee 2012: 77). Some 37.3 per cent of China's liquefied natural gas (LNG) imports, 46 per cent of gas imports and 59 per cent of oil imports pass via the IOR and the Strait of Malacca. Chinese strategists have tried to maintain good relations with Indonesia, Malaysia and Singapore – the three IORA countries in the region. It has recently been reported that China's Export-Import (Exim) Bank has agreed to finance 85 per cent of the 48.69 km-long Malacca–Malaysia–Dumai–Indonesia bridge project across the Strait of Malacca (Shen Qing 2013). China's naval capability is not on par with the US navy in the region. Besides, in view of the sensitivities relating to the sovereignty issues of littoral states around the Malacca Strait like Indonesia and Malaysia, China has tried to act more as a responsible maritime power than influencing these chokepoints in its favour entirely (Chen Shaofeng 2010: 16).

Beyond these three chokepoints, the IOR itself as a whole is vital to China's economic and maritime interests. China has a strong connection with the 51 littoral states in IOR. The IOR littoral countries offer Beijing a range of opportunities to construct ports and bases. In recent times, the PLA has been focusing on constructing 'overseas strategic points'. One report even indicates that Beijing proposes to establish three categories of strategic points in the IOR (see Map 10.1): (i) a northern supply line connecting countries like Pakistan, Sri Lanka and Myanmar; (ii) a western supply chain involving Djibouti, Yemen, Oman, Kenya, Tanzania and Mozambique; and (iii) a southern supply chain connecting countries like Seychelles and Madagascar.[7] Eight IORA member countries will be involved with this Chinese planning. Recently, China signed a deal to develop the Tanzanian port of Bagamoyo, which has the potential to emerge as a naval base (*wantchinatimes.com* 2013b). Xi Jinping visited Tanzania during his first overseas trip after assuming power as President of China. Placing this Chinese reach within a broader context, maritime strategists in China have constructed a policy that combines national defence and maritime security strategy.

The Chinese urgency with regard to the IOR is linked to the growing military presence of other powers in this region. China sees ocean politics as a 'new frontier' of power contestation and is of the view that an intense competition among the major powers is emerging with regard to ocean development and the ability to protect maritime security interests (Gao Zugui 2010: 80). In course of time, China's maritime security policies have gone through some significant changes, under which protecting China's 'maritime rights and interests' has become an important issue (Zou Wentao 2014). For China, IORA countries such as Bangladesh, Mauritius, Seychelles, Maldives and Sri Lanka, and non-IORA countries like Pakistan and Myanmar are critical in this pursuit, and China has been studiously developing strong ties with them. China's principal approach is to construct a polygonal perspective that will in the long run enable it to emerge as a global power in the IOR region.

Both sea transportation and the securing of maritime routes have received urgent attention in China. Besides, the Western vigilance on China's maritime activities has compelled Beijing to balance its maritime expansion policy and marine economic drive. The current Chinese construction activities involving ports, highways, pipelines and airports in IOR littoral states are part of China's classic strategy of 'going global' (Chunhao Lou 2012: 631). It may also be noted that Beijing's real strategic focus is the Pacific rather than the Indian Ocean (Chunhao Lou 2013). It needs to be acknowledged, on the other hand, that the core of China's energy security policy is attached to the Indian Ocean; that China's internal stability is closely linked with its unshackled economic development, which is critically dependent on secure energy supplies through the Indian Ocean. China's white paper, *China's Energy Policy 2012*, does acknowledge that 'expanding international cooperation' is one of the basic aspects of China's energy security policy (*gov.cn* 2012).

China is emerging as a commercial power through the construction of ports, pipelines, infrastructure up-gradation and commercial bases in the IORA member states as well as in some South Asian countries, some of whom are India's neighbours. States in IOR are contemplating expanded trade and even FTAs with China.[8] Details of China's ventures in IOR help in understanding how China is becoming a

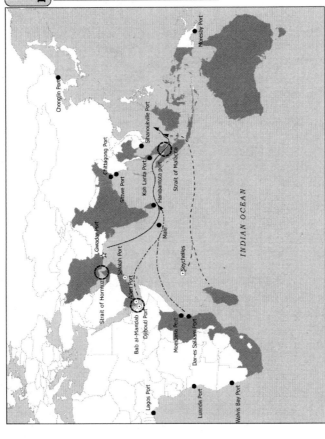

Map 10.1 China's strategic bases in the Indian Ocean: focus on IORA countries.

prominent trading country (Table 10.2), and why it is currently the world's largest exporter and second-largest importer. Not only does Beijing account for the world's biggest container ports; it also controls a fifth of the world's container fleet. Reports suggest that almost 41 per cent of the ships built in 2012 were made in China (*The Economist* 2013). More interesting are the figures for China's bilateral trade with IORA countries (Figure 10.1). Going by World Bank figures (*worldbank.org* n.d.), the US is the largest world economy, with GDP of $16.24 trillion in 2012 – almost double that of China and nine times that of India. But China had a total bilateral trade of $668 billion in 2012 with IORA members, which was more than double that of America's trade and three times that of India's. Since China's induction into IORA as a dialogue partner, the trade volume between China and IORA has been increasing almost constantly. In 2003, the China–IORA trade accounted for 12 per cent (around $100 billion) of China's total trade volume. The proportion increased to 13.4 per cent in 2006 ($236 billion), 15.2 per cent in 2008 ($390 billion) and 17.3 per cent in 2011 ($633 billion).[9]

In the backdrop of China's maritime and geostrategic pre-eminence in the IOR, two broad discourses emerge: *first*, China's emergence as a maritime power in the IOR, where it is expanding its naval presence, checking India's authority and the American presence in the region; *second*, the enhancement of its economic opportunities in this region through trade and commercial dealings, that are a key to its rise as a global power (Hartley 2010; see also Walgreen 2006).

Table 10.2 China's foreign direct investment in IORA countries (in US$10,000)

Sl. No.	Country	2011	2012
1	Australia	30,953	33,797
2	Bangladesh	495	227
3	Comoros	–	–
4	India	4217	4406
5	Indonesia	4607	6378
6	Iran	787	410
7	Kenya	235	209
8	Madagascar	–	–
9	Malaysia	35,828	31,751
10	Mauritius	113,921	95,873
11	Mozambique	–	–
12	Oman	–	–
13	Seychelles	43,333	36,507
14	Singapore	609,681	630,508
15	South Africa	1323	1605
16	Sri Lanka	68	20
17	Tanzania	–	–
18	Thailand	10,120	7772
19	United Arab Emirates	7140	12,963
20	Yemen	888	287

Source: *China Statistical Yearbook 2013*, National Bureau of Statistics, Beijing: China Statistics Press, 2013, pp. 244–6.

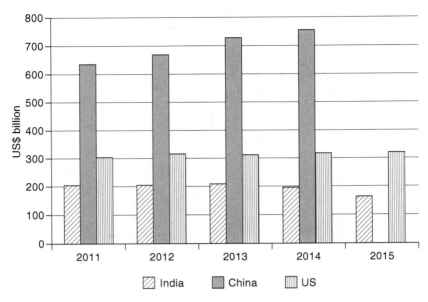

Figure 10.1 Comparison of India, China and US total bilateral trade with IORA, 2011–2015 (US$ billion) (sources: International Trade Centre, www.trademap. org/tm_light/Bilateral_TS.aspx; Department of Commerce, Government of India, http://commerce.nic.in; East African Community Trade Helpdesk, http://tradehelpdesk.eac.int/Reports/Table2a.php; US Census Bureau, www. census.gov/foreign-trade/balance/c7830.html#2011).

Note
Data for total trade of China not available for 2015.

The People's Liberation Army Navy (PLAN) has been vigilant and active in addressing the non-traditional security issues, such as piracy, in the IOR. It has emerged as a leading force, to not only protect China's own sea-lanes of communication but also to contribute to international security operations ever since it revised its concept of 'security' in 1996 to include common security, comprehensive security and cooperative security, to tackle both traditional and non-traditional security issues, including terrorism. In this regard, building alliances, partnerships and trust has become a priority in the Chinese perspective. Beijing has employed these arguments while dealing with IORA countries. The underlying Chinese motive in this endeavour is to push a comprehensive maritime diplomacy, which will combine both hard-power and soft-power elements of its policy approach.

The India factor: IORA and Beijing's inter-regional approach

There are two mainstream schools of thought in China with regard to India in the context of the Indian Ocean. One school, consisting of liberals, with marginal impact, believes that India does not oppose China's maritime interests in the Indian Ocean and advocates accepting and accommodating India in the regional maritime politics. India is not considered as a naval competitor in China's regional maritime drive, nor is Beijing capable of building a navy that is capable of looking after the security environment of the IOR (Penghong 2010: 78). The other group, comprising realists who dominate China's decision-making process, believe that India is competing with China's maritime interests in the region. It has an alarmist perception of India's position in the Indian Ocean, linking the issue with the changing course of geopolitics in the region, that combines the United States' 'pivot' to Asia, American maritime presence in the region, India's Look East (now Act East) policy, and India's strong connection with countries like Australia, Japan, and the US (Wang Lirong 2009: 48–50).

In the Chinese contestation, there is scope for China and India to coexist in the Indian Ocean. Joint naval exercises are an effective confidence-building measure (CBM) in this regard. In order to counter non-traditional security issues in the region and protect its maritime interests in region, China has to put in place a strong maritime policy in the Indian Ocean, which must welcome India. But Chinese experts also acknowledge that the Chinese moves regarding the IOR pose a challenge for India, because India has always considered the Indian Ocean as its own sphere of influence (Ma Jiali 2010; see also Ma and Shu 2009: 50). The dominant Chinese view is to remain vigilant regarding India's moves in the Indian Ocean and to explore where and how the PLAN must capitalise on, and enhance its own presence in the ocean. Officially, China takes India's Act East policy and India's military relations with Australia and Japan quite seriously.

India and IORA

Since its establishment in 1995–1996, and till recently, the IOR-ARC used to be seen more as an association for addressing soft security issues concerning the IOR (Gupta 2013) and was more or less dormant. Of late, though, IORA appears to be transforming into an important multilateral body that could affect China's strategic interests in the region. New non-traditional security threats, conventional and non-conventional security challenges and the strategic presence and posture of major powers – the US, China and India – not only make the Indian Ocean region vital, but give IORA a considerable standing. The vitality of IORA lies in its comprehensive agenda that encompasses the maritime regions of Africa, Asia and Australia.

Given the commercial and strategic significance of IOR, there is no doubt that both China and India will take their quest for enhanced maritime influence to a new level, opening up another avenue of power politics in the Sino-Indian maritime complexity. India has been a leading country in IOR-ARC, but has not been unequivocally forthcoming about the future of this organisation until recently. Given China's increasing clout in the IOR and future prospects of Chinese membership in IORA, New Delhi must upgrade and review its own standing both in IORA and in IOR. The Indian authority may be challenged if Beijing demands membership or greater involvement with IORA.

India on its part has tried to revitalise IORA through new ideas. For example, the Gurgaon Business Forum in October–November 2012 proposed an Economic and Business Conference to prepare the ground for strong trade and economic contacts among IORA members. This proposal was followed up by the first Economic and Business Conference in Mauritius on 4–5 July 2013, under the IOR-ARC mechanism. India's then Minister of Commerce and Industry, Anand Sharma, co-chaired the conference. This conference discussed the concept of 'open regionalism', which was meant to promote 'trade as an important factor in promoting economic cooperation' in the region (*commerce.nic.in* 2013). The idea was to institute trade practices in line with international norms and implement less rigid trade barriers in the Indian Ocean (ibid.). These, to some extent, have to be in line with the growing multilateral temper that India wants to employ in IOR. Though India seems resolute about revitalising its approach to IORA through a 'regional cooperative maritime framework' where the thrust is more on the security aspect in IOR (Kahangama 2013), this approach has to be implemented jointly with the concept of 'open regionalism'. The strategy should focus on 'trade security', to coalesce India's security as well as maritime interests. Capitalizing on the Indian Ocean Naval Symposium (IONS) will be a key in this regard. Under Prime Minister Modi, India's approach to the IOR countries have been steadily revived. In his opening remarks at Forum for India Pacific Island Countries (FIPIC), Prime Minister Modi stated ardently that: 'Ocean is critical to India's future. That is why, in the past year, I have focussed a lot on ocean economy, in India and international engagement' (Modi 2015).

India took the lead in holding the first IONS in 2008 to structure 'non-discriminatory norms and institutions' in IOR. With 35 members, IONS represents the majority of Indian Ocean littorals and is considered to be an 'inclusive and consultative forum' (*indiannavy.nic.in* 2013). Terming this initiative a vital landmark in India's quest for a 'cooperative and inclusive world order', the then Prime Minister Manmohan Singh, while inaugurating the IONS initiative, stressed the importance of 'freedom of the seas' and 'deepening trade and economic linkages' in IOR (*pib.nic.in* 2008). It is more than seven years since IONS was initiated, but India still lags behind China in terms of trade and economic contacts with the IOR countries. IONS also presents a dilemma for India between 'cooperative security' and 'balancing security'. The IONS agenda talks about 'cooperative security'; but New Delhi needs to decide whether this type of security can be achieved without China, especially considering that Beijing has emerged as a cooperative partner for many IOR countries. If the thrust is on 'balancing security', which is equivalent to checking the Chinese influence in the region, India not only has to firm up security tie-ups with the littoral countries but also has to maximise its trade and economic dealings with the littoral members. On both fronts of 'cooperative security' and 'balancing security', India appears to be vacillating.

The contours

Beijing's tryst with IORA mirrors the classic contemporary diplomacy that China usually deploys with regard to most multilateral bodies. This includes building strong economic bridges with member states while exploiting the political, strategic and security bearings involved with them. China's approach to IORA forms part of its broader foreign policy comprising economic globalisation, regional economic integration and harmonious world thesis. These concepts and terminologies have often been used in the Chinese foreign policy construct and in China's dialogue and perspective with regard to important multilateral bodies like ASEAN, SCO and Boao Forum. The advocacy of a 'harmonious ocean' is derived from China's 'harmonious world' concept while economic globalisation and regional economic integration have been the two prime foreign policy dialogues of China, since the time of Hu Jintao. Beijing may not adopt a special policy tactic towards IORA per se; but the dialogues and perspectives China carries forward are certainly within the limits and parameters of its greater foreign policy objectives.

In a way, the stability issue in the Indian Ocean will hinge not only on how the major and minor powers coexist in the region but also on to what extent IORA accommodates those powers' interests. In this milieu, China's and India's power influence and dynamics will invite greater institutional involvement in IOR. The challenge for India is whether it can pursue an objective and autonomous policy on IORA without taking sides, which in the current dispensation is not possible. India would at the same time prefer a multilateral cooperative framework to push for greater peace and stability in the region. Where maritime politics in the IOR is concerned, New Delhi accords considerable importance to IORA and IONS. But will that really work in India's favour? India must pursue an astute and comprehensive policy that will involve both bilateralism and multilateralism in its engagement with IORA and IOR countries. Vis-à-vis Beijing, India's main objective must be to not concede too much space to China in the IOR and to systematically and sagaciously renounce Beijing's growing clout in the region. Three broad policy imperatives will be key for India in this regard: (i) capitalise on enhancing political understanding with IOR countries while maximising trade and economic contacts; (ii) revitalise IORA and other related multilateral mechanisms in the region; and (iii) adopt a comprehensive policy approach that will help sustain and promote India's authority in the region.

Notes

1 This chapter has been published earlier in *Strategic Analysis*, 38(5), 2014, pp. 668–87.
2 China was inducted as a dialogue partner, along with the UK, at the first IOR-ARC Ministerial Council meeting, held in January 2000 at Muscat, Oman. The IOR-ARC's Working Group on Trade and Investment (WGTI) also met for the first time on the sidelines of this meeting.
3 The 'going global' or 'going out' (*zouchuquzhanlue*) strategy has been a hallmark of the Chinese government's policy approach since 1999. Its main aspect is to encourage outward foreign investment. See Zweig 2010; see also Lee 2012: 83.
4 China's current interest in the Indian Ocean is linked with its security-related interests in African affairs. China offered material assistance as well as military training to a number of African liberation groups in the late 1950s. It was during that period that China developed an interest in the Indian Ocean. See Shinn 2012.
5 China and Djibouti established diplomatic relations on 8 January 1979. Since then, a number of high-level Chinese political leaders and military officials have travelled to Djibouti. Recently, Hassan Darar Houffaneh, Djibouti's Defence Minister, visited China. He discussed with his Chinese counterpart Chang Wanquan ways to further expand the two countries' military-to-military relationship and to forge an understanding on strategic affairs. See Yan and Liang 2013; see also *china.org.cn* 2006.
6 China has faced a lot of difficulties in the Malacca Strait region because of the tense situation in the East China Sea, South China Sea and to some extent because of the Taiwan issue. See Chen Shaofeng 2010: 2.
7 This report, written by freelance writer Hai Tao, appeared in the *International Herald Leader* (23 December 2011), a newspaper published from Beijing. See http://news.xinhuanet.com/herald/2011-12/23/c_131321310.htm (accessed on 14 January 2014). Other similar news reports are *wantchinatimes.com* 2013b and Yu Renze 2013.
8 Among the IORA members, China has an FTA only with Singapore, which was signed on 23 October 2008 during the Singapore Prime Minister's visit to China. For details, see *China FTA Networks* n.d.
9 In 2009, the China–IORA trade decreased slightly. However, IORA's bilateral trade share in China's total trade volume increased from 15.2 per cent in 2008 to 15.7 per cent in 2009.

References

Anquan, Jiang and Zhang Jianbo, 2013. 'Djibouti welcomes China to build a military base' (translated from the Chinese), *Global Times*, 11 March, www.chinaafricaproject.com/djibouti-welcomes-china-to-build-a-military-base-translation/ (accessed on 13 January 2014).
Chen Shaofeng, 2010. 'China's self-extrication from the "Malacca dilemma" and implications', *International Journal of China Studies*, 1(1), January, pp. 1–24.
China FTA Networks, n.d. 'China's Free Trade Agreements', *China FTA Networks*, http://fta.mofcom.gov.cn/topic/ensingapore.shtml (accessed on 1 February 2014).
china.org.cn, 2006. 'Djibouti', Chinese Foreign Ministry, 10 October, www.china.org.cn/english/features/focac/183543.htm (accessed on 13 January 2014)
Chunhao, Lou, 2012. 'US–India–China relations in the Indian Ocean: a Chinese perspective', *Strategic Analysis*, 36(4): 624–39.
Chunhao, Lou, 2013. 'Power politics in the Indian Ocean: don't exaggerate the China threat', *East Asia Forum*, 24 October, www.eastasiaforum.org/2013/10/24/power-politics-in-the-indian-ocean-dont-exaggerate-the-china-threat/ (accessed on 29 January 2014).

commerce.nic.in, 2013. 'IOR-ARC economic and business conference press communiqué', Department of Commerce: Ministry of Commerce & Industry, Government of India, 5 July, http://commerce.nic.in/PressRelease/pressrelease_detail.asp?id=3036 (accessed on 29 January 2014).

Dikshit, Sandeep, 2012. 'Seeking to energise itself, grouping of Indian Ocean rim states admits U.S. as dialogue partner', *The Hindu*, 3 November, www.thehindu.com/news/national/seeking-to-energise-itself-grouping-of-indian-ocean-rim-states-admits-us-as-dialogue-partner/article4058303.ece (accessed on 30 December 2013).

The Economist, 2013. 'China's foreign ports: the new masters and commanders', *The Economist*, 8 June, www.economist.com/news/international/21579039-chinas-growing-empire-ports-abroad-mainly-about-trade-not-aggression-new-masters (accessed on 14 January 2014).

focac.org, 2013. 'Remarks by H.E. Director-General Lu Shaye at the 13th Meeting of the Council of Ministers of the Indian Ocean Rim Association', 1 November, Forum on China–Africa Cooperation (13 November 2013), www.focac.org/eng/zxxx/t1098484.htm (accessed on 3 January 2014).

Gao Zugui, 2010. 'International strategy and security environmental development trends over the next 5 to 10 years', *Contemporary International Relations*, Special Issue (In Commemoration of the 30th Anniversary of CICIR), China Institute of Contemporary International Relations, September.

gov.cn, 2012. 'II. Policies and goals of energy development', *China's Energy Policy 2012* (full text), Information Office of the State Council: The People's Republic of China, October, Beijing, www.gov.cn/english/official/2012-10/24/content_2250497_3.htm (accessed on 29 January 2014).

Gupta, Arvind, 2013. 'Build identity in Indian Ocean', *New Indian Express*, 13 November, www.newindianexpress.com/opinion/Build-identity-in-Indian-ocean/2013/11/13/article1887143.ece (accessed on 21 January 2014).

Hartley, John, 2010. 'Differing perceptions of China's role in the Indian Ocean' (Chapter 4), in *Indian Ocean: A Sea of Uncertainty*, Future Directions International, 21 June, pp. 95–9.

indiannavy.nic.in, 2013. 'Emerging maritime interests in Asia Pacific: an Indian perspective', Address by Chief of the Naval Staff (CNS) – Galle Dialogue 2013, 25 November, http://indiannavy.nic.in/cns-speeches/galle-dialogue-2013-emerging-maritime-interests-asia-pacific-indian-perspective-sri-lan (accessed on 1 August 2014).

iora.net, 2004. Address by H.E. Ambassador Wang Yusheng, China at the fifth meeting of the Council of Ministers of the Indian Ocean Rim Association for Regional Cooperation, August, Sri Lanka, www.iora.net/documents/speeches.aspx (accessed on 3 January 2014).

iora.net, 2007. Speech by H.E. Liu Zhentang, Ambassador Extraordinary and Plenipotentiary of the People's Republic of China to the Islamic Republic of Iran and head of Chinese Delegation, on the occasion of the 7th Council of Ministers of Indian Ocean Rim Association for Regional Cooperation, 7 March, Tehran, www.iora.net/documents/speeches.aspx (accessed on 3 January 2014).

iora.net, 2010. Address at the Tenth Conference of the Council of Ministers of the Indian Ocean Rim-Association for Regional Cooperation (IOR-ARC), H.E. Ambassador Shu Zhan, 5 August, Sana'a, www.iora.net/documents/speeches.aspx (accessed on 3 January 2014).

Kahangama, Iranga, 2013. 'India, Sri Lanka & Maldives: Chinese influence and regional maritime security issues', *Daily Mirror*, 1 August, www.dailymirror.lk/business/

features/33156-india-sri-lanka-a-maldives-chinese-influencenand-regional-maritime-security-issues-.html (accessed on 29 January 2014).

Krishnan, Ananth, 2013. 'China details Indian Ocean strategy and interests', *The Hindu*, 9 June, www.thehindu.com/news/international/world/china-details-indian-ocean-strategy-and-interests/article4795550.ece (accessed on 14 January 2014).

Lee, John, 2012. 'China's geostrategic search for oil', *The Washington Quarterly*, 35(3), Summer, pp. 75–92.

Ma Jiali, 2010. 'Progress and questions in Sino-India security relationship', *China.org.cn*, 10 March, www.china.org.cn/opinion/2010-03/26/content_19693647.htm (accessed 1 February 2014).

Ma Jiali and Shu Jun, 2009. 'India's maritime outlook and its maritime strategy', *Asia and Africa Review*, 2.

mea.gov.in, 2013. 'Perth Communiqué – 13th Meeting of the Council of Ministers of the Indian Ocean Rim Association, Perth, Australia, November 1, 2013', Ministry of External Affairs, Government of India, 6 November, www.mea.gov.in/bilateral-documents.htm?dtl/22443/Perth+Communiqu13th+Meeting+of+the+Council+of+Ministers+of+the+Indian+Ocean+Rim+Association (accessed on 5 January 2014).

Modi, Narendra, 2015. 'PM's opening remarks at Forum for India Pacific Island Countries (FIPIC) Summit', Jaipur, 21 August 2015, www.narendramodi.in (accessed on 8 January 2016).

Mountain, Thomas C., 2011. 'Choke point Bab el-Mandeb: understanding the strategically critical Horn of Africa', *Foreign Policy Journal*, 19 November, www.foreignpolicyjournal.com/2011/11/19/choke-point-bab-el-mandeb-understanding-the-strategically-critical-horn-of-africa/ (accessed on 13 January 2014).

Penghong, Cai, 2010. 'Regional maritime security environment: a Chinese perspective', in Sam Bateman and Joshua Ho (eds), *Southeast Asia and the Rise of Chinese and Indian Naval Power: Between Rising Naval Powers*, London: Routledge, pp. 72–9.

pib.nic.in, 2008. 'PM inaugurates Indian Ocean Naval Symposium Seminar – 2008', Press Information Bureau, Prime Minister's Office, Government of India, 14 February, http://pib.nic.in/newsite/PrintRelease.aspx (accessed on 3 January 2014).

Shen Qing, 2013. 'Malaysia, Indonesia plan to build bridge across Strait of Malacca', *English.news.cn*, 16 October, http://news.xinhuanet.com/english/world/2013-10/16/c_132803947.htm (accessed on 14 January 2014).

Shinn, David, 2012. 'China's security policy in Africa and the Western Indian Ocean', *China in Africa*, 26 July, www.sinoafrica.org/en/print/2063 (accessed on 29 January 2014).

Walgreen, David, 2006. 'China in the Indian Ocean Region: lessons in PRC grand strategy', *Comparative Strategy*, 25(2): 55–73.

Wang Chenyan and Hu Yinan, 2012. 'China opposes "extreme action" in Strait of Hormuz', *China Daily*, 20 January, www.chinadaily.com.cn/cndy/2012-01/20/content_14479613.htm (accessed on 13 January 2014).

Wang Lirong, 2009. 'The Indian Ocean and China's sea lane security strategy', *South Asian Studies*, No. 3, pp. 48–50.

Wang Xianglin, 2010. 'On China's marine safety', *Contemporary International Relations*, 20(1): 96–101.

wantchinatimes.com, 2013a. 'China issues first Indian Ocean regional development blue book', *WantChinaTimes*, 10 June, www.wantchinatimes.com/news-subclass-cnt.aspx?id=20130610000043&cid=1101 (accessed on 14 January 2014).

wantchinatimes.com, 2013b. 'Xi adds Tanzanian pearl to Indian Ocean strategy', *Want China Times*, 28 March, www.wantchinatimes.com/news-subclass-cnt.aspx?id=20130328000010&cid=1101 (accessed on 14 January 2014).

worldbank.org, n.d. World Bank database, http://data.worldbank.org/indicator/NY.GDP.MKTP.CD (accessed on 17 January 2014).

Yan Meng and Liang Jun, 2013. 'Chinese defence chief holds talks with Djibouti counterpart', *People's Daily*, 5 December, http://english.people.com.cn/90786/8475348.html (accessed on 13 January 2014).

Yu Renze, 2013, 'Chinese navy expected to build strategic bases in Indian Ocean', *SINA English*, 7 January, http://english.sina.com/china/2013/0106/545538.html (accessed on 6 January 2014).

Zhou Yan, 2012. 'Oil pipes to bypass Strait of Hormuz', *People's Daily*, 17 January, http://english.people.com.cn/90883/7707067.html (accessed on 13 January 2014).

Zou Wentao, 2014. 'Restructuring China's maritime security: lofty ambition, little progress', *RSIS Commentaries*, No. 007/2014, 13 January.

Zweig, David, 2010. 'The rise of a new "trading nation"', in Lowell Dittmer and George T. Yu (eds), *China, the Developing World, and the New Global Dynamic*, Boulder, CO: Lynne Rienner, pp. 37–59.

11 Between RCEP and TPP

ASEAN+6 and Asia-Pacific intricacies

Multilateral trade in Asia is entering a new chapter of interaction and integration with the Regional Comprehensive Economic Partnership (RCEP) initiated by ASEAN and the US-centred Trans-Pacific Partnership (TPP). Two compelling regional issues – trade liberalisation and economic integration – have been at the core of these initiatives.[1] The backdrop of these efforts is the US 'pivot to Asia' vis-à-vis 'rebalancing' strategy, prevailing maritime disputes in the region and a range of free trade agreements (FTAs).[2] This chapter is aimed at explaining the politics, policies and nuances that both India and China attach to RCEP and TPP. It argues that India's association with China under the RCEP negotiation is an opportunity for India to maximise its 'Act East' policy, and uphold the dialogue of East Asian community building under the premise of ASEAN+6 and beyond, which has so far wilted under constant Chinese opposition.

RCEP and TPP: the politics and economics

The fundamentals of RCEP and TPP are not necessarily in conflict but are essentially contrasting economic models, primarily on negotiation fronts. RCEP is linked to the economic and political supremacy of China and ASEAN at the moment; TPP highlights the American worldview. They differ from each other in the exclusivity of their design, principles, volume and membership (Wilson 2013). RCEP is mostly ASEAN-centric and is East/South-East Asia-centred currently where China is the biggest economy; whereas TPP is a US-led Pacific Rim or Asia-Pacific initiative, covering or centring mostly APEC countries. Currently, TPP is seen as a 'comprehensive and high-standard' FTA (Fergusson *et al.* 2013). The mandate of TPP was to move beyond WTO commitments and liberalise trade in nearly all goods and services (ibid.).

RCEP has generally come into the limelight after TPP became a matter of discussion. It is primarily based on the ASEAN+1 FTA formula. It was launched formally in November 2012 during the East Asian Summit.[3] It combines the ten ASEAN countries and their six major trading partners, which includes India. RCEP would form the world's largest free trade bloc, covering 3.5 billion people (*China Daily* 2013).[4] TPP on the other hand covers a population of only 500–600 million (ibid.). (Figure 11.1 portrays the comparative

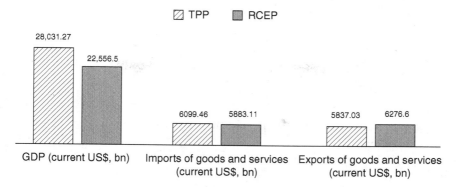

Figure 11.1 TPP vs RCEP: economy and trade, 2014 (source: World Development Indicators, The World Bank, http://databank.worldbank.org/data/views/reports/tableview.aspx).

economic volume and strength of RCEP and TPP.) More notably, RCEP combines three major drivers of market growth: China, India and ASEAN. One of its core aims is to generate economic growth and partnerships among its members at a much higher level than the existing ASEAN FTAs (Basu Das 2012). RCEP is generally seen as an 'ASEAN++' formula, combining East Asia FTA (EAFTA) and the Comprehensive Economic Partnership in East Asia (CEPEA) (ibid.; see also Hsu 2013: 42). EAFTA is based on ASEAN+3 (ASEAN + China, Japan and South Korea), which has always been backed by China. CEPEA, based on ASEAN+6, is supported by Japan (Basu Das 2012). Formalisation of RCEP was likely to take place by 2015 but it is expected sometime in 2016–2017. Its core spirit is based on 'open accession clause' (Hsu 2013: 42; see also Basu Das 2013: 2, Wignaraja 2013a).

American advocacy of TPP is linked to its 'pivot to Asia'/'rebalancing' strategy,[5] and its global design and aim of integrating the American economy more closely with the regional economies. TPP aimed to put in place various global rules to lower or reduce the hidden barriers to overseas competition.[6] It is based on a 'WTO-plus' approach (Basu Das 2013: 2; see also *ustr.gov* 2011), goes beyond the conformist WTO norms and is an experiment in 'multilateralising regionalism'.[7] Essentially a multilateral FTA, TPP was signed on 3 June 2005, and formally entered into force on 28 May 2006. Brunei, Chile, New Zealand and Singapore were the first signatories. In 2008, Vietnam, United States, Peru, Malaysia and Australia joined formally. The *CRS Report for Congress* had stated earlier that the TPP negotiations on 29 chapters were aimed to eliminate tariff and non-tariff barriers in key areas like goods, services and agriculture (Fergusson *et al.* 2013).[8] The TPP negotiations were concluded in October 2015. RCEP, in contrast, will follow the rules and norms mostly attuned to ASEAN conventions and guidelines, built on a consensus (Basu Das 2013: 3).[9] The RCEP, as it looks currently, is a much more liberal and flexible trade negotiating process that aims to accommodate both developed and developing economies. In order to bring more liberalisation that will be suitable for its member countries, China along with ASEAN may, partially or fully, deregulate its domestic market conditions or the prevailing economic systems to advance the RCEP negotiation process (Terada 2013: 2).

ASEAN is central in both these trade liberalising models. While RCEP is based on an extended 'ASEAN++' approach which brings ASEAN's FTA partners on board, TPP too has tried to include vital ASEAN members. ASEAN is strongly connected with most regional and extra-regional powers in trade and economic dealings (see Figure 11.2).

Traditionally, ASEAN members prefer to engage economically with the 'Chinese world', while politically, most of them identify themselves as 'pro-US world' countries. The latter is partly on account of the maritime realities they have to live with. For instance, Vietnam, Brunei, Singapore, Indonesia and Philippines may agree to the broader ASEAN agenda of RCEP model of regional economic integration; but they have in principle supported the TPP. Singapore, Brunei, Vietnam and Malaysia are an integral part of the TPP.

For powers like India, Japan, Australia and New Zealand, these multilateral prospects of RCEP and TPP present a range of regional and global opportunities. For instance, both Japan and South Korea are members of RCEP, but showed interest in being part of the TPP-led regional economic integration (and Japan joined at a later stage). The idea and ethos of integrating the East Asian economies under ASEAN+6 has not succeeded so far, and the three big economies – China, Japan and South Korea – have not agreed in principle on the ASEAN+6 mechanism for the East Asian community building. Maritime disputes in the region and power politics have brought into question the ASEAN+6 notion: whether the economic ethos of building an East Asian community will ultimately help reduce the existing political differences.

The Chinese perspective between RCEP and TPP

Chinese experts describe RCEP as a 'prototype of an Asian FTA', a timely mechanism to forge cooperation, think about regional economic integration and an opportunity for ASEAN and its dialogue partners to become free from dependence on the Western economic sphere,[10] but they anticipate a range of challenges in actualising the process of the RCEP. Maritime issues and the sensitivity of the ASEAN dialogue partners like Japan on protecting its agricultural sector and South Korea's rice industry could be possible barriers.[11] China has officially seen the arrival of RCEP primarily as an extension of Sino-ASEAN engagement. Beijing aimed at pushing RCEP between ASEAN and ASEAN+3, but realising that ASEAN countries are not really united, wants to push for an ASEAN+6 RCEP.

Rhetorically, Chinese officials have welcomed the American Asia-Pacific strategy and TPP, saying that there is always scope for constructive collaboration among countries and across regions. The media, scholarly discourse and expert opinion have, however, been quite critical of both (Szczudlik-Tatar 2012). It is argued that the US wants to disperse the unity and ethos of East Asian economic cooperation, and make inroads into East Asia more diligently and effectively (Guoyou and Wen 2012: 110). China links TPP to a broader American strategy in Asia, having a direct linkage to multiple factors: American strategic 'rebalancing' towards East Asia and Asia-Pacific, the US presence in Asia, and an attempt to contain China's rise and restrict its economic supremacy.[12]

The Indian perspective between RCEP and TPP

From the outset, India has supported the idea of RCEP and has participated in launching the RCEP negotiation process. India has shown keen interest in joining RCEP though it is still hesitant about an FTA with China, and there are worries that Chinese goods may flood the Indian market through RCEP (Chaulia 2012). Overall, ASEAN's significance in Indian foreign policy makes New Delhi take the RCEP negotiation seriously. RCEP would not only facilitate India's greater presence in the South-East or East Asian market; it will also facilitate and punctuate India's Act East policy massively in economic dealings. Not only does India share an FTA with ASEAN but also with two of the main dialogue partners of ASEAN – Japan and South Korea. RCEP will provide a substantial platform for India to maximise its trade profile and economic, services and communications contacts with the ASEAN communities, which will lead to greater cooperation in areas like banking, tourism and societal interactions (Wignaraja 2013b). Above all this, partaking in the RCEP will enhance India's Asia-Pacific undertaking.

The Indian perspective of TPP is equally an evolving one. TPP takes on board the ASEAN countries, a fact that is important for India and its 'Act East' policy. Currently, TPP does not really look to India as a possible member; but there is a discourse emerging in the West that countries like India may be asked to join in future if the negotiation process among the Asia-Pacific countries moves smoothly and successfully. India would not like to join TPP in its current form, as TPP rules compel member countries to amend their domestic rules and norms with regard to climate change, environment and human rights to WTO+ standards (Malhotra 2012). Besides, what restricts India's overall approach to TPP is that India is still not a member of APEC.

The evolving India–China upsurge

The Chinese and Indian perspectives of RCEP and TPP discussed so far are fundamental for a variety of reasons: (i) the US is a dividing factor between China and India; (ii) ASEAN's massive engagement with both China and India; (iii) India's newly envigorated 'Act East' policy; and (iv) maritime politics, mainly the South China Sea disputes.

The US factor

Chinese scholars and experts view India as a 'pro-US' country along with Japan and Australia. The Chinese acuity over RCEP and TPP is part and parcel of its broader regional view and understanding of this 'four-nation alliance' (Zhao Qinghai 2007). Also, while both the region of South-East Asia and the institutions of ASEAN are economically beholden to China, they support US geostrategic aims and objectives. There is a conviction in China that the US is on an active role to divide ASEAN for its own benefit. India's perspective should be closely linked to its broader design of 'Look East' or 'Act East' policy. The RCEP would be expected to permit greater India–China economic bonding in ASEAN. It is, however, yet to be known to what extent China will accommodate broader Indian political and economic interests in East or South-East Asia.

ASEAN engagement

Associating with ASEAN has been one of the main foreign policy planks of China and India in regional politics. The Chinese engagement in this regard is seen under ASEAN+1, ASEAN+3 and ASEAN+6. Historically, Beijing has always been keener to engage economically with ASEAN rather than the other way around.[13] India's engagement with ASEAN has been under ASEAN+6, FTA and the newly crafted strategic partnership under its 'Look East'/'Act East' policy. India sees itself as a potential security provider, which is an important aspect of its current 'Act East' policy where the China factor holds the prime cosmos behind India's ambition. Beijing in its turn currently seems to be more serious towards ASEAN and South-East Asia than ever, for two reasons: (i) prevailing maritime disputes and (ii) the US return to Asia-Pacific. Beijing not only wants to consolidate its hold over ASEAN but wants to have a good grasp over greater South-East Asian communities. In recent years, China has developed a range of 'practical cooperation' with South-East Asia in the fields of economics, trade, capital, information, transport, culture, infrastructure and people-to-people exchanges. The trade and economic contacts between China and ASEAN, in particular, have grown rapidly and are constantly rising (see Figure 11.2). Beijing also enjoys healthy trade contacts with the main ASEAN dialogue partners (see Figure 11.3).

India's 'Act East' policy and China

The arrival of both RCEP and TPP creates a golden juncture for India to advance its 'Act East' policy because there is a strong possibility that China might be induced to agree to an ASEAN+6 mechanism in the region with the lead of RCEP. But the prime task for India would be to maintain a balance between the emerging politics and economics, and identify areas of cooperation on key policy areas at a time when regional politics is rapidly changing and the ASEAN countries are looking to India seriously as a regional power. In crafting a more

Between RCEP and TPP 169

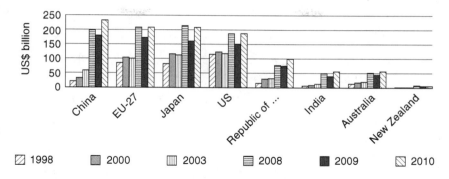

Figure 11.2 ASEAN total trade with selected trading partners, 1998–2010 (source: Asean Community in Figures, 2011, www.asean.org).

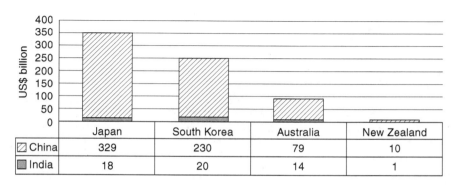

Figure 11.3 Comparative trade contact of China and India with main ASEAN dialogue partners, 2012 (US$bn) (source: www.nzchinacouncil.com/downloads/Partnership%20Forum%202013%20%20MOFCOM%20Wang%20Chao.pdf; also see http://dfat.gov.au/publications/tgs/index.html, www.asianz.org.nz/node/4697).

decisive policy towards ASEAN, India must capitalise on maximising trade and economic contacts with it. The India–ASEAN trade and economic contact has seen rapid and sustained progress recently (see Figure 11.4); associating with RCEP and its negotiation will certainly boost further these contacts. By joining RCEP, India can further expand the mode of liberalising the India–ASEAN economic engagement, and simultaneously enter into bilateral FTA negotiations with China, Australia and New Zealand (Hsu 2013: 49). Besides, the established 'strategic partnership' between India and ASEAN must move to the next stage of trade and economic contacts. Actualising ASEAN+6, RCEP will help further its objectives of the 'Act East' policy.

India's 'Look East'/'Act East' policy has gone beyond the conformist way of engaging with ASEAN alone. New Delhi has developed comprehensive and special strategic engagement with Japan and South Korea, and has taken equally

170 *Regional contours*

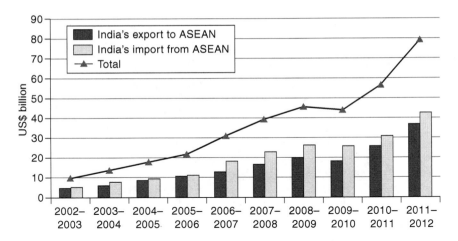

Figure 11.4 India–ASEAN trade, 2002/2003–2012/2013 (US$ billion) (source: Dept. of Commerce: Ministry of Commerce and Industry, Govt. of India).

seriously its relationship with Australia and New Zealand. India has also constructively developed a strong security engagement with ASEAN countries and with countries in East Asia like Japan. The only impediment in New Delhi's 'Act East' policy is China and its obsessive resistance to India's greater role in the East Asian region. India's growing rapport with Japan in the region has also caused unease in China all this while.[14]

Four correlated insights can be pointed out in China's approach to India's 'Look East'/'Act East' policy, which are relevant in the context of RCEP and TPP. *First*, China is of the view that India has expanded its outreach to ASEAN and the South-East Asian region constructively. Chinese officials, experts and media reports suggest that India's earlier 'Look East' policy was more 'economic-centric', whereas now India's tryst with ASEAN and the countries in the region is quite comprehensive (Li Hongmei 2010). This makes China uncomfortable given that Beijing always wants to remain the dominant power in this region.

Second, China relates the US factor quite closely to India's 'Look East'/'Act East' policy. Though Chinese experts and commentators have argued that India's current serious commitment to both ASEAN and South-East Asia existed before the US's current 'pivot to Asia' policy, still the Americans always encouraged India to pursue an intensive policy towards South-East Asia and ASEAN in order to restrict the Chinese reach in the region (*china.org.cn* 2012).

Third, China locates India's policy approach to ASEAN and South-East Asia with the Japan factor and the Japanese strategic presence. It sees India as Japan's trusted and assured partner on regional security and military issues and in the broader ASEAN politics (Li Hongmei 2010). India's informal security alliance or bonding with Japan, Australia and the US has always disquieted China.

Fourth, China locates India's current approach to the region as being China-centric. It is argued that India today proactively angles its policies in the South China Sea and other issues in the region to take advantage of China's problematic relations with countries like Vietnam, Philippines, Japan, the US and some ASEAN countries.[15] It is because of the growing India–ASEAN maritime understanding and India's recent oil exploration agreement with Vietnam that Beijing is vigilant about and antagonistic to India's involvement in ASEAN and in South-East Asian regional politics.

Tying up with India under RCEP will help China counterbalance not only the broader US design of building an economic ring with the major economies in the region, but also check India's progressive policy in this region. The key Chinese strategy here is: stay engaged and deny (Zhao Hong 2007: 136).

RCEP and Chinese acuity of India–China maritime politics

Connecting with powers like India under RCEP will help China keep an eye on and monitor the Indian calculus in the region more deliberately and institutionally. It will also help Beijing impede and control Indian moves in maritime politics, more specifically in the South China Sea zone. Chinese policymakers understand that in South-East Asia, India's prime strategic interest is to maximise trade and commercial dealings. At the same time, India has seriously maximised its maritime interests in the region. It is obvious that China will continue to be vigilant about India in South-East Asia as well as in East Asia.

Briefly stated, in the course of the evolution of RCEP and TPP, three important structural developments in the East Asian or broader Asia-Pacific regional order have taken place which have strategic implications for India–China ties. *First*, a direct Sino-US rivalry seems to be emerging on trade and economic fronts. In this rivalry, the ASEAN community is somewhat disunited. This aspect did exist before the emergence of RCEP and TPP, but it has been much more perceptible recently.

Second, in the ASEAN-led regional multilateral politics, engaging with ASEAN and its dialogue partners will be the priority for several countries, including India. ASEAN's centrality would continue to dominate both the political and economic bearings of regional politics, and that will have direct implications for Asia's two heavyweights, China and India. Therefore, Sino-Indian relations will be one of the highlights of regional politics in future.

Third, China will continue to place most of its foreign policy thrust and emphasis on ASEAN and South-East Asia. Though China's engagement with ASEAN will continue to decide the greater part of East Asian politics, India will continue to emerge as a deciding power, and RCEP will be a favourable factor for India in the context of its 'Act East' policy.

On the whole, the politics of RCEP and TPP are pushing regional power play to a new level. China believes that the US will eventually invite India, its traditional partner in Asia, to join TPP (Jin Baisong 2013). Since TPP is likely to pose a serious challenge to Beijing's regional trade and economic supremacy, the Chinese policymakers will make every effort to push regional FTA negotiation through RCEP or may actively promote the idea of FTAAP. As the progressive nature of the Asia-Pacific politics suggests, China will be left with fewer options and may eventually concede to the ASEAN+6 mechanism. Also, it will be compelled to forge an understanding with India in signing an FTA in the near future. For India, this would be an appropriate occasion to discuss the issue of trade deficit with China at the bilateral level.

Beijing's APEC call on India: a new twist in India–China ties?

Are India–China relations in Asia-Pacific entering a new level of engagement? During the first meeting between President Xi Jinping and Prime Minister Modi on the sidelines of the sixth BRICS summit in Brazil during 14–16 July 2014, China invited India to attend the APEC Summit meeting that was scheduled to be held in Beijing in November 2014. The Indian side viewed this as a 'significant gesture' and a 'serious and important invitation' (MEA 2014).[16] But why did China extend this invitation to India unilaterally?

First, President Xi tried to impress Prime Minister Modi, who had just taken over power in India, about China's vision of Asia and global affairs. Xi said, 'as two leading emerging countries, if China and India voice a common position, the whole world would listen' and that 'China and India could be partners instead of competitors' (Wu Jiao 2014). Xi's expression was a political and strategic one, aiming to convey that China wants to collaborate with India at bilateral as well as regional and global levels. This was noticed on the issue of permanent membership for India in the SCO. Without committing himself, President Xi told the Indian Prime Minister that India must be prepared to accept greater responsibility in the SCO, if offered. The attempt was to win some level of trust at political and diplomatic levels that China wants a 'cooperative' partnership with India at regional or global levels.[17]

Second, Beijing's invitation was a 'political statement', which expounded a 'leadership position' that China aims to carry forward with regard to Asia-Pacific. It is not for the first time that China surprised many countries, including India, through this kind of open invitation. Beijing today is known to take a 'unilateral' call on many global affairs, which can sometimes be quite startling. A prominent example of this was China's lobbying for and eventual induction of South Africa during the 2011 Sanya BRICS leadership summit.

Third, China's invitation is linked with the current crux of China's regional foreign policy strategy where both 'connectivity' and 'partnership' are two important themes (see, for example, Feng and Huang 2014; Yang Jiechi 2014). The official Chinese-proposed APEC theme for the November 2014 meeting was: *Shaping the future through Asia-Pacific Partnership*.[18] Regional economic integration, innovative growth and connectivity and infrastructure development were some of the overarching themes of the summit (*ncapec.org* 2014). On most of these issues, India factored in China's Asia-Pacific and regional stratagem.

Through the 'partnership' theme China factors India as a developing country as well as an emerging economy within a variety of global politics that includes Asia-Pacific as well. In Beijing's regional Economic Corridor projects and Maritime Silk Route (MSR) projects India is an important factor. China is also engaged with India in the Bangladesh–China–India–Myanmar Economic Corridor (BCIM-EC) project.

Fourth, China's invitation was meant to advocate that New Delhi must review its Western orientation or 'anti-China' mindset in its foreign policy orientation. The Barack Obama administration has constantly seen India as a 'potential ally' in the US's 'pivot Asia' policy. The Chinese offer came just before the round of the India–US strategic dialogue which was scheduled for the end of July 2014. It was also timed ahead of Prime Minister Modi's visit to Japan as Prime Minister.

Fifth, the TPP issue may have also driven China to issue this invitation to India. The APEC Beijing meeting discussed regional economic integration, where much of the focus was on TPP (Tang and Wang 2014). Even though the Chinese strategic circles see TPP as being linked with the US's 'pivot Asia'/ 'rebalancing' strategy to balance China in some way, they are open to China joining TPP if the trade rules and negotiation styles are relaxed in favour of emerging economies. Recently, some experts and groups in the US have pushed ahead the dialogue of India's possible APEC membership (Ayres 2014; see also *mydigitalfc.com* 2014): that India's inclusion in APEC will not only enhance the current Asia-Pacific economic integration process but will simplify India–US economic dealings where the American companies' market access concerns can be addressed (ibid.). For China, a better understanding with India on regional trading mechanisms may eventually compel the APEC economies, especially the US, to relax the norms and make TPP negotiations flexible in favour of the developing economies in future. China has also pushed forward the idea of RCEP, mostly in response to TPP, where India factors under the ASEAN+6 mechanism.[19] Compared to the US, China is still the most influential economic power both within and outside APEC (see Figure 11.5).

India and APEC: does China's support really matter?

India's tryst with APEC has been a two-decade-long struggle so far. In 1997, India was not inducted when the issue of inducting new members in APEC was in its prime debate. India repeated its membership request in 2007, which is still pending. APEC membership basically requires a consensus on the application by all existing members. India was mainly denied APEC admission on the ground that its economy was not integrated into the global system and India was unable to gain confidence among APEC members. In later years, there was a membership freeze within APEC.

As of now, Beijing may not oppose India's bid for APEC membership for a variety of reasons. *First*, there will be a galloping set of support for India on present conditions, including from the US, Japan and South-East Asian countries. *Second*, India has developed a good chain of contacts with most APEC

174 *Regional contours*

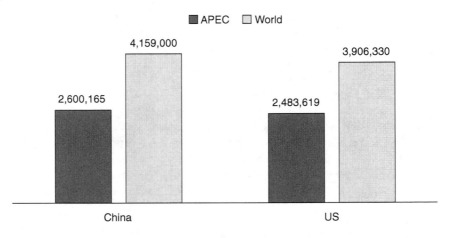

Figure 11.5 China, US comparative merchandise trade status with APEC and the world, 2013 (US$ million) (source: *StatsAPEC*, Asia-Pacific Economic Cooperation, http://statistics.apec.org/index.php/bilateral_linkage/index).

members. And *third*, APEC membership criteria are based on consensus mode, far from any technical or 'enforcement mechanisms' to which China can resort to oppose India's case. However, in pragmatic terms, India needs China's support along with that of the US and Japan to win consensus in its favour for APEC entry.

APEC's importance in Chinese foreign policy has grown substantially over the years. From the inception of APEC in 1989, Beijing has actively participated in APEC and has pushed forward many new ideas and initiatives as a leading economy.[20] Chinese leaders have used APEC as an effective channel to promote China's foreign economic policies and relations. Most APEC dealings are based on building consensus, and in this arrangement, a peer group networking is most important. Chinese leaders have used this to their advantage for policy consensus, trade as well as economic expansion. Not only is China a leading economy of APEC but also is the biggest trading partner, largest export market and a major source of investment for many APEC economies (*fmcoprc.gov.hk* 2013). Reports suggest that nine out of the top ten trading partners of China are APEC members (Kai Zhou 2011). Also, in aggregate, APEC members account for almost 70 per cent of FDI in China today (ibid.). Given these facts, China's opinion will matter for most of the APEC dealings no matter how much the US and other Pacific economies dominate APEC.

Collectively, the total volume of Asian economies constitutes a higher proportion than the non-Asian economies within APEC (see Figure 11.6), in which China has a better share with the Asian economies than the non-Asian economies (Figure 11.7). Beijing continues to bring an Asian identity to APEC, and the Chinese leadership has promoted the 'Asian spirit' within APEC (Liu Zhenmin 2014).

Between RCEP and TPP 175

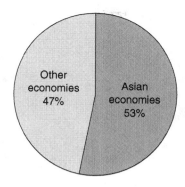

Figure 11.6 Share of Asian and other non-Asian economies in APEC's total GDP (PPP) (source: *World Development Indicators*, World Bank Data, http://data.worldbank.org/indicator/NY.GDP.MKTP.PP.CD).

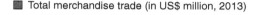
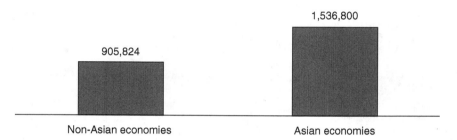

Figure 11.7 China's total merchandise trade with Asian and non-Asian APEC economies, 2013 (US$ million) (source: *StatsAPEC*, Asia-Pacific Economic Cooperation, http://statistics.apec.org/index.php/bilateral_linkage/index (accessed 28 July 2014)).

To sum up, China's overture to India as regards APEC merits thoroughgoing policy contemplation. It has implications for Asia-Pacific as well as for India–China bilateral ties. China's invitation to India is a 'forwarding' approach that is deliberate and a potent one. India will be continually tested with this kind of economic proposal in coming times, as Beijing pursues an active, assertive and forward-looking foreign policy. India must also capitalise on its own campaigning to promote its bid in this Asia-Pacific economic grouping with other bigger and smaller countries in APEC, including the US and other Pacific economies.

Notes

1 For an excellent discussion on the issue of trade liberalisation, see Hicks and Soo 2012.
2 In the current debate on Asian integration, the debate on East Asian integration is the foremost one. The socio-cultural and historical bonding among the East Asian community is at the core of this prevalent thesis. Ironically, it is the same set of issues and politics in the post-cold war period that placed them apart. See Gwi-Ok Kim 2012.
3 RCEP negotiations were first held among the ASEAN countries and ASEAN's FTA partners on 20 November 2012, on the sidelines of the East Asia Summit in Phnom Penh, Cambodia, though discussions over the idea started in 2011. The 19th ASEAN Economic Ministers (AEM) meeting discussed a roadmap for RCEP in Hanoi, Vietnam in March 2013. See *Global Times* 2013. It is argued that RCEP is expected to be more flexible than TPP in accommodating new members. It also permits different timeframes in implementing provisions for developing countries, unlike TPP. See Drysdale 2013.
4 Kristy Hsu argues that RCEP is a much more liberal initiative, as it allows 'external economic partners' beyond ASEAN+6, if they manage to sign FTAs with ASEAN. RCEP may involve external powers like the US and Russia in future if they manage to conduct FTA negotiations with ASEAN. See Hsu 2013: 42.
5 Barack Obama explicitly articulated the 'pivot' or 'rebalance' strategy during his visit to the Asia-Pacific region in late 2011. For an excellent analysis of this aspect, see Paal 2013. Fergusson *et al.* 2013 also note how TPP is linked with the Obama administration's 'pivot' Asia policy.
6 American experts like Claude Barfield hold this view. See Wilson 2013.
7 Baldwin 2006 argues that the 'TPP is an experiment in "multilateralising regionalism", intended to make the mess of PTAs in the region more consistent with the multilateral, rule-based system of non-discriminatory trade relations' governed by WTO. See Capling and Ravenhill 2011: 554.
8 Capling and Ravenhill 2011: 554 argue that the aim of the TPP negotiators is to produce 'a comprehensive, high-quality, multi-party agreement that could help to tame the tangle of PTAs' and be a potential stepping stone to achieving the long-term APEC goal of liberalising trade among its member economies.
9 Also for an excellent comparison between RCEP and TPP, see Hsu 2013.
10 This is the view of Xu Liping, who is a Research Fellow at the Institute of Asia-Pacific Studies of CASS, Beijing. See Yu Lintao 2012.
11 This is the view of Zhang Jie, who is a researcher at the Institute of Asia-Pacific Studies at CASS. Pointing to the internal differences that exist among the ASEAN countries, Zhang Jie also argues that countries like Philippines are rigid over the South China Sea dispute, and this could be a possible barrier to gather consensus and unity to build RCEP. See Yu Lintao 2012.
12 Chinese experts see the American 'pivot to Asia' policy as similar to that of 'rebalancing' strategy in Asia-Pacific. See Fu Mengzi 2012. The domestic discourse in China suggests that the American Asia-Pacific strategy is linked to two main broader strategies: (i) to take adequate advantage of Asia's economic conditions and (ii) to check and counter China's influence in the region. See Szczudlik-Tatar 2012: 4.
13 One principal example of this is the China–ASEAN FTA. Chinese premier Zhu Rongji first suggested it in November 2000. See Dosch 2010: 74.
14 For instance, the tour of then Prime Minister Manmohan Singh to Japan was closely watched by Chinese strategists. Some vituperative pieces also appeared in the Chinese media about the growing India–Japan relations. See, for example, Cai Hong 2013.
15 For example, Ju Hailong 2012 argues: 'taking a stronger role in South China Sea disputes and taking advantage of China's territorial conflicts with its neighbouring countries are India's strategic means to counter China'.

16 When India requested membership in APEC, it received support from Australia, Japan and the US. But these countries did not pursue India's case further. Mainly it was cited that India was not a Pacific economy and India's economy was not well integrated with the Asia-Pacific economies. Besides, APEC decided not to admit new members till 2010. Later, India was invited to become an observer in November 2011. See *nis-glonass.ru* 2011.

17 Author's impression from an interaction with a few well-known Chinese experts on India in Shanghai. The author thanks the experts in the Shanghai Institute for International Studies (SIIS) and Shanghai Academy of Social Science (SASS) for sharing their insights on the subject. The author met them during his trip to Shanghai on 21–23 July 2014.

18 APEC announced the 2014 theme: 'Shaping the future through Asia-Pacific partnership', *apec.org* 2014. See *ncapec.org* 2014.

19 For more on the debate on the Chinese perspectives on RCEP and TPP and how India factors in this formulation, see Panda 2014.

20 In keeping with the criterion for APEC membership that the applicant country must be a 'separate economy' rather than a 'separate state', officially, APEC members are known as member economies rather than member countries. Taiwan's entry to APEC was made possible by this criterion: it was termed as 'Chinese Taipei'. In November 1991, the People's Republic of China (PRC), Hong Kong (China) and 'Chinese Taipei' were inducted as three new member economies. The entry of Hong Kong, which is now a Special Administrative Region of the PRC, to APEC was made possible as a 'British colony'. India was invited to attend as an observer at the APEC meeting in November 2011. Currently, a number of economies like Pakistan, Cambodia, Costa Rica, Colombia, Panama, Ecuador, Bangladesh, Macau, Sri Lanka, Mongolia and Laos are looking for APEC membership along with India. Information extracted from various sources, such as *international.gc.ca*; *apec.org*.

References

apec.org, 2014. 'Issued by the APEC Informal Senior Officials' Meeting, Asia-Pacific Economic Cooperation, Beijing, China, December 13, 2013', www.apec.org/Press/News-Releases/2013/1213_theme.aspx (accessed on July 28 2014).

Ayres, Alyssa, 2014.'Bringing India inside the Asian trade tent', *Council on Foreign Relations, Policy Innovation Memorandum*, No. 46, June, www.cfr.org/india/brining-india-asian-trade-tent/p33173 (accessed on 30 July 2014).

Baldwin, Richard, 2006. 'Multilateralising regionalism: spaghetti bowls as building blocs on the path to global free trade', *The World Economy*, 29(11): 1451–1518.

Basu Das, Sanchita, 2012. 'Asia's regional comprehensive economic partnership', *East Asia Forum*, 27 August, www.eastasiaforum.org (accessed on 2 June 2013).

Basu Das, Sanchita, 2013. 'RCEP and TPP: comparisons and concerns', *ISEAS Perspectives*, Singapore, No. 2, 7 January.

Cai Hong, 2013. 'Japan, India eager to forge closer ties', *China Daily*, 30 May, www.chinadaily.com.cn/cndy/2013-05/30/content_16545844.htm (accessed on 2 June 2013).

Capling, Ann and John Ravenhill, 2011. 'Multilateralising regionalism: what role for the Trans-Pacific Partnership Agreement?', *The Pacific Review*, 24(5): 553–75.

Chaulia, Sreeram, 2012. 'Trade bloc blues: can India draw the maximum advantage out of the RCEP and TPP tussle?' *Economic Times*, 15 December, http://articles.economictimes.indiatimes.com/2012-12-14/news/35820026_1_rcep-free-trade-regional-comprehensive-economic-partnership (accessed on 27 May 2013).

China Daily, 2013. 'Indonesia may prefer RCEP to TPP', *China Daily*, 30 January, www.chinadaily.com.cn/xinhua/2013-01-30/content_8175420.html (accessed on 21 May 2013).

china.org.cn, 2012. 'India's "Look East Policy"', *China.org.cn*, 6 April, www.china.org.cn/opinion/2012-04/06/content_25075354.htm (accessed on 24 May 2013).

Dosch, Jorn, 2010. 'China and Southeast Asia: a new regional order in the making?', in Lowell Dittmer and George T. Yu (eds), *China, the Developing World, and the New Global Dynamic*, Boulder, CO: Lynne Rienner, pp. 61–82.

Drysdale, Peter, 2013. 'Asia and the international trade regime', *East Asia Forum*, 7 January, pp. 1–3.

Feng Zhongping and Huang Jing, 2014. 'China's strategic partnership diplomacy: engaging with a changing diplomacy', *Working Paper 8*, EGMONT, FRIDE, European Strategic Partnership Observatory, June, pp. 1–19.

Fergusson, Ian F., William H. Cooper, Remy Jurenas and Brock R. Williams, 2013. 'The Trans-Pacific Partnership negotiations and issues for Congress' (Summary), *CRS Report for Congress: Congressional Research Service*, 7–5700, R42694, 21 August, www.fas.org/sgp/crs/row/R42694.pdf (accessed on 22 December 2015).

fmcoprc.gov.hk, 2013. 'Deepen reform and opening up and work together for a Better Asia Pacific', Address by H.E. Xi Jinping, President of the People's Republic of China to the APEC CEO Summit, 9 October, www.fmcoprc.gov.hk/eng/xwdt/zt/xzxcxytjh/t1088517.htm (accessed on 26 July 2014).

Fu Mengzi, 2012. 'Path paved for Clinton successor', *China Daily*, 6 December, www.china.org.cn/opinion/2012-12/06/content_27327911_2.htm (accessed on 24 May 2013).

Global Times, 2013. 'ASEAN eyes bigger role in global economy with RCEP: Malaysian official', *Global Times*, 21 March, www.globaltimes.cn/DesktopModules/DnnForge%20-%20NewsArticles/Print.aspx?tabid=99&tabmoduleid=94&articleId=769663&moduleId=405&PortalID=0 (accessed on 27 May 2013).

Guoyou Song and Wen Jin Yuan, 2012. 'China's Free Trade Agreement strategies', *The Washington Quarterly*, 35(4), Fall, pp. 107–19.

Gwi-Ok Kim, 2012. 'Building a peaceful East Asian Community: origins of a regional concept and visions for a global age', *Asian Perspective*, 37(2), April–June, pp. 233–54.

Hicks, Raymond and Soo Yeon Kim, 2012. 'Reciprocal trade agreements in Asia: credible commitment to trade liberalization or paper tigers?' *Journal of East Asian Studies*, 12(1), January–April, pp. 1–29.

Hsu, Kristy, 2013. 'The RCEP: integrating India into the Asian economy', *Indian Foreign Affairs Journal*, 8(1), January–March, pp. 41–51.

international.gc.ca, 2014. 'History and membership of APEC', *Foreign Affairs, Trade and Development Canada*, Government of Canada, www.international.gc.ca/apec/map-carte.aspx (accessed on 26 July 2014).

Jin Baisong, 2013. 'The futility of US designs', *China Daily*, 27 May, www.china.org.cn/opinion/2013-05/27/content_28941237.htm (accessed on 31 May 2013).

Ju Hailong, 2012. 'India playing long game in South China Sea', *Global Times*, 9 April, www.globaltimes.cn/NEWS/tabid/99/ID/703944/India-playing-long-game-in-South-China-Sea.aspx (accessed on 23 May 2013).

Kai Zhou, 2011. 'Integration into the APEC region', *Importance of APEC to China*, APEC 2011, University of Hawaii System, UNERO, uhero.hawaii.edu/74 (accessed on 14 November 2014).

Li Hongmei, 2010. 'India's "Look East Policy" means "Look to encircle China"?', *People's Daily*, 27 October, http://english.peopledaily.com.cn/90002/96417/7179404.html (accessed on 24 May 2013).

Liu Zhenmin, 2014. 'Insisting on win-win cooperation and forging the Asian Community of common destiny together', *China International Studies*, vol. 45, March–April, pp. 5–25.

Malhotra, Jyoti, 2012. 'In RCEP vs. TPP alphabet trade bloc soup, India refuses to choose', *Business Standard*, 25 November, www.business-standard.com/article/economy-policy/in-rcep-vs-tpp-alphabet-trade-bloc-soup-india-refuses-to-choose-112112503008_1.html (accessed on 21 May 2013).

MEA, 2014. 'Transcript of media briefing by official spokesperson in Fortaleza on Prime Minister's ongoing visit', MEA, 15 July, http://mea.gov.in/in-focus-article.htm?23630/Transcript+of+Media+Briefing+by+Official+Spokesperson+in+Fortaleza+on+Prime+Ministers+ongoing+visit (accessed on 26 July 2014).

mydigitalfc.com, 2014. 'US urged to support India's inclusion in APEC forum', my digitalfc.com, 26 June, www.mydigitalfc.com/print/336385 (accessed on 26 July 2014).

ncapec.org, 2014. 'National Centre for APEC', *The Voice of U.S. Business in the Asia-Pacific*, www.ncapec.org/events/ (accessed on 30 July 2014).

nis-glonass.ru, 2011. 'Workshop: GNSS application for seamless transport supply chain connectivity in APEC', Asia Pacific Economic Cooperation, www.nis-glonass.ru/apec/Member.php (accessed on 28 July 2014).

Paal, Douglas, 2013. 'The United States and Asia in 2012: domestic politics takes charge', *Asian Survey*, 53(1), January–February, pp. 12–21.

Panda, Jagannath P., 2014. 'Factoring the RCEP and the TPP: China, India and the politics of regional integration', *Strategic Analysis*, 38(1), January–February, pp. 49–67.

Szczudlik-Tatar, Justyna, 2012. 'China's response to the United States' Asia-Pacific Strategy', *Policy Paper*, The Polish Institute of International Affairs, No. 41, October, pp. 1–8.

Tang Guoqiang and Wang Zhenyu, 2014. 'Prospects for Asia Pacific economic integration', *China International Studies*, January–February, pp. 64–87.

Terada, Takashi, 2013. 'A golden opportunity for Japan's regional integration policy: TPP, RCEP, and CJK', *AJISS Commentary*, The Association of Japanese Institutes of Strategic Studies, No. 173, 26 March, pp. 1–4.

ustr.gov, 2011. www.ustr.gov/about-us/press-office/fact-sheets/2011/november/united-states-trans-pacific-partnership (accessed on 1 January 2013).

Wignaraja, Ganeshan, 2013a. 'Why Indian business should embrace the RCEP', *Asia Pathways* (A blog of the Asian Development Bank Institute), 11 July, www.asiapathways-adbi.org/2013/07/why-indian-business-should-embrace-the-rcep/ (accessed on 29 July 2013).

Wignaraja, Ganeshan, 2013b. 'RCEP is huge for Indian businesses which should scale up': Surojit Gupta's Interview with Ganeshan Wignaraja, *Times of India*, 6 February, http://articles.timesofindia.indiatimes.com/2013-02-06/interviews/36765453_1_rcep-indian-businesses-regional-comprehensive-economic-partnership (accessed on 27 May 2013).

Wilson, Karl, 2013. 'A tangled mess', *China Daily* (Asia Weekly), 4(10), 15–21 March, http://epaper.chinadailyasia.com/pools/2-20130315-001.pdf (accessed on 20 May 2013).

Wu Jiao, 2014. 'China's Xi, India's Modi meet with upbeat tone', *China Daily*, 15 July, http://usa.chinadaily.com.cn/epaper/2014-07-15/content_17782213.htm (accessed on 26 July 2014).

Yang Jiechi, 2014. 'China's new foreign relations for a complex world', *China International Studies*, January/February, pp. 5–17.

Yu Lintao, 2012. 'RCEP makes a difference', *Beijing Review*, 29 November, www.bjreview.com.cn/quotes/txt/2012-11/27/content_503600.htm (accessed on 20 May 2013).

Zhao Hong, 2007. 'India and China: rivals or partners in Southeast Asia?', *Contemporary Southeast Asia: A Journal of International and Strategic Affairs*, 29(1), April, pp. 121–42.

Zhao Qinghai, 2007. 'The four-nation alliance: concept vs. reality', *China International Studies*, no. 7, winter, pp. 11–24.

12 East Asian dynamism

India as a security provider and China[1]

In the current interplay of world politics, the new discussion in India is how India must push forward its reach in East Asia through its newly devised 'Act East' policy than just the previously stated 'Look East' policy.[2] The countries of the region expect India to become a possible security provider for them through greater strategic and military engagements. Japan and South Korea, two of India's 'extended neighbours' and 'special partners', for example, perceive India's presence as being conducive to their strategic interests. Besides, the Americans have advocated that New Delhi must play a proactive role in East Asia. Given the interests of these different powers, the Indian political as well as official circles also recognise that India now sees itself as a net security provider.[3] This chapter outlines how India and China are balancing each other between Beijing's commanding politics in East Asia and India's quest for greater power status, search for energy resources in the region as well as the quest to emerge as a possible security provider.

East Asia in India's 'extended neighbourhood' diplomacy

New Delhi's East Asian reach is a construct of its 'extended neighbourhood' conception (*mea.gov.in* 2014; see also Scott 2009). The official parlance of this concept was outlined in 2006 by the then Minister of External Affairs, Pranab Mukherjee. He said that India's political, economic and defence engagement with West Asia, Central Asia, South-East Asia as well as in the IOR explained this phenomenon (Mukherjee 2006). This concept of 'extended neighbourhood' signifies a classic mixture of soft power as well as hard-power projection with continuous multilateral political, economic and ideational engagements that India steadily employs in different parts of Asia.

ASEAN remains the main threshold in India's East Asia policy. Not only does ASEAN enhance India's 'extended neighbourhood' policy in the East Asian region, it equally provides India an institutional base to engage with the region structurally (Scott 2009).[4] India was inducted as a sectoral partner of ASEAN in 1992, dialogue partner in 1996 and summit-level partner in 2002. In 2003, the two sides signed the Instrument of Accession to the Treaty of Amity and Cooperation in South-East Asia, and a Joint Declaration for Cooperation to

Combat International Terrorism and a Framework Agreement on Comprehensive Economic Cooperation at the Bali Summit. In 2004, the two sides signed the ASEAN–India Partnership for Peace, Progress and Shared Prosperity. This was followed by a Plan of Action that was implemented from 2004 to 2010; its second phase was in progress from 2010 to 2015. India's previous Look East policy was advanced further with the December 2012 India–ASEAN Commemorative Summit marking 20 years of India's association with ASEAN and the tenth anniversary of India–ASEAN summit-level partnership, to upgrade the bilateral ties to a 'strategic partnership' (*aseanindia.com* 2012). The crux of this Commemorative Summit was an evolving security understanding between the two sides, mainly on the aspect of maritime cooperation.

But India still continues to remain a cautious power when it comes to defence- and security-centred issues in East Asia. India does not necessarily have to take a position on most security- or conflict-driven issues; yet given the security outlook and policy perspective that it shares with East Asia, New Delhi must rise to the occasion and express a leadership position. Given the growing security dynamics and maritime politics in East Asia, India and ASEAN have nevertheless upgraded their partnership to a 'strategic' one, where ASEAN member countries like Vietnam, the Philippines and Singapore expect India to play a leadership role. For instance, praising the active policy of the new Indian government under Prime Minister Narendra Modi and viewing India as a key 'strategic partner' in the evolving South-East Asian security architecture, the Deputy Prime Minister and Foreign Minister of Vietnam, Pham Binh Minh, has appealed to India for a greater role in 'freedom of navigation, maritime safety and security in the South China Sea region' (*zeenews.india.com* 2014).

In East Asia, India enjoys a good thrust of 'strategic partnership' with Japan, South Korea and ASEAN, the last being the most important. This 'strategic partnership', formally launched in 2012, is still in the process of consolidation. For a long time, the South-East Asian community has seen India's presence on a 'positive scale' (Brewster 2013: 151), particularly as an alternate power with regard to China. India and ASEAN have engaged earlier with a set of dialogue mechanisms, high-level visits of defence personnel, training and education, coordinated patrols, joint military exercises, etc. Most of these engagements have, however, been 'bilateral centric' (ibid.; see also Scott 2009).

A prime aspect of India's defence diplomacy with ASEAN member states is its maritime approach with the region. ASEAN members like Myanmar, Singapore, Thailand, Malaysia and Indonesia are important to India's maritime diplomacy in the north-east Indian Ocean, where India has usually maintained its maritime authority. The core of India–ASEAN naval engagement all these years has evolved through joint naval exercises, bilateral dialogues and exercises and a few exercises like MILAN (*indiannavy.nic.in* 2012; see Table 12.1). India has deployed at regular intervals its vessels and fleets in the South China Sea region as well as in the Malacca Strait and Sunda Strait. Further, the Indian Navy travels at regular intervals to ports of Thailand, Vietnam, Philippines, Cambodia, Singapore and Indonesia. Currently, India has stepped up cooperation with

Table 12.1 India's naval exercises with ASEAN members

Name and mode	Countries involved/year commenced	Major focus
Singapore–India Maritime Bilateral Exercise (SIMBEX): Annual	• Singapore, 1993–1994	• Enhance inter-operability and mutual understanding • Maritime search, security and rescue operations
MILAN (Multi-nation)	• 1995; 17 countries participated in 2014, 7 of them ASEAN members (Singapore, Vietnam, Thailand, Malaysia, Indonesia, Brunei and Philippines)	• Humanitarian assistance and disaster relief • Peace and rescue operations
India–Indonesia coordinated Patrol Naval Exercise (INDINDO CORPAT)	• Indonesia • Biannual exercise • Started in 2000	• Held along the International Maritime Boundary Line • Held normally in April and October • Joint patrol for sea search, coordination against piracy, armed robbery, poaching, illegal immigration, human trafficking, drug trafficking, etc. • Launched in line with India's Look East policy
Indo-Thai Coordinated Patrol (CORPAT)	• Thailand • Started in 2005	• Counter piracy, poaching and arms smuggling • Enhance inter-operability • Effective implementation of the Law of the Sea to prevent illegal activities
KOMODO	• Seventeen countries including India, Indonesia, the US, China, Russia, New Zealand, South Korea, Japan, Singapore, Malaysia, Brunei, Thailand, Vietnam, the Philippines and Laos participated • Inaugural multilateral naval exercise	• Humanitarian assistance/disaster relief (HA/DR) exercise • The second exercise to focus on peacekeeping operations under the UN flag
RIMPAC (Rim of the Pacific Exercise)	• Australia, Brunei, Canada, Chile, Colombia, France, India, Indonesia, Japan, Malaysia, Mexico, Netherlands, New Zealand, Norway, People's Republic of China, Peru, Republic of Korea, Philippines, Singapore, Tonga, the UK and US • Began in 1971	• Cooperation of the combined forces and improve individual war fighting competencies • India sent ship for the first time in 2014 • This year also marked the first time hospital ships participated • People's Republic of China also participated for the first time in 2014

Source: information compiled from open sources like Press Information Bureau, Ministry of Defence: Government of India, *The Hindu*, *Times of India*, Embassy of India in Thailand, *Jakarta Post*, etc.

Vietnam in the maritime sector. Importantly, India has built a few bases south of Visakhapatnam for its Eastern Fleet, and a new naval airbase, known as INS *Baaz*, south of Andaman and Nicobar Islands. Its territory of Andaman and Nicobar Islands allows India to maintain a psychological advantage to reach quickly the Bay of Bengal region as well as the Malacca Strait. To increase the scope of maritime surveillance in the region, the Indian Navy opened a new 'forward airbase' on Greater Nicobar in July 2012 (*indiannavy.nic.in* 2012).[5] India has also sent INS *Sudershini* as part of an India–ASEAN commemorative expedition to mark the ancient and contemporary maritime linkages between the two sides (*aseanindia.com* n.d.). These have been soft-power approaches by India to make its presence felt in the ASEAN region. Opportunities and options exist for India to emerge as a stronger security and military power in East Asia. A foremost attempt in this endeavour could be to advance further the multilateral and institutional presence that India shares with the East Asian region. India's current forte in East Asia is linked with its longstanding engagement not only with ASEAN and its members, but also with other great powers in the region such as Japan and South Korea.

China's policy gambit in East Asia

In East Asia, Beijing has always given priority thrust to ASEAN since the crafting of the 'strategic partnership' in 2003. China's core aim has been how to generate confidence and optimism over its rise. Vietnam and Philippines in particular have seen the 'rise of China' as not being 'peaceful' for the region (Ng and Chen 2014). Meanwhile, the 'peaceful rise' of China projection, which was floated by Zheng Bijian, the then Vice-Principal of the Central Party School of China during the Boao Forum for Asia in 2003, has moved concurrently with the Sino-ASEAN strategic partnership.

Since 2003, time and again, the leaderships in China and ASEAN have discussed China's rise and developmental model, and have brought new insights to advance mutual trust, reduce tensions and uphold peace and stability. In October 2003, the Sino-ASEAN strategic partnership was forged through a joint declaration, titled *A Strategic Partnership for Peace and Prosperity* (*asean.org* 2003). Since then the two sides have signed numerous agreements to boost this partnership, but an inclusive Sino-ASEAN engagement is still missing. From 2003 onwards, the core of this strategic engagement has been trade and economic relationship, and the tenth anniversary event witnessed both sides acknowledging the importance of this aspect. Meanwhile, Beijing has emerged as ASEAN's biggest trading partner and ASEAN as China's third-largest trading partner. Statistics suggest that their bilateral trade has increased fourfold since 2002. China and ASEAN had expressed ambitiously to push the bilateral trade figure to US$500 billion by 2015 (Zhao and Zhong 2014).

It may be noted, however, that elsewhere in the world strategic partnership is not all about trade contacts and economic engagement. Objectively, a strategic partnership must also have political and strategic bearings of a bilateral relationship. In the Sino-ASEAN strategic partnership, this seems to be quite problematic currently, specifically given the dispute over the South China Sea. The 2012 ASEAN summit in Cambodia failed to evolve a code of conduct (COC), exposing ASEAN's internal divisions over the issue.

Without compromising on China's claims, the leadership in Beijing wants to become judicious and moderate in resolving the dispute. China insists on an 'Asia Way' and advocates an 'ASEAN Way' (Tang Qifang 2015) for two correlated reasons. *First*, China does not want the ASEAN countries to seek outside powers' intervention on maritime issues, mainly of the US (*chinadaily.com.cn* 2014).

Second, Beijing wants to keep outside powers away from the regional politics, so that it can easily remain the predominant power in the regional politics. India is a factor in that. Even though the Chinese leadership has been cautious in branding India as an 'outside' power in the ASEAN region, it has given enough hints that New Delhi must keep itself detached in the South China Sea zone.

Beijing's leadership vision remains the core of its East Asian reach. China has gradually argued in favour of 'Asian integration' in which 'ASEAN community building' remains central. For China, the 'Asian integration' process is a difficult entity to achieve, whereas 'ASEAN community building' is viable economically though not politically. Beijing nevertheless pursues the discussion of 'Asian integration' to establish a leadership case. This is noticed in China's constant backing for the establishment of an integrated South-East Asian community (Bai Shi 2015). For instance, the Chinese Foreign Minister Wang Yi stated at the 2015 Boao Forum that 'by the end of 2015, ASEAN will establish three communities – political-security, economic and socio-cultural community – which are important milestones of Asian integration' (*fmprc.gov.cn* 2015). Beijing sees that ASEAN countries are important to its economic fortune; the ASEAN community also reciprocates China's economic pursuits in the region.

Taking this state of affairs a step forward, the Chinese leadership has proposed a '2+7' framework to augment China's interaction with ASEAN. The Chinese Premier Li Keqiang proposed this framework during the 16th China–ASEAN Leaders Meeting held in Brunei in 2013. The '2' entails political consensus on two aspects: deepening strategic trust and improving economic developmental cooperation; the '7' refers to cooperation in areas like politics, trade and economy, interconnection and building trust, finance, security, ocean, and humanity (Wang Yuzhu 2014). Further on, China's Foreign Minister Wang Yi has made a 'ten-point' proposal of China–ASEAN cooperation.[6]

Chinese maritime assertiveness

Geographically, the South China Sea is a slice of the Pacific Ocean, encompassing the waters from Singapore to the Taiwan Strait in the north-east. Three correlated factors that drive the Chinese to take a somewhat aggressive stance on the issue are: (i) this is a key maritime transportation zone for China's future energy and maritime posture; (ii) it is an energy-resourceful region; and (iii) the legality of this sea zone is a vital factor in maritime diplomacy. Crucial for the Chinese is the unique distinction of the South China Sea as the 'maritime transportation' zone between Asia-Pacific and the rest of the world.

Debate continues whether China's recent actions in the South China Sea replicate an assertive policy (Swaine and Fravel 2011; Jian Zhang 2013). Land reclamation on islands and reefs in the South China Sea and building facilities on artificial islands that Beijing has created would help it to mount several tasks that include military defence (Holmes 2015; Hunt 2015). These actions are provocative from the perspective of South-East Asia, especially in the view of Vietnam and Philippines.

India's multilateral presence: need for maritime foresight

New Delhi's thrust so far has been on building closer relations with ASEAN, ADMM+, ARF, Indian Ocean Rim Association (IORA) and Indian Ocean Naval Symposium (IONS) to propel a good understanding on maritime security issues, including other security and governance issues that are keys to the East Asian regional architecture. India's official advocacy is to thrust the focus on ASEAN and commit to peace and stable regional security architecture through forums like ARF and ADMM+, including expanded maritime interactions. Historically, the South-East Asian countries were initially lukewarm to India's entry into ARF. In the post-Cold War phase, India slowly raised its engagement with ASEAN and joined ARF in 1996. Gradually, ASEAN members realised India's importance and standing and started seeing India's emergence as a vital factor in South-East Asian security. Some of them, like Singapore, started viewing India as a possible counterbalance to the rising Chinese presence in the region (Batabyal 2006). Since then, through its institutional bonding with ASEAN, India has deepened its engagement with ARF and ADMM+.

East Asian Integration (EAI), from an Indian perspective, for example, highlights New Delhi's approach to the East Asian community as well as Asia-Pacific. In India's official policy phraseology, 'The East Asia Summit is the forum for building an open, inclusive and transparent architecture of regional cooperation in the Asia Pacific region' (*mea.gov.in* 2011). The context and importance of EAS is implied and argued in Indian foreign policy mainly within a construct of realising the importance of ARF and ADMM+ (ibid.). India's official perception of ARF was aptly outlined by the speech of its then Minister for External Affairs at the 20th ARF meeting in Brunei Darussalam: *first*, ARF as a dialogue forum is a useful mechanism provided it is backed with commitments by all nations; *second*, ARF can be a conduit of hope and solution for addressing security issues, including terrorism and maritime security; and *third*, ARF can be pushed ahead as a multilateral cultural tactic to address Asia's growing security and political dynamics (*mea.gov.in* 2013a). This official dialogue is, however, mostly rhetorical: neither has ARF been forthcoming about its perception of regional peace and stability nor has it helped in uniting the thoughts and spirit of its constituents the way it was originally meant to address. Besides, India is still not sure what its role should be in ARF and how it should approach ARF as a forum.

Compared to ARF, ADMM+ is a relatively new security mechanism. It is supposed to be a confidence-building mechanism and to uphold peace and stability through dialogue and discussion. ADMM+ has promoted a 'new mode of multilateralism' combining ASEAN members as well as eight dialogue partners (Australia, China, Japan, India, South Korea, New Zealand, Russia and the US) in the Asia-Pacific region. Counterterrorism, building cooperation in areas of humanitarian assistance and disaster relief, peacekeeping and maritime security have been the main areas of discussion in this forum. In ADMM+ meetings India has raised the issue of the South China Sea dispute but has not advocated a perspective that will augment its own position on freedom of navigation and oil exploration (*pib.nic.in* 2013).

It may be noted that actors like Vietnam and the Philippines who are parties to the South China Sea disputes, along with Taiwan, Brunei and Malaysia, which have some disquiet over the issue, are concerned about the Chinese authority and do not want to sit at the negotiating table with China. In the South China Sea, the Chinese authorities have unilaterally proposed 'joint development' of oil or energy exploration in disputed areas. The Chinese Defence Ministry has also cautioned that countries that want to carry out projects for their self-interest in the South China Sea region should confine them to the range of freedom of navigation; besides, freedom of navigation should not be a factor in 'territorial and ocean rights' of the countries involved (*chinadaily.com.cn* 2013).

There is scope for India to shape a well-crafted maritime drive over the South China Sea region. In this, a coordinated approach with likeminded countries like Vietnam and the Philippines, which share strategic interests similar to those of India and see India as a power, would be useful. The Vision Statement of the ASEAN–India Commemorative Summit points out that both ASEAN and India look to each other in 'strengthening cooperation to ensure maritime security and freedom of navigation' and 'safety of SLOCs for unfettered movement of trade in accordance with international law, including the UNCLOS [United Nations Convention on the Law of the Sea]' (*asean.org* 2012).

In its vision of ADMM+, India has stressed two key aspects: the vitality of ARF and the scope of ADMM+ in the regional security architecture. There is huge scope for these two multilateral frameworks to emerge as effective confidence-building mechanisms to address the security environment of the region. India's future outlook with regard to these two institutions should be on how to safeguard its maritime interests in this region through their intervention. Besides, India must pursue the dialogue of regional integration prudently through ARF and ADMM+. The progression of regional economic integration should forge with the ASEAN+6 mechanism and should converge with the sentiments of EAS, where India is a factor.

The China factor and India's potential leadership role

A politics of interdependence and inter-reliability along with new multilateral understanding is taking place in East Asia, where North-East Asia is an important factor (Zhang Tuosheng 2014). In this region, there is subtle competition between the US and China to maintain their respective regional supremacy (Kang Seung Woo 2014). Both Japan and South Korea are important factors in this power politics. If India has to enhance its East Asian reach further, boosting defence and strategic cooperation with these two countries must be a priority for it. Sharing rapport with them on matters of strategic and security affairs along with concrete and vigorous defence and strategic ties with East Asia on the whole will enhance India's strategic reach in the region.

With South Korea, the Foreign Policy and Security Dialogue (FPSD) promotes discussion and further cooperation in the field of space and nuclear cooperation, collaboration in defence production, maritime and cyber security along with cultural exchanges and people-to-people contacts (*mea.gov.in* 2013b). Any support from South Korea in the East Asian dynamics will be an added advantage to New Delhi. The regional order in Asia has become fragmented and there is a necessity for a liberal order in East Asia. India and South Korea can work together for a 'multipolar East Asia' (Tayal 2014: 5). North Korea and its denuclearisation can be a common factor for the two countries to cooperate under a 'comprehensive security' structure in East Asia.

In addition, India has to maximise its presence through participation and presence in East Asia. The Seoul Defence Dialogue (SDD) is a recently established forum where India must aim to participate. The SDD is the highest-ranking multilateral security dialogue platform at the level of vice minister, which has been hosted by the Republic of Korea's Ministry of Defence since November 2012. It addresses issues concerning peace and security in the broader Asia-Pacific, and in particular in the Korean Peninsula. China has not shown much interest in the SDD and has been passively partaking in the North-East Asian multilateral forums (Jaeho Hwang 2014). India must aim to fill that gap.

Relations with Japan are another important endeavour in this regard. The Senkaku/Diaoyu dispute between China and Japan does not seem to be getting anywhere to resolution. The US National Defence Authorization Act for Fiscal Year 2013, which outlined that East China Sea disputes are subject to the Treaty of Mutual Cooperation and Security between the US and Japan, has further complicated matters. The recent Japanese revision of its pacifist constitution and collective national self-defence doctrine has also compelled the Chinese to review the conditions in the East China Sea region and become more aggressive over the dispute.

India's official idiom is that the issue must be 'peacefully' resolved. India values China as an 'immediate neighbour' and as an 'economic powerhouse', and Japan as a valuable 'strategic and economic' regional and global partner. But are India's strategic and maritime interests in East or South-East Asia secured and enhanced by not taking a position on this dispute? Leading powers that aim to offer a leadership role cannot afford a cautious or conservative posture on disputes, especially those that need serious contemplation. India must have a greater vision and may contemplate to conditionally revise its customary standpoint on the Sino-Japanese maritime dispute. India's strategic treatise, if not actual official position, must have some resemblance to the Japanese stake in the dispute. This also makes practical sense given China's obsessive resistance to India's oil exploration and commercial activities in the South China Sea.

Key features of the current India–Japan defence partnership are: 2+2 dialogues involving the Foreign and Defence Secretaries, bilateral maritime exercises, Tokyo's regular partaking in the India–US Malabar exercise, transfer of defence technology and equipment to India, and notably, Joint Working Group (JWG) cooperation in the US2 amphibian aircraft and its technology, etc. (MEA 2014). Amongst all this, there is certain recognition and commitment on the part of both India and Japan to issues like maritime security, freedom of navigation and over flights. At the same time, India's support to Japan should not become a one-sided affair. In return, India must urge Japan to proactively support India's strategic character in East Asia and keep up the cooperation with India under the EAS.

The other factor that India must review and reassess is the evolving security dynamics in East Asia. East Asia is undergoing radical power transitions. The US role in the region is relatively declining and China–Russia understanding is growing. In addition, rising tensions between China and Japan, prevailing maritime disputes, tensions in Korean peninsula and unresolved North Korean nuclear issues are important factors that need serious appraisal. What makes the conditions in East Asia important for India is the simmering power balance between itself, China and Japan. No matter how much neutrality India maintains in East Asia, China will continue to identify India as a power closer to Japanese strategic interests. India must also introspect as to what extent China has appreciated India's 'neutrality' in the East Asian maritime disputes. The North Korean nuclear affair is another issue, which India must consider and proactively respond to as a regional power. The Tokyo Declaration between India and Japan has taken note of North Korea's denuclearisation. Both countries have urged North Korea to take 'concrete measures towards denuclearisation' and comply with global obligations (MEA 2014). Maintaining a strong bilateral understanding with Japan and South Korea would help India not only to address some of these security dynamics in East Asia but also to have a strong presence in East Asian affairs. That may compel Beijing to perceive India more pragmatically than earlier, which is important for India's emergence in the region.

Notes

1 This chapter is a revised version of Panda 2015. A portion of it has also been published in Panda 2014.
2 In a brainstorming session of 15 Indian Heads of Mission in East Asia and South-East Asia in Hanoi, India's Minister for External Affairs said that it was time now that India must 'Act East and not just Look East'. See *dnaindia.com* 2014.

3 Ashok K. Kantha, then Secretary (East), has been quoted saying: 'India has vital stakes in the Indian Ocean and in harnessing its capabilities as net security provider.' See *Business Standard* 2013.
4 Almost 26 India–ASEAN intergovernmental mechanisms exist, covering a range of areas such as security, political, economic and institutional engagements.
5 The Government of India has recently launched a number of infrastructure steps and projects in the Andaman and Nicobar chain of islands, notably, forwarding operating bases in Kamorta in Nicobar and in Diglipur in Andaman.
6 These comprise: dialogue, implement the spirit of Joint Declaration, treaty on China–ASEAN good-neighbourliness, international production capacity cooperation, connectivity, maritime cooperation, promote sub-regional cooperation, aim to sign nuclear weapon-free zone, defence and security cooperation, and peace and stability in the South China Sea. See *chinese-embassy.no* 2015.

References

asean.org, 2003. 'Joint Declaration of the Heads of State/Government of the Association of Southeast Asian Nations and the People's Republic of China on Strategic Partnership for Peace and Prosperity', 8 October, www.asean.org/news/item/external-relations-china-joint-declaration-of-the-heads-of-stategovernment-of-the-association-of-southeast-asian-nations-and-the-people-s-republic-of-china-on-strategic-partnership-for-peace-and-prosperity-bali-indonesia-8-october-2003 (accessed on 11 August 2015).

asean.org, 2012. 'Vision Statement ASEAN–India Commemorative Summit', 21 December, www.asean.org/news/asean-statement-communiques/item/vision-statement-asean-indiacommemorative-summit (accessed on 22 September 2013).

aseanindia.com, n.d. 'Navy Expedition' ASEAN–India: progress and prosperity', www.aseanindia.com/navy/about/ (accessed on 23 September 2014).

aseanindia.com, 2012. 'ASEAN–India Commemorative Summit 2012, ASEAN India: progress & prosperity', www.aseanindia.com/summit-2012/ (accessed on 3 September 2014).

Bai Shi, 2015. 'Renewing partnership', *Beijing Review*, No. 33, 10 August, www.bjreview.com/world/txt/2015-08/10/content_699381.htm (accessed on 13 August 2015).

Batabyal, Anindya, 2006. 'Balancing China in Asia: a realist assessment of India's Look East strategy', *China Report*, 42(2): 179–97.

Brewster, David, 2013. 'India's defence strategy and the India ASEAN relationship', *India Review*, 12(3): 151–64.

Business Standard, 2013. 'India stepping up role as net security provider in Indian Ocean', *Business Standard*, 19 September, www.business-standard.com/article/news-ians/india-stepping-up-role-as-net-security-provider-in-indian-ocean-113091900569_1.html (accessed on 7 September 2014).

chinadaily.com.cn, 2013. 'Freedom of navigation in South China Sea unaffected', *China Daily*, 29 August, www.chinadaily.com.cn/ethnic/china/2013-08/29/content_16930540.htm (accessed on 7 October 2013).

chinadaily.com.cn, 2014. 'China far from being "aggressive" in South China Sea', *China Daily*, 13 May, www.chinadaily.com.cn/china/2014-05/13/content_17505247.htm (accessed on 13 August 2015).

chinese-embassy.no, 2015. 'Wang Yi brought forth a ten-point proposal on China–ASEAN cooperation', Embassy of the People's Republic of China in the Kingdom of Norway, 6 August, www.chinese-embassy.no/eng/zyxw/t1286715.htm (accessed on 13 August 2015).

dnaindia.com, 2014. 'Sushma Swaraj tells Indian envoys to Act East and not just Look East', *Daily News and Analyses*, 26 August, www.dnaindia.com/india/report-sushma-swaraj-tells-indian-envoys-to-act-east-and-not-just-look-east-2013788 (accessed on 3 September 2014).

fmprc.gov.cn, 2015. 'Speech by Foreign Minister Wang Yi at the session "ASEAN Community: a major milestone for Asian integration"' of the Boao Forum for Asia Annual Conference 2015, 28 March, Ministry of Foreign Affairs of the People's Republic of China, www.fmprc.gov.cn/mfa_eng/wjb_663304/wjbz_663308/2461_663310/t1252648.shtml (accessed on 13 August 2015).

Holmes, Oliver, 2015. 'China nears completion of controversial airstrip in South China Sea', *Guardian*, 2 July, www.theguardian.com/world/2015/jul/02/china-controversial-airstrip-south-china-sea-spratly-islands (accessed 13 August 2015).

Hunt, Katie, 2015. 'Beijing: island building in South China Sea "almost complete"', *CNN*, 17 June, http://edition.cnn.com/2015/06/17/asia/china-south-china-sea-land-reclamation/ (accessed on 13 August 2015).

indiannavy.nic.in, 2012. 'New naval air station INS *Baaz* commissioned by CNS', 31 July, http://indiannavy.nic.in/print/1431 (accessed on 20 September 2014).

Jaeho Hwang, 2014. 'Seoul Defence Dialogue: new horizons for Korea's diplomacy', *Korea Herald*, Brookings, 13 November, www.brookings.edu/research/opinions/2013/11/13-seoul-defense-dialogue-hwang (accessed on 23 September 2014).

Jian Zhang, 2013. 'China's growing assertiveness in the South China Sea: a strategic shift?', *The South China Sea and Australia's Regional Security Environment*, National Security College Occasional Paper No. 5, Leszek Buszynski and Christopher Roberts (eds), National Security College, 24 May, pp. 18–25, http://nsc.anu.edu.au/documents/occasional-5-brief-4.pdf (accessed on 13 August 2015).

Kang Seung Woo, 2014. 'Political dynamics of Northeast Asia shifting', *The Korea Times*, 7 July, www.koreatimes.co.kr/www/news/nation/2014/09/180_160530.html (accessed on 23 September 2014).

MEA, 2014. 'Tokyo Declaration for India Japan Special Strategic and Global Partnership', 1 September, Ministry of External Affairs, Government of India.

mea.gov.in, 2011. 'Statement by PM at the 6th East Asia Summit Plenary Session', Bali, 19 November, Ministry of External Affairs, Government of India, www.mea.gov.in/in-focus-article.htm?6974/Statement+by+PM+at+the+6th+East+Asia+Summit+Plenary+Session (accessed on 11 September 2014).

mea.gov.in, 2013a. 'External Affairs Minister's intervention on "exchange of views on regional and international issues"', 20th ARF meeting in Brunei Darussalam, Ministry of External Affairs, Government of India, 2 July, www.mea.gov.in/in-focus-article.htm?21891/External+Affairs+Ministers+Intervention+on+Exchange+of+views+on+re gional+and+international+issues+at+20th+ASEAN+Regional+Forum+ARF+meeting+in+Brunei+Darussalam (accessed on 11 September 2014).

mea.gov.in, 2013b. '3rd India Republic of Korea Foreign Policy and Security Dialogue', Ministry of External Affairs, Government of India, 2 September, http://mea.gov.in/press-releases.htm?dtl/22144/3rd+India++Republic+of+Korea+Foreign+Policy+and+S ecurity+Dialogue (accessed on 20 September 2014).

mea.gov.in, 2014. 'Keynote address by Secretary (East) at 6th IISS-MEA Dialogue on "India's Extended Neighbourhood: Prospects and Challenges", lecture delivered at IDSA, New Delhi, Media Centre, Ministry of External Affairs, Government of India, New Delhi', 4 March, http://mea.gov.in/Speeches-Statements.htm?dtl/23030 (accessed on 3 September 2014).

Mukherjee, Pranab, 2006. 'Indian foreign policy: a road map for the decade ahead', Speech, 46th National Defence College Course, MEA Media Centre, 15 November, www.mea.gov.in/Speeches-Statements.htm?dtl/2395/ (accessed on 3 September 2014).

Ng, Teddy and Andrea Chen, 2014. 'Xi Jinping says world has nothing to fear from awakening of "peaceful lion"', *South China Morning Post*, 28 March, www.scmp.com/news/china/article/1459168/xi-says-world-has-nothing-fear-awakening-peaceful-lion?page=all (accessed on 11 August 2015).

Panda, Jagannath P., 2014. 'India's security outlook and views on multilateral cooperation: the emerging Asia-Pacific theater', in *Prospects of Multilateral Cooperation in the Asia-Pacific: To Overcome the Gap of Security Outlooks*, NIDS International Symposium on Security Affairs 2013: The National Institute for Defense Studies, Japan, October, pp. 69–86.

Panda, Jagannath P., 2015. 'India in East Asia: reviewing the role of a security provider', in S.D. Muni and Vivek Chadha (eds), *Asian Strategic Review 2015: India as a Security Provider*, New Delhi: Pentagon Press and IDSA, pp. 213–29.

pib.nic.in, 2013. 'Second ASEAN Defence Ministers' Meeting (Plus) Joint Declaration', Press Information Bureau, Government of India, 29 August, http://pib.nic.in/newsite/erelease.aspx?relid=98856 (accessed on 23 September 2014).

Scott, David, 2009. 'India's "extended neighbourhood" concept: power projection for a rising power', *India Review*, 8(2), April–June, pp. 107–43.

Swaine, Michael D. and M. Taylor Fravel, 2011. 'China's assertive behaviour, Part Two: the maritime periphery', The Massachusetts Institute of Technology, *The China Leadership Monitor*, 35, pp. 1–29.

Tang Qifang, 2015. 'Foreign Minister's view on South China Sea reasonable and clear', *China Daily*, 13 August, http://usa.chinadaily.com.cn/opinion/2015-08/13/content_21583229.htm (accessed on 13 August 2015).

Tayal, Skand, 2014. 'Emerging security architecture in East Asia: India's strategy towards the Koreas and Japan', *Issue Brief*, No. 246, Institute of Peace and Conflict Studies (IPCS), February.

Wang Yuzhu, 2014. 'Premier Li improves prospects of China–ASEAN relationship', *CCTV.com*, 18 November, http://english.cntv.cn/2014/11/18/ARTI1416299817197110.shtml (accessed on 13 August 2015).

zeenews.india.com, 2014. 'Vietnam seeks greater role for India in South China Sea', Zee News India, 25 August, http://zeenews.india.com/news/nation/vietnam-seeks-greater-role-for-india-in-south-china-sea_957303.html (accessed on 3 September 2014).

Zhang Tuosheng, 2014. 'The changing regional order in East Asia', *China & US Focus*, 4 January, www.chinausfocus.com/print/?id=3472 (accessed on 9 September 2014).

Zhao Yinan and Zhong Nan, 2014. 'China, ASEAN set 2015 as goal for upgrading free trade agreement', *China Daily*, 14 November, http://usa.chinadaily.com.cn/china/2014-11/14/content_18911804.htm (accessed on 12 August 2015).

Part IV
Cross-continental contemporaries

13 BRICS and the emerging powers identity

This chapter argues that the India–China construct within BRICS is based on mutual appreciation and reciprocation of shared global interests that are keys to their 'developing world' identity.[1] These shared global interests are planned to achieve national security interests that are continental and global in nature and are important to their own international positioning and status bearing.

BRICS (which commenced as BRIC – Brazil, Russia, India and China) began in 2001 as a conceptual formulation of Goldman Sachs, which was later highlighted in *Dreaming with BRICS: The Path to 2050*, that the collective output of BRIC would outshine the G-7 economies in US dollar terms in less than 40 years. BRICS's strength lies in its collective three billion people, who constitute almost 43 per cent of the global population (Zheng Xinli 2011). It has combined approximate US$4 trillion foreign reserves and GDP of $13.7 trillion. BRICS accounts for almost 18 per cent of world economic aggregate, which is vital enough for various financial reform politics (ibid.). It is also predicted that by the year 2015, BRICS's GDP will increase to almost 23 per cent of the world figure, and touch almost 31 per cent by 2020 (ibid.). At a basic political level, BRICS's exclusivity is about 'emerging powers' and more aptly about the 'developing world' thesis in the existing North–South divide. As an 'emerging powers' club, BRICS is under the global spotlight and has become institutionalised slowly (see Table 13.1).

The rise of BRICS countries has been impressive, particularly that of China and India. More than China's and India's economic growth trajectory, their political influence has placed BRICS in the limelight. Russia's relation with China and India under BRICS is another major highlight of BRICS, both positively and negatively. From a political perspective, BRICS bonds together three immediate neighbours – Russia, China and India. Though they are closely interconnected at the regional level in the RIC (Russia–India–China) structure, RIC has been overshadowed to some extent by BRICS's rise and progress.[2]

BRICS's dynamism for China is a matter of global importance, and the thesis links to the politics of multipolarism. In the view of many Chinese scholars, two vital trends may be noticed with the rise of a multipolar world order: *first*, intense global economic, trade and financial integration or alliance; and *second*, multipolarisation in global politics and international relations across the continents and

Table 13.1 BRICS summits and major issues discussed

Summit date	Location, host	Theme and major issues discussed	Key outcomes, new action plans
First Summit 16 June 2009	Yekaterinburg, Russia	First *Joint Statement* released; How to resolve global financial crisis; Reform of the global financial institutions; Sustainable development	Urge and need for a 'global reserve currency' that is 'diversified, stable and predictable'
Second Summit 15–16 April 2010	Brasilia, Brazil	Second *Joint Statement* released; Common vision and global governance; International trade and development; Energy, climate change, terrorism	First meeting of the Development Bank; Meeting of the Think-Tanks
Third Summit 14 April 2011	Sanya, Hainan, China	First Declaration released known as 'Sanya Declaration'; Comprehensive reform of the UN; Continue cooperation in the UNSC on Libya; Reform IMF and other financial institutions	New Action Plan for strengthening BRICS; New areas of cooperation (first BRICS Friendship Cities and Local Governments Cooperation)
Fourth Summit 29 March 2012	New Delhi, India	Theme: 'BRICS Partnership for Global Stability, Security and Prosperity'; Call for a more representative international financial architecture; Concern over slow pace of quota and governance reform at the IMF; Discussion on climate change, Iran, Afghanisthan, etc.	Delhi Action Plan; First meeting of the BRICS Urbanisation Forum; Meeting of BRICS High Representative responsible for National Security

Fifth Summit 27 March 2013	Durban, South Africa	Theme: 'BRICS and Africa: Partnership for Development, Integration and Industrialisation' Engagement and cooperation with non-BRICS countries, particularly with the emerging market and developing countries (EMDCs)	BRICS Virtual Secretariat; BRICS Public Diplomacy Forum; BRICS Anti-Corruption Cooperation; BRICS Youth Policy Dialogue
Sixth Summit 15 July 2014	Fortaleza, Brazil	Theme: 'Inclusive Growth: Sustainable Solutions' Furthering cooperation between BRICS and South America; Agreement establishing the New Development Bank (NDB); Announcing the Treaty for the Establishment of the BRICS Contingent Reserve Arrangement (CRA)	New areas of cooperation like foreign policy planning dialogue; Mutual recognition of higher education degrees and diplomas; Establishment of the BRICS Development Bank
Seventh Summit 9 July 2015	Ufa, Russia	Theme: 'BRICS Partnership – a Powerful Factor of Global Development' Establishment of BRICS financial institutions: the New Development Bank and the Contingent Reserves Arrangement (CRA); Possible engagement with Eurasian Economic Union (EEU) and the Shanghai Cooperation Organisation (SCO)	Ufa Action Plan; Working Group on the creation of the Multilateral Contingent Reserve Arrangement (CRA); New areas of cooperation to be explored like BRICS Dialogue on Peacekeeping, Establishment of the BRICS Council of Regions, and Cooperation and Exchange of Experiences among BRICS media professionals

countries (Shen Qiang 2010: 35). In the Chinese perspective, BRICS's rise has resulted in the relative decline of the influence and dominance of the US (ibid.). Chinese scholars further argue that with BRICS's rise, American authoritative control over the three mainstream financial bodies – the WTO, IMF and the World Bank – has significantly eroded (ibid.).

BRICS is a platform for China to associate with the developing world, most importantly with the emerging economies, and act in concert against the Western power blocs, especially against the US. India is seen in that context as a vital partnering country for China, though in limited scale, mainly in the context of economic multilateralism. The Indian undertaking of BRICS is important for a variety of reasons. *First*, currently, the Indian economy stands next to the Chinese economy. *Second*, India connects with individual BRICS countries on separate spectrums, both at regional and global levels. Through India–Brazil–South Africa (IBSA), it is closely connected to both Brazil and South Africa at the intercontinental level; it is equally connected at the regional level with Russia and China in RIC. India is also attached to Brazil, South Africa and China in the BASIC climate forum. India will soon become formally a member of the Shanghai Cooperation Organisation (SCO) in which both China and Russia are core members. *Third*, amongst BRICS countries, though India is seen as a 'pro-Western' country, its foreign policy dialogue has mostly been 'South–South' vis-à-vis developing-world centric, a central theme that remains core to the IBSA, BASIC and BRICS bearings.

India's course in BRICS has been more economic-centric, attempting to bring equity in the current global order in global governance issues. Reform of the global financial and political institutions has been one of the most demanding aspects of India's approach within and outside BRICS. During the Plenary Session of the Fourth BRICS Summit in New Delhi, the then Prime Minister Manmohan Singh in his statement contemplated three specific things: (i) intra-BRICS complementarity and cooperation; (ii) infrastructure development in developing countries; and (iii) addressing the deficiencies in global governance (*pmindia.nic.in* 2012b).

China's tryst with BRICS

The prime Chinese interest within BRICS is to be labelled as a developing country.[3] *Second*, China has always seen its global interests in anti-American terms. The BRICS countries' articulated determination to reform the global political and financial architecture in favour of the Southern countries becomes convenient here. Both historically and in contemporary times, China has tried to adhere intimately, though reluctantly, with Asian and international affairs through different means: notably as a *developing country*, as a *socialist country* and as a *revolutionary country* (Gurtov 2010: 13). Its self-projection as a revolutionary and socialist country has enabled it to build some temporary alliances against capitalist nations and against imperialist tendencies; and its claim of being largely a developing country has given China considerable elbowroom in contemporary international politics.

China's partaking in a multilateral grouping like BRICS, with a competitive power like India and remote countries like Brazil and South Africa, increasingly confirms its multilateral strategy and foreign policy stratagem as an 'emerging economy'. This becomes even more apparent when there is firm acknowledgement in China that BRICS is not entirely an economic entity, that strategic components are an essential part of it.

China's approach to BRICS is partly political and partly economic, aiming to maximise its own global interests and objectives rather than bringing anything new and specific in favour of the 'developing world' (Panda 2011).[4] In the Chinese perception, BRICS's rise is a thesis of 'emerging countries', based on the dialogue of 'modernisation' and the attempt to transform them from mainly 'agricultural to industrial economies' (Canrong 2011). China asks for better space at the global level for the developing world where it can equally maximise its national interests and a few strategic objectives in global financial institutions (He Dan 2012). Three main issues that eloquently explain the Chinese strategy and approach within BRICS are: Chinese currency promotion strategy; Chinese politics with the US and Europe in Bretton Woods institutions; and the tactic of holding the identity of a developing country or emerging power.

Since at least the Chinese accession to the WTO in September 2001, currency has been a hot debating issue between China and the Western countries. Through BRICS, the Chinese are aiming to not only score over the West in the debate but also in promoting the Yuan (RMB) steadily as an international currency, in the process attenuating the imbalances resulting from US fiscal deficits and authoritarian monetary policies of the West (see Qu Bo 2012). There is a direct link between China's domestic reforms, its dialogue of reforming the international institutions and promoting the Yuan as a currency (Plasschaert 2012; see also Qu Bo 2012). Beijing is aiming primarily to keep its internal inflation down, limit the appreciation of the RMB and modify exchange rates in favour of the RMB. This is to be achieved through declining US domestic prices and its financial instability (Wolf 2010).[5]

Much of China's current account conundrum is with the US (Plasschaert 2012: 175). At the heart of the matter is the global current account imbalance, which is mainly a result of the sizeable US trade deficit with China. At the same time, Chinese diplomats and experts are conscious about the US intention to cooperate with China to help itself out of the economic crisis (see Qu Bo 2012). They argue, however, that 'the West exaggerates the fall of America and the rise of China' (Liu Ming 2010). China remains the biggest debt holder for America, with more than $800 billion and accounts for 7 per cent of US public debt (ibid.). If China can convince the 'emerging markets' to have the Yuan as a medium of trade exchange in place of the US dollar, the Yuan can easily become an international currency. In fact, China has successfully consolidated the Yuan against the dollar in last few years (see Figure 13.1).

The Chinese have worked hard for many years to promote the Yuan at the global level. At present, the RMB has 19 bilateral local currencies swap

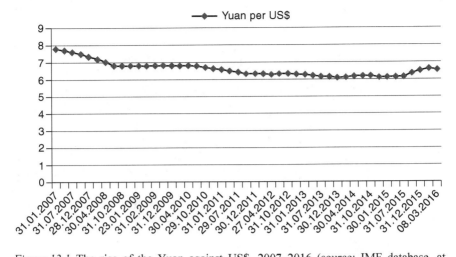

Figure 13.1 The rise of the Yuan against US$, 2007–2016 (source: IMF database, at www.imf.org/external/np/fin/data/param_rms_mth.aspx).

arrangements (ibid.; see Table 13.2). Moreover, the Chinese economy is so ingrained into some of the regional economies that it becomes easy for the Yuan to take over from the dollar. For example, the East Asian countries have formed a 'renminbi bloc', abandoning the dollar and fixing their currencies to the Yuan, a concentrated effort in internalising the Chinese currency (Gao Changxin 2012). The rise of the Yuan will be facilitated by the fact that the BRICS countries feel that they are in a 'dollar trap' (McDowell 2012).

The rise of 'China Inc.' over the last 30 years has also made the Yuan more attractive for trade transactions (Cottingham 2012). Since the 2008 global economic crisis, the value, influence and attraction of the Yuan has grown consistently across continents. Many in China see the dominance of the dollar in the Chinese domestic market as an affront to their country's international image as an economic power (Otero-Iglesias 2011). Shyam Saran notes that a number of countries like Nigeria, Russia, Belarus, Mongolia, Malaysia, Republic of Korea and the Philippines are now holding the Yuan as part of their global reserves. They were earlier over-dependent on the dollar (Saran 2012). Nineteen countries now have currency swap arrangements with China (see Table 13.2), and this list is likely to expand. The New Delhi BRICS summit agreed that the member countries' currencies would be used as the direct medium for intra-BRICS trade transactions. That again is a step in the direction of internationalising the Yuan vis-à-vis the dollar.[6] The idea of establishing a multi-currency financial order and reducing the authority of the US dollar and euro in global transactions has been unfolding within BRICS for some time. Taking this idea forward, the 2015 Ufa BRICS summit created a currency pool under the Contingency Reserve Arrangement (CRA) and officially launched BRICS's New Development Bank (NDB).

Table 13.2 China's RMB swap deals

Sl. no.	Countries having currency swap deal with China	Month/year swap deal signed	Amount	Bilateral trade figures (in US$ billion)
1	Argentina	March 2009	RMB70 billion; US$10.2 billion	14.8 (2011)
2	Australia	March 2012	US$31 billion; RMB200 billion; A$30 billion	113.3 (2010–2011)
3	Belarus	March 2009	RMB20 billion; US$2.9 billion Br 8 trillion	2.5 (2010)
4	Brazil	June 2012	US$29 billion; R$60 billion	77 (2011)
5	Hong Kong	January 2009	US$29 billion; RMB200 billion	283.5 (2011)
6	Iceland	June 2010	RMB3.5 billion; US$512 million ISK66 billion	0.18 (2012)
7	Indonesia	March 2009	RMB100 billion; IDR175 trillion	60 (2011)
8	Japan	March 2002	3 billion Yen-RMB	347 (2011)
9	Kazakhstan	June 2011	RMB7 billion; US$1.08 billion	22.519 (January–November 2011)
10	Malaysia	February 2009	RMB80 billion; MYR40 billion	90 (2011)
11	New Zealand	April 2011	RMB25 billion; US$3.83 billion	13.3 (2011)
12	Pakistan	December 2011	RMB10 billion; PKR140 billion	10.6 (2011)
13	Singapore	July 2010	RMB150 billion; US$22.12 billion	80.5 (2011)
14	South Korea	June 2002	US$2 billion	246 (2011)
15	Thailand	December 2011	RMB70 billion; US$11.06 billion	64.7 (2011)
16	Turkey	February 2012	US$1.6 billion	18.7 (2011)
17	Ukraine	June 2012	RMB15 billion; UKH19 billion US$2.38 billion	8.5 (2011)
18	United Arab Emirates	January 2012	RMB35 billion; US$5.54 billion	35 (2011)
19	Uzbekistan	April 2011	RMB700 million; US$106 million	2.48 (2011)

Sources: collated from various open news media and government sources like *Xinhua*, *Forbes*, *Tribune*, *China Daily*, Ministry of Commerce of the PRC, China.org.cn, *Financial Times*, *People's Daily*, *The Diplomat*, etc.

With the NDB headquarters stationed in Shanghai, the Yuan will have considerable influence in the bank's daily transactions. The IMF has recently announced to include the RMB in the Special Drawing Rights (SDR) in the reserve currency basket along with the Dollar, Euro, Yen and Pound/Sterling. The work report of the Chinese government, released in March 2015, had given an assurance to work more intently to make the Yuan fully convertible (*Xinhuanet* 2015; see also *english.gov.cn* 2015).

Meanwhile, talks on the formation of an SCO Development Bank are reviving between China and Russia. To reduce transactions in the US dollar, China and Russia have been scheming the strategy of local currency transaction since 2000. Bilaterally, the two countries began avoiding conversion of mutual payments in dollars and euro, testing the initiative first in the China–Russia border areas. With the Yuan–Rouble trade platform becoming more stable and established, the Russians are now acknowledging the prominence of the Yuan. Given the current Western sanctions on Russia in the wake of the Ukraine crisis, the banks in Russia have found it difficult to operate since the corresponding accounts in the US have transactions in US dollars. That has paved the way for the Yuan to gain a standing as an alternative currency. Beijing has permitted the Russian commercial lenders and companies to invest in the Chinese financial boards and organisations with the first line of credit in the Yuan. Sberbank, Russia's biggest commercial lender, has teamed up with the Export Import Bank of China to offer its first line of credit in Yuan to Russian companies and business bodies.

India's advocacy in BRICS

Unlike China, India does not compete with the US nor does it see the EU in adversarial terms to its global perspective. The Indian Rupee is neither in competition with the US dollar nor in conflict with the Euro. The Rupee has not in fact consolidated its position against the US dollar (see Figure 13.2).

India's approach to BRICS so far has been more eloquent in addressing global economic and political governance issues rather than in addressing the global politics that exists between the developing and developed countries. The Indian Prime Ministers' speeches in various BRICS forums explain this phenomenon. Three perspectives may be outlined here. *First*, India has asked vigorously to reform the global financial structure, and has advocated improving the stake and quota for the developing countries in these multilateral financial bodies. India has also raised the issue of UN reform, including UNSC reform. *Second*, India has tried to promote the 'South–South' spirit, advocating the establishment of a BRICS Development Bank, which has finally been established as New Development Bank (NDB), and has raised the issue of infrastructure development in developing countries. But though India wants to promote the issue of NDB, it has also asked for the expansion of the capital base of the World Bank and other multilateral banks for financing appropriate infrastructure development in poor and developing countries. Beijing on the other hand wanted to have a

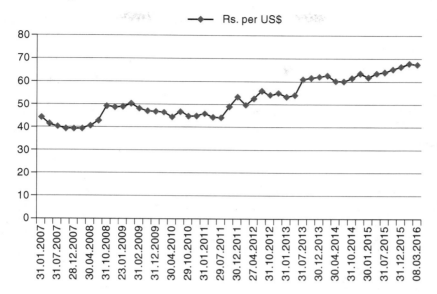

Figure 13.2 Indian rupee vs US dollar (Rs per US$) (source: IMF database, at www.imf.org/external/np/fin/data/param_rms_mth.aspx).

BRICS Development Bank without really addressing the existing problems in the IMF and other multilateral banks. *Third*, India has raised issues of global governance matters more openly in BRICS forums. At the New Delhi BRICS summit, India raised the issue of urbanisation as a matter of challenge; other issues of energy, climate change, food, social equality, health, unemployment and poverty have also been raised in various BRICS forums and leadership summits (*pmindia.gov.in* 2009).

The Indian perspective with regard to BRICS is similar to its approach to and perspective of G-20. India has raised the vitality of G-20 in almost all BRICS summits. G-20 is an ideal platform for both the developed and developing world to discuss and develop new mechanisms towards the governance issues beyond politics. India's core dialogue with regard to G-20 is to improve and enhance the global financial decision-making process and improve the stake, claim and quota of the emerging economies in the global financial bodies and institutions. India's constant reiteration in various BRICS forums that G-20 should act as a binding force between developing and developed worlds explains New Delhi's perspective of North–South politics and India's interest with regard to the BRICS and G-20 institutional cooperation.

Three points have been raised by New Delhi in various G-20 forums. *First*, the importance of accelerating governance reforms in global financial institutions; and also the need to review and implement new mechanisms of 'quota formula' in global financial institutions as per the economic weight of a particular country (*pmindia.gov.in* 2012a). *Second*, India advocates clearly that there is a need to improve infrastructure in developing and underdeveloped countries. In G-20 forums, it has highlighted the Los Cabos declaration, which talked of infrastructure development in developing countries, which would help radically in improving global financial conditions. For this, New Delhi had proposed multilateral development banks and a BRICS development bank (*pmindia.gov.in* 2012c). This advocacy was emphasised during the New Delhi and Durban BRICS summits. *Third*, India has vigorously advocated against 'protectionist tendencies' of rich and industrialised countries, which in its view have only raised the level of unemployment across the world and have stunted growth rate (*pmindia.gov.in* 2012a). Accordingly, India has asked for more open and free markets for the emerging economies (*BRICS Post* 2013). Stressing the G-20 mechanism for greater international collaboration, India has emphasised four productive aspects: (i) avoiding competitive devaluation and resisting protectionism; (ii) advanced deficit countries following policies of fiscal consolidation; (iii) the need for structural reforms of the global financial institutions; and (iv) the need to focus on exchange rate flexibility and reserve currencies (*pmindia.gov.in* 2010b).

What the India–China construct in BRICS points to

A coherent common strategy to maximise the developing-world cause between India and China did not exist until recently. But with the recent growth of cross-regional parameters, mainly through BRICS, the two countries are jointly engaged in a number of matters related to global governance. This is for two reasons: (i) both realise the benefits of having a mutual understanding at the *global* or *cross-continental* or *cross-regional* level in an evolving multipolar world order; (ii) the rising import of the developing world in global politics makes them inter-reliant. While the idea of a multipolar world structure is a thesis beneficial to both, what really unites them, at least temporarily, is the logic and vitality of the developing world. BRICS suffices this case of 'developing world' more appropriately than anything else.

Scholars place the India–China discourse within the broader spectrum of 'civilisational course'. They argue that

> the prime contradiction of our epoch while assessing the relationship between China and India needs to be reconceptualised as one between forces of *swaraj* and *jiefang* (liberation), on the one hand, and forces of hegemony led by global capitalism, on the other.
>
> (Mohanty 2010: 104)

This sufficiently indicates that there are many facets to India–China relations.[7] One of these is the cross-regional dialogue like BRICS, which binds different continents in their relevant multilateral relationship bonding and discourse.

Conventional global politics suggests that building an alliance is the most effective way to check the dominance of certain countries and construct a balance in global power politics.[8] But this is a difficult enterprise in the post-cold war era, where a number of powers possess 'nuclear strength', strong militaries, and project different national security strategies and diverse interests and objectives. Two factors that have tactical implications in the current global politics are *ideology* and *identity*, apart from economic and political strength. While on one hand these two factors restrict India and China from forming a credible alliance against any particular nation or region, they also help them to sit together and think practically to have a combined opinion, groupings and partnership against the conventional Western dominance in the global Bretton Woods structure. The basic premise here remains that both India and China have been associating with each other for greater global bargaining power against the Western hegemonic multilateral systems and financial institutions through BRICS, BASIC, RIC, and now under the SCO, etc.

Overall, these groupings are central to the two countries' global profile as 'developing countries' and 'developing economies'. Multilateralism through different modes and mediums has been the pivot of most contemporary powers' global strategy (O'Keohane 1990). By jointly associating with various global, cross-regional or regional bodies temporarily or permanently, India and China make a statement that associating with adversary powers is possible in current global politics.

BRICS, IBSA and the India–China divide

The India–China shared perspective under BRICS is surely a rejuvenated fact for developing-world politics. But there are different perspectives between the two countries with regard to BRICS and IBSA at present, which restricts their cooperation. Rising as a continental grouping that was mainly stung by the Western powers' obstinacy at the Doha Round of trade talks, and more vitally to push the cause of developing countries at the cross-continental level, IBSA has been promoted by India as an institution of democratic countries (Dikshit 2011a).

The nature, spirit and objectives of both IBSA and BRICS are complementary in many respects. BRICS constitutes a superset of developing countries that IBSA as a forum initially represented. IBSA essentially depicts a broader South–South solidarity, harnessing a 'tripartite' continental framework among three large multicultural democracies of three major continents. On the other hand, BRICS broadly defines three things in world politics: *first*, as a multilateral forum it belongs to rapidly emerging economies; *second*, its core members, except Russia probably, are well-known powers from the developing world; and *third*, it is a grouping based more on the North–South divide, and aims to bring reforms to the global financial institutions in favour of the developing world. What places IBSA in a stream separate from BRICS is its 'democratic' ethos.[9] Notably, IBSA members are linked with China in climate politics of the BASIC framework.

While India continues to stress the importance of IBSA in its cross-continental reach, China has tried to sideline the IBSA by developing closer contacts with its members Brazil and South Africa. China has also taken serious note of the political and security issues that IBSA has so far been trying to cover.[10] Two factors make the politics of IBSA urgent for China. *First*, IBSA has coordinated in security and political issues more closely than BRICS. Its declarations place enormous weightage on the interests of the developing countries and discuss developmental as well as political and security issues. Under IBSAMAR, the navies of IBSA countries have held joint exercises in the Indian Ocean in 2008, 2010, 2012, 2014 and 2016. China's maritime posture in the Indian Ocean has also expanded rapidly in recent years. Carrying out offshore military manoeuvres, escort missions and anti-piracy exercises in various parts of the Indian Ocean has been a core strategy of the PLA Navy (*Xinhua* 2012). China would not want to permit India much advantage as a sole power in this ocean and it has placed stress on Russia's maritime activity as a BRICS country in this ocean. An example is a *Xinhua* piece, which noted that a Russian sailing vessel, *Pallada*, was on a 'tour of the Pacific and Indian Oceans' as part of its 'African Odyssey', and its 'main event' would be 'the BRICS summit in Durban' in March 2013 (*People's Daily* 2013).

Second, IBSA demands UN and UNSC reforms unanimously (see, for example, *ibsa-trilateral.org* 2003). China's stance in this matter is different (see Chapter 16). China mostly perceives BRICS's rise as an opportunity to prune other power blocs, mainly the Western dominance in global financial and political institutions. It would not want IBSA to steal a march over it in these matters, where Beijing may lose its tag as leader of the developing world.

BRICS is a notion of 'revisionist' powers, with the association of two P-5 nations, while IBSA is more about 'middle power' arrangements (Kornegay 2012: 1). For India, IBSA is a 'unique', democratic, novel initiative meant for 'special' global causes (Dikshit 2011b). China on its part seeks the merger of IBSA and BRICS as a consolidated voice of the developing world to establish a credible intercontinental approach to tackle the Western dominance at various levels of global politics. In China's perception the existence of IBSA as a separate grouping weakens the developing countries' cause.

The prevailing Indian dialogue and China

Given its asymmetry of power politics with the major power blocs, India's approach to BRICS has been a statement more of economics and less political, in sharp contrast to China's vision of BRICS. Through BRICS, Beijing wants to promote both economic issues that have a political bearing for its global dealings, along with other political and security issues.[11] India does not want to be seen as being closely allied with China multilaterally. An order based on massive political and economic engagement between the developing world at cross-regional and global levels has been India's immediate priority. In this context, BRICS is a staid entity in Indian foreign policy along with IBSA and BASIC (see the next chapter for BASIC).

In general, three imperatives explain India's approach to BRICS: (i) pursue the dialogue of the developing world, with China as a possible partner; (ii) maximise economic and political contacts at the cross-regional level, without really merging or mixing the dealings between BRICS, IBSA and BASIC; and (iii) be a part of the emerging order for global issues without affecting the relations with power blocs like the US and EU. The US is a 'traditional ally' and, markedly, a strategic partner in India's broader global strategic and security design, whereas China is just a partner and a constant security concern for both. India does see BRICS's rise as a 'strategic reality', a fitting mechanism that suits not only its own policy designs but also for greater developing- or emerging-world dialogue.[12] With the rapid evolution of multilateral politics and security alignment building, India has begun to realise and emphasise the virtues of multilateralism at different levels and forming strategic coalitions with concurring countries on issues of common interest (Panda 2012c). Unlike China, India is neither in political conflict with the American world nor shares problematic ties with the European world.

India's approach to BRICS is best explained in terms of its democratic dialogue. BRICS members ask for 'democratisation' of the global order, but not all BRICS members really adhere to or practise democratic principles. China's growing relations with Brazil and South Africa also prompt India to believe more in a non-BRICS world, at least in political if not in economic terms. For India, IBSA is a coordinating mechanism, based on soft-power dealings, having three objectives: democratic ethos, developing-country spirit, and acting together globally for socio-economic dealings (Panda 2012c). This distinct Indian approach will keep New Delhi politically and to some extent economically attractive globally, even if the Chinese will strengthen their ties with both Brazil and South Africa through trade and commercial dealings. IBSA not only enhances India's democratic ethos, but also helps build its identity as a country that does not necessarily belong to the Chinese world that trumpets a 'hard power' cudgel. Though the broader governance objectives and issues that both BRICS and IBSA have tried to address have much in common, for India, IBSA is largely a 'people's project' (*ibsa-trilateral.org* 2010). India sees IBSA as a forum not only for political consultation among the three large democracies, but equally as a multilateral forum to promote the cause, practice and spirit of the developing world. Cross-continental groupings like BRICS, IBSA and BASIC are important for India's global rise and profile. Through these bodies India tries to advocate its 'developing country' label even if it has to share much of these foreign policy bearings with adverse powers like China.[13]

The future[14]

From a regional outlook, though Russia, India and China are located close to each other, strategic vis-à-vis foreign policy contradictions hardly help them form any substantial credible alliance. Combined with these strategic contradictions is China's rapid growth and potential in surpassing other BRICS members while using this grouping as a platform for its own objectives. In the context of BRICS, India and China lack any insightful perspectives for common global deliberations currently. For example, they are still to push for any common perspective or ground to manage the global financial institutions. Their conflicting perspectives on issues like maritime security, energy politics, climate change dialogue and trade protectionism have also been well known (Bajpayee 2010: 7). On a vital issue like climate change, they had a go-it-alone approach till recently (ibid.). Beijing under Xi Jinping's leadership has been quite open and forthcoming to multilateral politics and its global bearings, whereas India remains a relatively cautious power. Though India must continue to see BRICS as a serious cross-continental multilateral forum simultaneously with IBSA, it must put its act together with regard to BRICS and China.

Notes

1 This chapter is an extension and an updated version of several earlier writings. Reference is made here to Panda 2013a and Panda 2013b.
2 Contrary to the conventional notion, this author thinks that RIC is still a 'valid entity' in regional politics. See Panda 2012a.
3 Lowell Dittmer argues:

> For the past three decades, the People's Republic of China (PRC) has taken a renewed interest in the five-sixths of the world that is still developing, famously christened the 'Third World' in the dawn of the Cold War to refer to those still-developing countries whose political and economic trajectories remained uncertain. And although at times it seemed to have been eclipsed by security concerns superimposed by threatening superpowers or by lucrative economic opportunities elsewhere, China's identification with the developing world has never wavered.
>
> (Dittmer 2010: 1)

4 Certain conjectures made in Panda (2011) have been proved correct in course of time, such as China's effort to bring South Africa into BRICS. Some other conjectures, it is expected, will prove correct in the near future. It is acknowledged here that the core essentials of this study have been extensively borrowed from this source.
5 Experts argue that 'China has opted for a partial convertibility of the RMB, i.e. not extended to the capital account. It partly retains therefore the possibility of controlling its exchange rate through pegging the RMB to the dollar in varied guises.' See Defraigne 2012: 141.
6 China's effort within BRICS is not only to place its currency as a predominant one among the BRICS countries but also to limit the scope and influence of the US dollar and the Euro. The CDB is looking forward to signing an MoU with other BRICS nations to lend them RMB loans instead of dollars. See *Reuters* 2012.
7 Alka Acharya argues: 'the dominant paradigm in which India–China relations are generally analysed is essentially one of competitive power politics'. See Acharya 2000.
8 For details on this thesis, see Walt 1987.
9 This section draws on Panda 2013c.
10 The Chinese media have covered the politics of IBSA widely. A few examples are: *People's Daily* 2010a, 2010b, 2011; *Xinhua* 2010.
11 I have argued this in a policy brief published by the ISDP in Stockholm, Sweden. The Indian part of the BRICS dialogue is an extension of this policy brief. See Panda 2012b.
12 For an exclusive discussion on this aspect, see Panda 2012c. The author sincerely acknowledges that most of this section draws on this article.

13 For an analysis of Indian foreign policy priorities, see Panda 2012d.
14 This part is derived largely from Panda 2012d. It is an extension of the broader dialogue and policy prescriptions that the author has made in public.

References

Acharya, Alka, 2000. 'A measured tread to the future', *Seminar*, 487, March, www.indiaseminar.com/2000/487/487%20alka%20acharya.htm (accessed on 28 June 2013).
Bajpayee, Chietigj, 2010. 'China–India relations: regional rivalry takes the world stage', *China Security*, 6(2): 41–58.
BRICS Post, 2013. 'India criticises US protectionist approach', *The BRICS Post*, 13 February, http://thebricspost.com/india-criticises-us-protectionist-approach/ (accessed on 22 March 2013).
Canrong, Jin, 2011. 'The essence of the rise of BRICS and its future', *China & US Focus*, 14 April, www.chinausfocus.com/print/?id=4229 (accessed on 14 January 2013).
Cottingham, Jonathan, 2012. 'The Yuan's potential as a medium of exchange', *www.e-ir.info*, 13 November, www.e-ir.info/2012/11/13/the-yuans-potential-as-a-medium-of-exchange/ (accessed on 9 January 2013).
Defraigne, Pierre, 2012. 'A monetary G3 with a multilateral perspective', in Jan Wouters, Tanguy de Wilde, Pierre Defraigne and Jean-Christophe Defraigne (eds), *China, European Union and Global Governance*, Cheltenham: Edward Elgar, pp. 125–46.
Dikshit, Sandeep, 2011a. 'IBSA needs to step up pace on trade within the grouping and security', *The Hindu*, 18 October, www.thehindu.com/news/national/ibsa-needs-to-step-up-pace-on-trade-within-the-grouping-and-security/article2546692.ece (accessed on 5 August 2015).
Dikshit, Sandeep, 2011b. '"IBSA must remain restricted to 3 countries": Manmohan', *The Hindu*, 19 October, www.thehindu.com/news/national/article2549580.ece?css=print (accessed on 3 August 2015).
Dittmer, Lowell, 2010. 'China and the developing world', in Lowell Dittmer and George T. Yu (eds), *China, the Developing World, and the New Global Dynamics*, Boulder, CO: Lynne Rienner, pp. 1–13.
english.gov.cn, 2015. *Report on the Work of the Government*, Delivered at the Third Session of the 12th National People's Congress on March 5, The State Council, The People's Republic of China, http://english.gov.cn/archive/publications/2015/03/05/content_281475066179954.htm (accessed on 5 September 2015).
Gao Changxin, 2012. 'Asian economies turn to yuan', *China Daily*, 24 October, www.chinadaily.com.cn/china/2012-10/24/content_15840495.htm (accessed on 7 January 2013).
Gurtov, Mel, 2010. 'Changing perspectives and policies', in Lowell Dittmer and George T. Yu (eds), *China, the Developing World, and the New Global Dynamics*, Boulder, CO: Lynne Rienner, pp. 13–36.
He Dan, 2012. 'Emerging economies should be "given bigger role"', *China Daily*, 17 December, www.chinadaily.com.cn/china/2012-12/17/content_16022032.htm (accessed on 3 August 2015).
ibsa-trilateral.org, 2003. Brasilia Declaration, IBSA, 3 June, www.ibsa-trilateral.org/index.php?option=com_content&task=view&id=48&Itemid=27 (accessed on 27 January 2013).
ibsa-trilateral.org, 2010. 'Prime Minister's opening remarks at the Press conference after the IBSA Summit', 19 April, www.ibsa-trilateral.org/index.php?option=com_content&task=view&id=128&Itemid=51.

Kornegay, Francis A., 2012. 'IBSA on the 10th anniversary of the Brasilia Declaration', *SAFPI Policy Brief*, South African Foreign Policy Initiative, Open Society Foundation for South Africa, (19), December, pp. 1–3.

Liu Ming, 2010. 'China should update foreign policy guidelines', *Zhongguo Wang* (Official portal, China Internet Information Centre under the China International Publishing Group and the State Council Information Group), 25 March, OSC Transcribed Text, *World News Connection* (dialog.com), 201003251477.1_401800896de0750d, accession number 296401778.

McDowell, Daniel, 2012. 'China turns to BRICS to globalize Yuan', *World Politics Review*, 15 March, www.worldpoliticsreview.com/articles/11735/china-turns-to-brics-to-globalize-yuan (accessed on 3 January 2012).

Mohanty, Manoranjan, 2010. 'China and India: competing hegemonies or civilizational forces of Swaraj and Jiefang?', *China Report*, 46(103): 103–11.

O'Keohane, Robert, 1990. 'Multilateralism: an agenda for research', *International Journal*, vol. 45, Autumn, pp. 401–34.

Otero-Iglesias, Miguel, 2011. 'The internationalization of the Renminbi: prospects and risks', *Area: International Economy and Trade*, ARI 73/2011, 18 April, www.academia.edu/697914/The_Internationalisation_of_the_Renminbi_Prospects_and_Risks (accessed on 8 January 2012).

Panda, Jagannath P., 2011. 'China's "new multilateralism" and the rise of BRIC: a realist interpretation of a "multipolar" world order', *Asia Paper* (Institute for Security and Development Policy, Sweden), February.

Panda, Jagannath P., 2012a. 'The import of Russia–India–China: still a valid entity?', *Russia and India Report*, 16 April, http://indrus.in/articles/2012/04/16/the_import_of_russia-India–China_still_a_valid_entity_15484.html (accessed on 6 August 2015).

Panda, Jagannath P., 2012b. 'India's call on BRICS: aligning with China without a deal', *ISDP Policy Brief*, No. 91, 9 March, www.isdp.eu/images/stories/isdp-main-pdf/2012_panda_indias-call-on-brics.pdf (accessed on 5 September 2015).

Panda, Jagannath, 2012c. 'A "BRICS" wall? The complexity of China–India multilateral politics', *Indian Foreign Affairs Journal*, 7(2), April–June, pp. 175–94.

Panda, Jagannath, 2012d. 'Revisiting India's policy priorities: Nonalignment 2.0 and the Asian matrix', *NBR Commentary*, 10 July, www.nbr.org/research/activity.aspx?id=260 (accessed on 24 June 2013).

Panda, Jagannath P., 2013a. *BRICS and the China–India Construct: A New World Order in Making?*, IDSA Monograph Series, No. 24, September.

Panda, Jagannath P., 2013b. 'Emerging powers: China and India in BRICS', in S.D. Muni and Vivek Chadha (eds), *Asian Strategic Review*, New Delhi: Pentagon Press/IDSA, pp. 107–21.

Panda, Jagannath P., 2013c. 'China and IBSA: possible BRICS overreach?', *Strategic Analysis*, 37(3), May–June, pp. 209–304.

People's Daily, 2010a. 'IBSA countries sign agreements on scientific areas', *People's Daily*, 16 April, http://english.peopledaily.com.cn/90001/90777/90852/6953422.html (accessed on 30 January 2013).

People's Daily, 2010b. 'IBSA summit ends with praise for growing forum relevance', *People's Daily*, 16 April, http://english.peopledaily.com.cn/90001/90777/90852/6953390.html (accessed on 30 January 2013).

People's Daily, 2011. 'IBSA calls for "immediate end to all violence" in Syria', *People's Daily*, 11 August, http://english.peopledaily.com.cn/90777/7566857.html (accessed on 30 January 2013).

People's Daily, 2013. 'Russian sailing vessel Pallada sets out on "African Odyssey"', 23 January, http://english.peopledaily.com.cn/90777/8104642.html# (accessed on 30 January 2013).

Plasschaert, Sylvain, 2012. 'Is the renminbi undervalued?', in Jan Wouters, Tanguy de Wilde, Pierre Defraigne and Jean-Christophe Defraigne (eds), *China, European Union and Global Governance*, Cheltenham: Edward Elgar, pp. 164–83.

pmindia.gov.in, 2009. 'PM's opening remarks at the Plenary Session of the BRIC Summit', Yekaterinburg, Russia, 16 June, http://pmindia.gov.in/content_print.php?nodeid=763&nodetype=2 (accessed on 22 March 2013).

pmindia.gov.in, 2010. 'PM's remarks at the Plenary Session of the G-20 Summit', Seoul, Republic of Korea, 12 November, http://pmindia.gov.in/content_print.php?nodeid=951&nodetype=2 (accessed on 22 March 2013).

pmindia.gov.in, 2012a. 'PM's statement to the media at the conclusion of the G20 summit in Los Cabos', Los Cabos, Mexico, 19 June, http://pmindia.gov.in/content_print.php?nodeid=1186&nodetype=2 (accessed on 22 March 2013).

pmindia.gov.in, 2012b. 'PM's statement at Second Plenary session of G-20 leaders on "Strengthening the international financial architecture and the financial system and promoting financial inclusion"', Los Cabos, Mexico, 19 June, http://pmindia.gov.in/content_print.php?nodeid=1185&nodetype=2 (accessed on 22 March 2012).

pmindia.gov.in, 2012c. 'PM's speech at the Plenary Session of G-20 Summit', Los Cabos, Mexico, 18 June, http://pmindia.gov.in/content_print.php?nodeid=1184&nodetype=2 (accessed on 22 March 2013).

pmindia.nic.in, 2012. 'PM's statement at the Plenary Session of the fourth BRICS Summit', New Delhi, 29 March, http://pmindia.nic.in/content_print.php?nodeid=1156&nodetype=2 (accessed on 22 March 2013).

Qu Bo, 2012. 'Dynamic engagement: China's participation in international monetary institutions', in Jan Wouters, Tanguy de Wilde, Pierre Defraigne and Jean-Christophe Defraigne (eds), *China, European Union and Global Governance*, Cheltenham: Edward Elgar, pp. 183–98.

Reuters, 2012. 'China to offer renminbi loans to BRICS nations – FT', *Reuters*, 7 March, www.reuters.com/article/2012/03/07/china-brics-loans-idUSL5E8E77I820120307 (accessed on 12 August 2015).

Saran, Shyam, 2012. 'The Asian future of reserves', *Business Standard*, 16 May, www.business-standard.com/india/printpage.php?autono=474401&tp= (accessed on 7 January 2012).

Shen Qiang, 2010. 'How to assess Obama Administration's new geo-strategy towards Asia', *Foreign Affairs Journal*, Chinese People's Institute of Foreign Affairs, 98, Winter, www.cpifa.org/en/q/listQuarterlyArticle.do;jsessionid=0221BFDAF1EBAE45029ECB0197FDC0EE?pageNum=4&articleId=189&quarterlyPageNum=18 (accessed on 3 July 2013).

Walt, Stephen M., 1987. *The Origin of Alliances*, Ithaca, NY: Cornell University Press.

Wolf, Martin, 2010. 'Why America is going to win the global currency battle', *Financial Times*, 13 October, p. 11.

Xinhua, 2010. 'Indian Navy warships leave for African visit', *Xinhua*, 20 August, http://news.xinhuanet.com/english2010/world/2010-08/20/c_13454822.htm (accessed on 30 January 2013).

Xinhua, 2012. 'Chinese Navy escort voyages fruitful', *Xinhua* (*China Daily*), 26 December, www.chinadaily.com.cn/china/2012-12/26/content_16055040.htm (accessed on 30 January 2013).

Xinhuanet, 2015. 'China focus: China to advance yuan's full convertibility', *Xinhuanet*, 6 March, http://news.xinhuanet.com/english/2015-03/06/c_134043190.htm (accessed on 5 September 2015).

Zheng Xinli, 2011. 'BRICS has to take up more challenges', *China Daily*, 14 April, www.chinadaily.com.cn/cndy/2011-04/14/content_12323057.htm (accessed on 5 September 2015).

14 BASIC and climate politics

Does the Brazil–South Africa–India–China (BASIC) forum symbolise the core of both India's and China's primary international positions on climate negotiations strategy or are there additional factors and nuances attached to their strategies? The issues involved are: (i) the import of BASIC in the context of the developing-world phenomenon, particularly in the context of India–China cross-continental interaction; and (ii) the complexity of these two Asian powers' policies and politics over climate change negotiations and governance in the context of the convergence and divergences that exist between their own domestic and international policy positions. This chapter argues that the India–China engagement in the BASIC setting is part of their perspective of the North–South divide, where both bargain hard to protect their individual terrain in the climate dialogue within the rubric of developing-world identity and dialogue. The developing-world identity helps both countries uphold their national interest while building a pressure cluster to tackle the Western pressure on the climate issue.

BASIC: the idea, origin and politics

BASIC owes its origin to a European Commission initiative, which funded an applied research project, named 'BASIC Project', bringing together a set of experts from the four BASIC countries. This project was carried out from January 2005 to June 2007. The European Commission's primary aim through this project was to figure out these four economies' national and international climate policies, negotiation strategy and support to the 'institutional capacity' of their climate policies. The BASIC Project gave rise to the Sao Paulo Proposal for an Agreement on Future Climate Policy. Realising the advantage of drawing up a combined platform on climate change dialogue, the BASIC member countries' experts started meeting regularly to discuss climate change negotiations before the Copenhagen summit in 2009 (Xinran Qi 2011) and presented a common platform as BASIC at the Copenhagen climate change dialogue (Masters 2012: 1). The conception of BASIC was reactionary, as a forum for the developing countries or emerging economies to protect their interests against the developed countries' pressure on climate change issues. COP15 (Conference of the Parties) created an ambience of stark variance and rift between the developing and developed worlds on climate negotiations, where the latter made it clear that it would not agree to initiate steps to reduce greenhouse gas (GHG) emissions if developing countries or emerging economies failed to do so. This dichotomy further promoted the identity politics at the cross-continental level between India and China as developing-world powers, which corroborated further with ideas like BRICS and IBSA.

The formation of BASIC signalled a kind of 'new territory' in climate negotiation geopolitics (Xinran Qi 2011: 295; see also Mejia 2010: 7). The spirit of BASIC is quite congruent with the G-77[1] emerging economies. These countries' rapid economic growth and rapid industrialisation have affected the climate where the focus has been on CO_2 emissions. Given their current economic growth, BASIC countries have surpassed many OECD countries in CO_2 emissions. BASIC as a grouping favour the stakes and claim of emerging economies, explaining that they need extra time, space and equity to meet climate change challenges. BASIC's climate change dialogue is based on the principle of 'equity', 'fairness' and 'common but differentiated responsibilities' (CBDR) (Xinran Qi 2011; Masters 2012: 2; Minas 2013). The core of this dialogue is linked to Article 3 of the United Nations Framework Convention on Climate Change (UNFCCC) of 1992,[2] which states:

> The Parties should protect the climate system for the benefit of present and future generations of humankind, on the basis of equity and in accordance with their [CBDR] and respective capabilities. Accordingly, the developed country Parties should take the lead in combating climate change and the adverse effects thereof.

Fundamentally, member countries of BASIC are emerging economies. Though they are major emitters of GHG (see Table 14.1), they have low per capita income and low per capita GHG emissions. Most of them depend upon fossil fuels for their energy needs. BASIC has put forward the following fundamental stance vis-à-vis climate change negotiations (BASIC 2010; see also Masters 2012: 2). *First*, 'BASIC is not just a negotiation coordinating forum, but also a forum for cooperative action on mitigation and adaptation including exchange of information and cooperation matters relating to climate technology and science.' *Second*, BASIC 'supports the Copenhagen Accord on climate negotiation and underlined the importance of the Accord as representing a high-level political understanding among the participants on contentious negotiation process'. *Third*, BASIC supports the core spirit and centrality of UNFCCC and the decision to implement the negotiation process as per the two-track Ad-hoc Working Groups (AWG), namely, AWG on Long-term Cooperative Action (AWG-LCA) and AWG for Fostering Emission Reduction Commitments for Annex-1 Parties under the Kyoto Protocol (AWG-KP). *Fourth*, the principle of CBDR must be respected as per UNFCCC. *Fifth*, adaptation issues should be given priority and importance equal to issues of mitigation. *Sixth*, equity, transparency and capacity building and technology transfer should be the hallmark of the negotiation

Table 14.1 Profile and climate status of BASIC members

Particulars	Brazil	South Africa	India	China
GDP (annual trillion US$)[1]	2.36	0.52	4.78	12.38
GDP growth (%)[2]	0.9	2.5	4.7	7.8
GDP based on PPP, share of world total (%)[3]	2.70	0.67	5.54	14.21
GDP per capita (GDP/population) in US$[4]	11,751	10,782	3919	9173
Total area (sq km)[5]	8,514,877	1,219,090	3,287,263	9,596,961
Population[6]	201,009,622	48,601,098	1,220,800,359	1,349,585,838
GDP in PPP (annual trillion US$)[7]	2.33	0.58	4.79	12.27
CO_2 emissions per capita (metric tons)[8]	2.15	9.04	1.66	6.19
Other GHG emissions, HFC, PFC and SF6 (thousand metric tons of CO_2 equivalent)[9]	10,621	3210	20,937	249,362
Primary energy supply (%)[10]	Oil and other liquid fuel: 47	Coal: 72	Coal: 41	Coal: 69
Main source of CO_2 emissions	Non-renewable fossil fuels			

Sources: 1, 4, 5, 6 – www.countryreports.org/data-tables/index.htm; 2, 3, 7, 8, 9 – World Bank Database; 10 – www.eia.gov/countries/.

process, etc. The creation of BASIC was facilitated by the fact that most of its member countries are linked with each other in other forums as well.

Though in principle BASIC countries agree that climate change negotiations should be carried out under the framework of UNFCCC, Kyoto Protocol and the Bali Roadmap, they realise that there is a need to have concrete understanding among themselves as a base for forming a credible grouping. At the same time, the different perspectives and fundamental contradictions in India's and China's foreign policy stances and on the issue of emission patterns put this in doubt.

BASIC and the perspectives of India and China

As a result of the creation of BASIC to generate a 'common negotiated position' in the UNFCCC to counter the pressure from the industrialised countries, in COP15 there was a 'fundamental shift in power' where the US had to negotiate with the BASIC member countries on voluntary mitigation targets apart from marking a deal with the EU on the issue (King *et al.* 2012: 2). In general, BASIC has more differences with the United States than with Europe, and the finalisation of the Copenhagen Accord was more of a 'political accord' between the BASIC countries and the United States. The Copenhagen Accord has no 'legal character' in the context of UNFCCC. Nevertheless, in the Copenhagen Accord developing countries committed themselves to support the adaptation and mitigation actions in their own territories and BASIC agreed on the issue of measuring, reporting and verifying (MRV) partially (Xinran Qi 2011: 307). Brazil announced to reduce emissions in the range of 36–39 per cent; China, 40–45 per cent; South Africa, 34–42 per cent; and India, 25–30 per cent (ibid.: 307–8). The December 2015 Paris climate conference (COP21) unveiled the first ever 'universal, legally binding global climate deal' as a global climate action plan where BASIC members endorsed it in principle (Paris Agreement 2015). In this context, both India and China have a shared understanding on climate change under BASIC.

India and climate dialogue

Fundamentally, India's international position on climate negotiation dialogue is congruent with the BASIC stance, which at the same time is linked with the domestic constituency of climate policies and politics. On the domestic front, India released the first National Action Plan on Climate Change (NAPCC) in 2008, on 30 June. The NAPCC identified eight core National Missions.[3] Earlier in 2006, the Indian government released the National Environmental Policy (NEP), which outlined crucial elements of India's response to climate change. There is also a high-level advisory group to assist and advise the Prime Minister in this matter. On the domestic front, India has tried to link climate policy with energy security, economic competitiveness and reducing local pollution along with land management and control (Bellevrat 2011: 9). In international negotiations, New Delhi has actively participated in many forums, starting with

UNFCCC in 1993. India acceded to the Kyoto Protocol in 2002. During the Copenhagen Accord negotiations, New Delhi committed to a *voluntary* – and *not legally binding* – 20–25 per cent reduction in emissions intensity by the year 2020, compared with the 2005 level. New Delhi has also said that this attempt at reducing emission patterns or intensity by 2020 will be pushed ahead with the concurrent acceptance of national principles and legislation and with the relevant provisions of UNFCCC (*pib.nic.in* 2010). There is a rider, however, that India's commitment to reduce its emissions intensity will happen with the help of technology and finance transfer (King *et al.* 2012: 29). Additional to these initiatives, in 2010 India agreed to the Listing in Chapeau of the Copenhagen Accord,[4] along with Brazil and South Africa. India maintains that getting into this listing will strengthen its international negotiation position on climate change (*pib.nic.in* 2010).

India forcefully maintains that climate change is a 'serious global environmental concern'; at the same time, it has its concerns linked to domestic issues such as agriculture, water storage, sea-level rise, habitations, floods and droughts, food security and water security (LARRDIS 2013: 1–2; see also *Economic Survey 2012–13*: 256–7). The principal account under which New Delhi advocates its principal climate position is that of a CBDR 'and respective capabilities and their specific regional and national development priorities, objectives and circumstances'. Submitting the country's National Communication (NATCOM) to the UNFCCC first in 2004 and next in 2012, India has explicitly noted the impact of climate change on sea-level rise and on air temperature (LARRDIS 2013: 8). Even on the Paris climate change agreement, India seems to be satisfied that it does not have any specific reference to 'historical responsibilities' and the 'all-important concept of "differentiation" has not been discarded altogether' (Sinha 2015).

India's official advocacy on the climate change negotiation process is linked with three principal outlines, as follows (King *et al.* 2012: 29). *First*, accelerated access to critical mitigation patterns and adaptation technologies and related intellectual property rights (IPR). In New Delhi's perspective, cost barriers make it difficult for developing countries to access IPR for climate-friendly technologies. *Second*, dialogue of equitable access to sustainable development. Asking for a constructive dialogue programme in COP17 and COP18, India has asked for better and uniform access to a sustainable development mechanism. *Third*, developed countries must not adhere to and follow unilateral trade measures while dealing with carbon border adjustments and taxes. This is an important issue because the EU had implemented unilateral carbon tax, which India criticised during the recent BASIC Ministers meeting.

China and climate dialogue

The National Development and Reform Commission (NDRC) is mainly responsible for China's domestic policy regarding climate and environment. The State Council is the country's supervisory body vis-à-vis domestic policies as also

China's international interface (Bellevrat 2011: 6). On the global platform, Beijing has always argued that there should be special categories to address climate challenge issues with regard to the interests and domestic priorities of the developing world (see Wei Zonglei 2009). Its recent annual report on the subject, titled *China's Policies and Actions for Addressing Climate Change*, reiterates China's 'proactive' participation in global negotiations on climate change under the following items: (i) participation in international negotiations under the UN framework; (ii) participation in relevant international dialogues and mechanisms like BRICS, BASIC and UNFCCC; and (iii) reiterating the spirit of the climate negotiations strategy in relevant conferences like the 2012 Doha conference (*china.org.cn* 2012).

China's dialogue and position on climate negotiation on the global platform starts from its domestic governance issues. Like India, it has argued in favour of CBDR. It is argued that China's pledge to the Paris climate negotiation is primarily an 'international reflection of China's domestic commitments' (Cecily Liu 2016). Officially, China has endorsed the Paris climate agreement stating that it is 'a new beginning in international cooperation and is fair in splitting responsibility between developed and developing countries' (*Xinhua* 2015). Currently, China is the largest emitter of CO_2 in the world and causes a quarter of the current global emissions (Figure 14.1). To protect itself against public opinion, Beijing has tried to develop the emerging world's combined dialogue on climate change through the advocacy of BASIC and BRICS forums. At the Doha Climate Change dialogue in 2012, the head of the Chinese delegation, Xie Zhenhua, reiterated the classic Chinese position that 'climate change is due to unrestricted emissions by developed countries in their process of industrialisation' and that 'Developing countries are the victims of climate change' (Harvey 2012).

China officially claims that it has taken the lead and responsibility to help developing countries, that it has: (i) helped them to deal with the climate

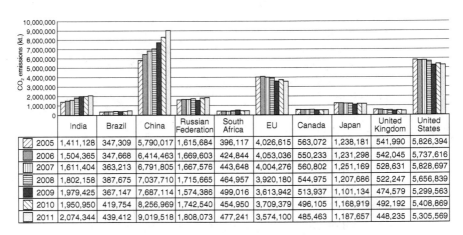

Figure 14.1 Major countries of CO_2 emissions (kt.) (source: World Bank Data, World Development Indicators, http://data.worldbank.org/).

challenge; (ii) earmarked $200 million for this cause; (iii) financed climate programmes in Africa, including some least developed countries (LDCs) and small island countries; and (iv) tried to bring a South–South perspective in its climate change challenge stance (*xinhuanet.com* 2012; *Xinhua* 2015). On the dialogue of sustainable development, China has taken a leading approach too. At the June 2012 Brazil Rio+20 summit, Premier Wen Jiabao stated that China would like to contribute US$6 million to a UN mission, named Environmental Programme Trust for Environmental Protection, which would enable the developing countries to raise their individual capacities to meet the new environmental challenges. Wen Jiabao also promised $31.7 million to help small-island, least developed and African countries to mitigate the climate change challenge affecting them (Cheng Guangjin 2012). For China, the crux is to coexist amicably with the developing world and back its position, slowly buying time for itself in terms of climate challenge issues.

India–China dynamics in BASIC

The India–China bonding on climate politics appears healthy. Both seem to share a strong and common perspective in the matter and seem to be taking a lead to protect the interests of the developing world. They have also pushed collectively the emerging and developing countries grouping through G-77 (*BRICS-POST* 2013). Besides, they have agreed and tried to build a common platform on this subject in a grouping like BRICS. However, whether their association within BASIC is entirely a climate-specific or developing-world arrangement needs to be understood in a broader context. The India–China agreement on climate change, signed on 21 October 2009, suggests that the international stakes and politics regarding the issue have compelled the two countries to forge a better bilateral understanding on the matter. The agreement was signed after the Copenhagen COP15 climate politics. Clearly, the understanding between the two countries on climate change is a post-BASIC initiative, with international or cross-continental political developments having a bearing on their transient bilateral relationship in today's context.

Officially known as the Agreement on Cooperation on Addressing Climate Change Between The Government of the Republic of India and The Government of the People's Republic of China, this agreement acknowledged the adverse consequences of climate change, which need not only bilateral consultation but also international cooperation. It recognised the UNFCCC and Kyoto Protocol as apposite mechanisms to discuss and address climate change. It also noted the concerns that exist between the developing and developed world. Pointedly, it reiterated the principle of CBDR for the larger developing world and stated that the developed countries must set an example in reducing their GHG emissions. It also stated that the developed countries needed to extend financial and technological support to developing countries on climate issues and help build capacity to tackle them.

Stating its objective as being to 'enhance dialogue, communication and pragmatic cooperation', the agreement stressed that the two countries needed to strengthen cooperation in areas like energy efficiency, renewable energy, clean energy, forest, and agriculture to build and achieve a sustainable development path. Article 1 of the agreement binds the two countries to hold ministerial consultations to discuss and review bilateral and international issues that relate to climate change. Article 2 mandates a Working Group to meet annually to discuss ongoing negotiations, both bilateral and international, on climate change. Article 3 states that the two sides agreed to exchange views on mitigation policies, technology development and matters related to GHG emissions. Cooperation is also aimed at extending to areas like energy, clean coal, transportation, management of forests and ecosystems, methane recovery and utilisation, sustainable habitats, etc. (*pib.nic.in* 2009).

During Prime Minister Modi's visit to China in May 2015, India and China released a Joint Statement on climate change, which emphasises greater bilateral cooperation and understanding on climate dialogue (*pib.nic.in* 2015). The Joint Statement not only stresses the importance of the 2009 Agreement but also equally takes note of the MoU between the two countries that was crafted in 2010 on Green Technologies (ibid.). It reiterates the significance of the UNFCCC and Kyoto Protocol and other relevant international climate frameworks. It highlights 'equity' and CBDR and calls for a 'leadership' position of developing countries for checking and reducing GHG emissions (ibid.).

The 2015 Joint Statement comes at a time when there was concern among the developing countries that China under Xi Jinping has entered into a special understanding with the US on climate change dialogue. Under Xi's leadership, Sino-US relations have seen some conditional improvement on global governance issues; climate change is one such matter. The November 2014 deal between China and US emphasises the need for an agreed perspective between the two countries on reducing GHG emission patterns and the deadline (Taylor and Branigan 2014). As per this deal, the Chinese government for the first time agreed to cap the emissions, whereas earlier China had expressed its willingness to check the rapid growth of emissions (ibid.; see also *whitehouse.gov* 2014).

The contours

While the BASIC members – separately and collectively – represent and encourage the expression of the developing-countries syndrome strongly, the engagement between India and China on climate change explains expressively the character and nuances that their relationship offers to global politics today. Understanding the India–China engagement within BASIC is important for a variety of reasons. *First*, not only is the role of BASIC important in the climate change negotiation process but also because of the character and motives of its member states. *Second*, though there is a strong variance in their perspective of climate change, the two countries have resolved to cooperate at a cross-continental level to face the stiff pressure of the developed world on this issue. *Third*, the India–China course reflects how these two Asian countries represent the developing countries' interests in a calculated design. This is a new experience and explains how world politics have become multilaterally polygonal. *Fourth*, the India–China discourse explains the versatility of their relationship. This interaction may not be cooperative always, but it raises expectations for collaboration at the global level. *Fifth*, both countries today distinguish their postures not only from the developed world but also from the poorer developing world. This raises the question whether their politics of developing-world identity is an enduring portent or just a temporary contrivance. Both India's and China's association within BASIC, along with Brazil and South Africa, explains the flexibility of their relationship discourse in a divided structure of the developing-developed world.

BASIC's progress in world politics will depend heavily upon the extent to which India and China continue to forge a common position on climate change. Differing intra-BASIC perspectives is one aspect that propels the debate whether BASIC's outlook on climate change is an enduring one. South Africa's differing stance on climate change has, for example, placed the unity of BASIC under a serious test. South Africa has declared that the 'global agreement on climate change should be concluded in the form of protocol with targets, commitments and actions for all parties' (Sethi 2013). This is closer to the Western stance, in contrast to the BASIC position, that the 'legally binding protocol on climate change should not be enforced until the context of the new climate deal is well known in public'. The progress and continuity of the BASIC climate dialogue depends heavily on to what extent the developing world is united on the issue and how India and China together represent its spirit.

Notes

1 Since UNFCCC 1992, emerging economies or developing countries, numbering around 131, have negotiated their climate dialogue under the framework of 'Group of 77 and China', popularly known as G-77.
2 BASIC, formed on 28 November 2009 on the sidelines of the Copenhagen climate summit, put forward the position that it would not be a part of the climate negotiation process if the developed countries did not accept its 'common minimum position' as per the UNFCCC of 1992 principle. See Xinran Qi 2011; Masters 2012; Minas 2013.
3 These are: (i) solar mission; (ii) for enhanced energy efficiency; (iii) on sustainable habitat; (iv) water mission; (v) for sustaining the Himalayan ecosystem; (vi) for a 'Green India'; (vii) for sustainable agriculture; and (viii) on strategic knowledge for climate change. See LARRDIS 2013: Reference Note: No. 25/RN/Ref./, p. 9.
4 According to the then India's Minister of State for Environment and Forests at the time, Jairam Ramesh, listing in Chapeau of the Accord 'implies that India participated in the Copenhagen Accord Negotiation and stands by the Accord'. See *pib.nic.in* 2010.

References

BASIC, 2010. 'Joint Statement issued at the conclusion of the Second Meeting of Ministers of BASIC Group, New Delhi, January 24, 2010'.
Bellevrat, Elie, 2011.*Climate Policies in China and India: Planning, implementation and linkages with international negotiations*, Working Paper, IDDRI, Sciences Po, Paris, France, No. 20/11, December.

BRICSPOST, 2013. 'China, India: wealthy nations must take climate change initiative', *The BRICSPOST*, 21 November, http://thebricspost.com/china-india-wealthy-nations-must-take-climate-change-initiative/ (accessed on 8 April 2014).

Cecily Liu, 2016. 'China's Paris climate pledges "reflect China's domestic desires"', *China Daily*, 25 January, at http://europe.chinadaily.com.cn/world/2016-01/25/content_23241278.htm (accessed on 21 February 2016).

Cheng Guangjin, 2012. 'China stepping out on world stage', *China Daily*, 31 December, www.chinadaily.com.cn/world/2012-12/31/content_16069903.htm (accessed on 17 January 2013).

china.org.cn, 2012. 'China's policies and actions for addressing climate change', Information Office of the State Council of the People's Republic of China, 21 November, www.china.org.cn/government/whitepaper/node_7172407.htm (accessed on 4 February 2013).

Economic Survey, 2012–13. Ministry of Finance, Government of India, New Delhi, pp. 256–7.

Harvey, Fiona, 2012. 'China pledges "due contribution" on emissions cuts', *Guardian*, 5 December, www.guardian.co.uk/environment/2012/dec/05/china-due-contribution-emissions-cuts (accessed on 4 February 2013).

King, Sir David, Megan Cole, Sally Tyldesley and Ryan Hogarth, 2012. *The Response of China, India and Brazil to Climate Change: A Perspective for South Africa*, Smith School of Enterprise and the Environment, University of Oxford, November.

LARRDIS, 2013. *Climate Change – India's Perspective*, Lok Sabha Secretariat: Parliamentary Library and Reference, Research, Documentation and Information Service (LARRDIS), Members Research Service, August.

Masters, Lesley, 2012. 'What future for BASIC? The emerging powers dimension in the international politics of climate change negotiations', *Global Insight*, Issue 95, March, Institute for Global Dialogue, pp. 1–5.

Mejia, D.A., 2010. 'The evolution of the climate change regime: Beyond a North–South divide?', *ICIP Working Paper*, No. 6, Barcelona: Institut Catala International per la Pau, pp. 1–48.

Minas, Stephen, 2013. 'BASIC positions: major emerging economies in the UN climate change negotiations', *FPC Briefing: The Foreign Policy Centre*, June.

Paris Agreement, 2015. 'Climate Action', at http://ec.europa.eu/clima/policies/international/negotiations/paris/index_en.htm (accessed on 21 February 2016).

pib.nic.in, 2009. 'India and China sign agreement on cooperation on addressing climate change', Ministry of Environment and Forests, 21 October, http://pib.nic.in/newsite/erelease.aspx?relid=53317 (accessed on 8 February 2014).

pib.nic.in, 2010. 'Suo Motu Statement in Lok Sabha by Minister of State for Environment and Forests (I/C) on some of the issues relating to the Copenhagen Accord in the light of recent developments', Press Information Bureau, Government of India, Ministry of Environment and Forests, 9 March, http://pib.nic.in/newsite/PrintRelease.aspx (accessed on 1 April 2014).

pib.nic.in, 2015. 'Joint Statement on Climate Change between India and China during Prime Minister's visit to China', Press Information Bureau, Government of India, 15 May, http://pib.nic.in/newsite/PrintRelease.aspx?relid=121754 (accessed on 2 August 2015).

Sethi, Nitin, 2013. 'Breaking ranks with BASIC, South Africa calls for legally binding protocol on climate change', *The Hindu*, 10 October.

Sinha, Amitabh, 2015. 'Paris climate talks: differentiation of developed and developing stays, India happy', *Indian Express*, 14 December, http://indianexpress.com/article/india/

india-news-india/paris-climate-talks-differentiation-of-developed-and-developing-stays-india-happy/ (accessed on 21 February 2016).

Taylor, Lenore and Tania Branigan, 2014. 'US and China strike deal on carbon cuts in push for global climate change pact', *Guardian*, 12 November, www.theguardian.com/environment/2014/nov/12/china-and-us-make-carbon-pledge (accessed on 2 August 2015).

UNFCCC, 1992. 'Principles', Article 3, United Nations Framework Convention on Climate Change, United Nations.

Wei Zonglei, 2009. 'Tackling climate change – a scientific view of development', *Contemporary International Relations*, vol. 19, Special Issue, March, pp. 68–88.

whitehouse.gov, 2014. 'U.S.–China Joint Announcement on Climate Change, Beijing: China, November 12, 2014', https://www.whitehouse.gov/the-press-office/2014/11/11/US–China-joint-announcement-climate-change (accessed on 2 August 2015).

Xinhua, 2015. 'China makes active contribution for breakthrough at Paris climate talks', *China Daily*, 14 December, www.chinadaily.com.cn/world/XiattendsParisclimateconference/2015-12/14/content_22710450.htm (accessed on 20 February 2016).

xinhuanet.com, 2012. 'China backs developing countries to combat climate change: official', *Xinhua*, 5 December, http://news.xinhuanet.com/english/china/2012-12/05/c_132020930.htm (accessed on 4 February 2013).

Xinran Qi, 2011. 'The rise of BASIC in UN climate change negotiations', *South African Journal of International Affairs*, 18(3), December, pp. 295–318.

15 Institutionalising the African reach[1]

This chapter examines the instrumental nature of comparative foreign policies of India and China within the charter of their pledge to multilateral outreach in Africa. This multilateral reach connotes a polygonal approach that harnesses bilateral, institutional and organisational chain of contacts together. The new mode of their multilateral contacts with the region through the African Union (AU) and multilateral forums like BRICS, BASIC and India–Brazil–South Africa (IBSA) reinforces this presence. This multilateral bonding provides the two countries various intercontinental benefits, strategic reach, opportunities for power positioning, posturing as well as distinctions that a merely bilateral approach does not necessarily provide.

There is a pervasive but subtle struggle for presence and partnership emerging between the two countries in Africa. This may not be a directly competitive one; nonetheless, their drive to institutionalise the African reach is allied to their power-building networks and cross-continental alliance politics. South Africa is a conspicuous example in this respect. Both China and India are driving to entice South Africa into their penumbra through a multilateral chain of contacts to establish their respective greater presence in the African continent. The Chinese approach has been more generous in funding projects and establishing strong economic linkages through 'aid and donor' approach; whereas the Indian approach is based more on a 'populist', 'third world', 'developing world' factor.

Recent literature on major powers' approaches to the African continent suggests that both India and China have emerged as the two most influential powers in Africa in the recent past. Some argue that the crux of this growing presence is the robust trade and economic contacts that both have employed (Broadman 2008; Chen Deming 2012; Meeking 2013). Others see the merits of the soft-power approach and see the two countries as influential actors of contemporary 'donors and partners' strategy (Naidu and Heyley 2008; Meeking 2013; Vickers 2013). The reach of these two Asian powers has been so pervasive in Africa in recent times that experts and scholars have been prompted to perceive a possible 'Asian' approach, distinct from the erstwhile colonial or Western approach towards Africa (see Iwata 2012).

Unlike the traditional Western 'donors or partners' approach that most countries have employed towards Africa, India's and China's approaches to the continent have evolved from a combination of history and contemporary dynamics. They combine the established 'Afro-Asian' multilateral bonding with the contemporary multilateral realities of economics, politics and diplomatic nuances and strategies. These involve a set of principles that combine a populist measure or approach, traditional 'donors and partners' contact and, most notably, a reliable international conglomerate that is multilateral and multipolar in nature, which is important both to Africa and to India and China as well. This multiple mode of reaching out to Africa helps the two countries enlarge their own presence in the continent while checking the other's influence. A comparative analysis of India's and China's contemporary approach to Africa would bear out this assertion.

Rising powers phenomenon

At present, other than the politics of energy and economics, the West is less concerned about Africa politically.[2] On the other hand, rising powers like China, India and Brazil see the African continent not only as an opportunity but also as an effective international partner for global partnership and for advancing their foreign policy objectives. South–South bonding today represents a political manifestation of the developing world relying on itself rather than the traditional mode of depending on the West (Sidiropoulos 2012: 1–2). In South–South solidarity, bilateralism becomes secondary and cross-continental bonding takes the lead, placing multilateralism and multilateral interests in the forefront. BRICS, BASIC and IBSA are representative of this portent. Likewise, the representation of AU as standing for Africa as a continent is reflected emphatically in China–AU, India–AU and Latin America–Africa summits.

This South–South spirit explains three policy directions. *First*, it is more about pan-continental frameworks, and explains the economic, diplomatic, cultural and political nuances attached to it. *Second*, the South–South spirit has got revitalised in the growing interests and political magnitude of the developing world, where these emerging countries are not necessarily reliant on the developed world (Sidiropoulos 2012: 2). *Third*, this bonding explains the increasing extent of multipolarism and multipolar world order, where nation-states seek to maximise their bilateral and multilateral foreign policy aims and objectives through coordinated positions and contacts. This generates a conditional 'global South foreign policy', which is noticed in the African states' relationship with the rest of the world (Persaud 2003: 55).

'Energy first' diplomacy: trade to maritime – the competing presence

Africa's strategic location and its resources are attractive to various countries to posit the continent as a leading factor in their foreign policy. *Energy in Africa*, a report by the World Bank, notes that despite the continent's abundant energy resources, nearly 25 African countries face an energy crisis (Masondo 2013).

226 Cross-continental contemporaries

Access to raw materials remains at the forefront of India's and China's reach in Africa, but the most effective device for the two countries in the continent is to have longer-term impact in creating human development conditionality and forging ahead institutional capabilities there (Gupta and Wang 2011). Manufacturing, services, infrastructure and telecommunications equally also provide massive opportunities.

China's trade recipe

The volume of trade and economic contacts between Africa and the two Asian countries is growingly rapidly. In 2000, China–Africa trade was around US$10.6 billion; in 2011 it jumped to $160 billion (Smith 2012; Wang Xiaotian 2012) (Figure 15.1). The China–Africa Cooperation Forum (CACF) has been a linchpin mechanism behind this growth. Trade and economic contacts have expanded to various areas such as tourism, finance, infrastructure and investment. It is also reported that by 2012, $20 billion has been accumulated as Chinese direct investment in Africa; some 75 per cent is going to sectors like agriculture, transportation and infrastructure, finance, manufacturing, etc. (Ma Xuequan 2013). Almost 2000 Chinese enterprises have reached Africa and have flooded their business in almost 50 African countries. Beijing has been generous in granting a huge amount of loans and aid in the last few years to Africa.

India's trade performance

There has been a steady growth in India's trade contacts with Africa in the last few years as well, growing by almost 20 times in the last decade. By 2011–2012, the bilateral trade figured around $67 billion, registering almost 28 per cent growth from 2010–2011 (*Hindu Business Line* 2013). Ambitiously, India aims

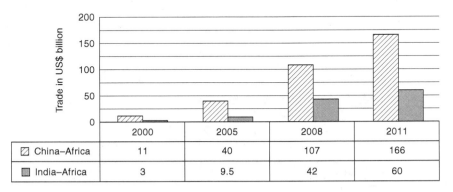

Figure 15.1 China–Africa and India–Africa bilateral trade, 2000–2011 (source: data collected from various open sources such as *China Daily, Xinhua, Financial Express, The Hindu Business Line, Economist, BBC, Times of India*, etc.).

Note
Figures are approximate.

to sign a free trade agreement (FTA) involving a limited number of goods with the Common Market for Eastern and Southern Africa (COMESA) (ibid.). The current Indian trade engagement with Africa is mainly in commodities and low-end manufactures. Statistics indicate that China accounted for 16.9 per cent of Africa's global trade and India for 5.2 per cent. Most of the African countries continue to enjoy a favourable trade balance with India (Banerjee 2013).

New Delhi is increasingly concerned about the 'cash diplomacy' that Beijing has promoted to woo and impress the African community for oil and energy diplomacy. There are a number of factors like money, premium payments while signing the deals, freedom of Chinese overseas oil exploration companies, the Chinese government's backing to these companies, and the value of the Chinese currency (RMB) which is stronger in the world market and puts China ahead of India in exploring energy in Africa and absorbing the African market (Katakey and Duce 2010). China pursues a business model that rotates around mostly infrastructure building, loans in exchange for accessing natural resources, and exploring new areas and markets and trade opportunities. Indian diplomacy in Africa so far has focused on areas like diamond and coal. India wants to promote its claim, stake and interests in areas like information technology, pharmaceuticals and automobiles (Kermeliotis 2011).

Prevailing maritime politics

Connecting to the Mediterranean Sea via the Suez Canal and the Red Sea, the Indian Ocean has been one of the prime political factors in China's and India's reach towards Africa (Map 15.1). The Indian Ocean and the Persian Gulf will remain the vital and critical route for China's and India's oil and energy diplomacy in the times to come. It is estimated that around 70–80 per cent of their oil imports will probably originate through the Persian Gulf. Major chokepoints in the Indian Ocean like the Straits of Hormuz, Malacca, the Mozambique Channel, Bab-el-Mandeb in the Gulf of Aden, Lombok and Sunda Straits, etc. constitute vital energy routes for China, India and the rest of the world (van Rooyen 2011: 8). Traditionally, neither China nor India has given strategic priority to these chokepoints (Potgieter 2012: 2).

Many have argued that Beijing has pursued a 'string of pearls' strategy around the Indian Ocean to protect its energy routes and concentrates heavily on its trade and energy routes with Africa. In contrast, India continues to keep its Navy active on the East African coast, which is known for continued maritime insecurity (Potgieter 2012: 18–19). India's maritime posture in the Indian Ocean has been more south-westward to the African littoral in recent years (Scott 2009: 117).

India set up in 2006–2007 a maritime monitoring station in northern Madagascar. Its objectives are not only to combat piracy and terrorist activities in the sea, but also to keep a close eye on the Chinese presence in the Indian Ocean. India has signed an agreement with Mozambique for regular maritime patrolling, and has provided 'seaward protection' for the AU at Mozambique (Pubby 2007).

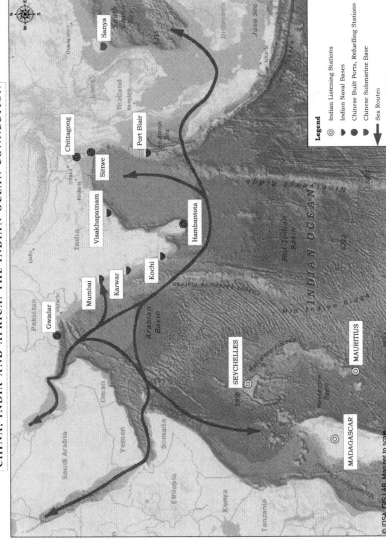

Map 15.1 China, India and Africa: the Indian Ocean connection (source: GIS Lab, IDSA).

Furthermore, India has carried out maritime exercises with Africa. India's involvement with South Africa in IBSA has facilitated raising maritime security issues vis-à-vis the African continent. IBSA has conducted IBSAMAR maritime exercises with India. India has also been active with regard to the Indian Ocean Rim Association for Regional Cooperation (IOR-ARC), which involves some of the key African states, including South Africa. The prime target of IOR-ARC (now renamed as Indian Ocean Regional Association, IORA) is to have a peaceful and stable maritime zone in the Indian Ocean Region (IOR). To address the security and defence issues, India has taken an initiative to create the Indian Ocean Naval Symposium (IONS), which includes a few African countries.

Tying up with AU: a sprint to institutionalise the bonding?

Though AU is a well-known 'continental body' (Murithi 2012: 666),[3] lack of consensus flowing from divergent national interests has affected its continental and global standing.[4] In reaching out to the AU, both China and India advocate greater unity and solidarity among the people of Africa. India has so far preferred to engage with only a few African countries bilaterally, while advocating greater institutional linkages between itself and Africa through the AU.

The Chinese institutional reach

China is politically better placed in Africa today than India. It has strong diplomatic relations and embassies and political offices across the continent.[5] China takes the African continent more seriously also because of the Taiwan factor: not all the African countries adhere to the one-China policy. It may be noted that the new AU headquarters in Addis Ababa in Ethiopia has been funded by China as a 'gift to the AU' (*BBC News*: *Africa* 2012).[6]

FOCAC: shaping the Sino-African bonding

By 2000, China had realised the importance of Africa; and Africa also mostly realised that China was emerging as an effective power in global politics and that it was vital to institutionalise the Sino-African engagement. The Forum of China–Africa Cooperation (FOCAC) was established in 2000 to take this engagement further (Yu 2010: 135). FOCAC has facilitated regular summits between China and African leaders, promoting innovation. Forty-eight African leaders attended the FOCAC meeting in Beijing, and reiterated their faith in a progressive Sino-African relationship. Trade, economic and political understanding and other areas like cultural engagement between the two sides have improved through FOCAC. As evidence of the cultural bonding between China and Africa, by the year 2012, a total of 29 Confucius Institutes were established in 20 countries in Africa (Yang Jiechi 2012).

India's outreach to AU

India's approach to Africa is based more on soft-power linkages, against the background of its cultural and historical experience of having been subjected to colonialism, which experience Africa also shares. India's approach to Africa has been based more or less on the 'developing world' formulations, where India has always denounced the 'donor-recipient' approach, and followed a 'developmental cooperation' framework (Saran 2012: 1–2). This 'developmental cooperative' structure is based on three broad foundations: idea of partnership, consultation where donorship comes secondary, and mutually beneficial interdependency (ibid.).

India's approach to the AU has been subtler than Beijing's. India has tried to build South–South solidarity with AU, including becoming a member of the AU Partner Group (AUPG). The India–AU relationship formally moved to the next level with the 2008 India–Africa Forum Summit (IAFS), in which 14 African leaders and the AU Commission participated.[7] This summit adopted the Delhi Declaration and India–Africa Framework for Cooperation. The second IAFS pushed ahead the bilateral relationship. This summit, held in May 2011 in Addis Ababa, was punctuated by the Addis Ababa Declaration and the Framework for Enhanced Cooperation. During this summit, India announced a grant of US$5 billion to Africa. The Addis Ababa declaration discussed not only cooperation between India and Africa but also a number of multilateral issues and concerns that both sides share. It also addressed various governance issues like climate change, poverty and the millennium development goals (MDGs) (*pib.nic.in* 2011). India has also launched 'Team 9 Initiative', which is aimed at forging better economic trust with French-speaking African countries.

Courting South Africa: the politics of BRICS, BASIC and IBSA

While multilateral networks and forging closer bonding with Africa have been a prime medium for both China and India at a wider level, networking with Africa has also been country specific. South Africa exemplifies this. South Africa is strategically important for China and India both for African politics and also for broader global and cross-continental politics. Scepticism persists over South Africa's potential regional and global prominence;[8] yet the Chinese and Indian linking with South Africa in various bilateral and multilateral forums has made this African nation a vital one in global politics today. South Africa is connected to India in IBSA, and with both China and India in BRICS. South Africa fits into the global discourse of 'developing world' and 'emerging economies' more than any other country in Africa. The historical Afro-Asian movement is a facilitator in this regard too.

For China, the association with South Africa in various multilateral forums is of utmost strategic importance. Bilaterally too, China has constantly upgraded its relationship with South Africa at several levels – political, diplomatic, economic

Institutionalising the African reach 231

and cultural. But the most astounding circumstance in the Sino-South African relationship was the Sanya (China) BRIC summit in 2011, where Beijing lobbied hard to induct South Africa as a member of BRIC, to emerge as BRICS (Donnelly and Benjamin 2013; Smith 2013). China has also managed to persuade South Africa that there is scope for maximising BRICS–IBSA cooperation, and perhaps a possible future merger of these two groups. President Jacob Zuma of South Africa encouraged this view by stating, 'We believe that the IBSA will get a better balance and become even stronger with South Africa now as a member of BRICS, more especially since the mandates of BRICS and IBSA complement each other' (Shao 2010). Whether in BRICS, IBSA or BASIC, South Africa remains the bonding factor for China and India in the African continent (Vickers 2013: 684).

BRICS's rapid institutionalisation process meanwhile seems to be overpowering IBSA's prominence (Panda 2013; Sidiropoulos 2013). Popularly known as a 'trading nation' (Zweig 2010: 37), China pursues intense trade (Figure 15.2) and diplomatic contacts with both South Africa and Brazil, to facilitate its energy and commercial needs, and takes BRICS seriously to promote the Yuan as an international currency. China's trade contacts with South Africa and Brazil are evidently much ahead of India's relations with these two countries (Figure 15.3).

BRICS and IBSA politics is not merely about associating with Africa or South Africa; it is about the growing Chinese and Indian influence in continental politics. For instance, the 2013 Durban BRICS summit focused a lot on Africa, and how there is scope for BRICS–Africa cooperation. Africa's vitality for BRICS countries was clearly visible in the theme of the summit, which was

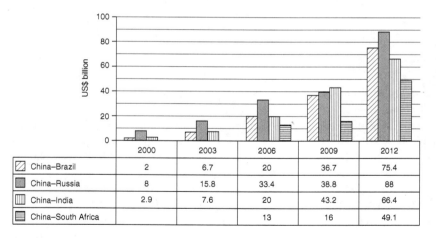

Figure 15.2 Trends of China's trade with BRICS countries, 2000–2012 (source: collated from various open sources like the *Times of India*, *Xinhua*, *Chinese Embassy in New Delhi*, *Ministry of Commerce of the PRC*, *Asia Times*, *Global Times*, *China Daily*, etc.).

Note
Figures are approximate. Data for China–South Africa trade in 2000 and 2003 are not available.

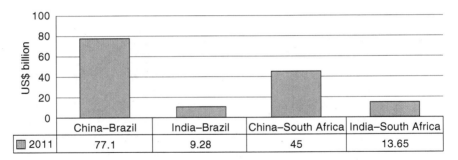

Figure 15.3 China's trade figures with IBSA members, 2011 (in US$ billion) (source: Collated from various sources like Secretariat for Social Communication – International Area, Presidency of the Federative Republic of Brazil, Embassy of the PRC in the Republic of South Africa, Ministry of Commerce & Industry and Ministry of Foreign Affairs, Government of India).

Note
All figures are approximate.

BRICS and Africa: Partnership for Development, Integration and Industrialisation. BRICS members also held a retreat with African leaders after the summit under the theme *Unlocking Africa's Potential: BRICS and Africa Cooperation on Infrastructure*, which suggests that most BRICS powers realise the need to establish better cooperation with Africa in order to exploit Africa's resource potential (*eThekwini Declaration* 2013). Two things were given utmost importance by the summit: to improve infrastructure in Africa, and carry out developmental projects through partnerships, to help improve human and societal conditions in the continent. In the summit, Africa was discussed exclusively, and much emphasis was given to tying up with Africa. But while the weight of Africa for BRICS powers is obvious, one wonders why BRICS did not discuss Africa earlier, given that BRICS is about the developing world.

A few factors need to be highlighted in this context. *First*, both China and India realise the importance of Africa and its continental representation that both BRICS and IBSA must have. *Second*, the politics of representation is a prodigious issue that divides India–China perspectives with regard to Africa. China, being a P-5 country, understands the complexity of reforming the UNSC and exploits the situation by advocating for greater continental representation, possibly from Africa. The Chinese advocacy is rhetorical, but Beijing benefits from the exercise in terms of public relations and goodwill in Africa. *Third*, the economic consequence of China–Africa relations is attached with the BRICS grouping too. Greater openness and impressive growth patterns of the Chinese economy are noticed among the African countries (Asongu and Aminkeng 2013; Grauwe *et al.* 2012). African countries see greater opportunities for themselves in this. *Fourth*, IBSA is an important project of India's cross-continental policy; and being known as a 'people's project', tends to promote Asian-African-Latin

American solidarity, which China finds little to its own interest. Both IBSA and BRICS embrace similar concerns on issues such as food security, social inclusiveness and energy issues, but India distinguishes IBSA's uniqueness as being largely a 'people's project' among democratic societies.

Explaining the China–India outreach to Africa: a comparative analysis

Bonding with Africa through the AU or through bilateral, cross-continental and organisational networks is a fresh stratagem for China and India. Overall, China's and India's networking engagement is a mixture of ideology, policy, politics and economic support that involves serious economic initiatives spurred by liberalisation. Both place their Africa policy in the context of their rising demand for energy resources and growing global political, diplomatic and economic ambitions.

Africa sees India positively, but values the Chinese presence even more. As discussed earlier, African leaders see the Chinese model much more favourably than the American model, which is currently dominant in global politics and in the global financial institutions (Power and Giles 2010). 'Business', 'resource politics' and 'resource diplomacy' occupy the primary place in current China–Africa relations (ibid.). India still continues to follow the traditional bilateral mode of reaching out to Africa, though New Delhi has started exploring new modes and mediums for this, mostly through institutional linkages and multilateral reach.

China has been quite positive and forthcoming in advocating a greater role for African countries in international affairs. It has openly backed the African countries for 'greater representation' in the UN, and pushed for African representation in global bodies like G-20 and BRICS. China has equally backed the African cause in the WTO Doha Round of Negotiations and helped African members on the way to attaining the MDGs (Yang Jiechi 2012).

The Chinese institutional reach in Africa explains four aspects: (i) the elucidation of a vital strategic relationship as a mode of pushing the relationship ahead; (ii) forging a common 'people-oriented' outlook to world affairs and international systems; (iii) cooperation building and establishing developing-world alliances; (iv) global identity building through South–South solidarity (Contessi 2009: 413). The main dialogue and ethos Beijing implements in the context of African bonding are to overcome the existing inequalities of globalisation and reforming global political and financial institutions in favour of the developing world.

India in its turn sees Africa as a key continent in achieving the politics of the developing world that it advocates globally. Besides, India locates its dialogue with Africa as a reliable partner for a range of socio-economic and global governance issues. The Non-Aligned Movement has been a common bond between India and Africa. India's connection with South Africa in the IBSA suggests that India wants to carry forward the 'people's projects' that both India and Africa have tried to advocate for long. Maritime security and politics in the IOR is one issue that brings India and Africa together. The recent maritime power posture in the Indian Ocean between China and India suggests that Africa will be an important factor in future IOR politics.

Four comparative policy imperatives can be seen in the context of Africa's current bonding with China and India. *First*, the 'ideological' prevalence that both countries seemed to be employing in the past has become secondary. Though South–South solidarity still remains the prime mode of reaching out to Africa, the spirit of its employment is highly subjective and covers a range of political, economic, diplomatic and strategic interests in Africa and in the region.

Second, Africa will continue to be a vital factor in China–India maritime politics in the Indian Ocean. Even though China is geographically disadvantaged in this matter relative to India, there is no doubt that China will continue to take Indian Ocean maritime zones seriously, as this is the key to China's oil diplomacy in Africa.

Third, the politics of BRICS and IBSA will gather momentum. One may even witness the AU forging cooperation with BRICS. A possibility in the longer run, with China's determined striving and with a little help from South Africa, is that BRICS and IBSA could either merge or establish a formal institutional linkage to discuss further governance issues.

Fourth, China and India will continue to prioritise their foreign policy strategies towards Africa, both to gain an advantage in terms of exploring energy resources and forging commercial dealings and also to form multilateral dealings with that continent. New trends and new patterns of engagement will be noticed in South–South politics, which may also shape and impact the emerging world order.

Notes

1 The *Journal of Asian and African Studies* (*JASS*), Sage Publications, Delhi, holds the copyright on this chapter. The author gratefully acknowledges the permission to publish it as a part of this book. It has been shortened to meet space requirements.
2 Occasionally, the West has been cautioning Africa about the 'new colonialism' of China and India that is designed to enhance their trade and economic contacts in the continent, conveniently oblivious of its own overarching reach and exploitation of African resources over centuries.
3 It is argued that as a 'continental body', the AU has a 'dual role' of establishing closer cooperation and unity among the member states of the African continent; and in promoting and advocating Africa's voice and stake internationally.
4 The AU is aimed at building harmony, solidarity, unity, peace and integrity among its 54 member states. It was established formally on 10 July 2002, replacing the erstwhile Organisation of African Unity (OAU). The main ethos and legacy of the AU are based on the pan-African movement.
5 China has embassies in 48 countries of Africa. With Somalia also it has diplomatic relations. Four countries do not have diplomatic relations with China because they have diplomatic relations with Taiwan. Forty-eight African countries have embassies in Beijing: Comoro Islands is the exception. For details, see *focac.org*, n.d. and Shinn 2011.

6 It is reported that the project cost $200 million. Most of the building materials were imported from China, including the furnishing. See *BBC News: Africa* 2012.
7 In this summit India offered 'unilateral duty-free and preferential market access for exports' from all 34 Least Developed Countries of Africa. A number of higher education agreements were also signed between the two sides. India offered more scholarships to African students to study in India. Conducting research and cooperation in bilateral R&D was also given prime importance. On the sidelines of this summit, a number of outreach activities were conducted, including (a) India–Africa Editors Conference; (b) joint performances by Indian and African troupes; (c) seminar and dialogue on India–Africa partnership; (d) business conclave; and (e) programme for youth and women from Africa.
8 Neither does South Africa's population, at around 50 million, match that of China or India; nor has its economy done substantially well over the last few years unlike the other BRICS countries. South Africa's GDP is ranked 28th in the world. Its economic growth record is even struggling to match some of its neighbours. For example, Nigeria may soon overtake South Africa as the biggest economy of Africa. See Donnelly and Benjamin (2013) and Smith (2013).

References

Asongu, Simplice A. and Gilbert A.A. Aminkeng, 2013. 'The economic consequences of China–Africa relations: debunking myths in the debate', *Journal of Chinese Economic and Business Studies*, 11(4): 261–77.

Banerjee, Chandrajit, 2013. 'Time to deepen trade ties with Africa'. *The Hindu Business Line*, 17 March, www.thehindubusinessline.com/opinion/time-to-deepen-trade-ties-with-africa/article4519137.ece (accessed on 17 April 2013).

BBC News: Africa, 2012. 'African Union opens Chinese-funded HQ in Ethiopia', 28 January, www.bbc.co.uk/news/world-africa-16770932?print=true (accessed on 8 March 2013).

Broadman, Harry G., 2008. 'China and India go to Africa', *Foreign Affairs*, March–April, www.foreignaffairs.com/print/63224 (accessed on 8 June 2014).

Chen Deming, 2012.'China and Africa poised to embrace a brighter future for economic cooperation and trade', Embassy of the People's Republic of China in the Federal Democratic Republic of Ethiopia, 18 July, http://et.china-embassy.org/eng/zfgx/t952599.htm (accessed on 8 March 2013).

Contessi, Nicola P., 2009. 'Experiments in soft balancing: China-led multilateralism in Africa and the Arab world, *Caucasian Review of International Affairs*, 3(4), Autumn, pp. 404–34.

Donnelly, Lynley and Chantelle Benjamin, 2013. 'China and SA cement relationship', *Mail & Guardian*, 22 March, http://mg.co.za/article/2013-03-22-00-china-and-sa-cement-relationship (accessed on 15 April 2013).

eThekwini Declaration, 2013. 'BRICS and Africa: partnership for development, integration and industrialisation', Fifth BRICS Summit, Durban, 26–27 March, www.brics5.co.za/about-brics/summit-declaration/fifth-summit/ (accessed on 3 July 2013).

focac.org, n.d. 'Forum on China–Africa Cooperation', www.focac.org/eng/xglj/zfsg/ (accessed on 21 April 2013).

Grauwe, Paul De, Romain Houssa and Giulia Piccillio, 2012. 'African trade dynamics: is China a different trading partner?' *Journal of Chinese Economic and Business Studies*, 10(1), February, pp. 15–45.

Gupta, Anil K. and Wang Haiyan, 2011. 'Myths about China and India's Africa race', *Bloomberg BusinessWeek*, 12 October, www.businessweek.com/asia/myths-about-china-and-indias-africa-race-09222011.html (accessed on 18 April 2013).

Hindu Business Line, 2013. 'India ups trade target with Africa to $100 billion by 2015', 18 March, www.thehindubusinessline.com/economy/india-ups-trade-target-with-africa-to-100-b-by-2015/article4522430.ece (accessed on 17 April 2013).

Iwata, Takuo, 2012. 'Comparative study on "Asian" approaches to Africa: an introductory reflection', *African Study Monographs*, 33(4), December, pp. 209–31.

Katakey, Rakteem and John Duce, 2010. 'India loses to China in Africa-to-Kazakhstan-to-Venezuela oil', *Bloomberg*, 29 June, www.bloomberg.com/news/2010-06-30/india-losing-to-china-in-africa-to-kazakhstan-to-venezuela-oil-purchases.html (accessed on 17 April 2013).

Kermeliotis, Teo, 2011. 'Why Asian giants scent opportunity in Africa', *CNN.com*, 4 August, http://edition.cnn.com/2011/BUSINESS/08/04/china.india.africa.overview/index.html (accessed on 17 April 2013).

Ma Xuequan, 2013.'Backgrounder: facts about China–Africa economic cooperation', *Xinhua*, 24 March, http://news.xinhuanet.com/english/africa/2013-03/24/c_124496942.htm (accessed on 17 April 2013).

Masondo, Happy, 2013.'South Africa: the wealth that lies beneath African soil', *mondaq.com*, 14 April, www.mondaq.com/x/233082/Renewables/The+wealth+that+lies+beneath+African+soil (accessed on 18 April 2013).

Meeking, Lincoln, 2013. 'The clash of two tigers: understanding Sino-Indian competition in Africa', *Consultancy Africa Intelligence*, 16 April, www.consultancyafrica.com/index.php?option=com_content&view=article&id=1267:the-clash-of-two-tigers-understanding-sino-indian-competition-in-africa-&catid=58:asia-dimension-discussion-papers&Itemid=264 (accessed on 10 July 2014).

Murithi, Tim, 2012. 'The African Union at ten: an appraisal', *African Affairs* (Briefings), 111/445.

Naidu, Sanusha and Herman Heyley, 2008. 'China and India in Africa: challenging the status quo?', *Pambazuka News*, issue 394, 3 September, www.pambazuka.org/en/category/comment/50252/print (accessed on 7 March 2013).

Panda, Jagannath P., 2013. 'China and IBSA: possible BRICS overreach?', *Strategic Analysis*, 37(3): 299–304.

Persaud, Randolph B., 2003. 'Conceptualizing the global south's perspective: the end of the Bandung spirit'. In J.A. Braveboy-Wagner (ed.), *The Foreign Policies of the Global South: Rethinking Conceptual Frameworks*, Boulder, CO: Lynne Rienner, pp. 49–64.

pib.nic.in, 2011.'Second Africa-India Forum Summit 2011: Addis Ababa Declaration', Press Information Bureau, Government of India, 25 May, http://pib.nic.in/newsite/erelease.aspx?relid=72319 (accessed on 16 July 2014).

Potgieter, T.D., 2012. 'The Indian Ocean: strategic context and eminence', *Institute for Security Studies Paper*, no. 236, August.

Power, Marcus and Mohan Giles, 2010.'Towards a critical geopolitics of China's engagement with African development', *Geopolitics*, 15(3): 462–95.

Pubby, Manu, 2007. 'India activates first listening post on foreign soil: radars in Madagascar', *Indian Express*, 17 July, www.indianexpress.com/news/india-activates-first-listening-post-on-foreign-soil-radars-in-madagascar/205416 (accessed on 21 April 2013).

Saran, Shyam, 2012.'India and Africa: development partnership', *RIS Discussion Papers*, No. 180, Research and Information System for Developing Countries, December.

Scott, David, 2009. 'India's "extended neighbourhood" concept: power projection for a rising power', *India Review*, 8(2): 107–43.
Shao, Haijun, 2010. 'BRICS will offer huge opportunities for S Africa, says President', *Xinhua*, 12 April, http://news.xinhuanet.com/english2010/indepth/2011-04/12/c_13824984.htm (accessed on 31 January 2013).
Shinn, David H., 2011. 'China–Africa relations: the big picture', *International Policy Digest*, 6 December, www.internationalpolicydigest.org/2011/12/06/China–Africa-relations-the-big-picture/ (accessed on 21 April 2013).
Sidiropoulos, Elizabeth, 2012. *Rising Powers, South-South Cooperation and Africa*. Policy Briefing: Global Powers and Africa Programme, no. 47, March, pp. 1–4.
Sidiropoulos, Elizabeth, 2013. 'IBSA: Avoiding being BRICked up', *Strategic Analysis*, 37(3): 285–90.
Smith, David, 2012. 'China's booming trade with Africa helps tone its diplomatic muscle', *Guardian*, 22 March, www.guardian.co.uk/world/2012/mar/22/chinas-booming-trade-africa-diplomatic (accessed on 17 April 2013).
Smith, David, 2013. 'South Africa: more of a briquette than a Bric?', *Guardian*, 24 March, www.guardian.co.uk/world/2013/mar/24/south-africa-bric-developing-economy (accessed on 15 April 2013).
van Rooyen, Frank, 2011. 'Africa and the geopolitics of Indian Ocean', *Occasional Paper* No. 78, South Africa Institute of International Affairs, February.
Vickers, Brendan, 2013. 'Africa and the rising powers: bargaining for the "marginalized many"', *International Affairs*, 89(3): 673–93.
Wang Xiaotian, 2012. 'Trade between China, Africa strengthening', *China Daily*, 19 July, www.chinadaily.com.cn/business/2012-07/19/content_15599626.htm (accessed on 17 April 2013).
Yang Jiechi, 2012.'Take the new type of China–Africa strategic partnership to a new high', Embassy of the People's Republic of China in the Federal Democratic Republic of Ethiopia, 18 July, htpp://et.china-embassy.org/eng/zfgx/t952597.htm (accessed on 8 March 2013).
Yu, George T., 2010. 'China's Africa policy: South–South unity and cooperation'. In Lowell Dittmer and George T. Yu (eds), *China, the Developing World, and the New Global Dynamic*, Boulder, CO: Lynne Rienner, pp. 129–56.
Zweig, David, 2010. 'The rise of a new "trading nation"'. In Lowell Dittmer and George T. Yu (eds), *China, the Developing World, and the New Global Dynamic*. Boulder, CO: Lynne Rienner, pp. 37–60.

Part V
The global colloquium

16 The global relationship

From Bretton Woods to alternative institution building

Reforming global institutions, particularly those of the Bretton Woods vintage, has been a persisting quest for India and China. Currently, they are pursuing this interest both bilaterally and at the regional level by establishing alternative institutions. This chapter deliberates whether the two countries are *interdependent* or *independent* in their approach to this matter.

Both India and China have supported in principle the current world order and have participated in the 'rules-based, liberal, post–World War II global economic and political order' (Gilboy and Heginbotham 2012: 128). At the same time, both hold the outlook that the current world order – mainly the international trade and financial system – is dominated by the US and the developed nations (ibid.). A reference to this effect is their joint resolution to demand reform of the Bretton Woods institutions. Table 16.1 presents details of the two countries' membership in various international organisations.

Table 16.1 India and China in Bretton Woods institutions

Institution	Joined in	
	India	China
African Development Bank	1983	1985
International Monetary Fund (IMF)	December 1945	December 1945
The World Bank Group	1944	April 1980
International Development Association (IDA)	September 1960	September 1960
International Finance Corporation (IFC)	July 1956	January 1969
International Bank for Reconstruction and Development (IBRD)	December 1945	December 1945
Multilateral Investment Guarantee Agency (MIGA)	January 1994	April 1988
International Centre for Settlement of Investment Disputes (ICSID)	(Not a Member)	February 1993
Asian Development Bank (ADB)	1966	1986
World Trade Organisation (WTO)	January 1995	December 2001

Reforming Bretton Woods[1]

India's tactic and advocacy of reforming the Bretton Woods institutions has been different from China's. The Indian approach is to bring reform in the current world order, democratise the decision-making process of world politics and bring parity between the developing and developed world. The Chinese approach and advocacy, on the other hand, is more politically tuned, being linked with Beijing's power rivalry with the US and Europe.

China has for long demanded a reformed IMF, which it has termed as a 'weak and ineffective' institution (Yu Yongding 2006: 520).[2] Its main objective is to increase its own quota and voting rights. China also points to the lack of transparency in the IMF, which is largely dominated by the EU, whereas China and the developing world is 'underrepresented' (Yu Yongding 2006; see also *Xinhuanet* 2009). It has advocated that the IMF member countries must increase the contribution as per their own economic situation, which must be based on 'voluntary principles' (*Xinhuanet* 2009).

The Chinese perspective on the WTO is on similar lines as that on the IMF. In acceding to the WTO (in September 2001), China had expected that its participation in the WTO would help it enhance its global financial stature and maximise its trade and economic deals (Zhihai Zheng 2003: 8). In reality, Chinese exporters have often confronted anti-dumping and countervailing problems from the US (Ka Zeng 2013). China's trade-related disputes have mostly been with the US or the EU.

With the World Bank, China's tryst has been a gradualist account of a rising economy integrating with the world economy and demanding better rights, contribution and access to the decision-making process. Since the 1970s, the World Bank has played a strong role in helping China's economic reform and transformation.[3] China's closer contacts with the World Bank have always been a boon for its greater access to international capital markets (Bottelier 2006: 1). But with the Chinese economy becoming a commanding economy, Beijing has followed a demanding approach with regard to World Bank reform, particularly for better voting rights for the emerging economies (*Bridges* 2010; Jin Lin 2010; Qu Bo 2012). Beijing has been of the view that there should be a periodic review of the shareholding in the International Bank for Reconstruction and Development (IBRD), as the IBRD continues to remain the original institution of the World Bank Group (Jin Lin 2010).

Where India is concerned, reforming the Bretton Woods institutions has long been a clearly expressed objective of its foreign policy (see MEA 2012; see also Mattoo and Subramanian 2008). With its rising economic strength, the Indian dialogue of reforming these institutions has primarily been carried out within the rubric of the developing-world discourse, where New Delhi recognises China as a developing-world partner.

India has raised two practical issues with regard to IMF reform: (i) the slow pace of quota review; and (ii) governance reforms (*Indian Express* 2012). In the WTO, India faces a pattern of cases similar to those faced by China, mostly from the developing countries. Politically, India has acknowledged that there is scope and opportunity for both developing countries to cooperate within the prism of the WTO (*BRICS Post* 2013). With regard to the World Bank, India too demands for its reform to become more developing-society friendly.

Three issues are central to India's perspective on this matter. *First*, India has been demanding a reformed governance process in order to provide more opportunity and representation for developing countries. For example, India has been advocating for a new application of the global financial institutions' 'quota formula', to be linked to the economic strength of a member country. *Second*, India's advocacy is linked to the need for more loans, grants, and funding for infrastructural development and for other projects in developing societies. *Third*, to minimise the protectionist tendencies of the industrialised countries. China's outlook on reforming the Bretton Woods institutions is concomitant to its vision of its own position in world affairs. Specifically, China seeks to maximise the strategic interests that are important to its rise and to check the prevailing American dominance regionally and globally.

New institutions: the alternative ideas

The common interest between India and China to reform the Bretton Woods institutions grew with their growing economic profile.[4] This development moulded three major structural developments in the current global governance system: *first*, global financial institutions or decision-making process became rather irrelevant, at least from the developing-world view; *second*, multiple power centres with the lead of India and China made the world order much more multipolar in nature; and *third*, the necessity of establishment of new institutions or the emergence of alternative ideas in world politics. The third aspect especially is an important aspect of the India–China global relationship course. India is strongly linked with China in the newly established institutions such as the New Development Bank (NDB) under BRICS and the Chinese-propelled Asian Infrastructure Investment Bank (AIIB), which seem to offer new alternative ideas and opportunities.

The NDB: India's presidency and China's premiership

Although, as noted by the Reserve Bank of India (RBI) Governor Raghuram Rajan, the NDB is not 'meant to challenge the existing multilateral institutions', it would help emerging economies explore new opportunities and avenues for long-term risk-oriented project investment (*The Hindu* 2014). This perspective is congruent with the overall BRICS outlook, which was reflected in BRICS's Fortaleza Declaration of 2014, which noted the continuous 'financing constraints to address infrastructure gaps and sustainable development needs' in emerging market economies and developing countries (MEA 2014a). The Fortaleza Declaration notes that the bank will have an initial authorised capital base of US$100 billion. Its opening subscribed capital of $50 billion will be shared equally among the founding members.

The NDB's structure is likely to give China a definite edge in shaping and determining the bank's operations, for several reasons. *First*, the bank's headquarters are in Shanghai, and hence China may have greater say in the bank's day-to-day affairs. China has more millionaires than other BRICS countries, and Shanghai has more millionaires than even Beijing. Unlike in democratic countries, the Chinese business community is heavily backed by the Communist Party and the government. *Second*, China is the third-largest contributor to the WTO's budget (see Figure 16.1), surpassed only by the United States and Germany. Given its economic weight, it would not be surprising if China demands greater rights or privileges in the NDB. *Third*, the NDB's Board of Governors and Board of Directors are chaired by Russia and Brazil, respectively. China maintains positive and stable relations with these countries. *Fourth*, China's far-reaching trade and economic contacts with Russia, Brazil and South Africa will contribute to limiting the Indian influence in the NDB. In terms of both commercial and merchandise global trade, China dominates the other BRICS countries (see Figures 16.2 and 16.3). *Fifth*, because China has emerged as a strong and influential factor in Africa, locating the NDB's regional centre in South Africa will likely help it to establish close ties with the regional centre. One of the factors contributing to China's ascendance in Africa is its strong advocacy of permanent African continental representation on the UNSC. In contrast with these concrete advantages, India's presidency of the bank is more symbolic in nature.

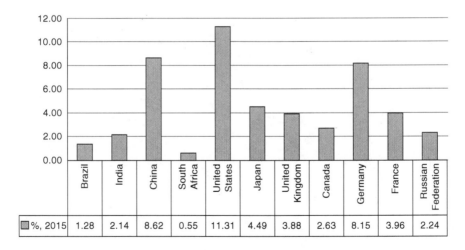

Figure 16.1 Contribution to WTO budget, 2015 (source: *Trade Profiles*, Statistical Database, WTO, Geneva, 2015; http://stat.wto.org/CountryProfile/WSDBCountryPFView.aspx?Language=E&Country=DE,FR; http://stat.wto.org/CountryProfile/WSDBCountryPFView.aspx?Language=E&Country=BR,CA,CN,IN,JP,RU,GB,US,ZA (accessed on 10 March 2016)).

Note
Figures are approximate.

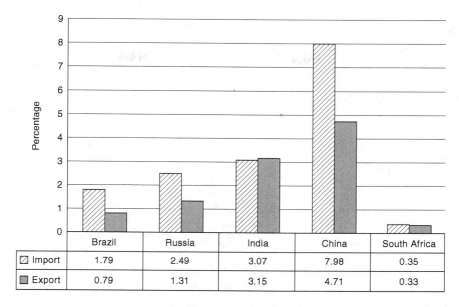

Figure 16.2 BRICS countries' share in world commercial trade, 2014 (source: *Trade Profiles*, Statistical Database, WTO, Geneva, 2014).

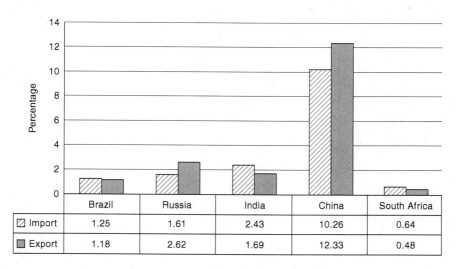

Figure 16.3 BRICS countries' share in world merchandise trade, 2014 (source: same as Figure 16.2).

China's economic advantages may help it not only influence the NDB's decisions, but also gradually dominate its proceedings. As regards funding sources, given its economic authority, China may want to fund most of the NDB projects, which India may not find palatable. With the exception of the recent agreements on establishing industrial parks and sister city or provincial level engagement at the bilateral level, India has been cautious with regard to China's investment and financial proposals.

The AIIB alternative

How does India view the AIIB, and principally its role in China's ambition of establishing a regional economic order congruent with its aspiration for an improved position in the global financial order? Politically, India has signed the Memorandum of Understanding (MoU) to join the AIIB, signalling to the world that it does not want to be left out of the emerging regional economic order. But diplomatically, there is a more nuanced significance attached to it. India's stance has to be understood mainly in terms of the changing discourse of regional politics, in which China is now an influential power and factor.

Given the two countries' conflicting stances on building infrastructure in various parts of Asia, including in both the maritime and land corridor domains, India's political decision to join the AIIB prompts a debate: Is India conceding to China's authority and influence both in Asia and elsewhere? India's rationale for going forward with this initiative becomes even more puzzling, considering that India has yet to accept the Chinese-proposed Maritime Silk Road (MSR) and Silk Road Economic Belt (SREB).

In deciding to join the AIIB, India has perhaps decided it does not wish to pass up the advantages and opportunities that the Chinese economy offers to Asia and the world. Pursuing trade and economic engagement and partnering with China in multilateral mechanisms have been stable aspects of India's China policy and overall India–China relations.

Three practical reasons may have induced India to decide to join the AIIB. *First*, the progression of India–China bilateral ties has been advanced as a 'developmental partnership'. The pledge of fostering a developmental partnership is contextualised at both the bilateral and regional levels (MEA 2014b). This developmental partnership may have its limitations, and we may instead witness only a 'limited partnership' as the strategic interests of the two countries clash at the regional level. Nevertheless, in regional and global economic engagement and interaction, there has been steady and progressive growth in India–China ties. India's decision to join the AIIB seems to be a part of this trend.

Second, India may foresee the AIIB becoming an important alternative institution that is beneficial to developing nations in Asia and beyond. It is in the common interest of India and China to work together in multilateral institutions or structures for mutual benefit. This approach has been seen in India's association with China in BRICS and its institutions, the Russia–India–China (RIC) trilateral framework, the BCIM sub-regional mechanism, and the ongoing trade liberalisation negotiation of the Regional Comprehensive Economic Partnership (RCEP, where India is linked to China through the ASEAN+6 mechanism). Another indicator of this mutual benefit was also seen in China's invitation to India to attend the APEC preparatory summit meeting in Beijing in 2014. Besides, India is now seeking membership in the SCO, where the SCO Development Bank is aiming to finance multilateral infrastructural projects connected to India (*tass.ru/en* 2014).

Third, aligning with China serves India's interest in reforming the Bretton Woods institutions. India's main intention here is to engage with China economically, though not strategically. Since China has become the main driver behind numerous economic initiatives, India cannot ignore its influence in Asia. The core goal of AIIB is to build infrastructure in Asia, something that is also being propelled by the Chinese through the One Belt, One Road (OBOR) initiative. As we have seen earlier, India's response to this initiative has been reticent. At the same time, India can better impede the Chinese financial projects from inside the AIIB rather than outside of it. This is a strategy that China previously sought to employ vis-à-vis loans to India and project proposals from ADB.

India seeks to associate, engage and align with China mostly in matters relating to economic governance. As far as security and strategic matters are concerned, India's approach is non-complementary to China's. India holds the distinction of maintaining its own independence when it comes to alliance politics, be it the US-led or Chinese-led order. Ultimately, between India and China, it boils down to the fact that India believes in a 'shared leadership' in Asia rather than a 'single leadership'.

Reforming the UN and UNSC reform[5]

The principality of 'alignment with China without an alliance' may be aptly explained in the India–China divided perspective with regard to UN reform and UNSC reform. China's resistance to unequivocally supporting India's bid for UNSC permanent membership, while pursuing a shared vision for reforming both the UN and UNSC, describes this chronicle. It points to the *independent* genre of politics that the two countries are engaged in as regards reforming the UN. India–China Joint Statements and official outlets have time and again paid obeisance to the two countries' interest in a 'comprehensive reform of the United Nations', acknowledging 'India's aim and aspirations to play a bigger role in the UN including the Security Council'.

Pragmatism prevails in this matter, however, over any pretence of reformism. This pragmatism entails: (i) a set of legal barriers; (ii) power rivalry between the existing P-5 and prospective members; and (iii) a range of global issues. The Chinese discourse about the expansion of UNSC permanent membership has been to support developing countries as such. While Germany, India, Japan and Brazil, popularly identified as G-4 countries, are generally considered as the frontrunners for UNSC permanent berths, the African countries' case has been openly supported by China.

The India factor in Beijing's official stance

On 11 December 1992, the 47th UN General Assembly (UNGA) adopted a resolution titled 'Question of equitable representation on and increase in the membership of the Security Council and related matters', which catalysed the UNSC reform debate. P-5 nations have shown some interest in the matter, acknowledging the need for reform, without taking a specific or formal stand. The then UN Secretary General Kofi Annan in his report titled *In Larger Freedom: Towards Development, Security and Human Rights for All* (2005) proposed two options for UNSC reform. *Option A* offered scope for six new permanent members without veto and three new two-year-term non-permanent seats, divided among the major regional areas; *Option B* offered no scope for new permanent members but offered a new category of eight four-year renewable-term seats and one new two-year non-permanent and non-renewable seat, divided among the major regional areas (see Table 16.2) ('Strengthening the United Nations' 2005). The US and China strongly opposed the proposal, with the Chinese Ambassador to the UN, Wang Guangya, terming it as 'immature' (*China Daily* 2005).

Broadly, the issue of UNSC reform involves five technicalities: membership categories; veto; regional representation; size; and working methods and modules. The expansion process and granting veto to new members require amendment of the UN Charter (Art. 108), official approval of two-thirds of UNGA, ratification by two-thirds of member states, and explicit endorsement of the P-5.

For the Chinese, expansion of UNSC membership is the core issue of UN reform. In the Chinese perspective, reform of both UNSC and UN needs to be seen as an integrated exercise. UN reform needs to be mainly directed towards enhancing the UN's authority for an effective global governance structure. On UNSC reform, however, China's approach remains conservative and ambiguous. It advocates reform but does not want to dilute the clout of the P-5; and it advocates greater representation for the 'developing world' without advocating veto for its members. More precisely, China advocates a 'transitional solution' to current UNSC membership rather than a complete change in the setup (see Table 16.3). As long as the non-permanent members win majority support, the scope of their term can be renewed indefinitely (*Beijing Review* 2010: 13).

The Chinese *Position Paper on UN Reform*, released in June 2005, outlines five fundamentals with regard to UNSC reform: (i) it should enhance the 'authority and efficiency of the Council'; (ii) representation of the developing countries should be given priority; (iii) rotating basis partaking in the decision-making process for small and medium-sized countries; (iv) geographic representation symbolising cultures and civilisations; and (v) regional groups should build a consensus on reform proposal with respect to their region and rotation method (see *Xinhua* 2005). The *Position Paper of the People's Republic of China at the 65th Session of the United Nations General Assembly* (2010) speaks about 'enhancing the authority and efficiency of the UNSC' and 'representation of developing countries, African countries in particular' (*fmprc.gov.cn* 2010). The

Table 16.2 Kofi Annan's proposal on UNSC reform and China's reaction

Model A

Region	No. of states	Existing permanent seats	New permanent seats	New two-year seats (non-renewable)	Total	
Africa	53	0	2	4	6	China's reaction: 'The proposal of an immature plan has deviated UNSC reform from a right track and has seriously undermined the overall development of the UN reform process and the preparation work for the September UN summit meeting' (Chinese Foreign Ministry spokesman, Liu Jianchao, *China Daily*, 10 June 2005)
Asia and Pacific	56	1	2	3	6	
Europe	47	3	1	2	6	
Americas	35	1	1	4	6	
Total	191	5	6	13	24	

Model B

Region	No. of states	Existing permanent seats	New four-year renewable seats	New two-year seats (non-renewable)	Total	
Africa	53	0	2	4	6	China's reaction: 'UNSC is not a board of directors and its composition should not be decided according to the financial contributions of its members' (Spokesperson of the Chinese Foreign Ministry, Kong Quan, *China Daily*, 22 September 2004)
Asia and Pacific	56	1	2	3	6	On Japan's bid: 'We believe that this issue should be dealt with in a gradual manner under the consensus reached by various parties. There should not be a rigid timetable for it' (Spokesperson of the Chinese Foreign Ministry, Kong Quan, *China Daily*, 22 September 2004)
Europe	47	3	2	1	6	
Americas	35	1	2	3	6	
Total	191	5	8	11	24	

250 *The global colloquium*

Table 16.3 China's perspective on UNSC membership reform

On reform
- UNSC reform involves the interests of various parties.
- Multipolarisation in the world community is still at an early stage and has yet to become the norm.
- It is extremely difficult and even impossible to shape the pattern of the UNSC for the next half century.

On membership expansion
- A 'transitional solution' is possible.
- UNSC should create 'semi-permanent members' instead of 'new permanent members'.
- 'Semi-permanent members' means 'non-permanent members who do not enjoy veto power but could be re-elected'.
- If non-permanent members win majority support, their term can be renewed and extended indefinitely. Though they may not hold the 'permanent member' status, eventually they will enjoy the status and privileges of the existing P-5 states.

On dividing UNSC membership
- 1st category: The existing P-5 nations: the US, the UK, China, Russia and France.
- 2nd category: 'Semi-permanent members' that will include India, Japan and others.
- 3rd category: Other non-permanent members that can serve only one term.

Source: Chen Jian, former President of the United Nations Association of China (interview in *Beijing Review*, 30 September 2010, pp. 10–13).

Chinese accent on reshaping the global order may particularly be noted here. Beijing explicitly advocates dialogue on globalisation and multipolarity and asks for greater democratisation of world affairs (Foot 2006: 92), particularly in global institutions like the UN.

Chinese scholars and strategists see the discourse on UNSC permanent membership expansion as a 'political game', having ramifications for 'redistribution of power' (Jiang and Fei 2006: 92). China is aware that the US does not believe in democratic accountability for its global actions;[6] it also does not trust the US advocacy of UNSC reform. But this state of affairs suits China. Among multilateral institutions, the UNSC offers China the veto as the most useful weapon to restrict US predominance in global issues.

Will China ever support India for UNSC?

Officially, China objects to the collective induction of G-4 in the UNSC as 'faulted' (Jiang and Fei 2006: 92) and has declared earlier through its *Position Paper on UN Reform* that it will veto such a proposal. Beijing's official objection is that (i) the group does not have representation from Africa; and (ii) Japan and Germany are not developing countries; the non-stated perception is that both Japan and Germany are US allies and India is increasingly becoming one.

Unlike other G-4 members, the Chinese perspective with regard to India's UNSC bid is conflicting. The Chinese experts themselves acknowledge it. Zhang Li states, for example: 'Beijing has held an ambiguous attitude towards India's desire to enter UNSC as a permanent member whereas, as a standard expression,

China backs India's expanding role in on-going global affairs and within the UN' (Zhang Li 2010: 23). Hong Lei, former Chinese Foreign Ministry spokesman, said once that 'China values the role India plays in international affairs, and China understands and supports India's willingness to play a bigger role at the UN' (*Xinhua* 2010). Evidently, Beijing's stance on India's UNSC bid is a blend of its past rivalry with India on the boundary dispute and plans to negate India the opportunity of enhancing its global profile and becoming a global power in the process.

China's perspective on the matter rests on some of the following parameters. *First*, India possesses the strength to become a global power that could eventually challenge the Chinese pre-eminence in Asia. *Second*, India's global profile as 'US supporter' is detrimental to China's global interests. China's discomfort in the matter was clearly demonstrated during the India-specific waiver at the Nuclear Supplies Group (NSG) and the Indo-US nuclear deal (Panda 2007). *Third*, Washington is vocally promoting a larger strategic role for India at the global stage in response to China's rising global ambitions (Karon 2010). *Fourth*, if China supports India's case, then there will be a likely expansion of the UNSC and African representation has to be there in the developing-world category. As opposed to its rhetorical statements, Beijing's real intention is to act as Big Brother to the African world to exploit the oil, gas, energy and trade benefits in the guise of advocating Africa for a greater space in world politics, but not a permanent seat at the UNSC (Panda 2011a: 29). *Fifth*, China mixes India's membership issue with the whole debate of UN reform. Experts play it safe by stating that 'If India manages to get two-thirds of the UN General Assembly support, China will support India's case' (Krishnan 2011). *Sixth*, China does not want to grant any leverage to India in the UN. China may even counter India's quest, citing allegations that India has violated the UNSC resolutions over Kashmir (Karon 2010): China's dialogue on Kashmir does suggest that.

History suggests that there is a close linkage between China's tryst with the UN and its global strategy and discourse of advancing the interest of the developing world, mainly with regard to reforming global financial and political institutions. Beijing's current backing for greater representation for the African nations in the UNSC is a result of historical dynamism and its steadfast developing-world strategy. Mao Zedong's newly established PRC in 1949 saw the developing world as an option to maximise Chinese political objectives in global fora such as opposing great-power interference, recovery of Taiwan, and regaining the lawful seat for the Chinese at the UN (Gurtov 2010: 14). The PRC has always identified and placed its interests quite closely with 'Third World' countries, in the belief that the globe is divided because of imperialist tendencies rather than ideological differences between the capitalist and socialist world (Clegg 2009: 49). In his memorable speech in 1974, Deng Xiaoping advocated a united fight against the hegemonism and superpower aggression of the US (see *marxists.org* 1974). In course of time, this speech has been elaborated as the Chinese strategy of the *Three Worlds Theory* (*Chairman Mao's Theory of the Differentiation...* 1977).[7]

To preserve its identity as a developing country, China makes it a point to take the initiative to protect and promote to some extent the interests of other developing countries (Chin 2008).[8] Fu Ziying, a former Vice Commerce Minister, has been quoted saying that 'China is the world's largest developing country and to strengthen relations with developing countries is a focal point of China's foreign policy' (*Renmin Ribao* 2010).

An assessment

China–India collaboration to reform the Bretton Woods institutions, mutual drive to establish new or alternative institutions and aim to establish new regional and global order are some concrete indications of a 'Chindia' spirit. In a rapidly evolving world order, India and China are not only exhibiting greater confidence in their political influence but also notably adopting new creative approaches for several types of engagements. China takes the lead in establishing these alternative institutions. The *authority* of the Chinese economy is the backbone of these propositions.

Even though the two countries have established a cooperative understanding in establishing new institutions, these are still early initiatives and lack apposite bilateral understanding. Moreover, both are yet to develop a common ground to manage the international financial institutions. A concrete understanding is still missing between them on various key global matters like trade protectionism, global economic crisis and the imbalance that still exists, and on global energy markets even though both are prime energy consumer countries.

Given the premise of a multipolar world order, will India–China global relations be enduring and sustainable? Xi Jinping's 'new type of major power relations' puts the vision of a multipolar world order in doubt from the Indian perspective, as China could be in a strong enough position to prefer a 'bipolar' design;[9] while from the Chinese perspective, India's constant 'Western prism' remains a troublesome factor. Both countries' interest in reforming the regional and global order may be *interdependent* on each other, but they follow an *independent* course of action when it relates to their national interests or foreign policy persuasion.

Notes

1 This portion of the chapter draws mainly on Panda 2015 and partially on Panda 2013a. Also see Panda 2013b.
2 Scholars argue that Beijing's participation in the IMF and the World Bank goes back to the 1980s, when China notified the IMF that it would

> realize current account convertibility, which means removing restrictions on current international payments and transfers. However, China took 16 years to fulfil its commitment to current account convertibility. During the period, China made various institutional adjustments in order to adapt to the consequences of domestic reform.
>
> (See Qu Bo 2012: 188)

3 Bottelier 2006 is an excellent paper on the subject.
4 Notable literature on the subject includes Chen and Chen 2010; Dahlman 2012; Gilboy and Heginbotham 2012.
5 This portion of the chapter is drawn on Panda 2011b.
6 Author's interaction with Chinese think-tank scholars in Beijing and Shanghai, 13–17 December 2010. (His visit was part of an IDSA initiative to send a delegation to Beijing and Shanghai to interact with various scholars and experts on bilateral and global issues.)
7 Mao's Three Worlds Theory was based on three entities: the First World (the superpowers, the US and the Soviet Union), the Second World (the superpowers' allies) and the Third World (non-aligned countries). It may be noted that in the Western theory of Three Worlds, the US belongs to the First World; the USSR to the Second World; and the neutral and non-aligned countries to the Third World.
8 Several other experts also hold a similar view.
9 Chinese experts acknowledge the special arrangements between China and the US on global governance matters; but reject the view that this arrangement will lead to a 'bipolar world structure'. For instance, Wu Xinbo, a leading academic and scholar in Fudan University is of the view that 'economically maybe China and the US are two special and powerful economies; but politically it is difficult for China and the US to monopolise world affairs. Russia, India, EU and ASEAN countries will not accept this bipolar order'. Author's interview with several Chinese experts in Beijing, Shanghai, Sichuan and Guangzhou during field study research in December 2014. This field study research was sponsored by the Indian Council of Social Science Research (ICSSR), New Delhi.

References

Beijing Review, 2010. 'China and the UN: a longstanding partnership', *Beijing Review*, 30 September.

Bottelier, Pieter, 2006. 'China and the World Bank: how a partnership was built', *Working Paper No. 277*, Stanford, CA: Stanford Centre for International Development, Stanford University, April, pp. 1–30.

BRICS Post, 2013. 'India, China should join hands at WTO reforms-EAM', *The BRICS Post*, 8 May, http://thebricspost.com/India–China-should-join-hands-at-wto-reforms-eam/#.VTs6cClCPFI (accessed on 25 April 2015).

Bridges, 2010. 'China wins new influence at the World Bank', *Bridges*, 14(15), 28 April.

Chairman Mao's Theory of the Differentiation of the Three Worlds is a Major Contribution to Marxism-Leninism, 1977. Peking: Foreign Languages Press.

Chen An and Chen Huiping, 2010. 'China–India cooperation, South–South coalition and the new international economic order: focus on the Doha Round', in Muthucumaraswamy Sornarajah and Jiangyu Wang (eds), *China, India and the International Economic Order*, Cambridge: Cambridge University Press, pp. 132–66.

Chin, Gregory T., 2008. 'China's evolving G8 engagement: complex interests and multiple identity in global governance reform', in Andrew F. Cooper and Agata Antkiewicz (eds), *Emerging Powers in Global Governance: Lessons from the Heiligendamm Process*, Waterloo, Ontario: Wilfrid Laurier University Press, pp. 83–114.

China Daily, 2005. 'China rejects pepped-over UNSC reform plan', *China Daily*, 10 June, www.chinadaily.com.cn/english/doc/2005-06/10/content_450207.htm (accessed on 14 March 2011).

Clegg, Jenny, 2009. *China's Global Strategy: Towards a Multipolar World*, New York: Pluto Press.

Dahlman, Carl J., 2012. *How China & India Are Influencing the Global Economy & Environment: The World Under Pressure*, Stanford, CA: Stanford University Press.

fmprc.gov.cn, 2010. 'II: UN Reform', Position Paper of the People's Republic of China at the 65th Session of the United Nations General Assembly, Ministry of Foreign Affairs of the People's Republic of China, 13 September, www.fmprc.gov.cn/eng/zxxx/t751986.htm (accessed on 28 January 2011).

Foot, Rosemary, 2006. 'Chinese strategies in a US-hegemonic global order: accommodating and hedging', *International Affairs*, 82(1), January, pp. 77–94.

Gilboy, George J. and Eric Heginbotham, 2012. *Chinese and Indian Strategic Behaviour: Growing Power and Alarm*, Cambridge: Cambridge University Press.

Gurtov, Mel, 2010. 'Changing perspectives and policies', in Lowell Dittmer and George T. Yu (eds), *China, the Developing World, and the New Global Dynamic*, Boulder, CO: Lynne Rienner, pp. 13–36.

The Hindu, 2014. 'BRICS bank not aimed at challenging IMF, WB: Rajan,' *The Hindu*, 7 September, www.thehindu.com/news/national/brics-bank-not-aimed-at-challenging-imf-wb-rajan/article6388363.ece (accessed on 16 March 2015).

Indian Express, 2012. 'India concerned over IMF quota reforms', *Indian Express*, 21 April, http://indianexpress.com/article/news-archive/web/india-concerned-over-imf-quota-reforms/ (accessed on 5 April 2015).

Jiang Zhenxi and Fei Xiaojun, 2006. 'A retrospect of the UN reform and its prospect', *International Strategic Studies* (translated by Gu Dong), Issue 2.

Jin Lin, 2010. 'Chinese minister: World Bank reform benefits world development', *CCTV.com*, 26 April, at http://english.cctv.com/20100426/103455.shtml (accessed on 16 April 2015).

Ka Zeng, 2013. 'High stakes: United States–China trade disputes under the World Trade Organization', *International Relations of the Asia-Pacific*, vol. 13, pp. 33–63.

Karon, Tony, 2010. 'India's Security Council seat: don't hold your breath', *Time*, 10 November, www.time.com/time/printout/0,8816,2030504,00.html (accessed on 15 March 2011).

Krishnan, Ananth, 2011. 'China doesn't favour G4 call on UNSC reforms', *The Hindu*, 15 February.

marxists.org, 1974. 'Deng Xiaoping, "Speech at the Special Session of the UN General Assembly", 10 April 1974', www.marxists.org/reference/archive/deng-xiaoping/1974/04/10.htm (accessed on 11 March 2011).

Mattoo, Aaditya and Arvind Subramanian, 2008. 'India and Bretton Woods II', *Economic and Political Weekly*, 8 November, pp. 62–70.

MEA, 2012. 'Speech by Foreign Secretary on building global security at the Institute of Peace and Conflict Studies (IPCS) – Konrad Adenauer Stiftung (KAS), April 16, 2012', www.mea.gov.in/Speeches-Statements.htm?dtl/19340/Speech+by+Foreign+Secretary+on+Building+Global+Security+at+the+Institute+of+Peace+and+Conflict+Studies+IPCS++Konrad+Adenauer+Stiftung+KAS (accessed on 23 July 2015).

MEA, 2014a. 'Sixth BRICS Summit – Fortaleza Declaration, July 15, 2014', http://brics6.itamaraty.gov.br/media2/press-releases/214-sixth-brics-summit-fortaleza-declaration (accessed on 21 August 2015).

MEA, 2014b. 'Joint Statement between the Republic of India and the People's Republic of China on building a closer developmental partnership, September 19, 2014', Ministry of External Affairs: Government of India, www.mea.gov.in/bilateral-documents.htm?dtl/24022/Joint+Statement+between+the+Republic+of+India+and+the+Peoples+Republic+of+China+on+Building+a+Closer+Developmental+Partnership (accessed on 17 March 2015).

Panda, Jagannath P., 2007. 'China's posture on the Indo–US nuclear deal', *IDSA Comment*, 10 October, www.idsa.in/idsastrategiccomments/ChinasPostureontheIndoUSnuclearDeal_JPPanda_101007 (accessed on 15 March 2011).

Panda, Jagannath P., 2011a. 'Beijing's perspective on UN Security Council reform: identity, activism and strategy', *Portuguese Journal of International Affairs*, Portugal, Spring/Summer, pp. 24–36.

Panda, Jagannath P., 2011b. 'China's stance on UNSC reform: the developing world factor', *ISDP Policy Brief*, No. 62, 23 March.

Panda, Jagannath P., 2013a. 'Deliberating a "cross-regional" perspective: China, India, and the emerging world order', in Victor F.S. Sit (ed.), *China–India Cooperation Prospects*, Enrich Series on China–India Issues: Papers presented at the 1st Academic Summit on China–India Cooperation in 2011, Singapore: Enrich Professional Publishing (S), pp. 241–58.

Panda, Jagannath P., 2013b. *BRICS and the China–India Construct: A New World Order in Making?*, IDSA Monograph Series, No. 24, September.

Panda, Jagannath P., 2015. 'India's China quandary on alternative institution building: alignment minus alliance', *Georgetown Journal of Asian Affairs*, Georgetown University, US, April.

Qu Bo, 2012. 'Dynamic engagement: China's participation in international monetary institutions', in Jan Wouters, Tanguy de Wilde d'Estmael, Pierre Defraigne and Jean-Christophe Defraigne (eds), *China, the European Union and Global Governance*, Cheltenham: Edward Elgar, pp. 183–200.

Renmin Ribao, 2010. 'Developing countries meet in Beijing, discuss financial crisis', *Renmin Ribao*, 20 May, OSC Transcribed Text, *World News Connection* (*dialogue.com*), 201005201477.1_c38600645a591869, accession number 299200180.

'Strengthening the United Nations', 2005. In *Larger Freedom: Towards Development, Security and Human Rights for All*, Report of the Secretary General: United Nations General Assembly, A/59/2005, Fifty-Ninth Session, Agenda Items 45 and 55, 21 March.

tass.ru/en, 2014. 'SCO Development Bank ready to finance projects in India, Iran', *Russian News Agency*, 17 October, http://tass.ru/en/economy/754510 (accessed on 16 March 2015).

Xinhua, 2005. 'Section IV: full text of China's position paper on UN reforms', *Xinhua*, 7 June, http://english.peopledaily.com.cn/200506/08/print20050608_189007.html (accessed on 26 January 2011).

Xinhua, 2010. 'China supports rational UN Security Council reform', *Xinhua*, 11 September, www.chinadaily.com.cn/china/2010-11/09/content_11524688.htm (accessed on 26 January 2011).

Xinhuanet, 2009. 'Premier Wen: increasing contribution to IMF not matter of a single country', *Xinhuanet*, 13 March, www.china.org.cn/government/NPC_CPPCC_2009/2009-03/13/content_17436675_19.htm (accessed on 30 March 2015).

Yu Yongding, 2006. 'IMF reform: a Chinese view', in Edwin M. Truman (ed.), *Reforming the IMF for the 21st Century*, Special Report 19, April, pp. 519–25.

Zhang Li, 2010. 'China–India relations: strategic engagement and challenges', *Asie. Visions*, September.

Zhihai Zheng, 2003. 'Economic globalization and development of China's foreign economic cooperation and trade', in Ding Lu, Guanzhong James Wen and Huizhong Zhou (eds), *China's Economic Globalization Through the WTO*, England: Ashgate.

17 Summing up

The focus of this book has been to highlight the enduring and emerging complexities in India–China relations. They are multi-layered and polygonal in nature, which are both a result and reflection of a multipolar world order. The book has tested the argument that India–China relations have crossed the conventional prism of 'competition-cooperation' premise, and have moved to new acmes of power dynamics that covers a complex web of 'competition, cooperation, conflict, collaboration, and coexistence'. This web of complexities is a significant segment of the relationship that they have established progressively at the bilateral, sub-regional, regional, cross-continental and global levels. These structural edifices explain the enduring vitality and layers of politics that India–China relations today are embedded in, which makes their relationship the most complicated, composite and compound one in the current global politics.

This book has also displayed how the spectrum of India–China relations in various structural edifices – bilateral, sub-regional, regional, cross-continental and global – reveals a multifaceted and multipronged dynamics of the relationships that is closely linked with the current multipolar world order. India–China relations in the BASIC climate grouping, the BRICS forum and in other multilateral forums have demonstrated that they are part and parcel of the evolving world structure. Relatively, Sino-US relations may be confined mostly to the space and scope of Chinese and American primacy in the current and future world politics (Wang Jisi 2015); but India–China relations are distinctive and have arrived at a stage where they shape and resolve the nature of world politics. As discussed at the beginning of this book, India–China relations are coupled heavily with the multipolar world order, which is both a reflection and result of multiple power centres and overwhelmingly shapes and influences the nature of current and future world politics. That prompts us to ask: What will be the future trajectory of India–China relations?

Given the transitional nature of these relations, it would be difficult to foresee and compute their exact nature in a definite context. Most of the analysis in this book has been far from any overt presumption. Given that India is still not entrenched fully in the global financial system and structure, there is a balancing politics emerging between the two. Five correlated scenarios, congenital in nature, may be consequential here.

Scenario One: At the bilateral level, the cooperative character will balance but not subdue the conflicting tendencies. The cooperative characters, as shown in Chapter 2 primarily, will be ordained by bilateral mechanisms, agreements and MoUs. This cooperative character will be visible in almost all spectrums, but primarily in economics and in the field of high-level political exchanges. This cooperative script can certainly balance their conflicting tendencies, but will not completely condense the possibility of small-scale conflicts, which may be minor, occasional and sporadic. These conflicts will either be noticed with regard to the traditional boundary dispute or bordering aspects of India–China disputes, where resources of land and water could be prime underlying aspects. These conflicts will noticeably arise because of 'threat perception' by either side and will also be linked with the 'historical enmity' (Tien-sze Fang 2014: 199). What makes these conflicting tendencies more pulsating in today's context is resource politics in border areas or trans-border areas, compounded by the label of 'nationalism' (as discussed in Chapters 2 and 3). Emotive and historically sensitive episodes like Tibet and the possible complexities that are associated with the post-Dalai Lama course may further intensify their antagonism. The cooperative character between India and China may push forward the 'developmental partnership' on what the current relationship is trying to focus on, but these may not be sufficient conditions to modulate the existing conflicting tendencies.

Scenario Two: Sub-regional crescendos will be more portentous with connectivity, corridors and conflicts. There is a return of serious focus on sub-regional dynamics in both countries. Bordering provinces on either side have been in the limelight for public and intellectual debate. The focus has been more on connectivity and corridors. BCIM-EC and the newly proposed Chinese initiative of 'One Belt, One Road' have been the important aspects of this sub-regional episode. Connectivity across the India–China border and launching connectivity across the Himalayan region may return to publicity for cooperation between the two sides. Still, given the security mistrust that exists between the two on the boundary dispute and on a range of bordering aspects, more than a cooperative effort, the sub-regional course may witness checks and balances between the two sides. With an advancing foreign policy and investment-oriented economy, China's focus would be more on connectivity and corridors. India with its active foreign policy would like to focus on its immediate neighbourhood to establish better political contacts. Nevertheless, much like the bilateral course, the sub-regional course between the two would be ostentatious. The sub-regional features would struggle to materialise to any real-time cooperation. Mechanisms like BCIM-EC may offer a cooperative sub-regional scenario. As discussed in Chapter 7, this may also prompt for a scenario of coexistence. Equally, the 'Silk Road' connectivity and corridor projects launched by the Chinese leadership offer a more compliant scenario, but from India's perspective, the security subtleties linked with OBOR projects will not be actualised or be beneficial for India–China relations in the immediate future. Third-party influences like Pakistan, India–China mutual mistrust and non-supportive approach over the South China Sea will limit the scope of any real-time sub-regional cooperation.

Amidst all this, three elaborations may be observed between the two sides at the sub-regional level. *First*, the neighbouring or trans-Himalayan or South Asian countries will play a strong role in influencing India–China relations and they will continue to emerge as vital factors. *Second*, corridors and connectivity will capture a lot of attention in the India–China sub-regional engagement, but real-time cooperation on connectivity across the borders and corridors across land and maritime domains will have their limitations and will fall short of any realistic cooperation. *Third*, new proposals and ideas may arrive between India and China at the sub-regional level for cooperation, prompting a case for coexistence.

Scenario Three: Regional contours would be based more on competitive aspects where the flashpoint will be maritime resource politics. Asymmetric growth in foreign policy dynamics and power posture between India and China at the regional level is the new contour of current Asian politics. One vital aspect of it is the multilateral power politics or engagement through which rising powers connect and integrate with regional vis-à-vis global conditions in order to contend and compete with each other's strategic interests and primacy. This Asian rendezvous is part and parcel of the rhetoric of liberalist sentiments, which realistically do not work in favour of the developing countries' relationships. In today's context, the increasing multilateral engagements between the two countries are a potential medium for denying space and holding an edge over each other's priority of acquiring assorted global resources, forming an Asian and a global identity, and conspicuously in securing respective national strategic objectives. The current foreign policy contours of these two countries are quite different from the previous order and politics. The boundary will continue to be the fundamental problem in their bilateral discourse, while the Asian discourse of Sino-Indian multilateral politics will be decided by their competition and power rivalry in resources.

Three specific patterns are noticeable in India–China relations. *First*, at the regional level, a multi-textured and multifaceted regional systemic power complexity with the lead of India and China has emerged. Searching for resources and cutting through each other's interests and presence seems to be the main aspect of their current regional politics in Asia. The India–China complexity at the Asian level shares two essential elements: an unprecedented competition for resources, and an institutionalised normative Asian region with a complex inter-reliant regional order. In this new regional scenario, both countries appear to be in tune with the logic of a new order, which combines the search for energy resources and diplomatic status with the quest for supremacy in Asia. That may bring their leadership perspectives into clash in Asia.

Second, the current context of multipolar world politics is one of global power trajectory, growth and shocks, principally pertaining to shrinking supply and ever-increasing prices of resources. It is not just a US-specific sub-prime crisis. On the other hand, global power politics is buoyed by India–China relations, especially at the multilateral levels. The political leadership on both sides states that 'China's and India's future prosperity lies in partnership, not rivalry'

(Li *et al.* 2010), in spite of the various aspects of their troubled relationship. One is also noticing the rise of the debate over the establishment of an 'Asian Century' where both India and China need to have a cooperative Asian partnership (*China Daily* 2015; see also *ndtv.com* 2015). These rhetorical judgements will continue to appear in the India–China discourse as trade and economic relations between the two are growing and both are getting associated in various multilateral mechanisms at the regional level. India's and China's rise may bring Asia into the limelight, and hence the 'Asian Century' debate may frequently crop up; but realistic cooperation to establish an 'Asian Century' primed by India–China cooperation may be a distant reality.

Third, identical regional ambitions in Asia put both India and China under a complex competitive periphery. Sino-Indian relations in Asia will be more complex in times to come, as the 'competing realities', like resource politics and authority politics that this book has discussed, are some of the subjects that are linked to their national security interests. The Indian and Chinese foreign policy behaviour in different segments of Asia has manifested that their rise and prominence has a characteristic of being obstructionist towards each other, irrespective of the issues or conditions with which they engage or compete. These include participation in various power politics in Asia, relations with the major powers or blocs in Asian political dynamics, and the search for avenues to explore or compete. As it is, getting access to major sources of resources in Asia – be it oil, gas, water, maritime or land – has always been a central factor in regional and global politics. The maritime domain will become the most competitive domain in Sino-Indian relations; hence, the spotlight will be on the Indian Ocean, South China Sea and the Bay of Bengal regions.

Scenario Four: Cross-continental contemporaries will witness more cooperative and collaborative politics under the rubric of 'developing world' identity: The rise of BRICS, continuity of BASIC, and the prominence of the African world along with India and China under the label of 'developing world' certainly prompt for an 'alternative' politics in a multipolar world order. Indeed, BRICS's rise explains a coordinated challenge to the Western dominance and supremacy in world politics and economics today. For the first time since the days of the non-aligned movement (NAM) and New Economic Order in the 1970s, there is a constructive and coordinated effort by the developing world to challenge the developed world's dominance in world politics (Desai 2013), and the BRICS movement has been the linchpin behind this effort. The India–China shared understanding within BRICS merits much credit for that. Indeed, the mortar that binds BRICS together is its rejection of the neo-liberal developmental model in world politics (ibid.), which implies the rejection of the Western-dominated financial institutions in world politics. Reforming global bodies like the IMF, WTO and World Bank will continue to be the pressing aspect where the India–China coordinated approach will be the most important aspect.

India and China may even reach a stage where they may represent a unified position of the developing world by campaigning strongly for reform of these political and financial institutions. Attaining various global governance objectives will also gain momentum in times to come. But realistically, these coordinated approaches may lack vigour and vitality due to the national interests that both India and China pursue globally. The two countries do not necessarily have a similar approach to world politics, but they have the identity politics of the developing world, where BRICS remains an appropriate forum for policy synchronisation and combined thrust. At the same time, given that national interests override collective wisdom and thinking in world politics, the unity and identity politics that India and China bring to the discourse of BRICS may be merely temporary and ad hoc. China will remain the predominant power in the BRICS formulation. To what extent this will affect the discourse and movement of BRICS will remain a matter of conjecture. India will also continue to draw attention.

At the same time, a BRICS-led world order is possible with unity and harmony among the BRICS members, especially between India and China. The new order being led by the two countries with BRICS will not change or rebuild any new world order per se, but it would affect the American and Western hegemonies in the existing world order. It will probably help build a new world order where developing countries will have a better and bigger say in world politics. But no world order is possible without binding India and China, the world's two largest economies and populous countries, together. India and China also must set an example for BRICS and developing countries on how to maximise and promote collective thinking and common objectives. A new world order will always be possible with India–China association, and not with India–China in isolation or in division. Further, India's rise and prominence, both within BRICS and outside, needs to be recognised by Beijing. The need is to assess and review the strength and weakness that both India and China hold towards each other in the spectrum of BRICS and outside. The identity of BRICS lies more with a joint India–China outlook than anything else, justifying the notion that the world structure is very much multipolar, where their relationships constitute a separate identity on their own.

Scenario Five: The relationship at the global colloquium will be one of power ambition and autonomy. A glimpse of the future of India–China global relations is perhaps noted appropriately in the May 2015 Joint Statement between the two countries, which says:

> As two major powers in the emerging world order, engagement between India and China transcends the bilateral dimension and has a significant bearing on regional, multilateral and global issues. Both Sides agreed to not only step up their consultations on developments affecting international peace, security and development but also coordinate their positions and work together to shape the regional and global agenda and outcomes.
>
> (*pib.nic.in* 2015)

The nuances attached to this comprehension mostly explain the overt India–China directives at the global level. They imply that India and China will forge a more cooperative effort at the global level and will shape the global decision-making process and agenda as they grow. The ambition and the spirit underlying this comprehension may sound positive and momentous, but a realistic consequence of their global colloquium as major powers points to a power dichotomy that is concurrent to their authority and influence in the global power structure. Both India and China as 'emerging' and rising powers will institute a more concerted cooperative relation at the global level. These will have severe limitations, however, as the world structure is still influenced and dictated by the Western powers and the West-dominated Bretton Woods institutions.

The US will continue to factor profoundly in India–China global relations. The American enduring dominance in global financial institutions will still affect their global cooperative drive. The rise of new or substitute financial institutions, as new avenues of cooperation and opportunities, primarily economic institutions, will generate a steady global relationship of understanding between the two sides. Nevertheless, given China's better assured integration in the global economic structure and most highly due to its prevailing influence in global politics being a P-5 nation in the UNSC, India will find it difficult to comply with China. To cite an example, as we viewed in Chapter 16, China may sound rational in supporting India's bid for UNSC permanent membership; still Beijing would not ideally like to see India making it to the board of this superlative institution. Furthermore, China's commanding and demanding aspects on global forte may not ever more be acceptable to India continuously. More importantly, China's ambition of establishing a parity of equal footing with the US as 'two world powers' will severely limit any realistic India–China global relations.

To conclude, India–China relations appear to be emerging as the most complex relationship in the current global politics. It is not a particular trend or a pattern that may be the prevailing aspect of this relationship. India–China relations will continue to impel multiple and multi-centric trends and patterns that are convoluted with the current and evolving world politics.

References

China Daily, 2015. 'Neighbours can usher in the Asian century', *China Daily*, 14 May, www.chinadaily.com.cn/opinion/2015-05/14/content_20711428.htm (accessed on 10 September 2015).

Desai, Radhika, 2013. 'The Brics are building a challenge to western economic supremacy', *Guardian*, 2 April, www.guardian.co.uk/commentisfree/2013/apr/02/brics-challenge-western-supremacy (accessed on 27 June 2013).

Li Xiaokun, Li Xiang and Ai Yang, 2010. 'World is big enough for China and India to grow', *China Daily*, 16 December, http://wo.chinadaily.com.cn/view.php?mid=31866&cid=81&isid=320 (accessed on 8 September 2015).

ndtv.com, 2015. '21st century belongs to Asia: PM Modi to Chinese media ahead of trip', 13 May, www.ndtv.com/india-news/21st-century-belongs-to-asia-pm-modi-to-chinese-media-ahead-of-trip-762679 (accessed on 10 September 2015).

pib.nic.in, 2015. 'Joint Statement between India and China during Prime Minister's visit to China', Press Information Bureau, Government of India, Prime Minister's Office, 15

May, http://pib.nic.in/newsite/PrintRelease.aspx?relid=121755 (accessed on 12 September 2015).

Tien-sze Fang, 2014. *Asymmetrical Threat Perceptions in India–China Relations*, New Delhi: Oxford University Press.

Wang Jisi, 2015. 'The "two orders" and the future of China–U.S. Relations', China File, 9 July, www.chinafile.com/reporting-opinion/two-way-street/two-orders-and-future-china-us-relations (accessed on 8 September 2015).

Index

Page numbers in *italics* denote tables, those in **bold** denote figures.

Abu Dhabi Crude Oil Pipeline 151
Acharya, Alka 2
'Act East' policy (India) 84, 104, 157, 164, 168; Chinese perspective on 168–71
Ad-hoc Working Groups (AWG) 214; Long-term Cooperative Action (AWG-LCA) 214
Addis Ababa Declaration 230
Afghanistan: 'Afghan-led, Afghan-owned' reconciliation process 126; India–China power politics in 125–7; Joint Statement (India–China, 2014) 126; presence in SAARC and SCO 126; SCO perspective on 144–5; terrorism, issue of 126; US troops withdrawal from 125
Afghan National Army (ANA) 126
African Development Bank *241*
African Union (AU) 224; bilateral trade with China and India **226**; cash diplomacy 227; China's trade recipe for 226; Chinese institutional reach to 229, 233; cultural bonding with China 229; energy crisis 225; 'energy first' diplomacy 225–9; free trade agreement (FTA) 227; Indian Ocean connection **228**; India's outreach to 230; India's trade contacts with 226–7; millennium development goals (MDGs) 230, 233; oil and energy diplomacy 227; prevailing maritime politics 227–9; reasons for China–India outreach to 233–4; Sino-African bonding 229
Afro-Asian movement 230
'Afro-Asian' multilateral bonding 225
Agreement on Trade and Intercourse (Tibet–India, 1954) 15
Aksai Chin 34–5, 37, 45, 47–8

al-Qaeda 126
Andaman and Nicobar Islands 184
Annan, Kofi 248; proposal on UNSC reform *249*
Antholis, William 5, 7–8
Archaeological Society of India (ASI) 85
Arunachal Pradesh 35, 37, 39–40; ADB loan for 39; China's claim on 48, 54, 60
ASEAN Regional Forum (ARF) 10, 186–7
ASEAN Way 185
ASEAN+3 (ASEAN + China, Japan and South Korea) 165
Asia Way 185
Asia-Pacific Economic Cooperation (APEC) 28; China's total merchandise trade with 175; Chinese perspective on India 172–5; India's bid for membership in 173–5; share of Asian and other non-Asian economies in **175**
'Asian Century' debate 259
Asian Community 27
Asian Development Bank (ADB) 146, *241*
Asian Highway Network (AHN) 110
Asian Infrastructure Investment Bank (AIIB) 27, 132, 137, 243, 246–7; goal of 247; India's decision to join 246; Memorandum of Understanding (MoU) 246
Asian Land Transport Infrastructure Development (ALTID) project 110
Asian-African-Latin American solidarity 232–3
Association of South-East Asian Nations (ASEAN) 7, 9, 105, 121, 159; '2 + 7' framework 185; ASEAN + 6 mechanism 247; Beijing's approach to *see* Sino–ASEAN bilateral relations; Chinese

264   Index

Association of South-East Asian Nations (ASEAN) *continued*
  maritime assertiveness 185–6; comparative trade contact of China and India with **169**; India–China economic bonding in 168; India's defence diplomacy with 182; India's naval exercises with 183; Regional Comprehensive Economic Partnership (RCEP) 164; total trade with selected trading partners **169**
AU Partner Group (AUPG) 230

Bab el-Mandeb 151, 152, 227
Bagamoyo port (Tanzania), development of 153
balance-of-power 3, 8, 99, 140
Bali Summit 182, 216
Bangladesh–China–India–Myanmar (BCIM) corridor 7, 48; BCIM forum 110n1; Chinese perspectives on 102–4; between connectivity and conflict 106–7; economic corridor 70, 99; economic interdependence *vs.* security syndrome 107–8; economic opportunities 99; 'engage but deny' strategy 109; forums *100–1*; global trade through 99; 'growth zone' concept 98–102; idea and construct of 98–102; idea of establishing 102; Indian perspectives on 104–5; Joint Study Group (JSG) meeting 99; Kunming Initiative 98; mechanism on India–China sub-regional interaction 98; peripheral diplomacy 104; between political cooperation and contradictions 108–10; principal element of 106; for regional development 99; revival of ancient silk route 106–7; soft-power phenomenon 104; Stillwell Road and car rally 106–7; strategic reasons for 99; tariff/non-tariff barriers 104; Track-II process 98; transnational cooperation 99
Bangladesh, India–China power politics in 129–30
Bay of Bengal 66, 104–5, 129–30, 184, 259
BCIM countries: China's bilateral trade with 109; India's bilateral trade with 109
Beijing Olympics 59
'belt and road' initiative *see* 'One Belt, One Road' (OBOR) initiative
Bhutan, India–China power politics in 127
BIMSTEC 99, 104–5, 111n8; China's interests and objectives in 105; FTA negotiations 105
Boao Forum (2015) 159, 184–5
Border Defence Cooperation Talks (BDCA) 45
border tourism 48
boundary demarcation, principles for 35, 39
boundary dispute, India–China: in Arunachal Pradesh 35, 37, 39–40; claims and reclaims of border 34–8, 36(map); comprehensive border settlement programme 39; confidence-building measures (CBMs) 41; contemporary years 43–5; core *vs.* contiguous 34–40; demarcation of border 35, 39; due to historical links with Tibet 48; in Eastern Sector 35; exchanging territory through a swap deal 47–9; initial years of negotiations 40–1; Joint Working Group 41, *42*; in Kashmir region 35; length of border 35; Line of Actual Control (LAC) 38–40; McMahon Line, legitimacy of 35; maintenance of status quo 47–9; middle years of negotiations 41–3; negotiation process to settle 40–5; 'package deal' offer 40; 'package settlement' through 'sectoral' approach 45–7; 'sector to sector' negotiation process 41; 'third party' factors 35
Brahmaputra (Yarlung Tsangpo) River 10, 48, 66–76, 129; India–China differences on 107
Brazil–Russia–India–China–South Africa (BRICS) 2, 16, 24, 259–60; China's tryst with 198; Contingency Reserve Arrangement (CRA) 200; cooperation with Africa 231; cooperation with IBSA 231; 'democratisation' of the global order 207; Development Bank 202; dynamism for China 195; financial reform politics 195; foreign reserves and GDP 195; formulation of 195; Fortaleza Declaration of 2014 243; future of 207–8; India–China construct in 27, 204–5; India–China divide 205–6; India's advocacy in 202–4; India's course in 198; intra-BRICS trade transactions 200; multi-currency financial order 200; New Development Bank (NDB) 137, 200, 202, 243; prevailing Indian dialogue and China 206–7; rapid institutionalisation process

231; rise of 195; share in world commercial trade **245**; share in world merchandise trade **245**; summits and major issues discussed *196–7*; trends of China's trade with **231**
Brazil–South Africa–India–China (BASIC) 7, 16, 24, 256, 259; Agreement on Cooperation on Addressing Climate Change 219; BASIC Project 213; climate change dialogue 214; contours of 220–1; creation of 216; emerging economies 214; idea, origin and politics 213–16; India–China relationship in 27, 219–20; perspectives of India and China on 216–19; profile and climate status of *215*; Sao Paulo Proposal for an Agreement on Future Climate Policy 213
Bretton Woods institutions 16–17, 27, 205, 241, 261; assessment of China–India collaboration on 252; decision-making process 243; India and China in *241*; new institutions and alternative ideas of 243–7; reformation of 242–3

carbon taxes 217
cash diplomacy 227
Central Asian Republics (CARs) 137
Centre for Policy Dialogue (CPD), Dhaka 105, 110n2
Chahbahar port, Iran 82
China: demand for energy 151; economic and political supremacy of 164; maritime assertiveness 185–6; as maritime power 151–6; perspective between RCEP and TPP 166–7
China Inc., rise of 200
China National Petroleum Corporation (CNPC) 151
China–Africa Cooperation Forum (CACF) 226
China–Central Asian engagement 145
China–Pakistan Economic Corridor (CPEC) 81, 91(map), 139; Boundary Agreement (2 March 1963) 92, 124; charting a course of action 92–3; Chinese justification with regard to 92; denouncing 'sovereignty' and 'history' in 90–2; Indian response to 82–3; land reclamation process 92
China–SAARC cooperation 121, 133
China–South Asia Expo 103
China–Tibet relations: 17-point agreement 53; on invasion of Tibet by China 53; on issue of Dalai Lama 53

China's Energy Policy 2012 153
China's foreign policy: 17-point agreement with Tibet 53; bilateral trade with other BCIM countries **109**; courting of South Africa 230–3; debate on foreign affairs 25; 'economic oriented' policy towards Tibet 58; 'Eurasian Pivot' strategy 81; good neighbour diplomacy 119; India's importance in 27; 'One Belt, One Road' (OBOR) initiative *see* 'One Belt, One Road' (OBOR) initiative; peripheral diplomacy, strategy of 102; 'silk road' diplomacy 85; 'string of pearls' strategy 227; towards Kashmir 123–4; 'Western Development' Scheme 58
China's India policy: debate on foreign affairs 25; dialogue on 24–9; on India's rise in East Asia 24; invitation to join OBOR initiative 24–9; media reporting on India 25–6; opposition to India's oil exploration in South China 86–90; perspective of India as a neighbour 25; policy of containment within engagement 27; 'string of pearls' strategy 227
China's Policies and Actions for Addressing Climate Change 218
Chindia: concept of 8, 252; discourse of 3, 6
Chinese Academy of Social Science (CASS) 38, 58
Chinese business communities, on Indian economy 26
Chinese citizens, perspective of India 26
Chinese leadership, account of India 26–7
Chinese media reporting, on India 25; on issue of Dalai Lama 26
Chinese People's Political Consultative Committee (CPPCC) 56
Chinese state treatise, about another country 25
Chumbi Valley 127
civil rivalry 6–7
civil–military relations, in China 47
climate change negotiations: Chinese perspectives on 217–19; Copenhagen Accord (2009) 213–14, 216; cost barriers 217; Doha Conference (2012) 205, 218; Indian perspectives on 216–17; intellectual property rights (IPR) 217; Kyoto Protocol (1992) 214, 216–17, 219–20; Paris Agreement (2015) 216–17
Clinton, Bill 132
code of conduct (COC) 185

common but differentiated responsibilities (CBDR) 214
Common Market for Eastern and Southern Africa (COMESA) 227
Communist Party of China (CPC) 26, 47; National Congress 25, 121
comparative profile, India–China *21*
comprehensive border settlement programme 39
Comprehensive Economic Partnership in East Asia (CEPEA) 165
Comprehensive Test Ban Treaty (CTBT) 67
confidence-building measures (CBMs) 41, 43, 157
Confucius Institutes 229
Contingency Reserve Arrangement (CRA) 200
COP15 (Conference of the Parties) 213, 216
Copenhagen Accord, on climate negotiation (2009) 213–14, 216–17; Listing in Chapeau of 217
cyber security 188

Dahlman, Carl J. 5
Dai, Bingguo 80
Dalai Lama 25–6, 35, 40, 48, 52, 54, 61, 129, 132; China's conditions-based talks with 58; escape to India 53; institution of (*Gaden Phodrang Labrang*) 54; power rivalry with Panchen Lama 56; reincarnation, practice of 54; succession issue 57; Their Holinesses *55*
Delhi Declaration 230
Deng, Xiaoping 40, 121, 251
Department of Economic Affairs of India 28–9
Depsang valley incident 45
'developing world' identity 9, 11, 195, 259
Development Research Centre of the State Council of the PRC 29
differentiation, theory of (1977) 251
Doha Conference (2012) 205, 218
Dreaming with BRICS: The Path to 2050 195
Durban BRICS summit (2013) 231

East Asia: China factor and India's potential leadership role in 188–9; China's policy gambit in 184–6; East Asia FTA (EAFTA) 165; in India's 'extended neighbourhood' diplomacy 181–4; India's multilateral presence in 186–7; Seoul Defence Dialogue (SDD) 188

East Asian Integration (EAI) 176n2, 186
East China Sea dispute 83, 188
East Turkistan Islamic Movement (ETIM) 144
Economic and Business Conference, Mauritius (July 2013) 158
Economic Corridor projects 173
economic globalisation 150–1, 159
'emerging economies' phenomena 17
emerging markets 83, 199, 243
emerging powers 1, 24, 195, 199
'energy first' diplomacy 225–9
energy resources, demand for 8
Environmental Programme Trust for Environmental Protection 219
Eurasia Economic Union 139
European Commission initiative 213
Export Import Bank of China 152, 202
extended neighbourhood, concept of 181

Farakka Barrage 129
Five Principles of Peaceful Coexistence *see* Panchsheel, principles of
flood management 70
food security 217, 233
Foreign Policy and Security Dialogue (FPSD), South Korea–India 188
Forum for India Pacific Island Countries (FIPIC) 158
Forum of China–Africa Cooperation (FOCAC) 229
four-nation alliance 168
Framework Agreement on Comprehensive Economic Cooperation 182
Framework for Enhanced Cooperation 230
free trade agreements (FTAs) 141, 164, 227
Free Trade Area (FTA): ASEAN FTA 99; China–ASEAN 99; India–ASEAN 99; negotiations among BIMSTEC countries 105
Fu, Ziying 252

'G-Zero' world situation, scenario of 8
Gandhi, Rajiv 41
Ganga–Brahmaputra–Meghna/Barak (GBM) basin 66
Gao, Zhenting 80
Garver, John 123–4
Gayoom, Abdulla Yameen Abdul 131
Global Times 38
Going Out Strategy 103, 110n6
Goldman Sachs 195
Gorbachev, Mikhail 41

Grand Western Water Diversion Plan 67–8
Greater Mekong Sub-region Growth Triangle 98, 102
'great game' politics 138
Green Technologies 220
greenhouse gas (GHG) emission 214, 219; major countries of **218**
Group of Twenty (G-20) 7, 203–4, 233
Gulf Cooperation Council (GCC) 84
Gulf of Aden 152, 227
Guo, Kai 68
Gurgaon Business Forum 158
Gwadar port, Pakistan 82
Gyatso, Sonam 54

Hong, Lei 89
Hong, Yuan 38
Hu, Jintao 21, 29, 82, 125, 159
Hua, Chunying 90
Huang, Hua 40
hydropower projects 67, 82, 128

identity politics 4, 8–9, 11, 214, 260
Import Export Code (IEC) 107
India–Africa Forum Summit (IAFS, 2008) 230
India–Africa Framework for Cooperation 230
India–African Union relationship 230
India–ASEAN relations: commemorative expedition 184; Commemorative Summit (2012) 182, 187; economic engagement 169, **170**; naval engagement 182; Partnership for Peace, Progress and Shared Prosperity 182
India–Bhutan relationship 127; Treaty of Friendship (1949) 127
India–Brazil–South Africa (IBSA) 198, 205–6, 224, 229; China's trade figures with **232**
India–Brazil–South Africa Maritime Exercise (IBSAMAR) 206, 229
India–China power politics, in South Asia: in Afghanistan 125–7; in Bangladesh 129–30; in Bhutan 127; emerging course of 132–3; factoring SAARC 121–3; on Kashmir issue 123–4; in Maldives 131; Modi and Xi 117–21; in Nepal 128–9; in Pakistan 123–5; rationale, resources and relationships 123–31; in Sri Lanka 130–1; terrorism-related problems 124; Western Development Strategy 132
India–China relations: advances in 28; Agreement on Cooperation on Addressing Climate Change 219; bilateral trade and trade imbalance **16**; in BRICS and BASIC 27; competitive aspects of 6; concept of 2–5; contemporary 5–8; developmental partnership 15, 28; dialogue, chronology of *18–19*; on economic engagement 27–8; fundamental conflict of interests 6; global relationship 8, 260; high points of India–China ties during Xi's visit 28; on India's bid for UNSC permanent membership 247–50, 261; on India's oil exploration in the South China sea 86–9; Joint Statement on 2, 15, 28; maritime rivalry 6; multipolar realities of 8–9; on mutual policies 21–9; over Gwadar port in Pakistan 82; rivalry in 6; stapled visa issue 125; strategic but not-so-cooperative partnership 16–20; structural convolution **4**; Tibetan refugees, implications of 61; US factor in 6
India–China Strategic and Cooperative Partnership of Peace and Prosperity 29
India–China trade: through Nathu La pass 107; trade balance **108**
India–Japan defence partnership 189
India–Nepal border 59
India–Pakistan boundary 93
India–Tibet–China tripartite relations 53; complexity of 15; India's next course and India–China relations 60–1; India's Tibet policy and China 53–4; Tibetan–Chinese dialogue and 57–60; on Tibetan refugees in India 60
India–US alliance 6–7; on India-specific waiver at NSG 251; Malabar exercise 189; nuclear deal 251
Indian Navy 182
Indian Ocean Naval Symposium (IONS) 158, 186, 229
Indian Ocean Region (IOR) 6, 83–4; Bab el-Mandeb 152; China–India maritime politics in 234; China–IORA trade 155; China's strategic bases in 154(map); Chinese access to 105; commercial and strategic significance of 157; India's cultural heritage across 85; India's maritime posture in 227; maritime and geostrategic pre-eminence of 155; maritime security and politics in 234; overseas strategic points 153; sea-lanes of communication 156; security environment of 157; Sino–Myanmar relations 151; Strait of Hormuz 151; Strait of Malacca 152; trade barriers in 158

Indian Ocean Research Group (IORG) 150
Indian Ocean Rim Association (IORA) 9, 186, 229; and Beijing's inter-regional approach 157; China's foreign direct investment in *155*; China's tryst with 150–1; comparison of India, China and US total bilateral trade with **156**; contours of 159; 'going global' strategy 151; hard-power and soft-power elements 156; India and 157–9; major chokepoints and key members *152*; Perth communiqué 150; security challenges 157; Working Group on Trade and Investment (WGTI) 160n2
Indian Ocean Rim Association for Regional Cooperation (IOR-ARC) *see* Indian Ocean Rim Association (IORA)
Indian Ocean Tourism Organisation (IOTO) 150
India's China policy: on 'balance' of competition-and-cooperation 23; in China's military and political power 22; on collaboration 24; dialogue on 21–4; mutual perceptions *23*; position on Tibet 37
India's foreign policy: 'Act East' policy 84; bid for UNSC permanent membership 247–50, 261; bilateral trade with other BCIM countries **109**; Cotton Route 84; courting of South Africa 230–3; Project Mausam 84, 85–6; Spice Route 84, 85
Indira Gandhi National Centre for Arts (IGNCA) 85
Indus River 69
Industrial Park, establishment of: Gujarat 28; Pune 28
INS *Airavat* incident (2011) 89
INS *Baaz* 184
INS *Sudershini* 184
Institute of Chinese Studies (ICS), New Delhi 110n1
Instrument of Accession to the Treaty of Amity and Cooperation in South-East Asia 181
intellectual property rights (IPR) 7, 217
International Bank for Reconstruction and Development (IBRD) 214, *241,* 242
International Centre for Settlement of Investment Disputes (ICSID) *241*
International Development Association (IDA) *241*
International Finance Corporation (IFC) *241*
International Monetary Fund (IMF) 146, *241,* 242, 259; Chinese participation in 252n2; Chinese perspective on 242; reserve currency basket 202
International North–South Transport Corridor (INSTC) 138
investment-oriented economy 257
Iran–Pakistan–India (IPI) pipeline 139
ISIS (Islamic State of Iraq and the Levant), rise of 126

Joint Declaration for Cooperation to Combat International Terrorism 181–2
Joint Economic Group (JEG) 17; India–China meetings, chronology of *20*

Kailash Mansarovar Yatra 28, 48
Kargil conflict, India–Pakistan 82, 124
Karot hydropower project 82
Kashmir: China's stance towards 123; dispute between India and Pakistan over 124; India's position on 124; people's right to self-determination 124; Simla agreement (India–Pakistan) 124
Khurshid, Salman 90, 122
Kohl, Helmut 128
Kunming Initiative 98, 110n1
Kyoto Protocol 214, 216–17, 219–20

Ladakh, Chinese interference in (1954) 15
Lakhvi, Zaki-ur-Rehman 139
Lashkar-e-Toiyaba (LeT) 139
Le, Yucheng 85
least developed countries (LDCs) 219, 235n7
Ledo Road 107
Lhasa Convention on Tibet (1904) 52
Lhasa–Shigatse rail line 59
Li, Keqiang 2, 25, 69, 185; idea of establishing BCIM-EC 102; tour to India 27
Li, Zhaoxing 121
Line of Actual Control (LAC) 34, 38–40; alignment of 38; clarification of 38–9; exchange of maps 38; Joint Working Group (JWG) on 38
Liu, Jianchao 68
local currency transaction, strategy of 202
Lombok and Sunda Straits 227
Look East policy (India) 104, 122, 132, 151, 168, 181
Los Cabos declaration 204

Ma, Zhaoxu 124
McMahon Line 25, 35, 37, 40, 52
Malacca Strait 182

Malacca–Malaysia–Dumai–Indonesia bridge project 152
Maldives, India–China power politics in 131
Mao, Zedong 21, 37, 67, 251
'maritime lifeline' of China 151
Maritime Silk Road (MSR) 79, 121, 130, 173, 246; financial backing 85; India and 83–6
Mekong Ganga Cooperation (MGC) 99
Mekong River Basin 72
MILAN naval exercise 182
millennium development goals (MDGs) 230, 233
Modi, Narendra 21, 24, 28–9, 80, 87, 137–8, 172, 182, 220; South Asian policy 117–21; visit to Central Asia 145; visit to Nepal 128
Mongol invasion of Tibet 54
Mongol Khans 54
Mozambique Channel 227
Mukherjee, Pranab 181
Multilateral Investment Guarantee Agency (MIGA) *241*
Mumbai terrorist attack (2008) 139

Nathu La pass (India–China border) 107, 111n9
National Action Plan on Climate Change (NAPCC), India 216
National Communication (NATCOM), India 217
National Defence Law (NDL), China 47
National Development and Reform Commission (NDRC), China 16, 217
National Environmental Policy (NEP), India 216
National Security Advisor (NSA) 43
Nehru, Jawaharlal 15, 21, 37
Nepal, India–China power politics in 128–9
Nepalese Constituent Assembly 128
New Development Bank (NDB) 202, 243; Chinese influence in 244, 246; funding sources 246; headquarters of 202; Indian influence in 244; India's presidency and China's premiership 243–6; investment and financial proposals 246; launching of 200; structure of 244
New Economic Order 259
Niti Aayog *see* Planning Commission of India
Non-Aligned Movement (NAM) 233, 259
North Korea 188–9

North-East Asian multilateral forums 188
Nuclear Supplies Group (NSG) 251

Obama, Barack 173, 176n5
oil and energy diplomacy 227
'One Belt, One Road' (OBOR) initiative 27, 59, 124, 137, 247, 257; China's national investment strategy and 80; comparison with Marshall Plan 79–80; components of 79; concept of 79–80; demographic objectives of 79–80; geographical objectives of 80; resource objectives of 80
one-China policy 70, 125, 127, 229
ONGC Videsh Limited (OVL) 89
Organisation of African Unity (OAU) 234n4

P-5 (permanent five) country 9, 206, 232
Pakistan, India–China power politics in 123–5
Pakistan-Occupied Kashmir (POK) 35, 82, 91(map), 123, 139; China's construction activities in 87, 124; livelihood project 90
Panchen Lama 61, 62n2; power rivalry with Dalai Lama 56
Panchsheel, principles of 3–4, 15–16, 21, 27, 29, 34, 123
Paris Agreement (2015) 216–17
'Peace Mission' exercises (China–Russia) 143
Peaceful Nuclear Explosion (PNE) 67
peaceful solution, principle of 40
People's Liberation Army (PLA) 38, 47–8, 53, 59, 153
People's Liberation Army Navy (PLAN) 156–7
people's project 207, 232–3
peripheral diplomacy, strategy of 102, 104, 117, 121
Petro Vietnam 89
piracy and terrorist activities 227
Plan of Action 130, 182
Planning Commission of India 16
political exchange of visits, between India and China *17*
power trade agreement (PTA), Nepal–India 128
Project Mausam 84, 85–6; *vs.* Maritime Silk Road initiative 85; theme of 85
Protocol on Modalities for the Implementation of Confidence-Building Measures (2005) 43

purchasing power parity (PPP) 7
Putin, Vladimir 139

Qi, Huaigao 122

Rajan, Raghuram 243
Regional Anti-Terrorist Structure (RATS) 141
Regional Comprehensive Economic Partnership (RCEP) 164; ASEAN agenda of 166, 168; 'ASEAN++' formula 165; and Chinese acuity of India–China maritime politics 171–2; Chinese perspective between TPP and 166–7; Indian perspective between TPP and 167; negotiations 133, 247; politics and economics 164–6; tariff and non-tariff barriers 165; *vs.* Trans-Pacific Partnership (TPP) 164–6; US factor 168
regional economic integration 99, 110, 150–1, 159, 166, 172–3, 187
Regulations on Religious Affairs (RRA) 56
religious freedom 56, 59–60
renminbi bloc 200
Renmin Ribao 37
Reserve Bank of India (RBI) 243
resource diplomacy 233
resource politics 9–11, 108, 117, 123, 233, 257–9
rising powers phenomenon 225
run-of-the-river project 67, 70
Russia–India–China (RIC) triangle 6, 16, 143, 145–6, 246; India–China interactions in 7

Sangay, Lobsang 54, 119
Sanya (China) BRIC summit (2011) 231
Sao Paulo Proposal for an Agreement on Future Climate Policy 213
Sberbank (Russia) 202
SCO Development Bank 202, 247
sea-lanes of communication 156
Senkaku/Diaoyu island dispute 80, 188
Seoul Defence Dialogue (SDD) 188
Shanghai Cooperation Organisation (SCO) 7, 9, 81, 83, 121, 125, 159, 198; Afghanistan factor 144–5; anti-Western and anti-NATO alliance 140; associating with India 143, 146; Beijing's perspective on 140–3; Chinese design of 142(map); connecting Central Asia 145; expansion of 141; free trade agreements 141; 'great game' politics 138; India's 'connect Central Asia' outlook post-Ufa 138–40; joint military exercises 144; membership of 137; 'Peace Mission' exercises (China–Russia) 143; post-Ufa triangular order 146–7; Regional Anti-Terrorist Structure (RATS) 141; security issues 143–4; Ufa summit 137–8
Shanghai Five 143
Sharma, Anand 158
Sichuan–Tibet railway link 59
Sikkim 43, 111n9, 127
silk road, concept of 83
Silk Road Economic Belt (SREB) 48, 79, 121, 137, 139, 246; challenges and opportunities for India 81–2; China–Pakistan Economic Corridor 48; China's invitation to India to join 81; components of 81; India and 80–3; neighbourhood dynamics, implications for 86–7; network of road and rail connection 81
Silk Road Fund (SRF) 81, 139
Silk Route connectivity, between India and China 106
Simla agreement (India–Pakistan) 124
Simla Convention of 1914 52
Singh, Jaswant 38
Singh, Manmohan 21, 29, 105, 198
Singh, V.K. 90
Sino–African relationship 229
Sino–ASEAN bilateral relations 83; Maritime Cooperation Fund 84; strategic partnership 184–5
Sino–India War (1962) 15, 22, 40, 53; reasons for 37
Sino–Japanese maritime dispute 189
Sino–Myanmar relations 151
Sino–Pakistani relations: Boundary Agreement (2 March 1963) 92, 124; on construction activities in POK 124; 'multi-dimensional' relationship 125; terrorism-related problems 124; Treaty for Friendship and Cooperation and Good Neighbourly Relations (2005) 125; *see also* China–Pakistan Economic Corridor (CPEC)
Sino–South African relationship 230–3
Sino–US relations 220
sister-city, establishment of 28; province cooperation MoUs/agreements *29*
Sixty Years since Peaceful Liberation of Tibet (2011) 59
Smith, Jeff 6–8

South Asia: Chinese power building exercise 119; global exports 119; good neighbour diplomacy 119; great-power diplomacy 121; India–China power politics in 117–21; India's exports to 119; strategic significance of 119
South Asian Association for Regional Cooperation (SAARC) 7, 9, 105, 117, 125; General Provisions of 123; institutional mechanisms 123; member profile vis-à-vis China *118*; prospective China membership 121–3; trade data compared with China *120*
South Asian Free Trade Area (SAFTA) 105
South Asian Growth Quadrangle 98
South China Growth Triangle 98
South China Sea (SCS) 83–4, 185; freedom of navigation 88, 90, 187; India's oil exploration in 86–90, 88(map); INS *Airavat* incident (2011) 89; nine-dash line 87; propriety of 'sovereignty' and 'history' in 87–90
South-East Asian nations 7, 87
South–North Water Diversion Project (SNWDP) 67–8; Indian perception of 68
Southern Silk Road initiatives 103, 106
Southern Tibet 39, 47
South–South bonding 225, 233
Special Drawing Rights (SDR) 202
Special Representatives (SRs) 43, 83; 'border management' talks 45; chronology of meetings *44*
Sri Lanka: Chinese nuclear submarine, issue of 131; Hambantota port 130; India–China power politics in 130–1; Peace Accord (1987), violation of 131; Plan of Action 130; Strategic Cooperative Partnership 130
stapled visa issue, between India and China 125
State Administration for Religious Affairs (China) 56
State Council of China 67, 85
Stillwell Road and car rally 106–7
Strait of Hormuz 151, 152
Strait of Malacca 80, 151–2
Strategic and Cooperative Partnership for Peace and Prosperity 3–4, 45
Strategic Economic Dialogue (SED) 16
Strategic Partnership for Peace and Prosperity, A 184
'string of pearls' strategy 227
Sunda Strait 182, 227

Sutlej River 69
Swaraj, Sushma 82

Taiwan's Economic and Cultural Council (TECC) 119
Taliban's Islamic Emirate 126
Tang Dynasty 103
Teesta River 129
Three Gorges Corp. 128
Three Gorges Dam 67
Three Worlds Theory, Chinese strategy of 251
Tibet–Sikkim border 35, 52
Tibetan Autonomous Region (TAR) 103; China's 'economic oriented' policy towards 58; Chinese invasion of 53; Chinese military presence in 59; conditions-based talks with China 58; connection through railway network 59; independence of 54; India's Tibet policy and China 53–4; Mongol invasion of 54; 'perpetual' and 'perceptual' dispute 52–6; resource endowment 59; Sino-Tibetan meetings *57*; Tibetan–Chinese dialogue 57–60
Tibetan Government in Exile (TGIE) 48, 54, 60, 119, 129
Tibetan protest movements 61
Tien-sze, Fang 6–8
Tirap-Changlang corridor 107
Tokyo Declaration 189
trade barriers, in the Indian Ocean 158
trade security 158
Trans-Arunachal Highway project 107
Trans-Asian Railway (TAR) 110
trans-boundary water resources: data sharing on 68–9; exploitation of 66; India–China experts level mechanism meetings on *71*; MoUs on water/hydrological data sharing *71*; river management 69
trans-national economies 66
trans-national energy resources 70
Trans-Pacific Partnership (TPP) 164; American advocacy of 165; Chinese perspective between RCEP and 166–7; evolving India–China upsurge in 167–72; Indian perspective between RCEP and 167; politics and economics 164–6; 'WTO-plus' approach 165
Treaty of Mutual Cooperation and Security, US–Japan 188
Turkmenistan–Afghanistan–Pakistan–India (TAPI) pipeline 138–9

Ufa summit 137–8, 139
UN General Assembly (UNGA) 248
UN Security Council (UNSC) 9; China's perspective on membership reform of *250*; Chinese reaction to Annan's proposal on 248, *249*; India factor in Beijing's official stance against permanent membership 248–50; India's bid for permanent membership of 247; Kofi Annan's proposal on reform of 248, *249*; perspective of Chinese support to India's bid for 250–2; pragmatism in reformation of 247; reformation of 247–52; technicalities in reformation of 248; veto power 248
United Nations (UN): Chinese *Position Paper on UN Reform* (2005) 248; Convention on Non-Navigational Uses of International Watercourses 69; Convention on the Law of the Sea (UNCLOS) 89, 187; Framework Convention on Climate Change (UNFCCC) 214, 217, 220; reformation of 247–52
United States (US): National Defence Authorization Act for Fiscal Year 2013 188; 'pivot' Asia policy 138–9, 146, 157, 164, 173; trade deficit with China 199; Trans-Pacific Partnership (TPP) 164; withdrawal of troops from Afghanistan 125
US dollars: *vs.* Indian rupee **203**; *vs.* Yuan (RMB) **200**
US–China Strategic and Economic Dialogue (S&ED) 20
Uyghurs 124, 126, 143

Vajpayee, A.B. 40, 53, 124
Vietnam 86–90, 93, 102–3, 133, 165–6, 171, 182, 184, 187
Vision and Action on Jointly Building Belt and Road (2015) 83
Visit China Year (2016) 29
Visit India Year (2015) 29
'vocal minority' perception 6

Wajed, Sheikh Hasina 130
Wangchuk, Jigme Khesar Namgyel 127
Wang, Guangqian 67
Wang, Guangya 248
Wang, Shucheng 68
Wang, Yi 185
water governance 69

water resource conflict: on Beijing's five-year energy plan 67; emerging scenarios 70–3; Experts Level Mechanism (ELM) 69; Grand Western Water Diversion Plan 67–8; hydropower projects 67; Indian concern and Chinese explanation over 68–9; Joint Statement on 69; mechanism for water sharing 73; MoU on hydrological data sharing 69; nuclear detonation in water diversion 67; perennial water scarcity, phase of 66; run-of-the-river project 67, 70; South–North Water Diversion Project (SNWDP) 67–8; Strengthening Cooperation on Trans-Border Rivers 69; trans-boundary water resources, exploitation of 66; water diversion project, dispute over 48; 'watershed' agreement 69–70; water war, forecast of 70; Yarlung Tsangpo water diversion projects 67
water security 217
Wen, Jiabao 16, 21, 151, 219
West Seti River hydropower project (Nepal) 128
'Western Development' Scheme 58
Western Development Strategy (China) 132
Working Mechanism for Consultation and Coordination on India–China Border Affairs (WMCC) 43, *46*
World Bank Group, The 146, 202, 225, *241, 259*; Chinese participation in 252n2; Chinese perspective on 242
World Trade Organisation (WTO) 141, *241, 259*; Chinese accession to 199; Chinese perspective on 242; contribution to **244**; Doha Round of Negotiations 233
Wu, Xinbo 253n9

Xi, Jinping 21, 25, 28–9, 59, 79, 84, 128, 130–1, 139, 208, 220, 252; agreements/MoUs signed with India 28; Beijing's foreign policy under 24; Chinese dream 72; high points during visit to India 28; 'neighbourhood' or 'peripheral' diplomacy 119, 121; 'new type of major-power relations,' idea of 20; proactive diplomacy 24; responsive diplomacy 25; South Asian policy 117–21; speech on 'China's Central Asia Strategy' 145; on stronger China–ASEAN community 83; visit to India

15, 28; visit to Pakistan 90; visit to Sri Lanka 130
Xie, Zhenhua 218
Xinjiang–Tibet road 37
Xinjiang Uyghur Autonomous Region (XUAR) 124, 143

Yang, Jiechi 39
Yarlung Tsangpo water diversion projects 67
Yuan (RMB) 227; appreciation of 199; promotion as an international currency 199–200; renminbi bloc 200; rise against US dollars **200**; swap deals *201*; Yuan–Rouble trade platform 202

Zhao, Nanqi 72
Zheng, He 84
Zhou, Enlai 15, 21, 40
Zuma, Jacob 231

Taylor & Francis eBooks

Helping you to choose the right eBooks for your Library

Add Routledge titles to your library's digital collection today. Taylor and Francis ebooks contains over 50,000 titles in the Humanities, Social Sciences, Behavioural Sciences, Built Environment and Law.

Choose from a range of subject packages or create your own!

Benefits for you
- Free MARC records
- COUNTER-compliant usage statistics
- Flexible purchase and pricing options
- All titles DRM-free.

Benefits for your user
- Off-site, anytime access via Athens or referring URL
- Print or copy pages or chapters
- Full content search
- Bookmark, highlight and annotate text
- Access to thousands of pages of quality research at the click of a button.

REQUEST YOUR FREE INSTITUTIONAL TRIAL TODAY

Free Trials Available
We offer free trials to qualifying academic, corporate and government customers.

eCollections – Choose from over 30 subject eCollections, including:

Archaeology	Language Learning
Architecture	Law
Asian Studies	Literature
Business & Management	Media & Communication
Classical Studies	Middle East Studies
Construction	Music
Creative & Media Arts	Philosophy
Criminology & Criminal Justice	Planning
Economics	Politics
Education	Psychology & Mental Health
Energy	Religion
Engineering	Security
English Language & Linguistics	Social Work
Environment & Sustainability	Sociology
Geography	Sport
Health Studies	Theatre & Performance
History	Tourism, Hospitality & Events

For more information, pricing enquiries or to order a free trial, please contact your local sales team:
www.tandfebooks.com/page/sales

The home of Routledge books

www.tandfebooks.com